FREE Study Skills Videos/DVD Offer

Dear Customer,

Thank you for your purchase from Mometrix! We consider it an honor and a privilege that you have purchased our product and we want to ensure your satisfaction.

As part of our ongoing effort to meet the needs of test takers, we have developed a set of Study Skills Videos that we would like to give you for FREE. These videos cover our *best practices* for getting ready for your exam, from how to use our study materials to how to best prepare for the day of the test.

All that we ask is that you email us with feedback that would describe your experience so far with our product. Good, bad, or indifferent, we want to know what you think!

To get your FREE Study Skills Videos, you can use the **QR code** below, or send us an **email** at studyvideos@mometrix.com with *FREE VIDEOS* in the subject line and the following information in the body of the email:

- The name of the product you purchased.
- Your product rating on a scale of 1-5, with 5 being the highest rating.
- Your feedback. It can be long, short, or anything in between. We just want to know your impressions and experience so far with our product. (Good feedback might include how our study material met your needs and ways we might be able to make it even better. You could highlight features that you found helpful or features that you think we should add.)

If you have any questions or concerns, please don't hesitate to contact me directly.

Thanks again!

Sincerely,

Jay Willis
Vice President
jay.willis@mometrix.com
1-800-673-8175

SCAN HERE

Mometrix
TEST PREPARATION

Mometrix
TEST PREPARATION

ACT®

Prep Book 2024-2025 with Practice Tests

ACT® Secrets Study Guide for the English, Math, Reading, Science, and Writing Sections

3 Full-Length Exams

250+ Online Video Tutorials

8th Edition

Written and edited by Mometrix Test Prep

Printed in the United States of America

This paper meets the requirements of ANSI/NISO Z39.48-1992 (Permanence of Paper).

Paperback
ISBN 13: 978-1-5167-2517-5
ISBN 10: 1-5167-2517-4

DEAR FUTURE EXAM SUCCESS STORY

First of all, **THANK YOU** for purchasing Mometrix study materials!

Second, congratulations! You are one of the few determined test-takers who are committed to doing whatever it takes to excel on your exam. **You have come to the right place.** We developed these study materials with one goal in mind: to deliver you the information you need in a format that's concise and easy to use.

In addition to optimizing your guide for the content of the test, we've outlined our recommended steps for breaking down the preparation process into small, attainable goals so you can make sure you stay on track.

We've also analyzed the entire test-taking process, identifying the most common pitfalls and showing how you can overcome them and be ready for any curveball the test throws you.

Standardized testing is one of the biggest obstacles on your road to success, which only increases the importance of doing well in the high-pressure, high-stakes environment of test day. Your results on this test could have a significant impact on your future, and this guide provides the information and practical advice to help you achieve your full potential on test day.

Your success is our success

We would love to hear from you! If you would like to share the story of your exam success or if you have any questions or comments in regard to our products, please contact us at **800-673-8175** or **support@mometrix.com**.

Thanks again for your business and we wish you continued success!

Sincerely,
The Mometrix Test Preparation Team

Need more help? Check out our flashcards at:
http://MometrixFlashcards.com/ACT

Dear Future Exam Success Story

TABLE OF CONTENTS

Introduction

Thank you for purchasing this resource! You have made the choice to prepare yourself for a test that could have a huge impact on your future, and this guide is designed to help you be fully ready for test day. Obviously, it's important to have a solid understanding of the test material, but you also need to be prepared for the unique environment and stressors of the test, so that you can perform to the best of your abilities.

For this purpose, the first section that appears in this guide is the **Secret Keys**. We've devoted countless hours to meticulously researching what works and what doesn't, and we've boiled down our findings to the five most impactful steps you can take to improve your performance on the test. We start at the beginning with study planning and move through the preparation process, all the way to the testing strategies that will help you get the most out of what you know when you're finally sitting in front of the test.

We recommend that you start preparing for your test as far in advance as possible. However, if you've bought this guide as a last-minute study resource and only have a few days before your test, we recommend that you skip over the first two Secret Keys since they address a long-term study plan.

Superscoring

ACT, Inc now has the option for superscoring. If you take the ACT more than once, your superscore is calculated using your best performance on each subject test. Just like the normal composite score, a superscore is the average of the subject tests rounded to the nearest whole number. For instance, Jahani has taken the ACT 3 times and the following table shows her scores and her superscore:

Date	**English**	**Math**	**Reading**	**Science**	**Composite**
December 5	31	25	28	28	28
April 17	29	27	36	27	30
June 12	33	29	25	27	29
Superscore					
Superset	**33**	**29**	**36**	**28**	**32**

It is important to note that colleges set their own policies and standards for the potential use of superscores. ACT, Inc strongly recommends that colleges use superscores, claiming that they are at least as good a predictor of first year performance as a single composite score, and often a better one.

Review Video Directory

As you work your way through this guide, you will see numerous review video links interspersed with the written content. If you would like to access all of these review videos in one place, click on the video directory link found on the bonus page: **mometrix.com/bonus948/act**

SCAN HERE

Secret Key #1 – Plan Big, Study Small

There's a lot riding on your performance. If you want to ace this test, you're going to need to keep your skills sharp and the material fresh in your mind. You need a plan that lets you review everything you need to know while still fitting in your schedule. We'll break this strategy down into three categories.

Information Organization

Start with the information you already have: the official test outline. From this, you can make a complete list of all the concepts you need to cover before the test. Organize these concepts into groups that can be studied together, and create a list of any related vocabulary you need to learn so you can brush up on any difficult terms. You'll want to keep this vocabulary list handy once you actually start studying since you may need to add to it along the way.

Time Management

Once you have your set of study concepts, decide how to spread them out over the time you have left before the test. Break your study plan into small, clear goals so you have a manageable task for each day and know exactly what you're doing. Then just focus on one small step at a time. When you manage your time this way, you don't need to spend hours at a time studying. Studying a small block of content for a short period each day helps you retain information better and avoid stressing over how much you have left to do. You can relax knowing that you have a plan to cover everything in time. In order for this strategy to be effective though, you have to start studying early and stick to your schedule. Avoid the exhaustion and futility that comes from last-minute cramming!

Study Environment

The environment you study in has a big impact on your learning. Studying in a coffee shop, while probably more enjoyable, is not likely to be as fruitful as studying in a quiet room. It's important to keep distractions to a minimum. You're only planning to study for a short block of time, so make the most of it. Don't pause to check your phone or get up to find a snack. It's also important to **avoid multitasking**. Research has consistently shown that multitasking will make your studying dramatically less effective. Your study area should also be comfortable and well-lit so you don't have the distraction of straining your eyes or sitting on an uncomfortable chair.

The time of day you study is also important. You want to be rested and alert. Don't wait until just before bedtime. Study when you'll be most likely to comprehend and remember. Even better, if you know what time of day your test will be, set that time aside for study. That way your brain will be used to working on that subject at that specific time and you'll have a better chance of recalling information.

Finally, it can be helpful to team up with others who are studying for the same test. Your actual studying should be done in as isolated an environment as possible, but the work of organizing the information and setting up the study plan can be divided up. In between study sessions, you can discuss with your teammates the concepts that you're all studying and quiz each other on the details. Just be sure that your teammates are as serious about the test as you are. If you find that your study time is being replaced with social time, you might need to find a new team.

Secret Key #2 – Make Your Studying Count

You're devoting a lot of time and effort to preparing for this test, so you want to be absolutely certain it will pay off. This means doing more than just reading the content and hoping you can remember it on test day. It's important to make every minute of study count. There are two main areas you can focus on to make your studying count.

Retention

It doesn't matter how much time you study if you can't remember the material. You need to make sure you are retaining the concepts. To check your retention of the information you're learning, try recalling it at later times with minimal prompting. Try carrying around flashcards and glance at one or two from time to time or ask a friend who's also studying for the test to quiz you.

To enhance your retention, look for ways to put the information into practice so that you can apply it rather than simply recalling it. If you're using the information in practical ways, it will be much easier to remember. Similarly, it helps to solidify a concept in your mind if you're not only reading it to yourself but also explaining it to someone else. Ask a friend to let you teach them about a concept you're a little shaky on (or speak aloud to an imaginary audience if necessary). As you try to summarize, define, give examples, and answer your friend's questions, you'll understand the concepts better and they will stay with you longer. Finally, step back for a big picture view and ask yourself how each piece of information fits with the whole subject. When you link the different concepts together and see them working together as a whole, it's easier to remember the individual components.

Finally, practice showing your work on any multi-step problems, even if you're just studying. Writing out each step you take to solve a problem will help solidify the process in your mind, and you'll be more likely to remember it during the test.

Modality

Modality simply refers to the means or method by which you study. Choosing a study modality that fits your own individual learning style is crucial. No two people learn best in exactly the same way, so it's important to know your strengths and use them to your advantage.

For example, if you learn best by visualization, focus on visualizing a concept in your mind and draw an image or a diagram. Try color-coding your notes, illustrating them, or creating symbols that will trigger your mind to recall a learned concept. If you learn best by hearing or discussing information, find a study partner who learns the same way or read aloud to yourself. Think about how to put the information in your own words. Imagine that you are giving a lecture on the topic and record yourself so you can listen to it later.

For any learning style, flashcards can be helpful. Organize the information so you can take advantage of spare moments to review. Underline key words or phrases. Use different colors for different categories. Mnemonic devices (such as creating a short list in which every item starts with the same letter) can also help with retention. Find what works best for you and use it to store the information in your mind most effectively and easily.

Secret Key #3 – Practice the Right Way

Your success on test day depends not only on how many hours you put into preparing, but also on whether you prepared the right way. It's good to check along the way to see if your studying is paying off. One of the most effective ways to do this is by taking practice tests to evaluate your progress. Practice tests are useful because they show exactly where you need to improve. Every time you take a practice test, pay special attention to these three groups of questions:

- The questions you got wrong
- The questions you had to guess on, even if you guessed right
- The questions you found difficult or slow to work through

This will show you exactly what your weak areas are, and where you need to devote more study time. Ask yourself why each of these questions gave you trouble. Was it because you didn't understand the material? Was it because you didn't remember the vocabulary? Do you need more repetitions on this type of question to build speed and confidence? Dig into those questions and figure out how you can strengthen your weak areas as you go back to review the material.

Additionally, many practice tests have a section explaining the answer choices. It can be tempting to read the explanation and think that you now have a good understanding of the concept. However, an explanation likely only covers part of the question's broader context. Even if the explanation makes perfect sense, **go back and investigate** every concept related to the question until you're positive you have a thorough understanding.

As you go along, keep in mind that the practice test is just that: practice. Memorizing these questions and answers will not be very helpful on the actual test because it is unlikely to have any of the same exact questions. If you only know the right answers to the sample questions, you won't be prepared for the real thing. **Study the concepts** until you understand them fully, and then you'll be able to answer any question that shows up on the test.

It's important to wait on the practice tests until you're ready. If you take a test on your first day of study, you may be overwhelmed by the amount of material covered and how much you need to learn. Work up to it gradually.

On test day, you'll need to be prepared for answering questions, managing your time, and using the test-taking strategies you've learned. It's a lot to balance, like a mental marathon that will have a big impact on your future. Like training for a marathon, you'll need to start slowly and work your way up. When test day arrives, you'll be ready.

Start with the strategies you've read in the first two Secret Keys—plan your course and study in the way that works best for you. If you have time, consider using multiple study resources to get different approaches to the same concepts. It can be helpful to see difficult concepts from more than one angle. Then find a good source for practice tests. Many times, the test website will suggest potential study resources or provide sample tests.

Practice Test Strategy

If you're able to find at least three practice tests, we recommend this strategy:

Untimed and Open-Book Practice

Take the first test with no time constraints and with your notes and study guide handy. Take your time and focus on applying the strategies you've learned.

Timed and Open-Book Practice

Take the second practice test open-book as well, but set a timer and practice pacing yourself to finish in time.

Timed and Closed-Book Practice

Take any other practice tests as if it were test day. Set a timer and put away your study materials. Sit at a table or desk in a quiet room, imagine yourself at the testing center, and answer questions as quickly and accurately as possible.

Keep repeating timed and closed-book tests on a regular basis until you run out of practice tests or it's time for the actual test. Your mind will be ready for the schedule and stress of test day, and you'll be able to focus on recalling the material you've learned.

Secret Key #4 – Pace Yourself

Once you're fully prepared for the material on the test, your biggest challenge on test day will be managing your time. Just knowing that the clock is ticking can make you panic even if you have plenty of time left. Work on pacing yourself so you can build confidence against the time constraints of the exam. Pacing is a difficult skill to master, especially in a high-pressure environment, so **practice is vital**.

Set time expectations for your pace based on how much time is available. For example, if a section has 60 questions and the time limit is 30 minutes, you know you have to average 30 seconds or less per question in order to answer them all. Although 30 seconds is the hard limit, set 25 seconds per question as your goal, so you reserve extra time to spend on harder questions. When you budget extra time for the harder questions, you no longer have any reason to stress when those questions take longer to answer.

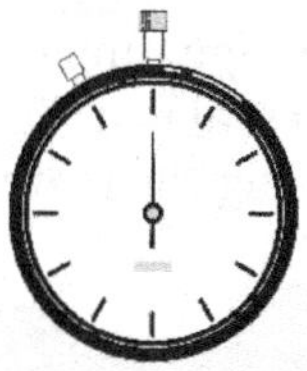

Don't let this time expectation distract you from working through the test at a calm, steady pace, but keep it in mind so you don't spend too much time on any one question. Recognize that taking extra time on one question you don't understand may keep you from answering two that you do understand later in the test. If your time limit for a question is up and you're still not sure of the answer, mark it and move on, and come back to it later if the time and the test format allow. If the testing format doesn't allow you to return to earlier questions, just make an educated guess; then put it out of your mind and move on.

On the easier questions, be careful not to rush. It may seem wise to hurry through them so you have more time for the challenging ones, but it's not worth missing one if you know the concept and just didn't take the time to read the question fully. Work efficiently but make sure you understand the question and have looked at all of the answer choices, since more than one may seem right at first.

Even if you're paying attention to the time, you may find yourself a little behind at some point. You should speed up to get back on track, but do so wisely. Don't panic; just take a few seconds less on each question until you're caught up. Don't guess without thinking, but do look through the answer choices and eliminate any you know are wrong. If you can get down to two choices, it is often worthwhile to guess from those. Once you've chosen an answer, move on and don't dwell on any that you skipped or had to hurry through. If a question was taking too long, chances are it was one of the harder ones, so you weren't as likely to get it right anyway.

On the other hand, if you find yourself getting ahead of schedule, it may be beneficial to slow down a little. The more quickly you work, the more likely you are to make a careless mistake that will affect your score. You've budgeted time for each question, so don't be afraid to spend that time. Practice an efficient but careful pace to get the most out of the time you have.

Secret Key #5 – Have a Plan for Guessing

When you're taking the test, you may find yourself stuck on a question. Some of the answer choices seem better than others, but you don't see the one answer choice that is obviously correct. What do you do?

The scenario described above is very common, yet most test takers have not effectively prepared for it. Developing and practicing a plan for guessing may be one of the single most effective uses of your time as you get ready for the exam.

In developing your plan for guessing, there are three questions to address:

- When should you start the guessing process?
- How should you narrow down the choices?
- Which answer should you choose?

When to Start the Guessing Process

Unless your plan for guessing is to select C every time (which, despite its merits, is not what we recommend), you need to leave yourself enough time to apply your answer elimination strategies. Since you have a limited amount of time for each question, that means that if you're going to give yourself the best shot at guessing correctly, you have to decide quickly whether or not you will guess.

Of course, the best-case scenario is that you don't have to guess at all, so first, see if you can answer the question based on your knowledge of the subject and basic reasoning skills. Focus on the key words in the question and try to jog your memory of related topics. Give yourself a chance to bring the knowledge to mind, but once you realize that you don't have (or you can't access) the knowledge you need to answer the question, it's time to start the guessing process.

It's almost always better to start the guessing process too early than too late. It only takes a few seconds to remember something and answer the question from knowledge. Carefully eliminating wrong answer choices takes longer. Plus, going through the process of eliminating answer choices can actually help jog your memory.

Summary: Start the guessing process as soon as you decide that you can't answer the question based on your knowledge.

How to Narrow Down the Choices

The next chapter in this book (**Test-Taking Strategies**) includes a wide range of strategies for how to approach questions and how to look for answer choices to eliminate. You will definitely want to read those carefully, practice them, and figure out which ones work best for you. Here though, we're going to address a mindset rather than a particular strategy.

Your odds of guessing an answer correctly depend on how many options you are choosing from.

Number of options left	5	4	3	2	1
Odds of guessing correctly	20%	25%	33%	50%	100%

You can see from this chart just how valuable it is to be able to eliminate incorrect answers and make an educated guess, but there are two things that many test takers do that cause them to miss out on the benefits of guessing:

- Accidentally eliminating the correct answer
- Selecting an answer based on an impression

We'll look at the first one here, and the second one in the next section.

To avoid accidentally eliminating the correct answer, we recommend a thought exercise called **the $5 challenge**. In this challenge, you only eliminate an answer choice from contention if you are willing to bet $5 on it being wrong. Why $5? Five dollars is a small but not insignificant amount of money. It's an amount you could afford to lose but wouldn't want to throw away. And while losing $5 once might not hurt too much, doing it twenty times will set you back $100. In the same way, each small decision you make—eliminating a choice here, guessing on a question there—won't by itself impact your score very much, but when you put them all together, they can make a big difference. By holding each answer choice elimination decision to a higher standard, you can reduce the risk of accidentally eliminating the correct answer.

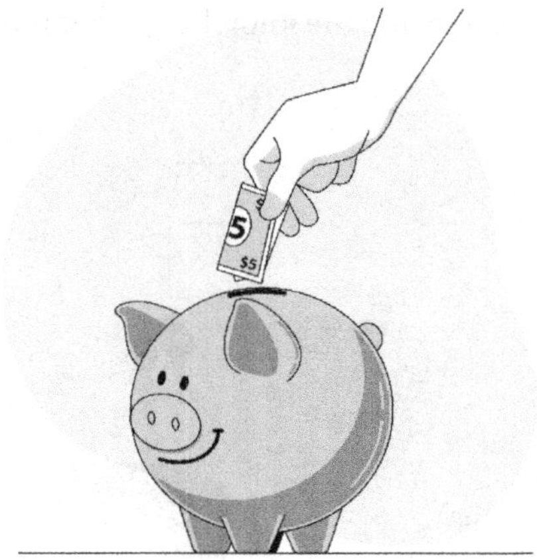

The $5 challenge can also be applied in a positive sense: If you are willing to bet $5 that an answer choice *is* correct, go ahead and mark it as correct.

Summary: Only eliminate an answer choice if you are willing to bet $5 that it is wrong.

Which Answer to Choose

You're taking the test. You've run into a hard question and decided you'll have to guess. You've eliminated all the answer choices you're willing to bet $5 on. Now you have to pick an answer. Why do we even need to talk about this? Why can't you just pick whichever one you feel like when the time comes?

The answer to these questions is that if you don't come into the test with a plan, you'll rely on your impression to select an answer choice, and if you do that, you risk falling into a trap. The test writers know that everyone who takes their test will be guessing on some of the questions, so they intentionally write wrong answer choices to seem plausible. You still have to pick an answer though, and if the wrong answer choices are designed to look right, how can you ever be sure that you're not falling for their trap? The best solution we've found to this dilemma is to take the decision out of your hands entirely. Here is the process we recommend:

Once you've eliminated any choices that you are confident (willing to bet $5) are wrong, select the first remaining choice as your answer.

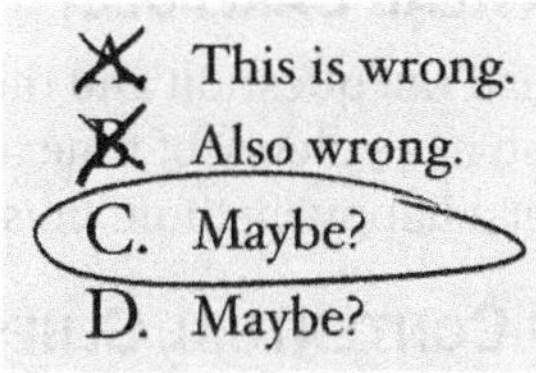

Whether you choose to select the first remaining choice, the second, or the last, the important thing is that you use some preselected standard. Using this approach guarantees that you will not be enticed into selecting an answer choice that looks right, because you are not basing your decision on how the answer choices look.

This is not meant to make you question your knowledge. Instead, it is to help you recognize the difference between your knowledge and your impressions. There's a huge difference between thinking an answer is right because of what you know, and thinking an answer is right because it looks or sounds like it should be right.

Summary: To ensure that your selection is appropriately random, make a predetermined selection from among all answer choices you have not eliminated.

Test-Taking Strategies

This section contains a list of test-taking strategies that you may find helpful as you work through the test. By taking what you know and applying logical thought, you can maximize your chances of answering any question correctly!

It is very important to realize that every question is different and every person is different: no single strategy will work on every question, and no single strategy will work for every person. That's why we've included all of them here, so you can try them out and determine which ones work best for different types of questions and which ones work best for you.

Question Strategies

✅ Read Carefully

Read the question and the answer choices carefully. Don't miss the question because you misread the terms. You have plenty of time to read each question thoroughly and make sure you understand what is being asked. Yet a happy medium must be attained, so don't waste too much time. You must read carefully and efficiently.

✅ Contextual Clues

Look for contextual clues. If the question includes a word you are not familiar with, look at the immediate context for some indication of what the word might mean. Contextual clues can often give you all the information you need to decipher the meaning of an unfamiliar word. Even if you can't determine the meaning, you may be able to narrow down the possibilities enough to make a solid guess at the answer to the question.

✅ Prefixes

If you're having trouble with a word in the question or answer choices, try dissecting it. Take advantage of every clue that the word might include. Prefixes can be a huge help. Usually, they allow you to determine a basic meaning. *Pre-* means before, *post-* means after, *pro-* is positive, *de-* is negative. From prefixes, you can get an idea of the general meaning of the word and try to put it into context.

✅ Hedge Words

Watch out for critical hedge words, such as *likely, may, can, sometimes, often, almost, mostly, usually, generally, rarely,* and *sometimes.* Question writers insert these hedge phrases to cover every possibility. Often an answer choice will be wrong simply because it leaves no room for exception. Be on guard for answer choices that have definitive words such as *exactly* and *always.*

✅ Switchback Words

Stay alert for *switchbacks.* These are the words and phrases frequently used to alert you to shifts in thought. The most common switchback words are *but, although,* and *however.* Others include *nevertheless, on the other hand, even though, while, in spite of, despite,* and *regardless of.* Switchback words are important to catch because they can change the direction of the question or an answer choice.

✅ Face Value

When in doubt, use common sense. Accept the situation in the problem at face value. Don't read too much into it. These problems will not require you to make wild assumptions. If you have to go beyond creativity and warp time or space in order to have an answer choice fit the question, then you should move on and consider the other answer choices. These are normal problems rooted in reality. The applicable relationship or explanation may not be readily apparent, but it is there for you to figure out. Use your common sense to interpret anything that isn't clear.

Answer Choice Strategies

⊘ ANSWER SELECTION

The most thorough way to pick an answer choice is to identify and eliminate wrong answers until only one is left, then confirm it is the correct answer. Sometimes an answer choice may immediately seem right, but be careful. The test writers will usually put more than one reasonable answer choice on each question, so take a second to read all of them and make sure that the other choices are not equally obvious. As long as you have time left, it is better to read every answer choice than to pick the first one that looks right without checking the others.

⊘ ANSWER CHOICE FAMILIES

An answer choice family consists of two (in rare cases, three) answer choices that are very similar in construction and cannot all be true at the same time. If you see two answer choices that are direct opposites or parallels, one of them is usually the correct answer. For instance, if one answer choice says that quantity *x* increases and another either says that quantity *x* decreases (opposite) or says that quantity *y* increases (parallel), then those answer choices would fall into the same family. An answer choice that doesn't match the construction of the answer choice family is more likely to be incorrect. Most questions will not have answer choice families, but when they do appear, you should be prepared to recognize them.

⊘ ELIMINATE ANSWERS

Eliminate answer choices as soon as you realize they are wrong, but make sure you consider all possibilities. If you are eliminating answer choices and realize that the last one you are left with is also wrong, don't panic. Start over and consider each choice again. There may be something you missed the first time that you will realize on the second pass.

⊘ AVOID FACT TRAPS

Don't be distracted by an answer choice that is factually true but doesn't answer the question. You are looking for the choice that answers the question. Stay focused on what the question is asking for so you don't accidentally pick an answer that is true but incorrect. Always go back to the question and make sure the answer choice you've selected actually answers the question and is not merely a true statement.

⊘ EXTREME STATEMENTS

In general, you should avoid answers that put forth extreme actions as standard practice or proclaim controversial ideas as established fact. An answer choice that states the "process should be used in certain situations, if..." is much more likely to be correct than one that states the "process should be discontinued completely." The first is a calm rational statement and doesn't even make a definitive, uncompromising stance, using a hedge word *if* to provide wiggle room, whereas the second choice is far more extreme.

⊘ BENCHMARK

As you read through the answer choices and you come across one that seems to answer the question well, mentally select that answer choice. This is not your final answer, but it's the one that will help you evaluate the other answer choices. The one that you selected is your benchmark or standard for judging each of the other answer choices. Every other answer choice must be compared to your benchmark. That choice is correct until proven otherwise by another answer choice beating it. If you find a better answer, then that one becomes your new benchmark. Once you've decided that no other choice answers the question as well as your benchmark, you have your final answer.

✓ Predict the Answer

Before you even start looking at the answer choices, it is often best to try to predict the answer. When you come up with the answer on your own, it is easier to avoid distractions and traps because you will know exactly what to look for. The right answer choice is unlikely to be word-for-word what you came up with, but it should be a close match. Even if you are confident that you have the right answer, you should still take the time to read each option before moving on.

General Strategies

✓ Tough Questions

If you are stumped on a problem or it appears too hard or too difficult, don't waste time. Move on! Remember though, if you can quickly check for obviously incorrect answer choices, your chances of guessing correctly are greatly improved. Before you completely give up, at least try to knock out a couple of possible answers. Eliminate what you can and then guess at the remaining answer choices before moving on.

✓ Check Your Work

Since you will probably not know every term listed and the answer to every question, it is important that you get credit for the ones that you do know. Don't miss any questions through careless mistakes. If at all possible, try to take a second to look back over your answer selection and make sure you've selected the correct answer choice and haven't made a costly careless mistake (such as marking an answer choice that you didn't mean to mark). This quick double check should more than pay for itself in caught mistakes for the time it costs.

✓ Pace Yourself

It's easy to be overwhelmed when you're looking at a page full of questions; your mind is confused and full of random thoughts, and the clock is ticking down faster than you would like. Calm down and maintain the pace that you have set for yourself. Especially as you get down to the last few minutes of the test, don't let the small numbers on the clock make you panic. As long as you are on track by monitoring your pace, you are guaranteed to have time for each question.

✓ Don't Rush

It is very easy to make errors when you are in a hurry. Maintaining a fast pace in answering questions is pointless if it makes you miss questions that you would have gotten right otherwise. Test writers like to include distracting information and wrong answers that seem right. Taking a little extra time to avoid careless mistakes can make all the difference in your test score. Find a pace that allows you to be confident in the answers that you select.

✓ Keep Moving

Panicking will not help you pass the test, so do your best to stay calm and keep moving. Taking deep breaths and going through the answer elimination steps you practiced can help to break through a stress barrier and keep your pace.

Final Notes

The combination of a solid foundation of content knowledge and the confidence that comes from practicing your plan for applying that knowledge is the key to maximizing your performance on test day. As your foundation of content knowledge is built up and strengthened, you'll find that the strategies included in this chapter become more and more effective in helping you quickly sift through the distractions and traps of the test to isolate the correct answer.

Now that you're preparing to move forward into the test content chapters of this book, be sure to keep your goal in mind. As you read, think about how you will be able to apply this information on the test. If you've already seen sample questions for the test and you have an idea of the question format and style, try to come up with questions of your own that you can answer based on what you're reading. This will give you valuable practice applying your knowledge in the same ways you can expect to on test day.

Good luck and good studying!

Five-Week ACT Study Plan

On the next few pages, we've provided an optional study plan to help you use this study guide to its fullest potential over the course of five weeks. If you have ten weeks available and want to spread it out more, spend two weeks on each section of the plan.

Below is a quick summary of the subjects covered in each week of the plan.

- Week 1: English
- Week 2: Math
- Week 3: Reading
- Week 4: Science
- Week 5: Writing (**If Applicable*)

Please note that not all subjects will take the same amount of time to work through.

Three full-length practice tests are included in this study guide. We recommend saving the third practice test and any additional tests for after you've completed the study plan. Take these practice tests timed and without any reference materials a day or two before the real thing as practice runs to get you in the mode of answering questions at a good pace.

**ACT Writing is an optional choice for the ACT that is not always required for college admission. Be sure to check with your college of choice for their admission requirements to verify if this is needed.*

Week 1: English

Instructional Content

First, read carefully through the English chapter in this book, checking off your progress as you go:

- ❑ Overview
- ❑ Conventions of Standard English
- ❑ Production of Writing
- ❑ Knowledge of Language

As you read, do the following:

- Highlight any sections, terms, or concepts you think are important
- Draw an asterisk (*) next to any areas you are struggling with
- Watch the review videos to gain more understanding of a particular topic
- Take notes in your notebook or in the margins of this book

After you've read through everything, go back and review any sections that you highlighted or that you drew an asterisk next to, referencing your notes along the way.

Practice Test #1

Now that you've read over the instructional content, it's time to take a practice test. Complete the English section of Practice Test #1. Take this test with **no time constraints**, and feel free to reference the applicable sections of this guide as you go. Once you've finished, check your answers against the provided answer key. For any questions you answered incorrectly, review the answer rationale, and then **go back and review** the applicable sections of the book. The goal in this stage is to understand why you answered the question incorrectly, and make sure that the next time you see a similar question, you will get it right.

Practice Test #2

Next, take the English section of Practice Test #2. This time, give yourself **45 minutes** (the amount of time you will have on the real ACT) to complete all 75 questions. You should again feel free to reference the guide and your notes, but be mindful of the clock. If you run out of time before you finish all of the questions, mark where you were when time expired, but go ahead and finish taking the practice test. Once you've finished, check your answers against the provided answer key and as before, review the answer rationale for any that you answered incorrectly and go back and review the associated instructional content. Your goal is still to increase understanding of the content but also to get used to the time constraints you will face on the test.

Week 2: Math

INSTRUCTIONAL CONTENT

First, read carefully through the math chapter in this book, checking off your progress as you go:

❑ Math Overview
❑ Number and Quantity
❑ Algebra
❑ Functions
❑ Geometry
❑ Statistics and Probability
❑ Integrating Essential Skills

As you read, do the following:

- Highlight any sections, terms, or concepts you think are important
- Draw an asterisk (*) next to any areas you are struggling with
- Watch the review videos to gain more understanding of a particular topic
- Take notes in your notebook or in the margins of this book

After you've read through everything, go back and review any sections that you highlighted or that you drew an asterisk next to, referencing your notes along the way.

PRACTICE TEST #1

Now that you've read over the instructional content, it's time to take a practice test. Complete the Math section of Practice Test #1. Take this test with **no time constraints**, and feel free to reference the applicable sections of this guide as you go. Once you've finished, check your answers against the provided answer key. For any questions you answered incorrectly, review the answer rationale, and then **go back and review** the applicable sections of the book. The goal in this stage is to understand why you answered the question incorrectly, and make sure that the next time you see a similar question, you will get it right.

PRACTICE TEST #2

Next, take the Math section of Practice Test #2. This time, give yourself **60 minutes** (the amount of time you will have on the real ACT) to complete all 60 questions. You should again feel free to reference the guide and your notes, but be mindful of the clock. If you run out of time before you finish all of the questions, mark where you were when time expired, but go ahead and finish taking the practice test. Once you've finished, check your answers against the provided answer key, and as before, review the answer rationale for any that you answered incorrectly and then go back and review the associated instructional content. Your goal is still to increase understanding of the content but also to get used to the time constraints you will face on the test.

Week 3: Reading

Instructional Content

First, read carefully through the reading chapter in this book, checking off your progress as you go:

❑ Reading Overview
❑ Key Ideas and Details
❑ Craft and Structure
❑ Integration of Knowledge and Ideas

As you read, do the following:

- Highlight any sections, terms, or concepts you think are important
- Draw an asterisk (*) next to any areas you are struggling with
- Watch the review videos to gain more understanding of a particular topic
- Take notes in your notebook or in the margins of this book

After you've read through everything, go back and review any sections that you highlighted or that you drew an asterisk next to, referencing your notes along the way.

Practice Test #1

Now that you've read over the instructional content, it's time to take a practice test. Complete the Reading section of Practice Test #1. Take this test with **no time constraints**, and feel free to reference the applicable sections of this guide as you go. Once you've finished, check your answers against the provided answer key. For any questions you answered incorrectly, review the answer rationale, and then **go back and review** the applicable sections of the book. The goal in this stage is to understand why you answered the question incorrectly, and make sure that the next time you see a similar question, you will get it right.

Practice Test #2

Next, take the Reading section of Practice Test #2. This time, give yourself **35 minutes** (the amount of time you will have on the real ACT) to complete all 40 questions. You should again feel free to reference the guide and your notes, but be mindful of the clock. If you run out of time before you finish all of the questions, mark where you were when time expired, but go ahead and finish taking the practice test. Once you've finished, check your answers against the provided answer key, and as before, review the answer rationale for any that you answered incorrectly and then go back and review the associated instructional content. Your goal is still to increase understanding of the content but also to get used to the time constraints you will face on the test.

Week 4: Science

Instructional Content

First, read carefully through the science chapter in this book, checking off your progress as you go:

❑ Science Overview
❑ Scientific Inquiry and Reasoning
❑ Physics
❑ Chemistry
❑ Biology
❑ Ecology
❑ Geology
❑ Earth Science and Weather
❑ Space Science

As you read, do the following:

- Highlight any sections, terms, or concepts you think are important
- Draw an asterisk (*) next to any areas you are struggling with
- Watch the review videos to gain more understanding of a particular topic
- Take notes in your notebook or in the margins of this book

After you've read through everything, go back and review any sections that you highlighted or that you drew an asterisk next to, referencing your notes along the way.

Practice Test #1

Now that you've read over the instructional content, it's time to take a practice test. Complete the Science section of Practice Test #1. Take this test with **no time constraints**, and feel free to reference the applicable sections of this guide as you go. Once you've finished, check your answers against the provided answer key. For any questions you answered incorrectly, review the answer rationale, and then **go back and review** the applicable sections of the book. The goal in this stage is to understand why you answered the question incorrectly, and make sure that the next time you see a similar question, you will get it right.

Practice Test #2

Next, take the Science section of Practice Test #2. This time, give yourself **35 minutes** (the amount of time you will have on the real ACT) to complete all 40 questions. You should again feel free to reference the guide and your notes, but be mindful of the clock. If you run out of time before you finish all of the questions, mark where you were when time expired, but go ahead and finish taking the practice test. Once you've finished, check your answers against the provided answer key, and as before, review the answer rationale for any that you answered incorrectly and then go back and review the associated instructional content. Your goal is still to increase understanding of the content but also to get used to the time constraints you will face on the test.

Week 5: Writing

Instructional Content

First, read carefully through the writing chapter in this book, checking off your progress as you go:

- ❑ Overview
- ❑ Brainstorm
- ❑ Strength Through Different Viewpoints
- ❑ Start Your Engines
- ❑ Don't Panic
- ❑ The Short Overview

As you read, do the following:

- Highlight any sections, terms, or concepts you think are important
- Draw an asterisk (*) next to any areas you are struggling with
- Watch the review videos to gain more understanding of a particular topic
- Take notes in your notebook or in the margins of this book

After you've read through everything, go back and review any sections that you highlighted or that you drew an asterisk next to, referencing your notes along the way.

Practice Test #1

Now that you've read over the instructional content, it's time to take a practice test. Complete the Writing section of Practice Test #1. Take this test with **no time constraints**, and feel free to reference the applicable sections of this guide as you go. Once you've finished, check your essay against the provided guide to make sure you have included all of the components of a well-constructed essay.

Practice Test #2

Next, take the Writing section of Practice Test #2. This time, give yourself **40 minutes** (the amount of time you will have on the real ACT) to complete your essay. You should again feel free to reference the guide and your notes, but be mindful of the clock. If you run out of time before you finish writing, mark where you were when time expired to have a reference for how much you will need to increase your pace in order to finish in time. Once you've finished, check your essay against the provided guide to make sure you have included all of the components of a well-constructed essay. Your goal is to improve your writing ability under pressure while also getting used to the time constraints you will face on the test.

English

Transform passive reading into active learning! After immersing yourself in this chapter, put your comprehension to the test by taking a quiz. The insights you gained will stay with you longer this way. Scan the QR code to go directly to the chapter quiz interface for this study guide. If you're using a computer, simply visit the bonus page at **mometrix.com/bonus948/act** and click the Chapter Quizzes link.

English Overview

The English portion of the ACT will have questions about underlined portions of text, with possible replacements as answer choices. Read the text four times, each time replacing the underlined portion with one of the choices. While reading the choices, read the sentence before, the sentence containing, and the sentence after the underlined portion. Sometimes an answer may not make sense until you read the following sentence and see how the two sentences flow together. Transitional words should create smooth, logical transitions and maintain a constant flow of text.

Some questions will be concerning sentence insertions. In those cases, do not look for the ones that simply restate what was in the previous sentence. New sentences should contain new information and new insights into the subject of the text. If asked for the paragraph to which a sentence would most naturally be added, find a key noun or word in that new sentence. Then, find the paragraph containing that exact word, or another word closely related to that key noun or word. That is the paragraph that should include the new sentence.

Some questions will ask what purpose a phrase fulfilled in a particular text. The answer depends upon the subject of the text. If the text is dramatic, then the phrase was probably used to show tension. If the text is comedic, then the phrase may have been there to relieve tension.

In related cases, you may be asked to provide a sentence that summarizes the text. Simple sentences, without wordy phrases, are usually best. If you are asked for a succinct answer, then the shorter the answer, the more likely it is correct.

Conventions of Standard English

PARTS OF SPEECH

NOUNS

A noun is a person, place, thing, or idea. The two main types of nouns are **common** and **proper** nouns. Nouns can also be categorized as abstract (i.e., general) or concrete (i.e., specific).

COMMON NOUNS

Common nouns are generic names for people, places, and things. Common nouns are not usually capitalized.

Examples of common nouns:

People: boy, girl, worker, manager

Places: school, bank, library, home

Things: dog, cat, truck, car

Review Video: What is a Noun?
Visit mometrix.com/academy and enter code: 344028

Proper Nouns

Proper nouns name specific people, places, or things. All proper nouns are capitalized.

Examples of proper nouns:

People: Abraham Lincoln, George Washington, Martin Luther King, Jr.

Places: Los Angeles, California; New York; Asia

Things: Statue of Liberty, Earth, Lincoln Memorial

Note: Some nouns can be either common or proper depending on their use. For example, when referring to the planet that we live on, *Earth* is a proper noun and is capitalized. When referring to the dirt, rocks, or land on our planet, *earth* is a common noun and is not capitalized.

General and Specific Nouns

General nouns are the names of conditions or ideas. **Specific nouns** name people, places, and things that are understood by using your senses.

General nouns:

Condition: beauty, strength

Idea: truth, peace

Specific nouns:

People: baby, friend, father

Places: town, park, city hall

Things: rainbow, cough, apple, silk, gasoline

Collective Nouns

Collective nouns are the names for a group of people, places, or things that may act as a whole. The following are examples of collective nouns: *class, company, dozen, group, herd, team,* and *public*. Collective nouns usually require an article, which denotes the noun as being a single unit. For instance, a choir is a group of singers. Even though there are many singers in a choir, the word choir is grammatically treated as a single unit. If we refer to the members of the group, and not the group itself, it is no longer a collective noun.

Incorrect: The *choir are* going to compete nationally this year.

Correct: The *choir is* going to compete nationally this year.

Incorrect: The *members* of the choir *is* competing nationally this year.

Correct: The *members* of the choir *are* competing nationally this year.

Pronouns

Pronouns are words that are used to stand in for nouns. A pronoun may be classified as personal, intensive, relative, interrogative, demonstrative, indefinite, and reciprocal.

Personal: *Nominative* is the case for nouns and pronouns that are the subject of a sentence. *Objective* is the case for nouns and pronouns that are an object in a sentence. *Possessive* is the case for nouns and pronouns that show possession or ownership.

Singular

	Nominative	Objective	Possessive
First Person	I	me	my, mine
Second Person	you	you	your, yours
Third Person	he, she, it	him, her, it	his, her, hers, its

Plural

	Nominative	Objective	Possessive
First Person	we	us	our, ours
Second Person	you	you	your, yours
Third Person	they	them	their, theirs

Intensive: I myself, you yourself, he himself, she herself, the (thing) itself, we ourselves, you yourselves, they themselves

Relative: which, who, whom, whose

Interrogative: what, which, who, whom, whose

Demonstrative: this, that, these, those

Indefinite: all, any, each, everyone, either/neither, one, some, several

Reciprocal: each other, one another

Review Video: Nouns and Pronouns
Visit mometrix.com/academy and enter code: 312073

Verbs

A verb is a word or group of words that indicates action or being. In other words, the verb shows something's action or state of being or the action that has been done to something. If you want to write a sentence, then you need a verb. Without a verb, you have no sentence.

Transitive and Intransitive Verbs

A **transitive verb** is a verb whose action indicates a receiver. **Intransitive verbs** do not indicate a receiver of an action. In other words, the action of the verb does not point to an object.

Transitive: He drives a car. | She feeds the dog.

Intransitive: He runs every day. | She voted in the last election.

A dictionary will tell you whether a verb is transitive or intransitive. Some verbs can be transitive or intransitive.

Action Verbs and Linking Verbs

Action verbs show what the subject is doing. In other words, an action verb shows action. Unlike most types of words, a single action verb, in the right context, can be an entire sentence. **Linking verbs** link the subject of a sentence to a noun or pronoun, or they link a subject with an adjective. You always need a verb if you want a complete sentence. However, linking verbs on their own cannot be a complete sentence.

Common linking verbs include *appear, be, become, feel, grow, look, seem, smell, sound,* and *taste.* However, any verb that shows a condition and connects to a noun, pronoun, or adjective that describes the subject of a sentence is a linking verb.

Action: He sings. | Run! | Go! | I talk with him every day. | She reads.

Linking:

Incorrect: I am.

Correct: I am John. | The roses smell lovely. | I feel tired.

Note: Some verbs are followed by words that look like prepositions, but they are a part of the verb and a part of the verb's meaning. These are known as phrasal verbs, and examples include *call off, look up*, and *drop off.*

Review Video: Action Verbs and Linking Verbs
Visit mometrix.com/academy and enter code: 743142

Voice

Transitive verbs may be in active voice or passive voice. The difference between active voice and passive voice is whether the subject is acting or being acted upon. When the subject of the sentence is doing the action, the verb is in **active voice**. When the subject is being acted upon, the verb is in **passive voice**.

Active: Jon drew the picture. (The subject *Jon* is doing the action of *drawing a picture.*)

Passive: The picture is drawn by Jon. (The subject *picture* is receiving the action from Jon.)

Verb Tenses

Verb **tense** is a property of a verb that indicates when the action being described takes place (past, present, or future) and whether or not the action is completed (simple or perfect). Describing an action taking place in the present (*I talk*) requires a different verb tense than describing an action that took place in the past (*I talked*). Some verb tenses require an auxiliary (helping) verb. These helping verbs include *am, are, is* | *have, has, had* | *was, were, will* (or *shall*).

Present: I talk	Present perfect: I have talked
Past: I talked	Past perfect: I had talked
Future: I will talk	Future perfect: I will have talked

Present: The action is happening at the current time.

Example: He *walks* to the store every morning.

To show that something is happening right now, use the progressive present tense: I *am walking.*

Past: The action happened in the past.

Example: She *walked* to the store an hour ago.

Future: The action will happen later.

Example: I *will walk* to the store tomorrow.

Present perfect: The action started in the past and continues into the present or took place previously at an unspecified time.

Example: I *have walked* to the store three times today.

Past perfect: The action was completed at some point in the past. This tense is usually used to describe an action that was completed before some other reference time or event.

Example: I *had eaten* already before they arrived.

Future perfect: The action will be completed before some point in the future. This tense may be used to describe an action that has already begun or has yet to begin.

Example: The project *will have been completed* by the deadline.

Review Video: Present Perfect, Past Perfect, and Future Perfect Verb Tenses
Visit mometrix.com/academy and enter code: 269472

Conjugating Verbs

When you need to change the form of a verb, you are **conjugating** a verb. The key forms of a verb are present tense (sing/sings), past tense (sang), present participle (singing), and past participle (sung). By combining these forms with helping verbs, you can make almost any verb tense. The following table demonstrate some of the different ways to conjugate a verb:

Tense	First Person	Second Person	Third Person Singular	Third Person Plural
Simple Present	I sing	You sing	He, she, it sings	They sing
Simple Past	I sang	You sang	He, she, it sang	They sang
Simple Future	I will sing	You will sing	He, she, it will sing	They will sing
Present Progressive	I am singing	You are singing	He, she, it is singing	They are singing
Past Progressive	I was singing	You were singing	He, she, it was singing	They were singing
Present Perfect	I have sung	You have sung	He, she, it has sung	They have sung
Past Perfect	I had sung	You had sung	He, she, it had sung	They had sung

Mood

There are three **moods** in English: the indicative, the imperative, and the subjunctive.

The **indicative mood** is used for facts, opinions, and questions.

Fact: You can do this.

Opinion: I think that you can do this.

Question: Do you know that you can do this?

The **imperative** is used for orders or requests.

Order: You are going to do this!

Request: Will you do this for me?

The **subjunctive mood** is for wishes and statements that go against fact.

Wish: I wish that I were famous.

Statement against fact: If I were you, I would do this. (This goes against fact because I am not you. You have the chance to do this, and I do not have the chance.)

Adjectives

An **adjective** is a word that is used to modify a noun or pronoun. An adjective answers a question: *Which one? What kind?* or *How many?* Usually, adjectives come before the words that they modify, but they may also come after a linking verb.

Which one? The *third* suit is my favorite.

What kind? This suit is *navy blue*.

How many? I am going to buy *four* pairs of socks to match the suit.

Review Video: Descriptive Text
Visit mometrix.com/academy and enter code: 174903

Articles

Articles are adjectives that are used to distinguish nouns as definite or indefinite. *A*, *an*, and *the* are the only articles. **Definite** nouns are preceded by *the* and indicate a specific person, place, thing, or idea. **Indefinite** nouns are preceded by *a* or *an* and do not indicate a specific person, place, thing, or idea.

Note: *An* comes before words that start with a vowel sound. For example, "Are you going to get an **u**mbrella?"

Definite: I lost *the* bottle that belongs to me.

Indefinite: Does anyone have *a* bottle to share?

Review Video: Function of Articles in a Sentence
Visit mometrix.com/academy and enter code: 449383

Comparison with Adjectives

Some adjectives are relative and other adjectives are absolute. Adjectives that are **relative** can show the comparison between things. **Absolute** adjectives can also show comparison, but they do so in a different way. Let's say that you are reading two books. You think that one book is perfect, and the other book is not exactly perfect. It is not possible for one book to be more perfect than the other. Either you think that the book is perfect, or you think that the book is imperfect. In this case, perfect and imperfect are absolute adjectives.

Relative adjectives will show the different **degrees** of something or someone to something else or someone else. The three degrees of adjectives include positive, comparative, and superlative.

The **positive** degree is the normal form of an adjective.

Example: This work is *difficult*. | She is *smart*.

The **comparative** degree compares one person or thing to another person or thing.

Example: This work is *more difficult* than your work. | She is *smarter* than me.

The **superlative** degree compares more than two people or things.

Example: This is the *most difficult* work of my life. | She is the *smartest* lady in school.

Review Video: What is an Adjective?
Visit mometrix.com/academy and enter code: 470154

Adverbs

An **adverb** is a word that is used to **modify** a verb, an adjective, or another adverb. Usually, adverbs answer one of these questions: *When? Where? How?* and *Why?* The negatives *not* and *never* are considered adverbs. Adverbs that modify adjectives or other adverbs **strengthen** or **weaken** the words that they modify.

Examples:

He walks *quickly* through the crowd.

The water flows *smoothly* on the rocks.

Note: Adverbs are usually indicated by the morpheme *-ly*, which has been added to the root word. For instance, *quick* can be made into an adverb by adding *-ly* to construct *quickly*. Some words that end in *-ly* do not follow this rule and can behave as other parts of speech. Examples of adjectives ending in *-ly* include: *early, friendly, holy, lonely, silly*, and *ugly*. To know if a word that ends in *-ly* is an adjective or adverb, check your dictionary. Also, while many adverbs end in *-ly*, you need to remember that not all adverbs end in *-ly*.

Examples:

He is *never* angry.

You are *too* irresponsible to travel alone.

Review Video: What is an Adverb?
Visit mometrix.com/academy and enter code: 713951

Review Video: Adverbs that Modify Adjectives
Visit mometrix.com/academy and enter code: 122570

Comparison with Adverbs

The rules for comparing adverbs are the same as the rules for adjectives.

The **positive** degree is the standard form of an adverb.

Example: He arrives *soon*. | She speaks *softly* to her friends.

The **comparative** degree compares one person or thing to another person or thing.

Example: He arrives *sooner* than Sarah. | She speaks *more softly* than him.

The **superlative** degree compares more than two people or things.

Example: He arrives *soonest* of the group. | She speaks the *most softly* of any of her friends.

Prepositions

A **preposition** is a word placed before a noun or pronoun that shows the relationship between that noun or pronoun and another word in the sentence.

Common prepositions:

about	before	during	on	under
after	beneath	for	over	until
against	between	from	past	up
among	beyond	in	through	with
around	by	of	to	within
at	down	off	toward	without

Examples:

The napkin is *in* the drawer.

The Earth rotates *around* the Sun.

The needle is *beneath* the haystack.

Can you find "me" *among* the words?

Review Video: Prepositions
Visit mometrix.com/academy and enter code: 946763

Conjunctions

Conjunctions join words, phrases, or clauses and they show the connection between the joined pieces. **Coordinating conjunctions** connect equal parts of sentences. **Correlative conjunctions** show the connection between pairs. **Subordinating conjunctions** join subordinate (i.e., dependent) clauses with independent clauses.

Coordinating Conjunctions

The **coordinating conjunctions** include: *and, but, yet, or, nor, for,* and *so*

Examples:

The rock was small, *but* it was heavy.

She drove in the night, *and* he drove in the day.

Correlative Conjunctions

The **correlative conjunctions** are: *either...or* | *neither...nor* | *not only...but also*

Examples:

Either you are coming *or* you are staying.

He *not only* ran three miles *but also* swam 200 yards.

Review Video: Coordinating and Correlative Conjunctions
Visit mometrix.com/academy and enter code: 390329

Review Video: Adverb Equal Comparisons
Visit mometrix.com/academy and enter code: 231291

Subordinating Conjunctions

Common **subordinating conjunctions** include:

after	since	whenever
although	so that	where
because	unless	wherever
before	until	whether
in order that	when	while

Examples:

I am hungry *because* I did not eat breakfast.

He went home *when* everyone left.

Review Video: Subordinating Conjunctions
Visit mometrix.com/academy and enter code: 958913

Interjections

Interjections are words of exclamation (i.e., audible expression of great feeling) that are used alone or as a part of a sentence. Often, they are used at the beginning of a sentence for an introduction. Sometimes, they can be used in the middle of a sentence to show a change in thought or attitude.

Common Interjections: Hey! | Oh, | Ouch! | Please! | Wow!

Agreement and Sentence Structure

Subjects and Predicates

Subjects

The **subject** of a sentence names who or what the sentence is about. The subject may be directly stated in a sentence, or the subject may be the implied *you*. The **complete subject** includes the simple subject and all of its modifiers. To find the complete subject, ask *Who* or *What* and insert the verb to complete the question. The answer, including any modifiers (adjectives, prepositional phrases, etc.), is the complete subject. To find the **simple subject**, remove all of the modifiers in the complete subject. Being able to locate the subject of a sentence helps with many problems, such as those involving sentence fragments and subject-verb agreement.

Examples:

simple subject

The small, red car is the one that he wants for Christmas.

complete subject

simple subject

The young artist is coming over for dinner.

complete subject

Review Video: Subjects in English
Visit mometrix.com/academy and enter code: 444771

In **imperative** sentences, the verb's subject is understood (e.g., [You] Run to the store), but is not actually present in the sentence. Normally, the subject comes before the verb. However, the subject comes after the verb in sentences that begin with *There are* or *There was.*

Direct:

John knows the way to the park.	Who knows the way to the park?	John
The cookies need ten more minutes.	What needs ten minutes?	The cookies
By five o'clock, Bill will need to leave.	Who needs to leave?	Bill
There are five letters on the table for him.	What is on the table?	Five letters
There were coffee and doughnuts in the house.	What was in the house?	Coffee and doughnuts

Implied:

Go to the post office for me.	Who is going to the post office?	You
Come and sit with me, please?	Who needs to come and sit?	You

PREDICATES

In a sentence, you always have a predicate and a subject. The subject tells who or what the sentence is about, and the **predicate** explains or describes the subject. The predicate includes the verb or verb phrase and any direct or indirect objects of the verb, as well as any words or phrases modifying these.

Think about the sentence *He sings.* In this sentence, we have a subject (He) and a predicate (sings). This is all that is needed for a sentence to be complete. Most sentences contain more information, but if this is all the information that you are given, then you have a complete sentence.

Now, let's look at another sentence: *John and Jane sing on Tuesday nights at the dance hall.*

subject — predicate

John and Jane sing on Tuesday nights at the dance hall.

Review Video: What is a Complete Predicate?
Visit mometrix.com/academy and enter code: 293942

SUBJECT-VERB AGREEMENT

Verbs must **agree** with their subjects in number and in person. To agree in number, singular subjects need singular verbs and plural subjects need plural verbs. A **singular** noun refers to **one** person, place, or thing. A **plural** noun refers to **more than one** person, place, or thing. To agree in person, the correct verb form must be chosen to match the first, second, or third person subject. The present tense ending *-s* or *-es* is used on a verb if its subject is third person singular; otherwise, the verb's ending is not modified.

Review Video: Subject-Verb Agreement
Visit mometrix.com/academy and enter code: 479190

NUMBER AGREEMENT EXAMPLES:

singular subject — singular verb

Single Subject and Verb: Dan calls home.

Dan is one person. So, the singular verb *calls* is needed.

plural subject — plural verb

Plural Subject and Verb: Dan and Bob call home.

More than one person needs the plural verb *call.*

PERSON AGREEMENT EXAMPLES:

First Person: I *am* walking.

Second Person: You *are* walking.

Third Person: He *is* walking.

COMPLICATIONS WITH SUBJECT-VERB AGREEMENT

WORDS BETWEEN SUBJECT AND VERB

Words that come between the simple subject and the verb have no bearing on subject-verb agreement.

Examples:

singular subject — singular verb

The joy of my life returns home tonight.

The phrase *of my life* does not influence the verb *returns.*

The question (singular subject) that still remains unanswered is (singular verb) "Who are you?"

Don't let the phrase *"that still remains..."* trouble you. The subject *question* goes with *is.*

Compound Subjects

A compound subject is formed when two or more nouns joined by *and*, *or*, or *nor* jointly act as the subject of the sentence.

Joined by And

When a compound subject is joined by *and*, it is treated as a plural subject and requires a plural verb.

Examples:

You and Jon (plural subject) are (plural verb) invited to come to my house.

The pencil and paper (plural subject) belong (plural verb) to me.

Joined by Or/Nor

For a compound subject joined by *or* or *nor*, the verb must agree in number with the part of the subject that is closest to the verb (italicized in the examples below).

Examples:

Today or tomorrow (subject) is (verb) the day.

Stan or Phil (subject) wants (verb) to read the book.

Neither the pen nor the book (subject) is (verb) on the desk.

Either the blanket or pillows (subject) arrive (verb) this afternoon.

Indefinite Pronouns as Subject

An indefinite pronoun is a pronoun that does not refer to a specific noun. Some indefinite pronouns function as only singular, some function as only plural, and some can function as either singular or plural depending on how they are used.

Always Singular

Pronouns such as *each*, *either*, *everybody*, *anybody*, *somebody*, and *nobody* are always singular.

Examples:

Each (singular subject) of the runners has (singular verb) a different bib number.

Is (singular verb) either (singular subject) of you ready for the game?

Note: The words *each* and *either* can also be used as adjectives (e.g., *each* person is unique). When one of these adjectives modifies the subject of a sentence, it is always a singular subject.

> Everybody (singular subject) grows (singular verb) a day older every day.

> Anybody (singular subject) is (singular verb) welcome to bring a tent.

Always Plural

Pronouns such as *both*, *several*, and *many* are always plural.

Examples:

> Both (plural subject) of the siblings were (plural verb) too tired to argue.

> Many (plural subject) have tried (plural verb), but none have succeeded.

Depend on Context

Pronouns such as *some*, *any*, *all*, *none*, *more*, and *most* can be either singular or plural depending on what they are representing in the context of the sentence.

Examples:

> All (singular subject) of my dog's food was (singular verb) still there in his bowl.

> By the end of the night, all (plural subject) of my guests were (plural verb) already excited about coming to my next party.

Other Cases Involving Plural or Irregular Form

Some nouns are **singular in meaning but plural in form**: news, mathematics, physics, and economics.

> The *news is* coming on now.

> *Mathematics is* my favorite class.

Some nouns are plural in form and meaning, and have **no singular equivalent**: scissors and pants.

> Do these *pants come* with a shirt?

> The *scissors are* for my project.

Mathematical operations are **irregular** in their construction, but are normally considered to be **singular in meaning**.

> *One plus one is* two.

> *Three times three is* nine.

Note: Look to your **dictionary** for help when you aren't sure whether a noun with a plural form has a singular or plural meaning.

Complements

A complement is a noun, pronoun, or adjective that is used to give more information about the subject or object in the sentence.

Direct Objects

A direct object is a noun or pronoun that tells who or what **receives** the action of the verb. A sentence will only include a direct object if the verb is a transitive verb. If the verb is an intransitive verb or a linking verb, there will be no direct object. When you are looking for a direct object, find the verb and ask *who* or *what.*

Examples:

> I took *the blanket.*
>
> Jane read *books.*

Indirect Objects

An indirect object is a noun or pronoun that indicates what or whom the action had an **influence** on. If there is an indirect object in a sentence, then there will also be a direct object. When you are looking for the indirect object, find the verb and ask *to/for whom or what.*

Examples:

> indirect object | direct object
>
> We taught the old dog a new trick.
>
> indirect object | direct object
>
> I gave them a math lesson.

Review Video: Direct and Indirect Objects
Visit mometrix.com/academy and enter code: 817385

Predicate Nominatives and Predicate Adjectives

As we looked at previously, verbs may be classified as either action verbs or linking verbs. A linking verb is so named because it links the subject to words in the predicate that describe or define the subject. These words are called predicate nominatives (if nouns or pronouns) or predicate adjectives (if adjectives).

Examples:

> subject | predicate nominative
>
> My father is a lawyer.
>
> subject | predicate adjective
>
> Your mother is patient.

Pronoun Usage

The **antecedent** is the noun that has been replaced by a pronoun. A pronoun and its antecedent **agree** when they have the same number (singular or plural) and gender (male, female, or neutral).

Examples:

antecedent pronoun

Singular agreement: John came into town, and he played for us.

antecedent pronoun

Plural agreement: John and Rick came into town, and they played for us.

To determine which is the correct pronoun to use in a compound subject or object, try each pronoun **alone** in place of the compound in the sentence. Your knowledge of pronouns will tell you which one is correct.

Example:

Bob and (I, me) will be going.

Test: (1) *I will be going* or (2) *Me will be going*. The second choice cannot be correct because *me* cannot be used as the subject of a sentence. Instead, *me* is used as an object.

Answer: Bob and I will be going.

When a pronoun is used with a noun immediately following (as in "we boys"), try the sentence **without the added noun**.

Example:

(We/Us) boys played football last year.

Test: (1) *We played football last ye*ar or (2) *Us played football last year*. Again, the second choice cannot be correct because *us* cannot be used as a subject of a sentence. Instead, *us* is used as an object.

Answer: We boys played football last year.

Review Video: Pronoun Usage
Visit mometrix.com/academy and enter code: 666500

Review Video: What is Pronoun-Antecedent Agreement?
Visit mometrix.com/academy and enter code: 919704

A pronoun should point clearly to the **antecedent**. Here is how a pronoun reference can be unhelpful if it is puzzling or not directly stated.

antecedent pronoun

Unhelpful: Ron and Jim went to the store, and he bought soda.

Who bought soda? Ron or Jim?

antecedent pronoun

Helpful: Jim went to the store, and he bought soda.

The sentence is clear. Jim bought the soda.

Some pronouns change their form by their placement in a sentence. A pronoun that is a **subject** in a sentence comes in the **subjective case**. Pronouns that serve as **objects** appear in the **objective case**. Finally, the pronouns that are used as **possessives** appear in the **possessive case**.

Examples:

Subjective case: *He* is coming to the show.

The pronoun *He* is the subject of the sentence.

Objective case: Josh drove *him* to the airport.

The pronoun *him* is the object of the sentence.

Possessive case: The flowers are *mine*.

The pronoun *mine* shows ownership of the flowers.

The word *who* is a subjective-case pronoun that can be used as a **subject**. The word *whom* is an objective-case pronoun that can be used as an **object**. The words *who* and *whom* are common in subordinate clauses or in questions.

Examples:

He knows who (subject) wants (verb) to come.

He knows the man whom (object) we want (verb) at the party.

Clauses

A clause is a group of words that contains both a subject and a predicate (verb). There are two types of clauses: independent and dependent. An **independent clause** contains a complete thought, while a **dependent (or subordinate) clause** does not. A dependent clause includes a subject and a verb, and may also contain objects or complements, but it cannot stand as a complete thought without being joined to an independent clause. Dependent clauses function within sentences as adjectives, adverbs, or nouns.

Example:

I am running (independent clause) because I want to stay in shape (dependent clause).

The clause *I am running* is an independent clause: it has a subject and a verb, and it gives a complete thought. The clause *because I want to stay in shape* is a dependent clause: it has a subject and a verb, but it does not express a complete thought. It adds detail to the independent clause to which it is attached.

Review Video: What is a Clause?
Visit mometrix.com/academy and enter code: 940170

Review Video: Independent and Dependent Clauses
Visit mometrix.com/academy and enter code: 556903

Types of Dependent Clauses

Adjective Clauses

An **adjective clause** is a dependent clause that modifies a noun or a pronoun. Adjective clauses begin with a relative pronoun (*who, whose, whom, which,* and *that*) or a relative adverb (*where, when,* and *why*).

Also, adjective clauses usually come immediately after the noun that the clause needs to explain or rename. This is done to ensure that it is clear which noun or pronoun the clause is modifying.

Examples:

I learned the reason (independent clause) why I won the award. (adjective clause)

This is the place (independent clause) where I started my first job. (adjective clause)

An adjective clause can be an essential or nonessential clause. An essential clause is very important to the sentence. **Essential clauses** explain or define a person or thing. **Nonessential clauses** give more information about a person or thing but are not necessary to define them. Nonessential clauses are set off with commas while essential clauses are not.

Examples:

A person who works hard at first (essential clause) can often rest later in life.

Neil Armstrong, who walked on the moon, (nonessential clause) is my hero.

Review Video: Adjective Clauses and Phrases
Visit mometrix.com/academy and enter code: 520888

Adverb Clauses

An **adverb clause** is a dependent clause that modifies a verb, adjective, or adverb. In sentences with multiple dependent clauses, adverb clauses are usually placed immediately before or after the independent clause. An adverb clause is introduced with words such as *after, although, as, before, because, if, since, so, unless, when, where*, and *while*.

Examples:

When you walked outside, (adverb clause) I called the manager.

I will go with you unless you want to stay. (adverb clause)

Noun Clauses

A **noun clause** is a dependent clause that can be used as a subject, object, or complement. Noun clauses begin with words such as *how, that, what, whether, which, who,* and *why*. These words can also come with an adjective clause. Unless the noun clause is being used as the subject of the sentence, it should come after the verb of the independent clause.

Examples:

noun clause: The real mystery is how you avoided serious injury.

noun clause: What you learn from each other depends on your honesty with others.

Subordination

When two related ideas are not of equal importance, the ideal way to combine them is to make the more important idea an independent clause and the less important idea a dependent or subordinate clause. This is called **subordination**.

Example:

Separate ideas: The team had a perfect regular season. The team lost the championship.

Subordinated: Despite having a perfect regular season, *the team lost the championship.*

Phrases

A phrase is a group of words that functions as a single part of speech, usually a noun, adjective, or adverb. A **phrase** is not a complete thought and does not contain a subject and predicate, but it adds detail or explanation to a sentence, or renames something within the sentence.

Prepositional Phrases

One of the most common types of phrases is the prepositional phrase. A **prepositional phrase** begins with a preposition and ends with a noun or pronoun that is the object of the preposition. Normally, the prepositional phrase functions as an **adjective** or an **adverb** within the sentence.

Examples:

prepositional phrase: The picnic is on the blanket.

prepositional phrase: I am sick with a fever today.

prepositional phrase: Among the many flowers, John found a four-leaf clover.

Verbal Phrases

A **verbal** is a word or phrase that is formed from a verb but does not function as a verb. Depending on its particular form, it may be used as a noun, adjective, or adverb. A verbal does **not** replace a verb in a sentence.

Examples:

verb: Correct: Walk a mile daily.

This is a complete sentence with the implied subject *you.*

verbal

Incorrect: To walk a mile.

This is not a sentence since there is no functional verb.

There are three types of verbal: **participles**, **gerunds**, and **infinitives**. Each type of verbal has a corresponding **phrase** that consists of the verbal itself along with any complements or modifiers.

PARTICIPLES

A **participle** is a type of verbal that always functions as an adjective. The present participle always ends with -*ing*. Past participles end with *-d, -ed, -n,* or *-t.* Participles are combined with helping verbs to form certain verb tenses, but a participle by itself cannot function as a verb.

verb | present participle | past participle

Examples: dance | dancing | danced

Participial phrases most often come right before or right after the noun or pronoun that they modify.

Examples:

participial phrase

Shipwrecked on an island, the boys started to fish for food.

participial phrase

Having been seated for five hours, we got out of the car to stretch our legs.

participial phrase

Praised for their work, the group accepted the first-place trophy.

GERUNDS

A **gerund** is a type of verbal that always functions as a **noun**. Like present participles, gerunds always end with *-ing*, but they can be easily distinguished from participles by the part of speech they represent (participles always function as adjectives). Since a gerund or gerund phrase always functions as a noun, it can be used as the subject of a sentence, the predicate nominative, or the object of a verb or preposition.

Examples:

gerund

We want to be known for teaching the poor.

object of preposition

gerund

Coaching this team is the best job of my life.

subject

gerund

We like practicing our songs in the basement.

object of verb

INFINITIVES

An **infinitive** is a type of verbal that can function as a noun, an adjective, or an adverb. An infinitive is made of the word *to* and the basic form of the verb. As with all other types of verbal phrases, an infinitive phrase includes the verbal itself and all of its complements or modifiers.

Examples:

infinitive: To join / noun: To join the team

To join the team is my goal in life.

The animals have enough food to eat for the night.

infinitive: to eat / adjective: to eat for the night

People lift weights to exercise their muscles.

infinitive: to exercise / adverb: to exercise their muscles

Review Video: Verbals
Visit mometrix.com/academy and enter code: 915480

Appositive Phrases

An **appositive** is a word or phrase that is used to explain or rename nouns or pronouns. Noun phrases, gerund phrases, and infinitive phrases can all be used as appositives.

Examples:

Terriers, hunters at heart, have been dressed up to look like lap dogs.

appositive: hunters at heart

The noun phrase *hunters at heart* renames the noun *terriers*.

His plan, to save and invest his money, was proven as a safe approach.

appositive: to save and invest his money

The infinitive phrase explains what the plan is.

Appositive phrases can be **essential** or **nonessential**. An appositive phrase is essential if the person, place, or thing being described or renamed is too general for its meaning to be understood without the appositive.

Examples:

Two of America's Founding Fathers, George Washington and Thomas Jefferson, served as presidents.

essential: George Washington and Thomas Jefferson

George Washington and Thomas Jefferson, two Founding Fathers, served as presidents.

nonessential: two Founding Fathers

Absolute Phrases

An absolute phrase is a phrase that consists of **a noun followed by a participle**. An absolute phrase provides **context** to what is being described in the sentence, but it does not modify or explain any particular word; it is essentially independent.

Examples:

The alarm ringing, he pushed the snooze button.

(noun: The alarm; participle: ringing; absolute phrase: The alarm ringing)

The music paused, she continued to dance through the crowd.

(noun: The music; participle: paused; absolute phrase: The music paused)

Parallelism

When multiple items or ideas are presented in a sentence in series, such as in a list, the items or ideas must be stated in grammatically equivalent ways. For example, if two ideas are listed in parallel and the first is stated in gerund form, the second cannot be stated in infinitive form. (e.g., *I enjoy reading and to study.* [incorrect]) An infinitive and a gerund are not grammatically equivalent. Instead, you should write *I enjoy reading and studying* OR *I like to read and to study*. In lists of more than two, all items must be parallel.

Example:

> **Incorrect**: He stopped at the office, grocery store, and the pharmacy before heading home.
>
> The first and third items in the list of places include the article *the*, so the second item needs it as well.
>
> **Correct**: He stopped at the office, *the* grocery store, and the pharmacy before heading home.

Example:

> **Incorrect**: While vacationing in Europe, she went biking, skiing, and climbed mountains.
>
> The first and second items in the list are gerunds, so the third item must be as well.
>
> **Correct**: While vacationing in Europe, she went biking, skiing, and *mountain climbing*.

Review Video: Parallel Sentence Construction
Visit mometrix.com/academy and enter code: 831988

Sentence Purpose

There are four types of sentences: declarative, imperative, interrogative, and exclamatory.

A **declarative** sentence states a fact and ends with a period.

> *The football game starts at seven o'clock.*

An **imperative** sentence tells someone to do something and generally ends with a period. An urgent command might end with an exclamation point instead.

> *Don't forget to buy your ticket.*

An **interrogative** sentence asks a question and ends with a question mark.

> *Are you going to the game on Friday?*

An **exclamatory** sentence shows strong emotion and ends with an exclamation point.

> *I can't believe we won the game!*

Sentence Structure

Sentences are classified by structure based on the type and number of clauses present. The four classifications of sentence structure are the following:

Simple: A simple sentence has one independent clause with no dependent clauses. A simple sentence may have **compound elements** (i.e., compound subject or verb).

Examples:

single subject | single verb

Judy watered the lawn.

compound subject | single verb

Judy and Alan watered the lawn.

single subject | compound verb | compound verb

Judy watered the lawn and pulled weeds.

compound subject | compound verb | compound verb

Judy and Alan watered the lawn and pulled weeds.

Compound: A compound sentence has two or more independent clauses with no dependent clauses. Usually, the independent clauses are joined with a comma and a coordinating conjunction or with a semicolon.

Examples:

independent clause | independent clause

The time has come, and we are ready.

independent clause | independent clause

I woke up at dawn; the sun was just coming up.

Complex: A complex sentence has one independent clause and at least one dependent clause.

Examples:

dependent clause | independent clause

Although he had the flu, Harry went to work.

independent clause | dependent clause

Marcia got married, after she finished college.

Compound-Complex: A compound-complex sentence has at least two independent clauses and at least one dependent clause.

Examples:

independent clause | dependent clause | independent clause

John is my friend who went to India, and he brought back souvenirs.

independent clause | independent clause | dependent clause

You may not realize this, but we heard the music that you played last night.

Review Video: Sentence Structure
Visit mometrix.com/academy and enter code: 700478

Sentence variety is important to consider when writing an essay or speech. A variety of sentence lengths and types creates rhythm, makes a passage more engaging, and gives writers an opportunity to demonstrate their writing style. Writing that uses the same length or type of sentence without variation can be boring or difficult to read. To evaluate a passage for effective sentence variety, it is helpful to note whether the passage contains diverse sentence structures and lengths. It is also important to pay attention to the way each sentence starts and avoid beginning with the same words or phrases.

Sentence Fragments

Recall that a group of words must contain at least one **independent clause** in order to be considered a sentence. If it doesn't contain even one independent clause, it is called a **sentence fragment**.

The appropriate process for **repairing** a sentence fragment depends on what type of fragment it is. If the fragment is a dependent clause, it can sometimes be as simple as removing a subordinating word (e.g., when, because, if) from the beginning of the fragment. Alternatively, a dependent clause can be incorporated into a closely related neighboring sentence. If the fragment is missing some required part, like a subject or a verb, the fix might be as simple as adding the missing part.

Examples:

Fragment: Because he wanted to sail the Mediterranean.

Removed subordinating word: He wanted to sail the Mediterranean.

Combined with another sentence: Because he wanted to sail the Mediterranean, he booked a Greek island cruise.

Run-on Sentences

Run-on sentences consist of multiple independent clauses that have not been joined together properly. Run-on sentences can be corrected in several different ways:

Join clauses properly: This can be done with a comma and coordinating conjunction, with a semicolon, or with a colon or dash if the second clause is explaining something in the first.

Example:

Incorrect: I went on the trip, we visited lots of castles.

Corrected: I went on the trip, and we visited lots of castles.

Split into separate sentences: This correction is most effective when the independent clauses are very long or when they are not closely related.

Example:

Incorrect: The drive to New York takes ten hours, my uncle lives in Boston.

Corrected: The drive to New York takes ten hours. My uncle lives in Boston.

Make one clause dependent: This is the easiest way to make the sentence correct and more interesting at the same time. It's often as simple as adding a subordinating word between the two clauses or before the first clause.

Example:

Incorrect: I finally made it to the store and I bought some eggs.

Corrected: When I finally made it to the store, I bought some eggs.

Reduce to one clause with a compound verb: If both clauses have the same subject, remove the subject from the second clause, and you now have just one clause with a compound verb.

Example:

Incorrect: The drive to New York takes ten hours, it makes me very tired.

Corrected: The drive to New York takes ten hours and makes me very tired.

Note: While these are the simplest ways to correct a run-on sentence, often the best way is to completely reorganize the thoughts in the sentence and rewrite it.

Review Video: Fragments and Run-on Sentences
Visit mometrix.com/academy and enter code: 541989

Dangling and Misplaced Modifiers

Dangling Modifiers

A dangling modifier is a dependent clause or verbal phrase that does not have a clear logical connection to a word in the sentence.

Example:

dangling modifier

Incorrect: Reading each magazine article, the stories caught my attention.

The word *stories* cannot be modified by *Reading each magazine article*. People can read, but stories cannot read. Therefore, the subject of the sentence must be a person.

gerund phrase

Corrected: Reading each magazine article, I was entertained by the stories.

Example:

dangling modifier

Incorrect: Ever since childhood, my grandparents have visited me for Christmas.

The speaker in this sentence can't have been visited by her grandparents when *they* were children, since she wouldn't have been born yet. Either the modifier should be clarified or the sentence should be rearranged to specify whose childhood is being referenced.

dependent clause

Clarified: Ever since I was a child, my grandparents have visited for Christmas.

adverb phrase

Rearranged: Ever since childhood, I have enjoyed my grandparents visiting for Christmas.

Misplaced Modifiers

Because modifiers are grammatically versatile, they can be put in many different places within the structure of a sentence. The danger of this versatility is that a modifier can accidentally be placed where it is modifying the wrong word or where it is not clear which word it is modifying.

Example:

modifier

Incorrect: She read the book to a crowd that was filled with beautiful pictures.

The book was filled with beautiful pictures, not the crowd.

modifier

Corrected: She read the book that was filled with beautiful pictures to a crowd.

Example:

modifier

Ambiguous: Derek saw a bus nearly hit a man on his way to work.

Was Derek on his way to work or was the other man?

modifier

Derek: On his way to work, Derek saw a bus nearly hit a man.

modifier

The other man: Derek saw a bus nearly hit a man who was on his way to work.

Split Infinitives

A split infinitive occurs when a modifying word comes between the word *to* and the verb that pairs with *to*.

Example: To *clearly* explain vs. *To explain* clearly | To *softly* sing vs. *To sing* softly

Though considered improper by some, split infinitives may provide better clarity and simplicity in some cases than the alternatives. As such, avoiding them should not be considered a universal rule.

Double Negatives

Standard English allows **two negatives** only when a **positive** meaning is intended. (e.g., The team was *not displeased* with their performance.) Double negatives to emphasize negation are not used in standard English.

Negative modifiers (e.g., never, no, and not) should not be paired with other negative modifiers or negative words (e.g., none, nobody, nothing, or neither). The modifiers *hardly, barely,* and *scarcely* are also considered negatives in standard English, so they should not be used with other negatives.

PUNCTUATION

END PUNCTUATION

PERIODS

Use a period to end all sentences except direct questions and exclamations. Periods are also used for abbreviations.

Examples: 3 p.m. | 2 a.m. | Mr. Jones | Mrs. Stevens | Dr. Smith | Bill, Jr. | Pennsylvania Ave.

Note: An abbreviation is a shortened form of a word or phrase.

QUESTION MARKS

Question marks should be used following a **direct question**. A polite request can be followed by a period instead of a question mark.

Direct Question: What is for lunch today? | How are you? | Why is that the answer?

Polite Requests: Can you please send me the item tomorrow. | Will you please walk with me on the track.

Review Video: Question Marks
Visit mometrix.com/academy and enter code: 118471

EXCLAMATION MARKS

Exclamation marks are used after a word group or sentence that shows much feeling or has special importance. Exclamation marks should not be overused. They are saved for proper **exclamatory interjections**.

Example: We're going to the finals! | You have a beautiful car! | "That's crazy!" she yelled.

Review Video: Exclamation Points
Visit mometrix.com/academy and enter code: 199367

COMMAS

The comma is a punctuation mark that can help you understand connections in a sentence. Not every sentence needs a comma. However, if a sentence needs a comma, you need to put it in the right place. A comma in the wrong place (or an absent comma) will make a sentence's meaning unclear.

These are some of the rules for commas:

Use Case	Example
Before a **coordinating conjunction** joining independent clauses	Bob caught three fish, and I caught two fish.
After an **introductory phrase**	After the final out, we went to a restaurant to celebrate.
After an **adverbial clause**	Studying the stars, I was awed by the beauty of the sky.
Between **items in a series**	I will bring the turkey, the pie, and the coffee.
For **interjections**	Wow, you know how to play this game.
After ***yes* and *no* responses**	No, I cannot come tomorrow.
Separate **nonessential modifiers**	John Frank, who coaches the team, was promoted today.
Separate **nonessential appositives**	Thomas Edison, an American inventor, was born in Ohio.
Separate **nouns of direct address**	You, John, are my only hope in this moment.
Separate **interrogative tags**	This is the last time, correct?
Separate **contrasts**	You are my friend, not my enemy.
Writing **dates**	July 4, 1776, is an important date to remember.
Writing **addresses**	He is meeting me at 456 Delaware Avenue, Washington, D.C., tomorrow morning.
Writing **geographical names**	Paris, France, is my favorite city.
Writing **titles**	John Smith, PhD, will be visiting your class today.
Separate **expressions like *he said***	"You can start," she said, "with an apology."

A comma is also used **between coordinate adjectives** not joined with *and*. However, not all adjectives are coordinate (i.e., equal or parallel). To determine if your adjectives are coordinate, try connecting them with *and* or reversing their order. If it still sounds right, they are coordinate.

Incorrect: The kind, brown dog followed me home.

Correct: The kind, loyal dog followed me home.

Review Video: When to Use a Comma
Visit mometrix.com/academy and enter code: 786797

Semicolons

The semicolon is used to join closely related independent clauses without the need for a coordinating conjunction. Semicolons are also used in place of commas to separate list elements that have internal commas. Some rules for semicolons include:

Use Case	Example
Between closely connected independent clauses **not connected with a coordinating conjunction**	You are right; we should go with your plan.
Between independent clauses **linked with a transitional word**	I think that we can agree on this; however, I am not sure about my friends.
Between items in a **series that has internal punctuation**	I have visited New York, New York; Augusta, Maine; and Baltimore, Maryland.

Review Video: How to Use Semicolons
Visit mometrix.com/academy and enter code: 370605

Colons

The colon is used to call attention to the words that follow it. When used in a sentence, a colon should only come at the **end** of a **complete sentence**. The rules for colons are as follows:

Use Case	Example
After an independent clause to **make a list**	I want to learn many languages: Spanish, German, and Italian.
For **explanations**	There is one thing that stands out on your resume: responsibility.
To give a **quote**	He started with an idea: "We are able to do more than we imagine."
After the **greeting in a formal letter**	To Whom It May Concern:
Show **hours and minutes**	It is 3:14 p.m.
Separate a **title and subtitle**	The essay is titled "America: A Short Introduction to a Modern Country."

Review Video: Using Colons
Visit mometrix.com/academy and enter code: 868673

Parentheses

Parentheses are used for additional information. Also, they can be used to put labels for letters or numbers in a series. Parentheses should be not be used very often. If they are overused, parentheses can be a distraction instead of a help.

Examples:

Extra Information: The rattlesnake (see Image 2) is a dangerous snake of North and South America.

Series: Include in the email (1) your name, (2) your address, and (3) your question for the author.

Review Video: Parentheses
Visit mometrix.com/academy and enter code: 947743

Quotation Marks

Use quotation marks to close off **direct quotations** of a person's spoken or written words. Do not use quotation marks around indirect quotations. An indirect quotation gives someone's message without using the person's exact words. Use **single quotation marks** to close off a quotation inside a quotation.

Direct Quote: Nancy said, "I am waiting for Henry to arrive."

Indirect Quote: Henry said that he is going to be late to the meeting.

Quote inside a Quote: The teacher asked, "Has everyone read 'The Gift of the Magi'?"

Quotation marks should be used around the titles of **short works**: newspaper and magazine articles, poems, short stories, songs, television episodes, radio programs, and subdivisions of books or websites.

Examples:

"Rip Van Winkle" (short story by Washington Irving)

"O Captain! My Captain!" (poem by Walt Whitman)

Although it is not standard usage, quotation marks are sometimes used to highlight **irony** or the use of words to mean something other than their dictionary definition. This type of usage should be employed sparingly, if at all.

Examples:

The boss warned Frank that he was walking on "thin ice."	Frank is not walking on real ice. Instead, he is being warned to avoid mistakes.
The teacher thanked the young man for his "honesty."	The quotation marks around *honesty* show that the teacher does not believe the young man's explanation.

Review Video: Quotation Marks
Visit mometrix.com/academy and enter code: 884918

Periods and commas are put **inside** quotation marks. Colons and semicolons are put **outside** the quotation marks. Question marks and exclamation points are placed inside quotation marks when they are part of a quote. When the question or exclamation mark goes with the whole sentence, the mark is left outside of the quotation marks.

Examples:

Period and comma	We read "The Gift of the Magi," "The Skylight Room," and "The Cactus."
Semicolon	They watched "The Nutcracker"; then, they went home.
Exclamation mark that is a part of a quote	The crowd cheered, "Victory!"
Question mark that goes with the whole sentence	Is your favorite short story "The Tell-Tale Heart"?

APOSTROPHES

An apostrophe is used to show **possession** or the **deletion of letters in contractions**. An apostrophe is not needed with the possessive pronouns *his, hers, its, ours, theirs, whose,* and *yours.*

Singular Nouns: David's car | a book's theme | my brother's board game

Plural Nouns that end with -*s*: the scissors' handle | boys' basketball

Plural Nouns that end without -*s*: Men's department | the people's adventure

Review Video: When to Use an Apostrophe
Visit mometrix.com/academy and enter code: 213068

Review Video: Punctuation Errors in Possessive Pronouns
Visit mometrix.com/academy and enter code: 221438

HYPHENS

Hyphens are used to **separate compound words**. Use hyphens in the following cases:

Use Case	Example
Compound numbers from 21 to 99 when written out in words	This team needs twenty-five points to win the game.
Written-out fractions that are used as adjectives	The recipe says that we need a three-fourths cup of butter.
Compound adjectives that come before a noun	The well-fed dog took a nap.
Unusual compound words that would be hard to read or easily confused with other words	This is the best anti-itch cream on the market.

Note: This is not a complete set of the rules for hyphens. A dictionary is the best tool for knowing if a compound word needs a hyphen.

Review Video: Hyphens
Visit mometrix.com/academy and enter code: 981632

DASHES

Dashes are used to show a **break** or a **change in thought** in a sentence or to act as parentheses in a sentence. When typing, use two hyphens to make a dash. Do not put a space before or after the dash. The following are the functions of dashes:

Use Case	Example
Set off parenthetical statements or an **appositive with internal punctuation**	The three trees—oak, pine, and magnolia—are coming on a truck tomorrow.
Show a **break or change in tone or thought**	The first question—how silly of me—does not have a correct answer.

ELLIPSIS MARKS

The ellipsis mark has **three** periods (…) to show when **words have been removed** from a quotation. If a **full sentence or more** is removed from a quoted passage, you need to use **four** periods to show the removed text and the end punctuation mark. The ellipsis mark should not be used at the beginning of a quotation. The ellipsis mark should also not be used at the end of a quotation unless some words have been deleted from the end of the final quoted sentence.

Example:

> "Then he picked up the groceries…paid for them…later he went home."

Brackets

There are two main reasons to use brackets:

Use Case	Example
Placing **parentheses inside of parentheses**	The hero of this story, Paul Revere (a silversmith and industrialist [see Ch. 4]), rode through towns of Massachusetts to warn of advancing British troops.
Adding **clarification or detail to a quotation** that is not part of the quotation	The father explained, "My children are planning to attend my alma mater [State University]."

Review Video: Brackets
Visit mometrix.com/academy and enter code: 727546

Common Usage Mistakes

Word Confusion

Which, That, and Who

The words *which*, *that*, and *who* can act as **relative pronouns** to help clarify or describe a noun.

Which is used for things only.

Example: Andrew's car, *which is old and rusty,* broke down last week.

That is used for people or things. *That* is usually informal when used to describe people.

Example: Is this the only book *that Louis L'Amour wrote?*

Example: Is Louis L'Amour the author *that wrote Western novels?*

Who is used for people or for animals that have an identity or personality.

Example: Mozart was the composer *who wrote those operas.*

Example: John's dog, *who is called Max,* is large and fierce.

Homophones

Homophones are words that sound alike (or similar) but have different **spellings** and **definitions**. A homophone is a type of **homonym**, which is a pair or group of words that are pronounced or spelled the same, but do not mean the same thing.

To, Too, and Two

To can be an adverb or a preposition for showing direction, purpose, and relationship. See your dictionary for the many other ways to use *to* in a sentence.

Examples: I went to the store. | I want to go with you.

Too is an adverb that means *also, as well, very,* or *in excess.*

Examples: I can walk a mile too. | You have eaten too much.

Two is a number.

Example: You have two minutes left.

There, Their, and They're

There can be an adjective, adverb, or pronoun. Often, *there* is used to show a place or to start a sentence.

Examples: I went there yesterday. | There is something in his pocket.

Their is a pronoun that is used to show ownership.

Examples: He is their father. | This is their fourth apology this week.

They're is a contraction of *they are.*

Example: Did you know that they're in town?

Knew and New

Knew is the past tense of *know.*

Example: I knew the answer.

New is an adjective that means something is current, has not been used, or is modern.

Example: This is my new phone.

Then and Than

Then is an adverb that indicates sequence or order:

Example: I'm going to run to the library and then come home.

Than is special-purpose word used only for comparisons:

Example: Susie likes chips more than candy.

Its and It's

Its is a pronoun that shows ownership.

Example: The guitar is in its case.

It's is a contraction of *it is.*

Example: It's an honor and a privilege to meet you.

Note: The *h* in honor is silent, so *honor* starts with the vowel sound *o*, which must have the article *an*.

Your and You're

Your is a pronoun that shows ownership.

Example: This is your moment to shine.

You're is a contraction of *you are.*

Example: Yes, you're correct.

Saw and Seen

Saw is the past-tense form of *see.*

Example: I saw a turtle on my walk this morning.

Seen is the past participle of *see.*

Example: I have seen this movie before.

Affect and Effect

There are two main reasons that *affect* and *effect* are so often confused: 1) both words can be used as either a noun or a verb, and 2) unlike most homophones, their usage and meanings are closely related to each other. Here is a quick rundown of the four usage options:

Affect (n): feeling, emotion, or mood that is displayed

Example: The patient had a flat *affect.* (i.e., his face showed little or no emotion)

Affect (v): to alter, to change, to influence

Example: The sunshine *affects* the plant's growth.

Effect (n): a result, a consequence

Example: What *effect* will this weather have on our schedule?

Effect (v): to bring about, to cause to be

Example: These new rules will *effect* order in the office.

The noun form of *affect* is rarely used outside of technical medical descriptions, so if a noun form is needed on the test, you can safely select *effect.* The verb form of *effect* is not as rare as the noun form of *affect,* but it's still not all that likely to show up on your test. If you need a verb and you can't decide which to use based on the definitions, choosing *affect* is your best bet.

Homographs

Homographs are words that share the same spelling, but have different meanings and sometimes different pronunciations. To figure out which meaning is being used, you should be looking for context clues. The context clues give hints to the meaning of the word. For example, the word *spot* has many meanings. It can mean "a place" or "a stain or blot." In the sentence "After my lunch, I saw a spot on my shirt," the word *spot* means "a stain or blot." The context clues of "After my lunch" and "on my shirt" guide you to this decision. A homograph is another type of homonym.

Bank

(noun): an establishment where money is held for savings or lending

(verb): to collect or pile up

Content

(noun): the topics that will be addressed within a book

(adjective): pleased or satisfied

(verb): to make someone pleased or satisfied

FINE

(noun): an amount of money that acts a penalty for an offense

(adjective): very small or thin

(adverb): in an acceptable way

(verb): to make someone pay money as a punishment

INCENSE

(noun): a material that is burned in religious settings and makes a pleasant aroma

(verb): to frustrate or anger

LEAD

(noun): the first or highest position

(noun): a heavy metallic element

(verb): to direct a person or group of followers

(adjective): containing lead

OBJECT

(noun): a lifeless item that can be held and observed

(verb): to disagree

PRODUCE

(noun): fruits and vegetables

(verb): to make or create something

REFUSE

(noun): garbage or debris that has been thrown away

(verb): to not allow

SUBJECT

(noun): an area of study

(verb): to force or subdue

TEAR

(noun): a fluid secreted by the eyes

(verb): to separate or pull apart

Commonly Misused Words and Phrases

A Lot

The phrase *a lot* should always be written as two words; never as *alot*.

Correct: That's a lot of chocolate!

Incorrect: He does that alot.

Can

The word *can* is used to describe things that are possible occurrences; the word *may* is used to described things that are allowed to happen.

Correct: May I have another piece of pie?

Correct: I can lift three of these bags of mulch at a time.

Incorrect: Mom said we can stay up thirty minutes later tonight.

Could Have

The phrase *could of* is often incorrectly substituted for the phrase *could have*. Similarly, *could of*, *may of*, and *might of* are sometimes used in place of the correct phrases *could have*, *may have*, and *might have*.

Correct: If I had known, I would have helped out.

Incorrect: Well, that could of gone much worse than it did.

Myself

The word *myself* is a reflexive pronoun, often incorrectly used in place of *I* or *me*.

Correct: He let me do it myself.

Incorrect: The job was given to Dave and myself.

Off

The phrase *off of* is a redundant expression that should be avoided. In most cases, it can be corrected simply by removing *of*.

Correct: My dog chased the squirrel off its perch on the fence.

Incorrect: He finally moved his plate off of the table.

Supposed To

The phrase *suppose to* is sometimes used incorrectly in place of the phrase *supposed to*.

Correct: I was supposed to go to the store this afternoon.

Incorrect: When are we suppose to get our grades?

Try To

The phrase *try and* is often used in informal writing and conversation to replace the correct phrase *try to*.

Correct: It's a good policy to try to satisfy every customer who walks in the door.

Incorrect: Don't try and do too much.

Production of Writing

The Writing Process

Brainstorming

Brainstorming is a technique that is used to find a creative approach to a subject. This can be accomplished by simple **free-association** with a topic. For example, with paper and pen, write every thought that you have about the topic in a word or phrase. This is done without critical thinking. You should put everything that comes to your mind about the topic on your scratch paper. Then, you need to read the list over a few times. Next, look for patterns, repetitions, and clusters of ideas. This allows a variety of fresh ideas to come as you think about the topic.

Free Writing

Free writing is a more structured form of brainstorming. The method involves taking a limited amount of time (e.g., 2 to 3 minutes) to write everything that comes to mind about the topic in complete sentences. When time expires, review everything that has been written down. Many of your sentences may make little or no sense, but the insights and observations that can come from free writing make this method a valuable approach. Usually, free writing results in a fuller expression of ideas than brainstorming because thoughts and associations are written in complete sentences. However, both techniques can be used to complement each other.

Planning

Planning is the process of organizing a piece of writing before composing a draft. Planning can include creating an outline or a graphic organizer, such as a Venn diagram, a spider-map, or a flowchart. These methods should help the writer identify their topic, main ideas, and the general organization of the composition. Preliminary research can also take place during this stage. Planning helps writers organize all of their ideas and decide if they have enough material to begin their first draft. However, writers should remember that the decisions they make during this step will likely change later in the process, so their plan does not have to be perfect.

Drafting

Writers may then use their plan, outline, or graphic organizer to compose their first draft. They may write subsequent drafts to improve their writing. Writing multiple drafts can help writers consider different ways to communicate their ideas and address errors that may be difficult to correct without rewriting a section or the whole composition. Most writers will vary in how many drafts they choose to write, as there is no "right" number of drafts. Writing drafts also takes away the pressure to write perfectly on the first try, as writers can improve with each draft they write.

Revising, Editing, and Proofreading

Once a writer completes a draft, they can move on to the revising, editing, and proofreading steps to improve their draft. These steps begin with making broad changes that may apply to large sections of a composition and then making small, specific corrections. **Revising** is the first and broadest of these steps. Revising involves ensuring that the composition addresses an appropriate audience, includes all necessary material, maintains focus throughout, and is organized logically. Revising may occur after the first draft to ensure that the following drafts improve upon errors from the first draft. Some revision should occur between each draft to avoid repeating these errors. The **editing** phase of writing is narrower than the revising phase. Editing a composition should include steps such as improving transitions between paragraphs, ensuring each paragraph is on topic, and improving the flow of the text. The editing phase may also include correcting grammatical errors that cannot be fixed without significantly altering the text. **Proofreading** involves fixing misspelled words, typos, other grammatical errors, and any remaining surface-level flaws in the composition.

Recursive Writing Process

However you approach writing, you may find comfort in knowing that the revision process can occur in any order. The **recursive writing process** is not as difficult as the phrase may make it seem. Simply put, the recursive writing process means that you may need to revisit steps after completing other steps. It also implies that the steps are not required to take place in any certain order. Indeed, you may find that planning, drafting, and revising can all take place at about the same time. The writing process involves moving back and forth between planning, drafting, and revising, followed by more planning, more drafting, and more revising until the writing is satisfactory.

Review Video: Recursive Writing Process
Visit mometrix.com/academy and enter code: 951611

OUTLINING AND ORGANIZING IDEAS

ESSAYS

Essays usually focus on one topic, subject, or goal. There are several types of essays, including informative, persuasive, and narrative. An essay's structure and level of formality depend on the type of essay and its goal. While narrative essays typically do not include outside sources, other types of essays often require some research and the integration of primary and secondary sources.

The basic format of an essay typically has three major parts: the introduction, the body, and the conclusion. The body is further divided into the writer's main points. Short and simple essays may have three main points, while essays covering broader ranges and going into more depth can have almost any number of main points, depending on length.

An essay's introduction should answer three questions:

1. What is the **subject** of the essay?

   If a student writes an essay about a book, the answer would include the title and author of the book and any additional information needed—such as the subject or argument of the book.

2. How does the essay **address** the subject?

   To answer this, the writer identifies the essay's organization by briefly summarizing main points and the evidence supporting them.

3. What will the essay **prove**?

   This is the thesis statement, usually the opening paragraph's last sentence, clearly stating the writer's message.

The body elaborates on all the main points related to the thesis, introducing one main point at a time, and includes supporting evidence with each main point. Each body paragraph should state the point in a topic sentence, which is usually the first sentence in the paragraph. The paragraph should then explain the point's meaning, support it with quotations or other evidence, and then explain how this point and the evidence are related to the thesis. The writer should then repeat this procedure in a new paragraph for each additional main point.

The conclusion reiterates the content of the introduction, including the thesis, to remind the reader of the essay's main argument or subject. The essay writer may also summarize the highlights of the argument or description contained in the body of the essay, following the same sequence originally used in the body. For example, a conclusion might look like: Point 1 + Point 2 + Point 3 = Thesis, or Point 1 → Point 2 → Point 3 → Thesis Proof. Good organization makes essays easier for writers to compose and provides a guide for readers to follow. Well-organized essays hold attention better and are more likely to get readers to accept their theses as valid.

MAIN IDEAS, SUPPORTING DETAILS, AND OUTLINING A TOPIC

A writer often begins the first paragraph of a paper by stating the **main idea** or point, also known as the **topic sentence**. The rest of the paragraph supplies particular details that develop and support the main point. One way to visualize the relationship between the main point and supporting information is by considering a table: the tabletop is the main point, and each of the table's legs is a supporting detail or group of details. Both professional authors and students can benefit from planning their writing by first making an outline of the topic. Outlines facilitate quick identification of the main point and supporting details without having to wade through the additional language that will exist in the fully developed essay, article, or paper. Outlining can also help readers to analyze a piece of existing writing for the same reason. The outline first summarizes the main idea in one sentence. Then, below that, it summarizes the supporting details in a numbered list. Writing the paper then consists of filling in the outline with detail, writing a paragraph for each supporting point, and adding an introduction and conclusion.

INTRODUCTION

The purpose of the introduction is to capture the reader's attention and announce the essay's main idea. Normally, the introduction contains 50-80 words, or 3-5 sentences. An introduction can begin with an interesting quote, a question, or a strong opinion—something that will **engage** the reader's interest and prompt them to keep reading. If you are writing your essay to a specific prompt, your introduction should include a **restatement or summarization** of the prompt so that the reader will have some context for your essay. Finally, your introduction should briefly state your **thesis or main idea**: the primary thing you hope to communicate to the reader through your essay. Don't try to include all of the details and nuances of your thesis, or all of your reasons for it, in the introduction. That's what the rest of the essay is for!

Review Video: Introduction
Visit mometrix.com/academy and enter code: 961328

THESIS STATEMENT

The thesis is the main idea of the essay. A temporary thesis, or working thesis, should be established early in the writing process because it will serve to keep the writer focused as ideas develop. This temporary thesis is subject to change as you continue to write.

The temporary thesis has two parts: a **topic** (i.e., the focus of your essay based on the prompt) and a **comment**. The comment makes an important point about the topic. A temporary thesis should be interesting and specific. Also, you need to limit the topic to a manageable scope. These three questions are useful tools to measure the effectiveness of any temporary thesis:

- Does the focus of my essay have enough interest to hold an audience?
- Is the focus of my essay specific enough to generate interest?
- Is the focus of my essay manageable for the time limit? Too broad? Too narrow?

The thesis should be a generalization rather than a fact because the thesis prepares readers for facts and details that support the thesis. The process of bringing the thesis into sharp focus may help in outlining major sections of the work. Once the thesis and introduction are complete, you can address the body of the work.

Review Video: Thesis Statements
Visit mometrix.com/academy and enter code: 691033

SUPPORTING THE THESIS

Throughout your essay, the thesis should be **explained clearly and supported** adequately by additional arguments. The thesis sentence needs to contain a clear statement of the purpose of your essay and a comment about the thesis. With the thesis statement, you have an opportunity to state what is noteworthy of this particular treatment of the prompt. Each sentence and paragraph should build on and support the thesis.

When you respond to the prompt, use parts of the passage to support your argument or defend your position. Using supporting evidence from the passage strengths your argument because readers can see your attention to the entire passage and your response to the details and facts within the passage. You can use facts, details, statistics, and direct quotations from the passage to uphold your position. Be sure to point out which information comes from the original passage and base your argument around that evidence.

Body

In an essay's introduction, the writer establishes the thesis and may indicate how the rest of the piece will be structured. In the body of the piece, the writer **elaborates** upon, **illustrates**, and **explains** the **thesis statement**. How writers arrange supporting details and their choices of paragraph types are development techniques. Writers may give examples of the concept introduced in the thesis statement. If the subject includes a cause-and-effect relationship, the author may explain its causality. A writer will explain or analyze the main idea of the piece throughout the body, often by presenting arguments for the veracity or credibility of the thesis statement. Writers may use development to define or clarify ambiguous terms. Paragraphs within the body may be organized using natural sequences, like space and time. Writers may employ **inductive reasoning**, using multiple details to establish a generalization or causal relationship, or **deductive reasoning**, proving a generalized hypothesis or proposition through a specific example or case.

Review Video: Drafting Body Paragraphs
Visit mometrix.com/academy and enter code: 724590

Paragraphs

After the introduction of a passage, a series of body paragraphs will carry a message through to the conclusion. Each paragraph should be **unified around a main point**. Normally, a good topic sentence summarizes the paragraph's main point. A topic sentence is a general sentence that gives an introduction to the paragraph.

The sentences that follow support the topic sentence. However, though it is usually the first sentence, the topic sentence can come as the final sentence to the paragraph if the earlier sentences give a clear explanation of the paragraph's topic. This allows the topic sentence to function as a concluding sentence. Overall, the paragraphs need to stay true to the main point. This means that any unnecessary sentences that do not advance the main point should be removed.

The main point of a paragraph requires adequate development (i.e., a substantial paragraph that covers the main point). A paragraph of two or three sentences does not cover a main point. This is especially true when the main point of the paragraph gives strong support to the argument of the thesis. An occasional short paragraph is fine as a transitional device. However, a well-developed argument will have paragraphs with more than a few sentences.

Methods of Developing Paragraphs

Common methods of adding substance to paragraphs include examples, illustrations, analogies, and cause and effect.

- **Examples** are supporting details to the main idea of a paragraph or a passage. When authors write about something that their audience may not understand, they can provide an example to show their point. When authors write about something that is not easily accepted, they can give examples to prove their point.
- **Illustrations** are extended examples that require several sentences. Well-selected illustrations can be a great way for authors to develop a point that may not be familiar to their audience.
- **Analogies** make comparisons between items that appear to have nothing in common. Analogies are employed by writers to provoke fresh thoughts about a subject. These comparisons may be used to explain the unfamiliar, to clarify an abstract point, or to argue a point. Although analogies are effective literary devices, they should be used carefully in arguments. Two things may be alike in some respects but completely different in others.

- **Cause and effect** is an excellent device to explain the connection between an action or situation and a particular result. One way that authors can use cause and effect is to state the effect in the topic sentence of a paragraph and add the causes in the body of the paragraph. This method can give an author's paragraphs structure, which always strengthens writing.

Types of Paragraphs

A **paragraph of narration** tells a story or a part of a story. Normally, the sentences are arranged in chronological order (i.e., the order that the events happened). However, flashbacks (i.e., an anecdote from an earlier time) can be included.

A **descriptive paragraph** makes a verbal portrait of a person, place, or thing. When specific details are used that appeal to one or more of the senses (i.e., sight, sound, smell, taste, and touch), authors give readers a sense of being present in the moment.

A **process paragraph** is related to time order (i.e., First, you open the bottle. Second, you pour the liquid, etc.). Usually, this describes a process or teaches readers how to perform a process.

Comparing two things draws attention to their similarities and indicates a number of differences. When authors contrast, they focus only on differences. Both comparing and contrasting may be done point-by-point, noting both the similarities and differences of each point, or in sequential paragraphs, where you discuss all the similarities and then all the differences, or vice versa.

Breaking Text into Paragraphs

For most forms of writing, you will need to use multiple paragraphs. As such, determining when to start a new paragraph is very important. Reasons for starting a new paragraph include:

- To mark off the introduction and concluding paragraphs
- To signal a shift to a new idea or topic
- To indicate an important shift in time or place
- To explain a point in additional detail
- To highlight a comparison, contrast, or cause and effect relationship

Paragraph Length

Most readers find that their comfort level for a paragraph is between 100 and 200 words. Shorter paragraphs cause too much starting and stopping and give a choppy effect. Paragraphs that are too long often test the attention span of readers. Two notable exceptions to this rule exist. In scientific or scholarly papers, longer paragraphs suggest seriousness and depth. In journalistic writing, constraints are placed on paragraph size by the narrow columns in a newspaper format.

The first and last paragraphs of a text will usually be the introduction and conclusion. These special-purpose paragraphs are likely to be shorter than paragraphs in the body of the work. Paragraphs in the body of the essay follow the subject's outline (e.g., one paragraph per point in short essays and a group of paragraphs per point in longer works). Some ideas require more development than others, so it is good for a writer to remain flexible. A paragraph of excessive length may be divided, and shorter ones may be combined.

Conclusion

Two important principles to consider when writing a conclusion are strength and closure. A strong conclusion gives the reader a sense that the author's main points are meaningful and important, and that the supporting facts and arguments are convincing, solid, and well developed. When a conclusion achieves closure, it gives the impression that the writer has stated all necessary information and points and completed the work, rather than simply stopping after a specified length. Some things to avoid when writing concluding paragraphs include:

- Introducing a completely new idea
- Beginning with obvious or unoriginal phrases like "In conclusion" or "To summarize"
- Apologizing for one's opinions or writing
- Repeating the thesis word for word rather than rephrasing it
- Believing that the conclusion must always summarize the piece

Review Video: Drafting Conclusions
Visit mometrix.com/academy and enter code: 209408

COHERENCE IN WRITING

COHERENT PARAGRAPHS

A smooth flow of sentences and paragraphs without gaps, shifts, or bumps will lead to paragraph **coherence**. Ties between old and new information can be smoothed using several methods:

- **Linking ideas clearly**, from the topic sentence to the body of the paragraph, is essential for a smooth transition. The topic sentence states the main point, and this should be followed by specific details, examples, and illustrations that support the topic sentence. The support may be direct or indirect. In **indirect support**, the illustrations and examples may support a sentence that in turn supports the topic directly.
- The **repetition of key words** adds coherence to a paragraph. To avoid dull language, variations of the key words may be used.
- **Parallel structures** are often used within sentences to emphasize the similarity of ideas and connect sentences giving similar information.
- Maintaining a **consistent verb tense** throughout the paragraph helps. Shifting tenses affects the smooth flow of words and can disrupt the coherence of the paragraph.

Review Video: How to Write a Good Paragraph
Visit mometrix.com/academy and enter code: 682127

SEQUENCE WORDS AND PHRASES

When a paragraph opens with the topic sentence, the second sentence may begin with a phrase like *first of all*, introducing the first supporting detail or example. The writer may introduce the second supporting item with words or phrases like *also*, *in addition*, and *besides*. The writer might introduce succeeding pieces of support with wording like, *another thing*, *moreover*, *furthermore*, or *not only that, but*. The writer may introduce the last piece of support with *lastly*, *finally*, or *last but not least*. Writers get off the point by presenting off-target items not supporting the main point. For example, a main point *my dog is not smart* is supported by the statement, *he's six years old and still doesn't answer to his name*. But *he cries when I leave for school* is not supportive, as it does not indicate lack of intelligence. Writers stay on point by presenting only supportive statements that are directly relevant to and illustrative of their main point.

Review Video: Sequence
Visit mometrix.com/academy and enter code: 489027

TRANSITIONS

Transitions between sentences and paragraphs guide readers from idea to idea and indicate relationships between sentences and paragraphs. Writers should be judicious in their use of transitions, inserting them sparingly. They should also be selected to fit the author's purpose—transitions can indicate time, comparison, and conclusion, among other purposes. Tone is also important to consider when using transitional phrases, varying the tone for different audiences. For example, in a scholarly essay, *in summary* would be preferable to the more informal *in short*.

When working with transitional words and phrases, writers usually find a natural flow that indicates when a transition is needed. In reading a draft of the text, it should become apparent where the flow is disrupted. At this point, the writer can add transitional elements during the revision process. Revising can also afford an opportunity to delete transitional devices that seem heavy handed or unnecessary.

Review Video: Transitions in Writing
Visit mometrix.com/academy and enter code: 233246

Types of Transitional Words

Time	afterward, immediately, earlier, meanwhile, recently, lately, now, since, soon, when, then, until, before, etc.
Sequence	too, first, second, further, moreover, also, again, and, next, still, besides, finally
Comparison	similarly, in the same way, likewise, also, again, once more
Contrasting	but, although, despite, however, instead, nevertheless, on the one hand... on the other hand, regardless, yet, in contrast
Cause and Effect	because, consequently, thus, therefore, then, to this end, since, so, as a result, if... then, accordingly
Examples	for example, for instance, such as, to illustrate, indeed, in fact, specifically
Place	near, far, here, there, to the left/right, next to, above, below, beyond, opposite, beside
Concession	granted that, naturally, of course, it may appear, although it is true that
Repetition, Summary, or Conclusion	as mentioned earlier, as noted, in other words, in short, on the whole, to summarize, therefore, as a result, to conclude, in conclusion
Addition	and, also, furthermore, moreover
Generalization	in broad terms, broadly speaking, in general

Review Video: Transition Words
Visit mometrix.com/academy and enter code: 707563

Review Video: How to Effectively Connect Sentences
Visit mometrix.com/academy and enter code: 948325

Common Types of Writing

Autobiographical Narratives

Autobiographical narratives are narratives written by an author about an event or period in their life. Autobiographical narratives are written from one person's perspective, in first person, and often include the author's thoughts and feelings alongside their description of the event or period. Structure, style, or theme varies between different autobiographical narratives, since each narrative is personal and specific to its author and his or her experience.

Reflective Essay

A less common type of essay is the reflective essay. **Reflective essays** allow the author to reflect, or think back, on an experience and analyze what they recall. They should consider what they learned from the experience, what they could have done differently, what would have helped them during the experience, or anything else that they have realized from looking back on the experience. Reflection essays incorporate both objective reflection on one's own actions and subjective explanation of thoughts and feelings. These essays can be written for a number of experiences in a formal or informal context.

Journals and Diaries

A **journal** is a personal account of events, experiences, feelings, and thoughts. Many people write journals to express their feelings and thoughts or to help them process experiences they have had. Since journals are **private documents** not meant to be shared with others, writers may not be concerned with grammar, spelling, or other mechanics. However, authors may write journals that they expect or hope to publish someday; in this case, they not only express their thoughts and feelings and process their experiences, but they also attend to their craft in writing them. Some authors compose journals to record a particular time period or a series of related events, such as a cancer diagnosis, treatment, surviving the disease, and how these experiences have changed or affected them. Other experiences someone might include in a journal are recovering from addiction, journeys of spiritual exploration and discovery, time spent in another country, or anything else someone wants to personally document. Journaling can also be therapeutic, as some people use journals to work through feelings of grief over loss or to wrestle with big decisions.

Examples of Diaries in Literature

The Diary of a Young Girl by Dutch Jew Anne Frank (1947) contains her life-affirming, nonfictional diary entries from 1942-1944 while her family hid in an attic from World War II's genocidal Nazis. *Go Ask Alice* (1971) by Beatrice Sparks is a cautionary, fictional novel in the form of diary entries by Alice, an unhappy, rebellious teen who takes LSD, runs away from home and lives with hippies, and eventually returns home. Frank's writing reveals an intelligent, sensitive, insightful girl, raised by intellectual European parents—a girl who believes in the goodness of human nature despite surrounding atrocities. Alice, influenced by early 1970s counterculture, becomes less optimistic. However, similarities can be found between them: Frank dies in a Nazi concentration camp while the fictitious Alice dies from a drug overdose. Both young women are also unable to escape their surroundings. Additionally, adolescent searches for personal identity are evident in both books.

Review Video: Journals, Diaries, Letters, and Blogs
Visit mometrix.com/academy and enter code: 432845

Letters

Letters are messages written to other people. In addition to letters written between individuals, some writers compose letters to the editors of newspapers, magazines, and other publications, while some write "Open Letters" to be published and read by the general public. Open letters, while intended for everyone to read, may also identify a group of people or a single person whom the letter directly addresses. In everyday use, the most-used forms are business letters and personal or friendly letters. Both kinds share common elements: business or personal letterhead stationery; the writer's return address at the top; the addressee's address next; a salutation, such as "Dear [name]" or some similar opening greeting, followed by a colon in business letters or a comma in personal letters; the body of the letter, with paragraphs as indicated; and a closing, like "Sincerely/Cordially/Best regards/etc." or "Love," in intimate personal letters.

Early Letters

The Greek word for "letter" is *epistolē*, which became the English word "epistle." The earliest letters were called epistles, including the New Testament's epistles from the apostles to the Christians. In ancient Egypt, the writing curriculum in scribal schools included the epistolary genre. Epistolary novels frame a story in the form of letters. Examples of noteworthy epistolary novels include:

- *Pamela* (1740), by 18th-century English novelist Samuel Richardson
- *Shamela* (1741), Henry Fielding's satire of *Pamela* that mocked epistolary writing.
- *Lettres persanes* (1721) by French author Montesquieu
- *The Sorrows of Young Werther* (1774) by German author Johann Wolfgang von Goethe
- *The History of Emily Montague* (1769), the first Canadian novel, by Frances Brooke

- *Dracula* (1897) by Bram Stoker
- *Frankenstein* (1818) by Mary Shelley
- *The Color Purple* (1982) by Alice Walker

Blogs

The word "blog" is derived from "weblog" and refers to writing done exclusively on the internet. Readers of reputable newspapers expect quality content and layouts that enable easy reading. These expectations also apply to blogs. For example, readers can easily move visually from line to line when columns are narrow, while overly wide columns cause readers to lose their places. Blogs must also be posted with layouts enabling online readers to follow them easily. However, because the way people read on computer, tablet, and smartphone screens differs from how they read print on paper, formatting and writing blog content is more complex than writing newspaper articles. Two major principles are the bases for blog-writing rules: The first is while readers of print articles skim to estimate their length, online they must scroll down to scan; therefore, blog layouts need more subheadings, graphics, and other indications of what information follows. The second is onscreen reading can be harder on the eyes than reading printed paper, so legibility is crucial in blogs.

Rules and Rationales for Writing Blogs

1. Format all posts for smooth page layout and easy scanning.
2. Column width should not be too wide, as larger lines of text can be difficult to read
3. Headings and subheadings separate text visually, enable scanning or skimming, and encourage continued reading.
4. Bullet-pointed or numbered lists enable quick information location and scanning.
5. Punctuation is critical, so beginners should use shorter sentences until confident in their knowledge of punctuation rules.
6. Blog paragraphs should be far shorter—two to six sentences each—than paragraphs written on paper to enable "chunking" because reading onscreen is more difficult.
7. Sans-serif fonts are usually clearer than serif fonts, and larger font sizes are better.
8. Highlight important material and draw attention with **boldface**, but avoid overuse. Avoid hard-to-read *italics* and ALL CAPITALS.
9. Include enough blank spaces: overly busy blogs tire eyes and brains. Images not only break up text but also emphasize and enhance text and can attract initial reader attention.
10. Use background colors judiciously to avoid distracting the eye or making it difficult to read.
11. Be consistent throughout posts, since people read them in different orders.
12. Tell a story with a beginning, middle, and end.

Specialized Types of Writing

Editorials

Editorials are articles in newspapers, magazines, and other serial publications. Editorials express an opinion or belief belonging to the majority of the publication's leadership. This opinion or belief generally refers to a specific issue, topic, or event. These articles are authored by a member, or a small number of members, of the publication's leadership and are often written to affect their readers, such as persuading them to adopt a stance or take a particular action.

Resumes

Resumes are brief, but formal, documents that outline an individual's experience in a certain area. Resumes are most often used for job applications. Such resumes will list the applicant's work experience, certification, and achievements or qualifications related to the position. Resumes should only include the most pertinent information. They should also use strategic formatting to highlight the applicant's most impressive experiences and achievements, to ensure the document can be read quickly and easily, and to eliminate both visual clutter and excessive negative space.

Reports

Reports summarize the results of research, new methodology, or other developments in an academic or professional context. Reports often include details about methodology and outside influences and factors. However, a report should focus primarily on the results of the research or development. Reports are objective and deliver information efficiently, sacrificing style for clear and effective communication.

Memoranda

A memorandum, also called a memo, is a formal method of communication used in professional settings. Memoranda are printed documents that include a heading listing the sender and their job title, the recipient and their job title, the date, and a specific subject line. Memoranda often include an introductory section explaining the reason and context for the memorandum. Next, a memorandum includes a section with details relevant to the topic. Finally, the memorandum will conclude with a paragraph that politely and clearly defines the sender's expectations of the recipient.

Technology in the Writing Process

Modern technology has yielded several tools that can be used to make the writing process more convenient and organized. Word processors and online tools, such as databases and plagiarism detectors, allow much of the writing process to be completed in one place, using one device.

Technology for Planning and Drafting

For the planning and drafting stages of the writing process, word processors are a helpful tool. These programs also feature formatting tools, allowing users to create their own planning tools or create digital outlines that can be easily converted into sentences, paragraphs, or an entire essay draft. Online databases and references also complement the planning process by providing convenient access to information and sources for research. Word processors also allow users to keep up with their work and update it more easily than if they wrote their work by hand. Online word processors often allow users to collaborate, making group assignments more convenient. These programs also allow users to include illustrations or other supplemental media in their compositions.

Technology for Revising, Editing, and Proofreading

Word processors also benefit the revising, editing, and proofreading stages of the writing process. Most of these programs indicate errors in spelling and grammar, allowing users to catch minor errors and correct them quickly. There are also websites designed to help writers by analyzing text for deeper errors, such as poor sentence structure, inappropriate complexity, lack of sentence variety, and style issues. These websites can help users fix errors they may not know to look for or may have simply missed. As writers finish these steps, they may benefit from checking their work for any plagiarism. There are several websites and programs that compare text to other documents and publications across the internet and detect any similarities within the text. These websites show the source of the similar information, so users know whether or not they referenced the source and unintentionally plagiarized its contents.

Technology for Publishing

Technology also makes managing written work more convenient. Digitally storing documents keeps everything in one place and is easy to reference. Digital storage also makes sharing work easier, as documents can be attached to an email or stored online. This also allows writers to publish their work easily, as they can electronically submit it to other publications or freely post it to a personal blog, profile, or website.

Knowledge of Language

Writing Style and Form

Writing Style and Linguistic Form

Linguistic form encodes the literal meanings of words and sentences. It comes from the phonological, morphological, syntactic, and semantic parts of a language. **Writing style** consists of different ways of encoding the meaning and indicating figurative and stylistic meanings. An author's writing style can also be referred to as his or her **voice**.

Writers' stylistic choices accomplish three basic effects on their audiences:

- They **communicate meanings** beyond linguistically dictated meanings,
- They communicate the **author's attitude**, such as persuasive or argumentative effects accomplished through style, and
- They communicate or **express feelings**.

Within style, component areas include:

- Narrative structure
- Viewpoint
- Focus
- Sound patterns
- Meter and rhythm
- Lexical and syntactic repetition and parallelism
- Writing genre
- Representational, realistic, and mimetic effects
- Representation of thought and speech
- Meta-representation (representing representation)
- Irony
- Metaphor and other indirect meanings
- Representation and use of historical and dialectal variations
- Gender-specific and other group-specific speech styles, both real and fictitious
- Analysis of the processes for inferring meaning from writing

Tone

Tone may be defined as the writer's **attitude** toward the topic, and to the audience. This attitude is reflected in the language used in the writing. The tone of a work should be **appropriate to the topic** and to the intended audience. While it may be fine to use slang or jargon in some pieces, other texts should not contain such terms. Tone can range from humorous to serious and any level in between. It may be more or less formal, depending on the purpose of the writing and its intended audience. All these nuances in tone can flavor the entire writing and should be kept in mind as the work evolves.

Word Selection

A writer's choice of words is a signature of their style. Careful thought about the use of words can improve a piece of writing. A passage can be an exciting piece to read when attention is given to the use of vivid or specific nouns rather than general ones.

Example:

General: His kindness will never be forgotten.

Specific: His thoughtful gifts and bear hugs will never be forgotten.

Active and Passive Language

Attention should also be given to the kind of verbs that are used in sentences. Active verbs (e.g., run, swim) are about an action. Whenever possible, an **active verb should replace a linking verb** to provide clear examples for arguments and to strengthen a passage overall. When using an active verb, one should be sure that the verb is used in the active voice instead of the passive voice. Verbs are in the active voice when the subject is the one doing the action. A verb is in the passive voice when the subject is the recipient of an action.

Example:

> Passive: The winners were called to the stage by the judges.
>
> Active: The judges called the winners to the stage.

Conciseness

Conciseness is writing that communicates a message in the fewest words possible. Writing concisely is valuable because short, uncluttered messages allow the reader to understand the author's message more easily and efficiently. Planning is important in writing concise messages. If you have in mind what you need to write beforehand, it will be easier to make a message short and to the point. Do not state the obvious.

Revising is also important. After the message is written, make sure you have effective, pithy sentences that efficiently get your point across. When reviewing the information, imagine a conversation taking place, and concise writing will likely result.

Appropriate Kinds of Writing for Different Tasks, Purposes, and Audiences

When preparing to write a composition, consider the audience and purpose to choose the best type of writing. Four common types of writing are persuasive, expository, and narrative. **Persuasive**, or argumentative writing, is used to convince the audience to take action or agree with the author's claims. **Expository** writing is meant to inform the audience of the author's observations or research on a topic. **Narrative** writing is used to tell the audience a story and often allows more room for creativity. **Descriptive** writing is when a writer provides a substantial amount of detail to the reader so he or she can visualize the topic. While task, purpose, and audience inform a writer's mode of writing, these factors also impact elements such as tone, vocabulary, and formality.

For example, students who are writing to persuade their parents to grant them some additional privilege, such as permission for a more independent activity, should use more sophisticated vocabulary and diction that sounds more mature and serious to appeal to the parental audience. However, students who are writing for younger children should use simpler vocabulary and sentence structure, as well as choose words that are more vivid and entertaining. They should treat their topics more lightly, and include humor when appropriate. Students who are writing for their classmates may use language that is more informal, as well as age-appropriate.

Review Video: Writing Purpose and Audience
Visit mometrix.com/academy and enter code: 146627

Formality in Writing

Level of Formality

The relationship between writer and reader is important in choosing a **level of formality** as most writing requires some degree of formality. **Formal writing** is for addressing a superior in a school or work environment. Business letters, textbooks, and newspapers use a moderate to high level of formality. **Informal writing** is appropriate for private letters, personal emails, and business correspondence between close associates.

For your exam, you will want to be aware of informal and formal writing. One way that this can be accomplished is to watch for shifts in point of view in the essay. For example, unless writers are using a personal example, they will rarely refer to themselves (e.g., "*I* think that *my* point is very clear.") to avoid being informal when they need to be formal.

Also, be mindful of an author who addresses his or her audience **directly** in their writing (e.g., "Readers, *like you*, will understand this argument.") as this can be a sign of informal writing. Good writers understand the need to be consistent with their level of formality. Shifts in levels of formality or point of view can confuse readers and cause them to discount the message.

CLICHÉS

Clichés are phrases that have been **overused** to the point that the phrase has no importance or has lost the original meaning. These phrases have no originality and add very little to a passage. Therefore, most writers will avoid the use of clichés. Another option is to make changes to a cliché so that it is not predictable and empty of meaning.

Examples:

> When life gives you lemons, make lemonade.
>
> Every cloud has a silver lining.

JARGON

Jargon is **specialized vocabulary** that is used among members of a certain trade or profession. Since jargon is understood by only a small audience, writers will use jargon in passages that will only be read by a specialized audience. For example, medical jargon should be used in a medical journal but not in a New York Times article. Jargon includes exaggerated language that tries to impress rather than inform. Sentences filled with jargon are not precise and are difficult to understand.

Examples:

> "He is going to *toenail* these frames for us." (Toenail is construction jargon for nailing at an angle.)
>
> "They brought in a *kip* of material today." (Kip refers to 1000 pounds in architecture and engineering.)

SLANG

Slang is an **informal** and sometimes private language that is understood by some individuals. Slang terms have some usefulness, but they can have a small audience. So, most formal writing will not include this kind of language.

Examples:

> "Yes, the event was a blast!" (In this sentence, *blast* means that the event was a great experience.)
>
> "That attempt was an epic fail." (By *epic fail*, the speaker means that his or her attempt was not a success.)

COLLOQUIALISM

A colloquialism is a word or phrase that is found in informal writing. Unlike slang, **colloquial language** will be familiar to a greater range of people. However, colloquialisms are still considered inappropriate for formal writing. Colloquial language can include some slang, but these are limited to contractions for the most part.

Examples:

"Can *y'all* come back another time?" (Y'all is a contraction of "you all.")

"Will you stop him from building this *castle in the air*?" (A "castle in the air" is an improbable or unlikely event.)

Academic Language

In educational settings, students are often expected to use academic language in their schoolwork. Academic language is also commonly found in dissertations and theses, texts published by academic journals, and other forms of academic research. Academic language conventions may vary between fields, but general academic language is free of slang, regional terminology, and noticeable grammatical errors. Specific terms may also be used in academic language, and it is important to understand their proper usage. A writer's command of academic language impacts their ability to communicate in an academic or professional context. While it is acceptable to use colloquialisms, slang, improper grammar, or other forms of informal speech in social settings or at home, it is inappropriate to practice non-academic language in academic contexts.

Chapter Quiz

Ready to see how well you retained what you just read? Scan the QR code to go directly to the chapter quiz interface for this study guide. If you're using a computer, simply visit the bonus page at **mometrix.com/bonus948/act** and click the Chapter Quizzes link.

Mathematics

Math Overview

The ACT mathematics test consists of 60 questions in 60 minutes, meaning you will have to maintain a one-question-per-minute pace to finish the math section on time. The questions you will encounter include the following:

Preparing for Higher Math (57-60%)

The Preparing for Higher Math category includes single-skill questions on the following topics:

- **Number and Quantity** (7-10%)
- **Algebra** (12-15%)
- **Functions** (12-15%)
- **Geometry** (12-15%)
- **Statistics and Probability** (8-12%)

Integrating Essential Skills (40-43%)

The Integrating Essential Skills category is made up of compound questions that require the integration of two or more skills to find the correct answer. These questions are likely to build on any of the skills listed in the Preparing for Higher Math section.

Topics likely to appear in the Integrating Essential Skills questions include the following:

- Rates and percentages
- Proportional relationships
- Area, surface area, and volume
- Average and median
- Expressing numbers in different ways

All of the questions on the ACT can be answered without a calculator, but a calculator is allowed. That means you'll have to use your best judgement on when and when not to use one to keep your pace for the test. The questions also vary by complexity.

Number and Quantity

Number Basics

Classifications of Numbers

Numbers are the basic building blocks of mathematics. Specific features of numbers are identified by the following terms:

Integer – any positive or negative whole number, including zero. Integers do not include fractions $\left(\frac{1}{3}\right)$, decimals (0.56), or mixed numbers $\left(7\frac{3}{4}\right)$.

Prime number – any whole number greater than 1 that has only two factors, itself and 1; that is, a number that can be divided evenly only by 1 and itself.

Composite number – any whole number greater than 1 that has more than two different factors; in other words, any whole number that is not a prime number. For example: The composite number 8 has the factors of 1, 2, 4, and 8.

Even number – any integer that can be divided by 2 without leaving a remainder. For example: 2, 4, 6, 8, and so on.

Odd number – any integer that cannot be divided evenly by 2. For example: 3, 5, 7, 9, and so on.

Decimal number – any number that uses a decimal point to show the part of the number that is less than one. Example: 1.234.

Decimal point – a symbol used to separate the ones place from the tenths place in decimals or dollars from cents in currency.

Decimal place – the position of a number to the right of the decimal point. In the decimal 0.123, the 1 is in the first place to the right of the decimal point, indicating tenths; the 2 is in the second place, indicating hundredths; and the 3 is in the third place, indicating thousandths.

The **decimal**, or base 10, system is a number system that uses ten different digits (0, 1, 2, 3, 4, 5, 6, 7, 8, 9). An example of a number system that uses something other than ten digits is the **binary**, or base 2, number system, used by computers, which uses only the numbers 0 and 1. It is thought that the decimal system originated because people had only their 10 fingers for counting.

Rational numbers include all integers, decimals, and fractions. Any terminating or repeating decimal number is a rational number.

Irrational numbers cannot be written as fractions or decimals because the number of decimal places is infinite and there is no recurring pattern of digits within the number. For example, pi (π) begins with 3.141592 and continues without terminating or repeating, so pi is an irrational number.

Real numbers are the set of all rational and irrational numbers.

Review Video: Classification of Numbers
Visit mometrix.com/academy and enter code: 461071

Review Video: Prime and Composite Numbers
Visit mometrix.com/academy and enter code: 565581

Numbers in Word Form and Place Value

When writing numbers out in word form or translating word form to numbers, it is essential to understand how a place value system works. In the decimal or base-10 system, each digit of a number represents how many of the corresponding place value—a specific factor of 10—are contained in the number being represented. To make reading numbers easier, every three digits to the left of the decimal place is preceded by a comma. The following table demonstrates some of the place values:

Power of 10	10^3	10^2	10^1	10^0	10^{-1}	10^{-2}	10^{-3}
Value	1,000	100	10	1	0.1	0.01	0.001
Place	thousands	hundreds	tens	ones	tenths	hundredths	thousandths

For example, consider the number 4,546.09, which can be separated into each place value like this:

4: thousands
5: hundreds
4: tens
6: ones
0: tenths
9: hundredths

This number in word form would be *four thousand five hundred forty-six and nine hundredths.*

Review Video: Place Value
Visit mometrix.com/academy and enter code: 205433

Rational Numbers

The term **rational** means that the number can be expressed as a ratio or fraction. That is, a number, r, is rational if and only if it can be represented by a fraction $\frac{a}{b}$ where a and b are integers and b does not equal 0. The set of rational numbers includes integers and decimals. If there is no finite way to represent a value with a fraction of integers, then the number is **irrational**. Common examples of irrational numbers include: $\sqrt{5}$, $(1+\sqrt{2})$, and π.

Review Video: Rational and Irrational Numbers
Visit mometrix.com/academy and enter code: 280645

Review Video: Ordering Rational Numbers
Visit mometrix.com/academy and enter code: 419578

Number Lines

A number line is a graph to see the distance between numbers. Basically, this graph shows the relationship between numbers. So a number line may have a point for zero and may show negative numbers on the left side of the line. Any positive numbers are placed on the right side of the line. For example, consider the points labeled on the following number line:

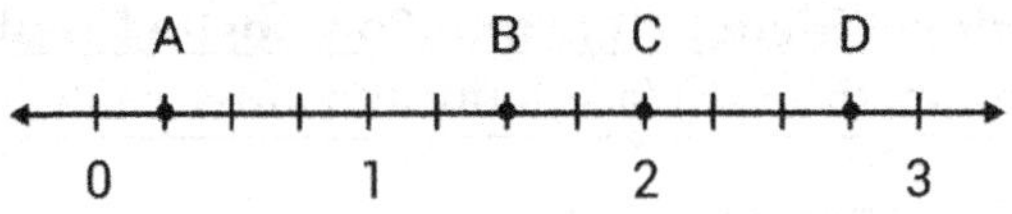

We can use the dashed lines on the number line to identify each point. Each dashed line between two whole numbers is $\frac{1}{4}$. The line halfway between two numbers is $\frac{1}{2}$.

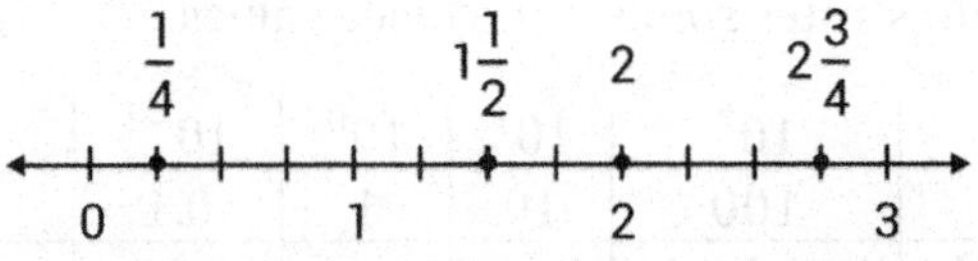

Review Video: The Number Line
Visit mometrix.com/academy and enter code: 816439

ABSOLUTE VALUE

A precursor to working with negative numbers is understanding what **absolute values** are. A number's absolute value is simply the distance away from zero a number is on the number line. The absolute value of a number is always positive and is written $|x|$. For example, the absolute value of 3, written as $|3|$, is 3 because the distance between 0 and 3 on a number line is three units. Likewise, the absolute value of –3, written as $|-3|$, is 3 because the distance between 0 and –3 on a number line is three units. So $|3| = |-3|$.

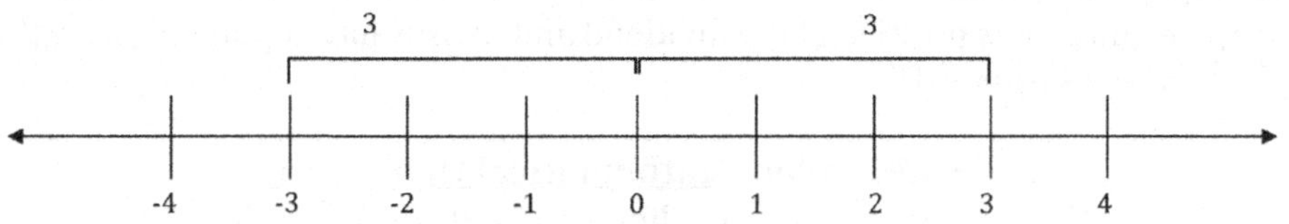

Review Video: Absolute Value
Visit mometrix.com/academy and enter code: 314669

OPERATIONS

An **operation** is simply a mathematical process that takes some value(s) as input(s) and produces an output. Elementary operations are often written in the following form: *value operation value*. For instance, in the expression $1 + 2$ the values are 1 and 2 and the operation is addition. Performing the operation gives the output of 3. In this way we can say that $1 + 2$ and 3 are equal, or $1 + 2 = 3$.

ADDITION

Addition increases the value of one quantity by the value of another quantity (both called **addends**). Example: $2 + 4 = 6$ or $8 + 9 = 17$. The result is called the **sum**. With addition, the order does not matter, $4 + 2 = 2 + 4$.

When adding signed numbers, if the signs are the same simply add the absolute values of the addends and apply the original sign to the sum. For example, $(+4) + (+8) = +12$ and $(-4) + (-8) = -12$. When the original signs are different, take the absolute values of the addends and subtract the smaller value from the larger value, then apply the original sign of the larger value to the difference. Example: $(+4) + (-8) = -4$ and $(-4) + (+8) = +4$.

SUBTRACTION

Subtraction is the opposite operation to addition; it decreases the value of one quantity (the **minuend**) by the value of another quantity (the **subtrahend**). For example, $6 - 4 = 2$ or $17 - 8 = 9$. The result is called the **difference**. Note that with subtraction, the order does matter, $6 - 4 \neq 4 - 6$.

For subtracting signed numbers, change the sign of the subtrahend and then follow the same rules used for addition. Example: $(+4) - (+8) = (+4) + (-8) = -4$

MULTIPLICATION

Multiplication can be thought of as repeated addition. One number (the **multiplier**) indicates how many times to add the other number (the **multiplicand**) to itself. Example: $3 \times 2 = 2 + 2 + 2 = 6$. With multiplication, the order does not matter, $2 \times 3 = 3 \times 2$ or $3 + 3 = 2 + 2 + 2$, either way the result (the **product**) is the same.

If the signs are the same, the product is positive when multiplying signed numbers. Example: $(+4) \times (+8) = +32$ and $(-4) \times (-8) = +32$. If the signs are opposite, the product is negative. Example: $(+4) \times (-8) = -32$ and $(-4) \times (+8) = -32$. When more than two factors are multiplied together, the sign of the product is determined by how many negative factors are present. If there are an odd number of negative factors then the product is negative, whereas an even number of negative factors indicates a positive product. Example: $(+4) \times (-8) \times (-2) = +64$ and $(-4) \times (-8) \times (-2) = -64$.

Division

Division is the opposite operation to multiplication; one number (the **divisor**) tells us how many parts to divide the other number (the **dividend**) into. The result of division is called the **quotient**. Example: $20 \div 4 = 5$. If 20 is split into 4 equal parts, each part is 5. With division, the order of the numbers does matter, $20 \div 4 \neq 4 \div 20$.

The rules for dividing signed numbers are similar to multiplying signed numbers. If the dividend and divisor have the same sign, the quotient is positive. If the dividend and divisor have opposite signs, the quotient is negative. Example: $(-4) \div (+8) = -0.5$.

Review Video: Mathematical Operations
Visit mometrix.com/academy and enter code: 208095

Parentheses

Parentheses are used to designate which operations should be done first when there are multiple operations. Example: $4 - (2 + 1) = 1$; the parentheses tell us that we must add 2 and 1, and then subtract the sum from 4, rather than subtracting 2 from 4 and then adding 1 (this would give us an answer of 3).

Review Video: Mathematical Parentheses
Visit mometrix.com/academy and enter code: 978600

Exponents

An **exponent** is a superscript number placed next to another number at the top right. It indicates how many times the base number is to be multiplied by itself. Exponents provide a shorthand way to write what would be a longer mathematical expression, Example: $2^4 = 2 \times 2 \times 2 \times 2$. A number with an exponent of 2 is said to be "squared," while a number with an exponent of 3 is said to be "cubed." The value of a number raised to an exponent is called its power. So 8^4 is read as "8 to the 4th power," or "8 raised to the power of 4."

Review Video: What is an Exponent?
Visit mometrix.com/academy and enter code: 600998

Roots

A **root**, such as a square root, is another way of writing a fractional exponent. Instead of using a superscript, roots use the radical symbol ($\sqrt{\ }$) to indicate the operation. A radical will have a number underneath the bar, and may sometimes have a number in the upper left: $\sqrt[n]{a}$, read as "the nth root of a." The relationship between radical notation and exponent notation can be described by this equation:

$$\sqrt[n]{a} = a^{\frac{1}{n}}$$

The two special cases of $n = 2$ and $n = 3$ are called square roots and cube roots. If there is no number to the upper left, the radical is understood to be a square root ($n = 2$). Nearly all of the roots you encounter will be square roots. A square root is the same as a number raised to the one-half power. When we say that a is the square root of b ($a = \sqrt{b}$), we mean that a multiplied by itself equals b: ($a \times a = b$).

A **perfect square** is a number that has an integer for its square root. There are 10 perfect squares from 1 to 100: 1, 4, 9, 16, 25, 36, 49, 64, 81, 100 (the squares of integers 1 through 10).

Review Video: Roots
Visit mometrix.com/academy and enter code: 795655

Review Video: Perfect Squares and Square Roots
Visit mometrix.com/academy and enter code: 648063

Word Problems and Mathematical Symbols

When working on word problems, you must be able to translate verbal expressions or "math words" into math symbols. This chart contains several "math words" and their appropriate symbols:

Phrase	Symbol
equal, is, was, will be, has, costs, gets to, is the same as, becomes	$=$
times, of, multiplied by, product of, twice, doubles, halves, triples	$\times$
divided by, per, ratio of/to, out of	$\div$
plus, added to, sum, combined, and, more than, totals of	$+$
subtracted from, less than, decreased by, minus, difference between	$-$
what, how much, original value, how many, a number, a variable	x, n, etc.

Examples of Translated Mathematical Phrases

- The phrase four more than twice a number can be written algebraically as $2x + 4$.
- The phrase half a number decreased by six can be written algebraically as $\frac{1}{2}x - 6$.
- The phrase the sum of a number and the product of five and that number can be written algebraically as $x + 5x$.
- You may see a test question that says, "Olivia is constructing a bookcase from seven boards. Two of them are for vertical supports and five are for shelves. The height of the bookcase is twice the width of the bookcase. If the seven boards total 36 feet in length, what will be the height of Olivia's bookcase?" You would need to make a sketch and then create the equation to determine the width of the shelves. The height can be represented as double the width. (If x represents the width of the shelves in feet, then the height of the bookcase is $2x$. Since the seven boards total 36 feet, $2x + 2x + x + x + x + x + x = 36$ or $9x = 36$; $x = 4$. The height is twice the width, or 8 feet.)

Subtraction with Regrouping

A great way to make use of some of the features built into the decimal system would be regrouping when attempting longform subtraction operations. When subtracting within a place value, sometimes the minuend is smaller than the subtrahend, **regrouping** enables you to 'borrow' a unit from a place value to the left in order to get a positive difference. For example, consider subtracting 189 from 525 with regrouping.

First, set up the subtraction problem in vertical form:

$$\begin{array}{r} 525 \\ -\ 189 \\ \hline \end{array}$$

Notice that the numbers in the ones and tens columns of 525 are smaller than the numbers in the ones and tens columns of 189. This means you will need to use regrouping to perform subtraction:

	5	2	5
–	1	8	9

To subtract 9 from 5 in the ones column you will need to borrow from the 2 in the tens columns:

	5	1	15
–	1	8	9
			6

Next, to subtract 8 from 1 in the tens column you will need to borrow from the 5 in the hundreds column:

	4	11	15
–	1	8	9
		3	6

Last, subtract the 1 from the 4 in the hundreds column:

	4	11	15
–	1	8	9
	3	3	6

Review Video: Subtracting Large Numbers
Visit mometrix.com/academy and enter code: 603350

ORDER OF OPERATIONS

The **order of operations** is a set of rules that dictates the order in which we must perform each operation in an expression so that we will evaluate it accurately. If we have an expression that includes multiple different operations, the order of operations tells us which operations to do first. The most common mnemonic for the order of operations is **PEMDAS**, or "Please Excuse My Dear Aunt Sally." PEMDAS stands for parentheses, exponents, multiplication, division, addition, and subtraction. It is important to understand that multiplication and division have equal precedence, as do addition and subtraction, so those pairs of operations are simply worked from left to right in order.

For example, evaluating the expression $5 + 20 \div 4 \times (2 + 3)^2 - 6$ using the correct order of operations would be done like this:

- **P:** Perform the operations inside the parentheses: $(2 + 3) = 5$
- **E:** Simplify the exponents: $(5)^2 = 5 \times 5 = 25$
  - The expression now looks like this: $5 + 20 \div 4 \times 25 - 6$
- **MD:** Perform multiplication and division from left to right: $20 \div 4 = 5$; then $5 \times 25 = 125$
  - The expression now looks like this: $5 + 125 - 6$
- **AS:** Perform addition and subtraction from left to right: $5 + 125 = 130$; then $130 - 6 = 124$

Review Video: Order of Operations
Visit mometrix.com/academy and enter code: 259675

Fractions, Decimals, and Percentages

Fractions

A **fraction** is a number that is expressed as one integer written above another integer, with a dividing line between them $\left(\frac{x}{y}\right)$. It represents the **quotient** of the two numbers "x divided by y." It can also be thought of as x out of y equal parts.

The top number of a fraction is called the **numerator**, and it represents the number of parts under consideration. The 1 in $\frac{1}{4}$ means that 1 part out of the whole is being considered in the calculation. The bottom number of a fraction is called the **denominator**, and it represents the total number of equal parts. The 4 in $\frac{1}{4}$ means that the whole consists of 4 equal parts. A fraction cannot have a denominator of zero; this is referred to as "*undefined.*"

Fractions can be manipulated, without changing the value of the fraction, by multiplying or dividing (but not adding or subtracting) both the numerator and denominator by the same number. If you divide both numbers by a common factor, you are **reducing** or simplifying the fraction. Two fractions that have the same value but are expressed differently are known as **equivalent fractions**. For example, $\frac{2}{10}, \frac{3}{15}, \frac{4}{20}$, and $\frac{5}{25}$ are all equivalent fractions. They can also all be reduced or simplified to $\frac{1}{5}$.

When two fractions are manipulated so that they have the same denominator, this is known as finding a **common denominator**. The number chosen to be that common denominator should be the least common multiple of the two original denominators. Example: $\frac{3}{4}$ and $\frac{5}{6}$; the least common multiple of 4 and 6 is 12. Manipulating to achieve the common denominator: $\frac{3}{4} = \frac{9}{12}; \frac{5}{6} = \frac{10}{12}$.

Review Video: Overview of Fractions
Visit mometrix.com/academy and enter code: 262335

Proper Fractions and Mixed Numbers

A fraction whose denominator is greater than its numerator is known as a **proper fraction**, while a fraction whose numerator is greater than its denominator is known as an **improper fraction**. Proper fractions have values *less than one* and improper fractions have values *greater than one.*

A **mixed number** is a number that contains both an integer and a fraction. Any improper fraction can be rewritten as a mixed number. Example: $\frac{8}{3} = \frac{6}{3} + \frac{2}{3} = 2 + \frac{2}{3} = 2\frac{2}{3}$. Similarly, any mixed number can be rewritten as an improper fraction. Example: $1\frac{3}{5} = 1 + \frac{3}{5} = \frac{5}{5} + \frac{3}{5} = \frac{8}{5}$.

Review Video: Proper and Improper Fractions and Mixed Numbers
Visit mometrix.com/academy and enter code: 211077

Adding and Subtracting Fractions

If two fractions have a common denominator, they can be added or subtracted simply by adding or subtracting the two numerators and retaining the same denominator. If the two fractions do not already have the same denominator, one or both of them must be manipulated to achieve a common denominator before they can be added or subtracted. Example: $\frac{1}{2}+\frac{1}{4}=\frac{2}{4}+\frac{1}{4}=\frac{3}{4}$.

Review Video: Adding and Subtracting Fractions
Visit mometrix.com/academy and enter code: 378080

Multiplying Fractions

Two fractions can be multiplied by multiplying the two numerators to find the new numerator and the two denominators to find the new denominator. Example: $\frac{1}{3}\times\frac{2}{3}=\frac{1\times2}{3\times3}=\frac{2}{9}$.

Dividing Fractions

Two fractions can be divided by flipping the numerator and denominator of the second fraction and then proceeding as though it were a multiplication problem. Example: $\frac{2}{3}\div\frac{3}{4}=\frac{2}{3}\times\frac{4}{3}=\frac{8}{9}$.

Review Video: Multiplying and Dividing Fractions
Visit mometrix.com/academy and enter code: 473632

Multiplying a Mixed Number by a Whole Number or a Decimal

When multiplying a mixed number by something, it is usually best to convert it to an improper fraction first. Additionally, if the multiplicand is a decimal, it is most often simplest to convert it to a fraction. For instance, to multiply $4\frac{3}{8}$ by 3.5, begin by rewriting each quantity as a whole number plus a proper fraction. Remember, a mixed number is a fraction added to a whole number and a decimal is a representation of the sum of fractions, specifically tenths, hundredths, thousandths, and so on:

$$4\frac{3}{8}\times 3.5=\left(4+\frac{3}{8}\right)\times\left(3+\frac{1}{2}\right)$$

Next, the quantities being added need to be expressed with the same denominator. This is achieved by multiplying and dividing the whole number by the denominator of the fraction. Recall that a whole number is equivalent to that number divided by 1:

$$=\left(\frac{4}{1}\times\frac{8}{8}+\frac{3}{8}\right)\times\left(\frac{3}{1}\times\frac{2}{2}+\frac{1}{2}\right)$$

When multiplying fractions, remember to multiply the numerators and denominators separately:

$$=\left(\frac{4\times8}{1\times8}+\frac{3}{8}\right)\times\left(\frac{3\times2}{1\times2}+\frac{1}{2}\right)$$

$$=\left(\frac{32}{8}+\frac{3}{8}\right)\times\left(\frac{6}{2}+\frac{1}{2}\right)$$

Now that the fractions have the same denominators, they can be added:

$$=\frac{35}{8}\times\frac{7}{2}$$

Finally, perform the last multiplication and then simplify:

$$=\frac{35\times7}{8\times2}=\frac{245}{16}=\frac{240}{16}+\frac{5}{16}=15\frac{5}{16}$$

Comparing Fractions

It is important to master the ability to compare and order fractions. This skill is relevant to many real-world scenarios. For example, carpenters often compare fractional construction nail lengths when preparing for a project, and bakers often compare fractional measurements to have the correct ratio of ingredients. There are three commonly used strategies when comparing fractions. These strategies are referred to as the common denominator approach, the decimal approach, and the cross-multiplication approach.

Using a Common Denominator to Compare Fractions

The fractions $\frac{2}{3}$ and $\frac{4}{7}$ have different denominators. $\frac{2}{3}$ has a denominator of 3, and $\frac{4}{7}$ has a denominator of 7. In order to precisely compare these two fractions, it is necessary to use a common denominator. A common denominator is a common multiple that is shared by both denominators. In this case, the denominators 3 and 7 share a multiple of 21. In general, it is most efficient to select the least common multiple for the two denominators.

Rewrite each fraction with the common denominator of 21. Then, calculate the new numerators as illustrated below.

$$\frac{2}{3} \overset{\times 7}{=} \frac{\mathbf{14}}{21} \qquad \frac{4}{7} \overset{\times 3}{=} \frac{\mathbf{12}}{21}$$

For $\frac{2}{3}$, multiply the numerator and denominator by 7. The result is $\frac{14}{21}$.

For $\frac{4}{7}$, multiply the numerator and denominator by 3. The result is $\frac{12}{21}$.

Now that both fractions have a denominator of 21, the fractions can accurately be compared by comparing the numerators. Since 14 is greater than 12, the fraction $\frac{14}{21}$ is greater than $\frac{12}{21}$. This means that $\frac{2}{3}$ is greater than $\frac{4}{7}$.

Using Decimals to Compare Fractions

Sometimes decimal values are easier to compare than fraction values. For example, $\frac{5}{8}$ is equivalent to 0.625 and $\frac{3}{5}$ is equivalent to 0.6. This means that the comparison of $\frac{5}{8}$ and $\frac{3}{5}$ can be determined by comparing the decimals 0.625 and 0.6. When both decimal values are extended to the thousandths place, they become 0.625 and 0.600, respectively. It becomes clear that 0.625 is greater than 0.600 because 625 thousandths is greater than 600 thousandths. In other words, $\frac{5}{8}$ is greater than $\frac{3}{5}$ because 0.625 is greater than 0.6.

Using Cross-Multiplication to Compare Fractions

Cross-multiplication is an efficient strategy for comparing fractions. This is a shortcut for the common denominator strategy. Start by writing each fraction next to one another. Multiply the numerator of the fraction on the left by the denominator of the fraction on the right. Write down the result next to the fraction on the left. Now multiply the numerator of the fraction on the right by the denominator of the fraction on the left. Write down the result next to the fraction on the right. Compare both products. The fraction with the larger result is the larger fraction.

Consider the fractions $\frac{4}{7}$ and $\frac{5}{9}$.

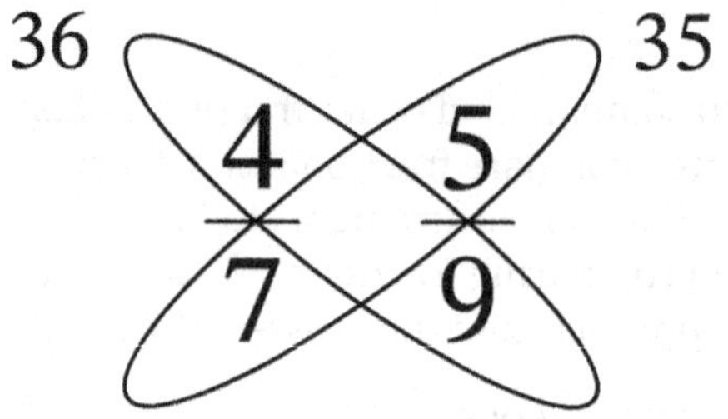

36 is greater than 35. Therefore, $\frac{4}{7}$ is greater than $\frac{5}{9}$.

Decimals

Decimals are one way to represent parts of a whole. Using the place value system, each digit to the right of a decimal point denotes the number of units of a corresponding *negative* power of ten. For example, consider the decimal 0.24. We can use a model to represent the decimal. Since a dime is worth one-tenth of a dollar and a penny is worth one-hundredth of a dollar, one possible model to represent this fraction is to have 2 dimes representing the 2 in the tenths place and 4 pennies representing the 4 in the hundredths place:

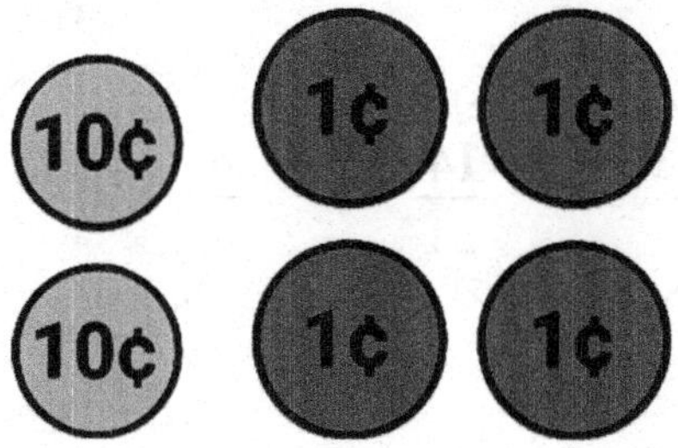

To write the decimal as a fraction, put the decimal in the numerator with 1 in the denominator. Multiply the numerator and denominator by tens until there are no more decimal places. Then simplify the fraction to lowest terms. For example, converting 0.24 to a fraction:

$$0.24 = \frac{0.24}{1} = \frac{0.24 \times 100}{1 \times 100} = \frac{24}{100} = \frac{6}{25}$$

Review Video: Decimals
Visit mometrix.com/academy and enter code: 837268

Operations with Decimals

Adding and Subtracting Decimals

When adding and subtracting decimals, the decimal points must always be aligned. Adding decimals is just like adding regular whole numbers. Example: $4.5 + 2.0 = 6.5$.

If the problem-solver does not properly align the decimal points, an incorrect answer of 4.7 may result. An easy way to add decimals is to align all of the decimal points in a vertical column visually. This will allow you to see exactly where the decimal should be placed in the final answer. Begin adding from right to left. Add each column in turn, making sure to carry the number to the left if a column adds up to more than 9. The same rules apply to the subtraction of decimals.

Review Video: Adding and Subtracting Decimals
Visit mometrix.com/academy and enter code: 381101

Multiplying Decimals

A simple multiplication problem has two components: a **multiplicand** and a **multiplier**. When multiplying decimals, work as though the numbers were whole rather than decimals. Once the final product is calculated, count the number of places to the right of the decimal in both the multiplicand and the multiplier. Then, count that number of places from the right of the product and place the decimal in that position.

For example, 12.3×2.56 has a total of three places to the right of the respective decimals. Multiply 123×256 to get 31,488. Now, beginning on the right, count three places to the left and insert the decimal. The final product will be 31.488.

Review Video: How to Multiply Decimals
Visit mometrix.com/academy and enter code: 731574

Dividing Decimals

Every division problem has a **divisor** and a **dividend**. The dividend is the number that is being divided. In the problem $14 \div 7$, 14 is the dividend and 7 is the divisor. In a division problem with decimals, the divisor must be converted into a whole number. Begin by moving the decimal in the divisor to the right until a whole number is created. Next, move the decimal in the dividend the same number of spaces to the right. For example, 4.9 into 24.5 would become 49 into 245. The decimal was moved one space to the right to create a whole number in the divisor, and then the same was done for the dividend. Once the whole numbers are created, the problem is carried out normally: $245 \div 49 = 5$.

Review Video: Dividing Decimals
Visit mometrix.com/academy and enter code: 560690

Review Video: Dividing Decimals by Whole Numbers
Visit mometrix.com/academy and enter code: 535669

Percentages

Percentages can be thought of as fractions that are based on a whole of 100; that is, one whole is equal to 100%. The word **percent** means "per hundred." Percentage problems are often presented in three main ways:

- Find what percentage of some number another number is.
  - Example: What percentage of 40 is 8?
- Find what number is some percentage of a given number.
  - Example: What number is 20% of 40?
- Find what number another number is a given percentage of.
  - Example: What number is 8 20% of?

There are three components in each of these cases: a **whole** (W), a **part** (P), and a **percentage** (%). These are related by the equation: $P = W \times \%$. This can easily be rearranged into other forms that may suit different questions better: $\% = \frac{P}{W}$ and $W = \frac{P}{\%}$. Percentage problems are often also word problems. As such, a large part of solving them is figuring out which quantities are what. For example, consider the following word problem:

In a school cafeteria, 7 students choose pizza, 9 choose hamburgers, and 4 choose tacos. What percentage of student choose tacos?

To find the whole, you must first add all of the parts: $7 + 9 + 4 = 20$. The percentage can then be found by dividing the part by the whole $\left(\% = \frac{P}{W}\right)$: $\frac{4}{20} = \frac{20}{100} = 20\%$.

Review Video: Computation with Percentages
Visit mometrix.com/academy and enter code: 693099

Converting Between Percentages, Fractions, and Decimals

Converting decimals to percentages and percentages to decimals is as simple as moving the decimal point. To *convert from a decimal to a percentage*, move the decimal point **two places to the right**. To *convert from a percentage to a decimal*, move it **two places to the left**. It may be helpful to remember that the percentage number will always be larger than the equivalent decimal number. Example:

$$0.23 = 23\% \qquad 5.34 = 534\% \qquad 0.007 = 0.7\%$$
$$700\% = 7.00 \qquad 86\% = 0.86 \qquad 0.15\% = 0.0015$$

To convert a fraction to a decimal, simply divide the numerator by the denominator in the fraction. To convert a decimal to a fraction, put the decimal in the numerator with 1 in the denominator. Multiply the numerator and denominator by tens until there are no more decimal places. Then simplify the fraction to lowest terms. For example, converting 0.24 to a fraction:

$$0.24 = \frac{0.24}{1} = \frac{0.24 \times 100}{1 \times 100} = \frac{24}{100} = \frac{6}{25}$$

Fractions can be converted to a percentage by finding equivalent fractions with a denominator of 100. Example:

$$\frac{7}{10} = \frac{70}{100} = 70\% \quad \frac{1}{4} = \frac{25}{100} = 25\%$$

To convert a percentage to a fraction, divide the percentage number by 100 and reduce the fraction to its simplest possible terms. Example:

$$60\% = \frac{60}{100} = \frac{3}{5} \quad 96\% = \frac{96}{100} = \frac{24}{25}$$

Review Video: Converting Fractions to Percentages and Decimals
Visit mometrix.com/academy and enter code: 306233

Review Video: Converting Percentages to Decimals and Fractions
Visit mometrix.com/academy and enter code: 287297

Review Video: Converting Decimals to Fractions and Percentages
Visit mometrix.com/academy and enter code: 986765

Review Video: Converting Decimals, Improper Fractions, and Mixed Numbers
Visit mometrix.com/academy and enter code: 696924

Complex Numbers

Complex numbers consist of a real component and an imaginary component. Complex numbers are expressed in the form $a + bi$ with real component a and imaginary component bi. The imaginary unit i is equal to $\sqrt{-1}$. That means $i^2 = -1$. The imaginary unit provides a way to find the square root of a negative number. For example, $\sqrt{-25}$ is $5i$. You should expect questions asking you to add, subtract, multiply, divide, and simplify complex numbers. You may see a question that says, "Add $3 + 2i$ and $5 - 7i$" or "Subtract $4 + i\sqrt{5}$ from $2 + i\sqrt{5}$." Or you may see a question that says, "Multiply $6 + 2i$ by $8 - 4i$" or "Divide $1 - 3i$ by $9 - 7i$."

Operations on Complex Numbers

Operations with complex numbers resemble operations with variables in algebra. When adding or subtracting complex numbers, you can only combine like terms—real terms with real terms and imaginary terms with imaginary terms. For example, if you are asked to simplify the expression $-2 + 4i - (-3 + 7i) - 5i$, you should first remove the parentheses to yield $-2 + 4i + 3 - 7i - 5i$. Combining like terms yields $1 - 8i$. One interesting aspect of imaginary numbers is that if i has an exponent greater than 1, it can be simplified. Example: $i^2 = -1$, $i^3 = -i$, and $i^4 = 1$. When multiplying complex numbers, remember to simplify each i with an exponent greater than 1. For example, you might see a question that says, "Simplify $(2 - i)(3 + 2i)$." You need to distribute and multiply to get $6 + 4i - 3i - 2i^2$. This is further simplified to $6 + i - 2(-1)$, or $8 + i$.

Simplifying Expressions with Complex Denominators

If an expression contains an i in the denominator, it must be simplified. Remember, roots cannot be left in the denominator of a fraction. Since i is equivalent to $\sqrt{-1}$, i cannot be left in the denominator of a fraction. You must rationalize the denominator of a fraction that contains a complex denominator by multiplying the numerator and denominator by the conjugate of the denominator. The conjugate of the complex number $a + bi$ is $a - bi$. You can simplify $\frac{2}{5i}$ by simply multiplying $\frac{2}{5i} \times \frac{i}{i}$, which yields $-\frac{2}{5}i$. And you can simplify $\frac{5+3i}{2-4i}$ by multiplying $\frac{5+3i}{2-4i} \times \frac{2+4i}{2+4i}$. This yields $\frac{10+20i+6i-12}{4-8i+8i+16}$ which simplifies to $\frac{-2+26i}{20}$ or $\frac{-1+13i}{10}$, which can also be written as $-\frac{1}{10} + \frac{13}{10}i$.

Matrix Basics

A **matrix** (plural: matrices) is a rectangular array of numbers or variables, often called **elements**, which are arranged in columns and rows. A matrix is generally represented by a capital letter, with its elements represented by the corresponding lowercase letter with two subscripts indicating the row and column of the element. For example, n_{ab} represents the element in row a column b of matrix N.

$$N = \begin{bmatrix} n_{11} & n_{12} & n_{13} \\ n_{21} & n_{22} & n_{23} \end{bmatrix}$$

A matrix can be described in terms of the number of rows and columns it contains in the format $a \times b$, where a is the number of rows and b is the number of columns. The matrix shown above is a 2×3 matrix. Any $a \times b$ matrix where $a = b$ is a square matrix. A **vector** is a matrix that has exactly one column (**column vector**) or exactly one row (**row vector**).

The **main diagonal** of a matrix is the set of elements on the diagonal from the top left to the bottom right of a matrix. Because of the way it is defined, only square matrices will have a main diagonal. For the matrix shown below, the main diagonal consists of the elements $n_{11}, n_{22}, n_{33}, n_{44}$.

$$\begin{bmatrix} n_{11} & n_{12} & n_{13} & n_{14} \\ n_{21} & n_{22} & n_{23} & n_{24} \\ n_{31} & n_{32} & n_{33} & n_{34} \\ n_{41} & n_{42} & n_{43} & n_{44} \end{bmatrix}$$

A 3×4 matrix such as the one shown below would not have a main diagonal because there is no straight line of elements between the top left corner and the bottom right corner that joins the elements.

$$\begin{bmatrix} n_{11} & n_{12} & n_{13} & n_{14} \\ n_{21} & n_{22} & n_{23} & n_{24} \\ n_{31} & n_{32} & n_{33} & n_{34} \end{bmatrix}$$

A **diagonal matrix** is a square matrix that has a zero for every element in the matrix except the elements on the main diagonal. All the elements on the main diagonal must be nonzero numbers.

$$\begin{bmatrix} n_{11} & 0 & 0 & 0 \\ 0 & n_{22} & 0 & 0 \\ 0 & 0 & n_{33} & 0 \\ 0 & 0 & 0 & n_{44} \end{bmatrix}$$

If every element on the main diagonal of a diagonal matrix is equal to one, the matrix is called an **identity matrix**. The identity matrix is often represented by the letter I.

$$I = \begin{bmatrix} 1 & 0 & 0 & 0 \\ 0 & 1 & 0 & 0 \\ 0 & 0 & 1 & 0 \\ 0 & 0 & 0 & 1 \end{bmatrix}$$

A **zero matrix** is a matrix that has zero as the value for every element in the matrix.

$$\begin{bmatrix} 0 & 0 & 0 & 0 \\ 0 & 0 & 0 & 0 \\ 0 & 0 & 0 & 0 \\ 0 & 0 & 0 & 0 \end{bmatrix}$$

The zero matrix is the *identity for matrix addition.* Do not confuse the zero matrix with the identity matrix.

The **negative of a matrix** is also known as the additive inverse of a matrix. If matrix N is the given matrix, then matrix $-N$ is its negative. This means that every element n_{ab} is equal to $-n_{ab}$ in the negative. To find the negative of a given matrix, change the sign of every element in the matrix and keep all elements in their original corresponding positions in the matrix.

If two matrices have the same order and all corresponding elements in the two matrices are the same, then the two matrices are **equal matrices**.

A matrix N may be **transposed** to matrix N^T by changing all rows into columns and changing all columns into rows. The easiest way to accomplish this is to swap the positions of the row and column notations for each element. For example, suppose the element in the second row of the third column of matrix N is $n_{23} = 6$. In the transposed matrix N^T, the transposed element would be $n_{32} = 6$, and it would be placed in the third row of the second column.

$$N = \begin{bmatrix} 1 & 2 & 3 \\ 4 & 5 & 6 \end{bmatrix}; \; N^T = \begin{bmatrix} 1 & 4 \\ 2 & 5 \\ 3 & 6 \end{bmatrix}$$

To quickly transpose a matrix by hand, begin with the first column and rewrite a new matrix with those same elements in the same order in the first row. Write the elements from the second column of the original matrix in the second row of the transposed matrix. Continue this process until all columns have been completed. If the original matrix is identical to the transposed matrix, the matrices are symmetric.

Basic Operations with Matrices

There are two categories of basic operations with regard to matrices: operations between a matrix and a scalar, and operations between two matrices.

Scalar Operations

A scalar being added to a matrix is treated as though it were being added to each element of the matrix. The same is true for subtraction, multiplication and division:

$$M + \mathrm{k} = \begin{bmatrix} m_{11} + k & m_{12} + k \\ m_{21} + k & m_{22} + k \end{bmatrix}$$
$$M - k = \begin{bmatrix} m_{11} - k & m_{12} - k \\ m_{21} - k & m_{22} - k \end{bmatrix}$$
$$M \times k = \begin{bmatrix} m_{11} \times k & m_{12} \times k \\ m_{21} \times k & m_{22} \times k \end{bmatrix}$$
$$M \div k = \begin{bmatrix} m_{11} \div k & m_{12} \div k \\ m_{21} \div k & m_{22} \div k \end{bmatrix}$$

Matrix Addition and Subtraction

All four of the basic operations can be used with operations between matrices (although division is usually discarded in favor of multiplication by the inverse), but there are restrictions on the situations in which they can be used. Matrices that meet all the qualifications for a given operation are called **conformable matrices**. However, conformability is specific to the operation; two matrices that are conformable for addition are not necessarily conformable for multiplication.

For two matrices to be conformable for addition or subtraction, they must be of the same dimension; otherwise, the operation is not defined. If matrix M is a 3×2 matrix and matrix N is a 2×3 matrix, the operations $M + N$ and $M - N$ are meaningless. If matrices M and N are the same size, the operation is as simple as adding or subtracting all of the corresponding elements:

$$\begin{bmatrix} m_{11} & m_{12} \\ m_{21} & m_{22} \end{bmatrix} + \begin{bmatrix} n_{11} & n_{12} \\ n_{21} & n_{22} \end{bmatrix} = \begin{bmatrix} m_{11} + n_{11} & m_{12} + n_{12} \\ m_{21} + n_{21} & m_{22} + n_{22} \end{bmatrix}$$

$$\begin{bmatrix} m_{11} & m_{12} \\ m_{21} & m_{22} \end{bmatrix} - \begin{bmatrix} n_{11} & n_{12} \\ n_{21} & n_{22} \end{bmatrix} = \begin{bmatrix} m_{11} - n_{11} & m_{12} - n_{12} \\ m_{21} - n_{21} & m_{22} - n_{22} \end{bmatrix}$$

The result of addition or subtraction is a matrix of the same dimension as the two original matrices involved in the operation.

Matrix Multiplication

The first thing it is necessary to understand about matrix multiplication is that it is not commutative. In scalar multiplication, the operation is commutative, meaning that $a \times b = b \times a$. For matrix multiplication, this is not the case: $A \times B \neq B \times A$. The terminology must be specific when describing matrix multiplication. The operation $A \times B$ can be described as A multiplied (or **post-multiplied**) by B, or B **pre-multiplied** by A.

For two matrices to be conformable for multiplication, they need not be of the same dimension, but specific dimensions must correspond. Taking the example of two matrices M and N to be multiplied $M \times N$, matrix M must have the same number of columns as matrix N has rows. Put another way, if matrix M has the dimensions $a \times b$ and matrix N has the dimensions $c \times d$, b must equal c if the two matrices are to be conformable for this multiplication. The matrix that results from the multiplication will have the dimensions $a \times d$. If a and d are both equal to 1, the product is simply a scalar. Square matrices of the same dimensions are always conformable for multiplication, and their product is always a matrix of the same size.

The simplest type of matrix multiplication is a 1×2 matrix (a row vector) times a 2×1 matrix (a column vector). These will multiply in the following way:

$$\begin{bmatrix} m_{11} & m_{12} \end{bmatrix} \times \begin{bmatrix} n_{11} \\ n_{21} \end{bmatrix} = m_{11}n_{11} + m_{12}n_{21}$$

The two matrices are conformable for multiplication because matrix M has the same number of columns as matrix N has rows. Because the other dimensions are both 1, the result is a scalar. Expanding our matrices to 1×3 and 3×1, the process is the same:

$$[m_{11} \quad m_{12} \quad m_{13}] \times \begin{bmatrix} n_{11} \\ n_{21} \\ n_{31} \end{bmatrix} = m_{11}n_{11} + m_{12}n_{21} + m_{13}n_{31}$$

Once again, the result is a scalar. This type of basic matrix multiplication is the building block for the multiplication of larger matrices.

To multiply larger matrices, treat each **row from the first matrix** and each **column from the second matrix** as individual vectors and follow the pattern for multiplying vectors. The scalar value found from multiplying the first-row vector by the first column vector is placed in the first row, first column of the new matrix. The scalar value found from multiplying the second-row vector by the first column vector is placed in the second row, first column of the new matrix. Continue this pattern until each row of the first matrix has been multiplied by each column of the second matrix.

Below is an example of the multiplication of a 3×2 matrix and a 2×3 matrix.

$$\begin{bmatrix} m_{11} & m_{12} \\ m_{21} & m_{22} \\ m_{31} & m_{32} \end{bmatrix} \times \begin{bmatrix} n_{11} & n_{12} & n_{13} \\ n_{21} & n_{22} & n_{23} \end{bmatrix} = \begin{bmatrix} m_{11}n_{11} + m_{12}n_{21} & m_{11}n_{12} + m_{12}n_{22} & m_{11}n_{13} + m_{12}n_{23} \\ m_{21}n_{11} + m_{22}n_{21} & m_{21}n_{12} + m_{22}n_{22} & m_{21}n_{13} + m_{22}n_{23} \\ m_{31}n_{11} + m_{32}n_{21} & m_{31}n_{12} + m_{32}n_{22} & m_{31}n_{13} + m_{32}n_{23} \end{bmatrix}$$

This process starts by taking the first column of the second matrix and running it through each row of the first matrix. Removing all but the first M row and first N column, we would see only the following:

$$[m_{11} \ m_{12}] \times \begin{bmatrix} n_{11} \\ n_{21} \end{bmatrix} = m_{11}n_{11} + m_{12}n_{21}$$

The first product would then be $m_{11}n_{11} + m_{12}n_{21}$. This process will be continued for each column of the N matrix to find the first full row of the product matrix, as shown below.

$$[m_{11}n_{11} + m_{12}n_{21} \quad m_{11}n_{12} + m_{12}n_{22} \quad m_{11}n_{13} + m_{12}n_{23}]$$

After completing the first row, the next step would be to simply move to the second row of the M matrix and repeat the process until all of the rows have been finished. The result is a 3×3 matrix.

$$\begin{bmatrix} m_{11} & m_{12} \\ m_{21} & m_{22} \\ m_{31} & m_{32} \end{bmatrix} \times \begin{bmatrix} n_{11} & n_{12} & n_{13} \\ n_{21} & n_{22} & n_{23} \end{bmatrix} = \begin{bmatrix} m_{11}n_{11} + m_{12}n_{21} & m_{11}n_{12} + m_{12}n_{22} & m_{11}n_{13} + m_{12}n_{23} \\ m_{21}n_{11} + m_{22}n_{21} & m_{21}n_{12} + m_{22}n_{22} & m_{21}n_{13} + m_{22}n_{23} \\ m_{31}n_{11} + m_{32}n_{21} & m_{31}n_{12} + m_{32}n_{22} & m_{31}n_{13} + m_{32}n_{23} \end{bmatrix}$$

If the operation were done in reverse ($N \times M$), the result would be a 2×2 matrix.

$$\begin{bmatrix} n_{11} & n_{12} & n_{13} \\ n_{21} & n_{22} & n_{23} \end{bmatrix} \times \begin{bmatrix} m_{11} & m_{12} \\ m_{21} & m_{22} \\ m_{31} & m_{32} \end{bmatrix} = \begin{bmatrix} m_{11}n_{11} + m_{21}n_{12} + m_{31}n_{13} & m_{12}n_{11} + m_{22}n_{12} + m_{32}n_{13} \\ m_{11}n_{21} + m_{21}n_{22} + m_{31}n_{23} & m_{12}n_{21} + m_{22}n_{22} + m_{32}n_{23} \end{bmatrix}$$

Review Video: Matrices: The Basics
Visit mometrix.com/academy and enter code: 516658

Algebra

LINEAR EXPRESSIONS

TERMS AND COEFFICIENTS

Mathematical expressions consist of a combination of one or more values arranged in terms that are added together. As such, an expression could be just a single number, including zero. A **variable term** is the product of a real number, also called a **coefficient**, and one or more variables, each of which may be raised to an exponent. Expressions may also include numbers without a variable, called **constants** or **constant terms**. The expression $6s^2$, for example, is a single term where the coefficient is the real number 6 and the variable term is s^2. Note that if a term is written as simply a variable to some exponent, like t^2, then the coefficient is 1, because $t^2 = 1t^2$.

LINEAR EXPRESSIONS

A **single variable linear expression** is the sum of a single variable term, where the variable has no exponent, and a constant, which may be zero. For instance, the expression $2w + 7$ has $2w$ as the variable term and 7 as the constant term. It is important to realize that terms are separated by addition or subtraction. Since an expression is a sum of terms, expressions such as $5x - 3$ can be written as $5x + (-3)$ to emphasize that the constant term is negative. A real-world example of a single variable linear expression is the perimeter of a square, four times the side length, often expressed: $4s$.

In general, a **linear expression** is the sum of any number of variable terms so long as none of the variables have an exponent. For example, $3m + 8n - \frac{1}{4}p + 5.5q - 1$ is a linear expression, but $3y^3$ is not. In the same way, the expression for the perimeter of a general triangle, the sum of the side lengths $(a + b + c)$ is considered to be linear, but the expression for the area of a square, the side length squared $(s^2)$is not.

LINEAR EQUATIONS

Equations that can be written as $ax + b = 0$, where $a \neq 0$, are referred to as **one variable linear equations**. A solution to such an equation is called a **root**. In the case where we have the equation $5x + 10 = 0$, if we solve for x we get a solution of $x = -2$. In other words, the root of the equation is -2. This is found by first subtracting 10 from both sides, which gives $5x = -10$. Next, simply divide both sides by the coefficient of the variable, in this case 5, to get $x = -2$. This can be checked by plugging -2 back into the original equation $(5)(-2) + 10 = -10 + 10 = 0$.

The **solution set** is the set of all solutions of an equation. In our example, the solution set would simply be -2. If there were more solutions (there usually are in multivariable equations) then they would also be included in the solution set. When an equation has no true solutions, it is referred to as an **empty set**. Equations with identical solution sets are **equivalent equations**. An **identity** is a term whose value or determinant is equal to 1.

Linear equations can be written many ways. Below is a list of some forms linear equations can take:

- **Standard Form**: $Ax + By = C$; the slope is $\frac{-A}{B}$ and the y-intercept is $\frac{C}{B}$
- **Slope Intercept Form**: $y = mx + b$, where m is the slope and b is the y-intercept
- **Point-Slope Form**: $y - y_1 = m(x - x_1)$, where m is the slope and (x_1, y_1) is a point on the line
- **Two-Point Form**: $\frac{y-y_1}{x-x_1} = \frac{y_2-y_1}{x_2-x_1}$, where (x_1, y_1) and (x_2, y_2) are two points on the given line

- **Intercept Form:** $\frac{x}{x_1} + \frac{y}{y_1} = 1$, where $(x_1, 0)$ is the point at which a line intersects the x-axis, and $(0, y_1)$ is the point at which the same line intersects the y-axis

Review Video: Slope-Intercept and Point-Slope Forms
Visit mometrix.com/academy and enter code: 113216

Review Video: Linear Equations Basics
Visit mometrix.com/academy and enter code: 793005

Solving Equations

Solving One-Variable Linear Equations

Multiply all terms by the lowest common denominator to eliminate any fractions. Look for addition or subtraction to undo so you can isolate the variable on one side of the equal sign. Divide both sides by the coefficient of the variable. When you have a value for the variable, substitute this value into the original equation to make sure you have a true equation. Consider the following example:

Kim's savings are represented by the table below. Represent her savings, using an equation.

X (Months)	Y (Total Savings)
2	$1,300
5	$2,050
9	$3,050
11	$3,550
16	$4,800

The table shows a function with a constant rate of change, or slope, of 250. Given the points on the table, the slopes can be calculated as $\frac{(2{,}050-1300)}{(5-2)}$, $\frac{(3{,}050-2{,}050)}{(9-5)}$, $\frac{(3{,}550-3{,}050)}{(11-9)}$, and $\frac{(4{,}800-3{,}550)}{(16-11)}$, each of which equals 250. Thus, the table shows a constant rate of change, indicating a linear function. The slope-intercept form of a linear equation is written as $y = mx + b$, where m represents the slope and b represents the y-intercept. Substituting the slope into this form gives $y = 250x + b$. Substituting corresponding x- and y-values from any point into this equation will give the y-intercept, or b. Using the point, $(2, 1{,}300)$, gives $1{,}300 = 250(2) + b$, which simplifies as $b = 800$. Thus, her savings may be represented by the equation, $y = 250x + 800$.

Rules for Manipulating Equations

Like Terms

Like terms are terms in an equation that have the same variable, regardless of whether or not they also have the same coefficient. This includes terms that *lack* a variable; all constants (i.e., numbers without variables) are considered like terms. If the equation involves terms with a variable raised to different powers, the like terms are those that have the variable raised to the same power.

For example, consider the equation $x^2 + 3x + 2 = 2x^2 + x - 7 + 2x$. In this equation, 2 and –7 are like terms; they are both constants. $3x$, x, and $2x$ are like terms, they all include the variable x raised to the first power. x^2 and $2x^2$ are like terms, they both include the variable x, raised to the second power. $2x$ and $2x^2$ are not like terms; although they both involve the variable x, the variable is not raised to the same power in both terms. The fact that they have the same coefficient, 2, is not relevant.

Review Video: Rules for Manipulating Equations
Visit mometrix.com/academy and enter code: 838871

Carrying Out the Same Operation on Both Sides of an Equation

When solving an equation, the general procedure is to carry out a series of operations on both sides of an equation, choosing operations that will tend to simplify the equation when doing so. The reason why the same operation must be carried out on both sides of the equation is because that leaves the meaning of the equation unchanged, and yields a result that is equivalent to the original equation. This would not be the case if we carried out an operation on one side of an equation and not the other. Consider what an equation means: it is a statement that two values or expressions are equal. If we carry out the same operation on both sides of the equation—add 3 to both sides, for example—then the two sides of the equation are changed in the same way, and so remain equal. If we do that to only one side of the equation—add 3 to one side but not the other—then that wouldn't be true; if we change one side of the equation but not the other then the two sides are no longer equal.

Advantage of Combining Like Terms

Combining like terms refers to adding or subtracting like terms—terms with the same variable—and therefore reducing sets of like terms to a single term. The main advantage of doing this is that it simplifies the equation. Often, combining like terms can be done as the first step in solving an equation, though it can also be done later, such as after distributing terms in a product.

For example, consider the equation $2(x + 3) + 3(2 + x + 3) = -4$. The 2 and the 3 in the second set of parentheses are like terms, and we can combine them, yielding $2(x + 3) + 3(x + 5) = -4$. Now we can carry out the multiplications implied by the parentheses, distributing the outer 2 and 3 accordingly: $2x + 6 + 3x + 15 = -4$. The $2x$ and the $3x$ are like terms, and we can add them together: $5x + 6 + 15 = -4$. Now, the constants 6, 15, and -4 are also like terms, and we can combine them as well: subtracting 6 and 15 from both sides of the equation, we get $5x = -4 - 6 - 15$, or $5x = -25$, which simplifies further to $x = -5$.

Review Video: Solving Equations by Combining Like Terms
Visit mometrix.com/academy and enter code: 668506

Canceling Terms on Opposite Sides of an Equation

Two terms on opposite sides of an equation can be canceled if and only if they *exactly* match each other. They must have the same variable raised to the same power and the same coefficient. For example, in the equation $3x + 2x^2 + 6 = 2x^2 - 6$, $2x^2$ appears on both sides of the equation and can be canceled, leaving $3x + 6 = -6$. The 6 on each side of the equation *cannot* be canceled, because it is added on one side of the equation and subtracted on the other. While they cannot be canceled, however, the 6 and -6 are like terms and can be combined, yielding $3x = -12$, which simplifies further to $x = -4$.

It's also important to note that the terms to be canceled must be independent terms and cannot be part of a larger term. For example, consider the equation $2(x + 6) = 3(x + 4) + 1$. We cannot cancel the x's, because even though they match each other they are part of the larger terms $2(x + 6)$ and $3(x + 4)$. We must first distribute the 2 and 3, yielding $2x + 12 = 3x + 12 + 1$. Now we see that the terms with the x's do not match, but the 12s do, and can be canceled, leaving $2x = 3x + 1$, which simplifies to $x = -1$.

Process for Manipulating Equations

Isolating Variables

To **isolate a variable** means to manipulate the equation so that the variable appears by itself on one side of the equation, and does not appear at all on the other side. Generally, an equation or inequality is considered to be solved once the variable is isolated and the other side of the equation or inequality is simplified as much as possible. In the case of a two-variable equation or inequality, only one variable needs to be isolated; it will not usually be possible to simultaneously isolate both variables.

For a linear equation—an equation in which the variable only appears raised to the first power—isolating a variable can be done by first moving all the terms with the variable to one side of the equation and all other terms to the other side. (*Moving* a term really means adding the inverse of the term to both sides; when a term is *moved* to the other side of the equation its sign is flipped.) Then combine like terms on each side. Finally, divide both sides by the coefficient of the variable, if applicable. The steps need not necessarily be done in this order, but this order will always work.

Review Video: Solving One-Step Equations
Visit mometrix.com/academy and enter code: 777004

Equations with More Than One Solution

Some types of non-linear equations, such as equations involving squares of variables, may have more than one solution. For example, the equation $x^2 = 4$ has two solutions: 2 and –2. Equations with absolute values can also have multiple solutions: $|x| = 1$ has the solutions $x = 1$ and $x = -1$.

It is also possible for a linear equation to have more than one solution, but only if the equation is true regardless of the value of the variable. In this case, the equation is considered to have infinitely many solutions, because any possible value of the variable is a solution. We know a linear equation has infinitely many solutions if when we combine like terms the variables cancel, leaving a true statement. For example, consider the equation $2(3x + 5) = x + 5(x + 2)$. Distributing, we get $6x + 10 = x + 5x + 10$; combining like terms gives $6x + 10 = 6x + 10$, and the $6x$-terms cancel to leave $10 = 10$. This is clearly true, so the original equation is true for any value of x. We could also have canceled the 10s leaving $0 = 0$, but again this is clearly true—in general if both sides of the equation match exactly, it has infinitely many solutions.

Equations with No Solution

Some types of non-linear equations, such as equations involving squares of variables, may have no solution. For example, the equation $x^2 = -2$ has no solutions in the real numbers, because the square of any real number must be positive. Similarly, $|x| = -1$ has no solution, because the absolute value of a number is always positive.

It is also possible for an equation to have no solution even if does not involve any powers greater than one, absolute values, or other special functions. For example, the equation $2(x + 3) + x = 3x$ has no solution. We can see that if we try to solve it: first we distribute, leaving $2x + 6 + x = 3x$. But now if we try to combine all the terms with the variable, we find that they cancel: we have $3x$ on the left and $3x$ on the right, canceling to leave us with $6 = 0$. This is clearly false. In general, whenever the variable terms in an equation cancel leaving different constants on both sides, it means that the equation has no solution. (If we are left with the *same* constant on both sides, the equation has infinitely many solutions instead.)

Features of Equations That Require Special Treatment

Linear Equations

A linear equation is an equation in which variables only appear by themselves: not multiplied together, not with exponents other than one, and not inside absolute value signs or any other functions. For example, the equation $x + 1 - 3x = 5 - x$ is a linear equation; while x appears multiple times, it never appears with an exponent other than one, or inside any function. The two-variable equation $2x - 3y = 5 + 2x$ is also a linear equation. In contrast, the equation $x^2 - 5 = 3x$ is *not* a linear equation, because it involves the term x^2. $\sqrt{x} = 5$ is not a linear equation, because it involves a square root. $(x - 1)^2 = 4$ is not a linear equation because even though there's no exponent on the x directly, it appears as part of an expression that is squared. The two-variable equation $x + xy - y = 5$ is not a linear equation because it includes the term xy, where two variables are multiplied together.

Linear equations can always be solved (or shown to have no solution) by combining like terms and performing simple operations on both sides of the equation. Some non-linear equations can be solved by similar methods, but others may require more advanced methods of solution, if they can be solved analytically at all.

SOLVING EQUATIONS INVOLVING ROOTS

In an equation involving roots, the first step is to isolate the term with the root, if possible, and then raise both sides of the equation to the appropriate power to eliminate it. Consider an example equation, $2\sqrt{x+1}-1=3$. In this case, begin by adding 1 to both sides, yielding $2\sqrt{x+1}=4$, and then dividing both sides by 2, yielding $\sqrt{x+1}=2$. Now square both sides, yielding $x+1=4$. Finally, subtracting 1 from both sides yields $x=3$.

Squaring both sides of an equation may, however, yield a spurious solution—a solution to the squared equation that is *not* a solution of the original equation. It's therefore necessary to plug the solution back into the original equation to make sure it works. In this case, it does: $2\sqrt{3+1}-1=2\sqrt{4}-1=2(2)-1=4-1=3$.

The same procedure applies for other roots as well. For example, given the equation $3+\sqrt[3]{2x}=5$, we can first subtract 3 from both sides, yielding $\sqrt[3]{2x}=2$ and isolating the root. Raising both sides to the third power yields $2x=2^3$; i.e., $2x=8$. We can now divide both sides by 2 to get $x=4$.

> **Review Video: Solving Equations Involving Roots**
> Visit mometrix.com/academy and enter code: 297670

SOLVING EQUATIONS WITH EXPONENTS

To solve an equation involving an exponent, the first step is to isolate the variable with the exponent. We can then take the appropriate root of both sides to eliminate the exponent. For instance, for the equation $2x^3+17=5x^3-7$, we can subtract $5x^3$ from both sides to get $-3x^3+17=-7$, and then subtract 17 from both sides to get $-3x^3=-24$. Finally, we can divide both sides by -3 to get $x^3=8$. Finally, we can take the cube root of both sides to get $x=\sqrt[3]{8}=2$.

One important but often overlooked point is that equations with an exponent greater than 1 may have more than one answer. The solution to $x^2=9$ isn't simply $x=3$; it's $x=\pm3$ (that is, $x=3$ or $x=-3$). For a slightly more complicated example, consider the equation $(x-1)^2-1=3$. Adding 1 to both sides yields $(x-1)^2=4$; taking the square root of both sides yields $x-1=2$. We can then add 1 to both sides to get $x=3$. However, there's a second solution. We also have the possibility that $x-1=-2$, in which case $x=-1$. Both $x=3$ and $x=-1$ are valid solutions, as can be verified by substituting them both into the original equation.

> **Review Video: Solving Equations with Exponents**
> Visit mometrix.com/academy and enter code: 514557

SOLVING EQUATIONS WITH ABSOLUTE VALUES

When solving an equation with an absolute value, the first step is to isolate the absolute value term. We then consider two possibilities: when the expression inside the absolute value is positive or when it is negative. In the former case, the expression in the absolute value equals the expression on the other side of the equation; in the latter, it equals the additive inverse of that expression—the expression times negative one. We consider each case separately and finally check for spurious solutions.

For instance, consider solving $|2x-1|+x=5$ for x. We can first isolate the absolute value by moving the x to the other side: $|2x-1|=-x+5$. Now, we have two possibilities. First, that $2x-1$ is positive, and hence $2x-1=-x+5$. Rearranging and combining like terms yields $3x=6$, and hence $x=2$. The other possibility is that $2x-1$ is negative, and hence $2x-1=-(-x+5)=x-5$. In this case, rearranging and combining like terms yields $x=-4$. Substituting $x=2$ and $x=-4$ back into the original equation, we see that they are both valid solutions.

Note that the absolute value of a sum or difference applies to the sum or difference as a whole, not to the individual terms; in general, $|2x-1|$ is not equal to $|2x+1|$ or to $|2x|-1$.

Spurious Solutions

A **spurious solution** may arise when we square both sides of an equation as a step in solving it or under certain other operations on the equation. It is a solution to the squared or otherwise modified equation that is *not* a solution of the original equation. To identify a spurious solution, it's useful when you solve an equation involving roots or absolute values to plug the solution back into the original equation to make sure it's valid.

Choosing Which Variable to Isolate in Two-Variable Equations

Similar to methods for a one-variable equation, solving a two-variable equation involves isolating a variable: manipulating the equation so that a variable appears by itself on one side of the equation, and not at all on the other side. However, in a two-variable equation, you will usually only be able to isolate one of the variables; the other variable may appear on the other side along with constant terms, or with exponents or other functions.

Often one variable will be much more easily isolated than the other, and therefore that's the variable you should choose. If one variable appears with various exponents, and the other is only raised to the first power, the latter variable is the one to isolate: given the equation $a^2 + 2b = a^3 + b + 3$, the b only appears to the first power, whereas a appears squared and cubed, so b is the variable that can be solved for: combining like terms and isolating the b on the left side of the equation, we get $b = a^3 - a^2 + 3$. If both variables are equally easy to isolate, then it's best to isolate the dependent variable, if one is defined; if the two variables are x and y, the convention is that y is the dependent variable.

Review Video: Solving Equations with Variables on Both Sides
Visit mometrix.com/academy and enter code: 402497

Systems of Equations

Solving Systems of Equations

A **system of equations** is a set of simultaneous equations that all use the same variables. A solution to a system of equations must be true for each equation in the system. **Consistent systems** are those with at least one solution. **Inconsistent systems** are systems of equations that have no solution.

Review Video: Solving Systems of Linear Equations
Visit mometrix.com/academy and enter code: 746745

Substitution

To solve a system of linear equations by **substitution**, start with the easier equation and solve for one of the variables. Express this variable in terms of the other variable. Substitute this expression in the other equation and solve for the other variable. The solution should be expressed in the form (x, y). Substitute the values into both of the original equations to check your answer. Consider the following system of equations:

$$x + 6y = 15$$
$$3x - 12y = 18$$

Solving the first equation for x: $x = 15 - 6y$

Substitute this value in place of x in the second equation, and solve for y:

$$3(15 - 6y) - 12y = 18$$
$$45 - 18y - 12y = 18$$
$$30y = 27$$
$$y = \frac{27}{30} = \frac{9}{10} = 0.9$$

Plug this value for y back into the first equation to solve for x:

$$x = 15 - 6(0.9) = 15 - 5.4 = 9.6$$

Check both equations if you have time:

$$\begin{aligned} 9.6 + 6(0.9) &= 15 \\ 9.6 + 5.4 &= 15 \\ 15 &= 15 \end{aligned} \qquad \begin{aligned} 3(9.6) - 12(0.9) &= 18 \\ 28.8 - 10.8 &= 18 \\ 18 &= 18 \end{aligned}$$

Therefore, the solution is (9.6,0.9).

Review Video: The Substitution Method
Visit mometrix.com/academy and enter code: 565151

Review Video: Substitution and Elimination
Visit mometrix.com/academy and enter code: 958611

ELIMINATION

To solve a system of equations using **elimination**, begin by rewriting both equations in standard form $Ax + By = C$. Check to see if the coefficients of one pair of like variables add to zero. If not, multiply one or both of the equations by a non-zero number to make one set of like variables add to zero. Add the two equations to solve for one of the variables. Substitute this value into one of the original equations to solve for the other variable. Check your work by substituting into the other equation. Now, let's look at solving the following system using the elimination method:

$$\begin{aligned} 5x + 6y &= 4 \\ x + 2y &= 4 \end{aligned}$$

If we multiply the second equation by -3, we can eliminate the y-terms:

$$\begin{aligned} 5x + 6y &= 4 \\ -3x - 6y &= -12 \end{aligned}$$

Add the equations together and solve for x:

$$\begin{aligned} 2x &= -8 \\ x &= \frac{-8}{2} = -4 \end{aligned}$$

Plug the value for x back in to either of the original equations and solve for y:

$$\begin{aligned} -4 + 2y &= 4 \\ y &= \frac{4+4}{2} = 4 \end{aligned}$$

Check both equations if you have time:

$$\begin{aligned} 5(-4) + 6(4) &= 4 \\ -20 + 24 &= 4 \\ 4 &= 4 \end{aligned} \qquad \begin{aligned} -4 + 2(4) &= 4 \\ -4 + 8 &= 4 \\ 4 &= 4 \end{aligned}$$

Therefore, the solution is $(-4,4)$.

Review Video: The Elimination Method
Visit mometrix.com/academy and enter code: 449121

GRAPHICALLY

To solve a system of linear equations **graphically**, plot both equations on the same graph. The solution of the equations is the point where both lines cross. If the lines do not cross (are parallel), then there is **no solution**.

For example, consider the following system of equations:

$$y = 2x + 7$$
$$y = -x + 1$$

Since these equations are given in slope-intercept form, they are easy to graph; the y-intercepts of the lines are $(0,7)$ and $(0,1)$. The respective slopes are 2 and –1, thus the graphs look like this:

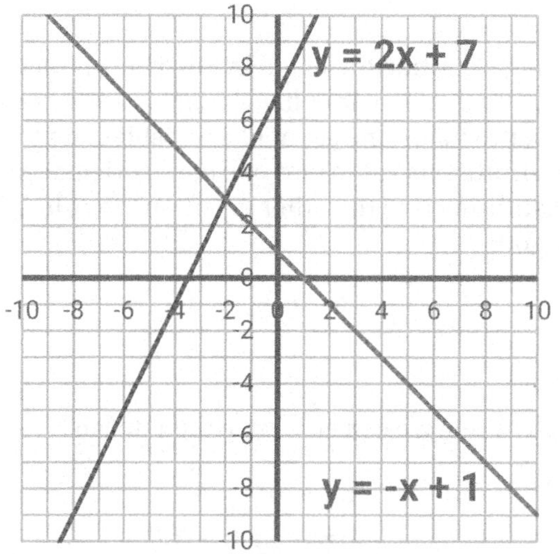

The two lines intersect at the point $(-2,3)$, thus this is the solution to the system of equations.

Solving a system graphically is generally only practical if both coordinates of the solution are integers; otherwise the intersection will lie between gridlines on the graph and the coordinates will be difficult or impossible to determine exactly. It also helps if, as in this example, the equations are in slope-intercept form or some other form that makes them easy to graph. Otherwise, another method of solution (by substitution or elimination) is likely to be more useful.

Review Video: Solving Systems by Graphing
Visit mometrix.com/academy and enter code: 634812

SOLVING SYSTEMS OF EQUATIONS USING THE TRACE FEATURE

Using the trace feature on a calculator requires that you rewrite each equation, isolating the y-variable on one side of the equal sign. Enter both equations in the graphing calculator and plot the graphs simultaneously. Use the trace cursor to find where the two lines cross. Use the zoom feature if necessary to obtain more accurate results. Always check your answer by substituting into the original equations. The trace method is likely to be less accurate than other methods due to the resolution of graphing calculators but is a useful tool to provide an approximate answer.

ADVANCED FUNCTIONS

STEP FUNCTIONS

The double brackets indicate a step function. For a step function, the value inside the double brackets is rounded down to the nearest integer. The graph of the function $f_0(x) = [\![x]\!]$ appears on the left graph. In comparison $f(x) = 2\left[\!\left[\frac{1}{3}(x-1)\right]\!\right]$ is on the right graph. The coefficient of 2 shows that it's stretched vertically by a factor of 2 (so there's a vertical distance of 2 units between successive "steps"). The coefficient of $\frac{1}{3}$ in front of the x shows that it's stretched horizontally by a factor of 3 (so each "step" is three units long), and the $x - 1$ shows that it's displaced one unit to the right.

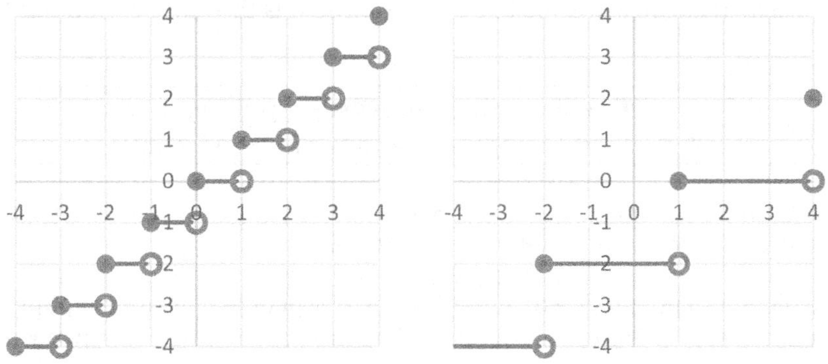

TRANSCENDENTAL FUNCTIONS

Transcendental functions are all functions that are non-algebraic. Any function that includes logarithms, trigonometric functions, variables as exponents, or any combination that includes any of these is not algebraic in nature, even if the function includes polynomials or roots.

EXPONENTIAL FUNCTIONS

Exponential functions are equations that have the format $y = b^x$, where base $b > 0$ and $b \neq 1$. The exponential function can also be written $f(x) = b^x$. Recall the properties of exponents, like the product of terms with the same base is equal to the base raised to the sum of the exponents $(a^x \times a^y = a^{x+y})$ and a term with an exponent that is raised to an exponent is equal to the base of the original term raised to the product of the exponents: $((a^x)^y = a^{xy})$. The graph of an example exponential function, $f(x) = 2^x$, is below:

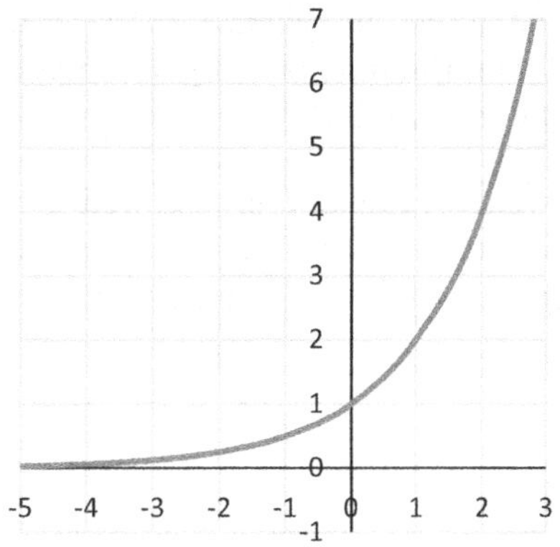

Note in the graph that the y-value approaches zero to the left and infinity to the right. One of the key features of an exponential function is that there will be one end that goes off to infinity and another that asymptotically approaches a lower bound. Common forms of exponential functions include:

Geometric sequences: $a_n = a_1 \times r^{n-1}$, where a_n is the value of the nth term, a_1 is the initial value, r is the common ratio, and n is the number of terms. Note that $a_1 \times r^{1-1} = a_1 \times r^0 = a_1 \times 1 = a_1$.

Population growth: $f(t) = ae^{rt}$, where $f(t)$ is the population at time $t \geq 0$, a is the initial population, e is the mathematical constant known as Euler's number, and r is the growth rate.

Review Video: Population Growth
Visit mometrix.com/academy and enter code: 109278

Compound interest: $f(t) = P\left(1 + \frac{r}{n}\right)^{nt}$, where $f(t)$ is the account value at a certain number of time periods $t \geq 0$, P is the initial principal balance, r is the interest rate, and n is the number of times the interest is applied per time period.

Review Video: Interest Functions
Visit mometrix.com/academy and enter code: 559176

General exponential growth or decay: $f(t) = a(1 + r)^t$, where $f(t)$ is the future count, a is the current or initial count, r is the growth or decay rate, and t is the time.

For example, suppose the initial population of a town was 1,200 people. The annual population growth is 5%. The current population is 2,400. To find out how much time has passed since the town was founded, we can use the following function:

$$2{,}400 = 1{,}200e^{0.05t}.$$

The general form for population growth may be represented as $f(t) = ae^{rt}$, where $f(t)$ represents the current population, a represents the initial population, r represents the growth rate, and t represents the time. Thus, substituting the initial population, current population, and rate into this form gives the equation above.

The number of years that have passed were found by first dividing both sides of the equation by 1,200. Doing so gives $2 = e^{0.05t}$. Taking the natural logarithm of both sides gives $\ln(2) = ln(e^{0.05t})$. Applying the power property of logarithms, the equation may be rewritten as $\ln(2) = 0.05t \times \ln(e)$, which simplifies as $\ln(2) = 0.05t$. Dividing both sides of this equation by 0.05 gives $t \approx 13.86$. Thus, approximately 13.86 years passed.

Logarithmic Functions

Logarithmic functions are equations that have the format $y = \log_b x$ or $f(x) = \log_b x$. The base b may be any number except one; however, the most common bases for logarithms are base 10 and base e. The log base e is the natural logarithm, or *ln*, expressed by the function $f(x) = \ln x$.

Any logarithm that does not have an assigned value of b is assumed to be base 10: $\log x = \log_{10} x$. Exponential functions and logarithmic functions are related in that one is the inverse of the other. If $f(x) = b^x$, then $f^{-1}(x) = \log_b x$. This can perhaps be expressed more clearly by the two equations: $y = b^x$ and $x = \log_b y$.

The following properties apply to logarithmic expressions:

Property	Description
$\log_b 1 = 0$	The log of 1 is equal to 0 for any base
$\log_b b = 1$	The log of the base is equal to 1
$\log_b b^p = p$	The log of the base raised to a power is equal to that power
$\log_b MN = \log_b M + \log_b N$	The log of a product is the sum of the log of each factor
$\log_b \frac{M}{N} = \log_b M - \log_b N$	The log of a quotient is equal to the log of the dividend minus the log of the divisor
$\log_b M^p = p \log_b M$	The log of a value raised to a power is equal to the power times the log of the value

The graph of an example logarithmic function, $f(x) = \log_2(x + 2)$, is below:

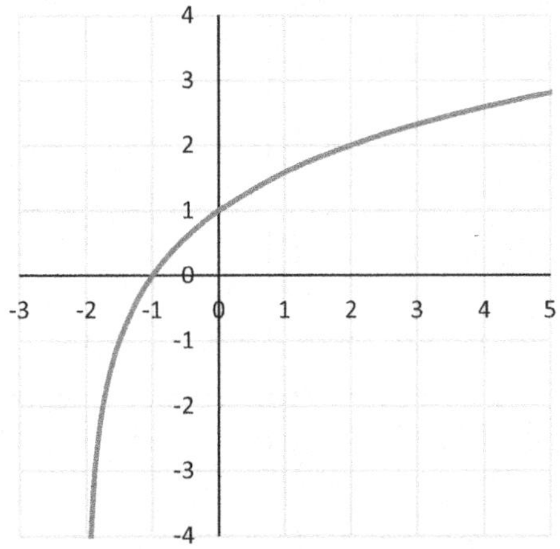

Review Video: Logarithmic Function
Visit mometrix.com/academy and enter code: 658985

Trigonometric Functions

Trigonometric functions are periodic, meaning that they repeat the same form over and over. The basic trigonometric functions are sine (abbreviated 'sin'), cosine (abbreviated 'cos'), and tangent (abbreviated 'tan'). The simplest way to think of them is as describing the ratio of the side lengths of a right triangle in relation to the angles of the triangle.

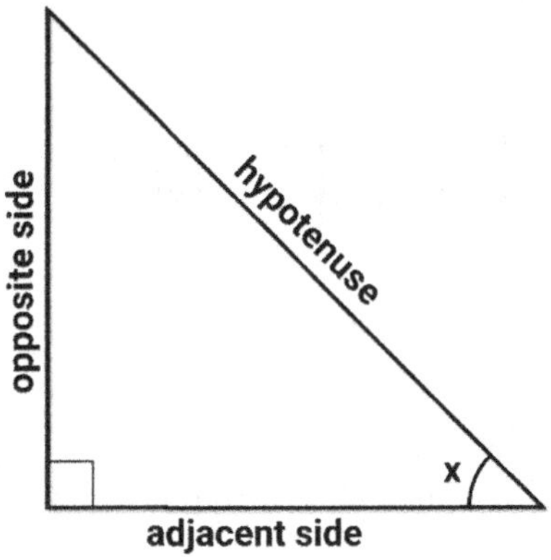

$$\sin x = \frac{\text{opposite side}}{\text{hypotenuse}}$$
$$\cos x = \frac{\text{adjacent side}}{\text{hypotenuse}}$$
$$\tan x = \frac{\text{opposite side}}{\text{adjacent side}}$$

Using sine as an example, trigonometric functions take the form $f(x) = A\sin(Bx + C) + D$, where the **amplitude** is simply equal to A. The **period** is the distance between successive peaks or troughs, essentially the length of the repeated pattern. In this form, the period is equal to $\frac{2\pi}{B}$. As for C, this is the **phase shift** or the horizontal shift of the function. The last term, D, is the vertical shift and determines the **midline** as $y = D$.

For instance, consider the function $f(x) = 2 + \frac{3}{2}\sin\left(\pi x + \frac{\pi}{2}\right)$. Here, $A = \frac{3}{2}$, $B = \pi$, $C = \frac{\pi}{2}$, and $D = 2$, so the midline is at $y = 2$, the amplitude is $\frac{3}{2}$, and the period is $\frac{2\pi}{\pi} = 2$. To graph this function, we center the sine wave on the midline and extend it to a height above and below the midline equal to the amplitude—so this graph would have a minimum value of $2 - \frac{3}{2} = \frac{1}{2}$ and a maximum of $2 + \frac{3}{2} = \frac{7}{2}$. So, the function would be graphed as follows:

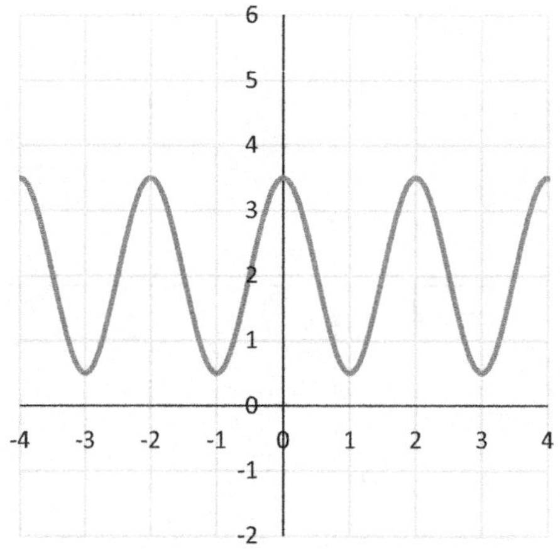

Matrix Systems

Solving Systems of Equations

Matrices can be used to represent the coefficients of a system of linear equations and can be very useful in solving those systems. Take for instance three equations with three variables where all a, b, c, and d are known constants:

$$a_1x + b_1y + c_1z = d_1$$
$$a_2x + b_2y + c_2z = d_2$$
$$a_3x + b_3y + c_3z = d_3$$

To solve this system, define three matrices:

$$A = \begin{bmatrix} a_1 & b_1 & c_1 \\ a_2 & b_2 & c_2 \\ a_3 & b_3 & c_3 \end{bmatrix};\ D = \begin{bmatrix} d_1 \\ d_2 \\ d_3 \end{bmatrix};\ X = \begin{bmatrix} x \\ y \\ z \end{bmatrix}$$

The three equations in our system can be fully represented by a single matrix equation:

$$AX = D$$

We know that the identity matrix times X is equal to X, and we know that any matrix multiplied by its inverse is equal to the identity matrix.

$$A^{-1}AX = IX = X;\ \text{thus } X = A^{-1}D$$

Our goal then is to find the inverse of A, or A^{-1}. Once we have that, we can pre-multiply matrix D by A^{-1} (post-multiplying here is an undefined operation) to find matrix X.

Systems of equations can also be solved using the transformation of an augmented matrix in a process similar to that for finding a matrix inverse. Begin by arranging each equation of the system in the following format:

$$a_1x + b_1y + c_1z = d_1$$
$$a_2x + b_2y + c_2z = d_2$$
$$a_3x + b_3y + c_3z = d_3$$

Define matrices A and D and combine them into augmented matrix A_a:

$$A = \begin{bmatrix} a_1 & b_1 & c_1 \\ a_2 & b_2 & c_2 \\ a_3 & b_3 & c_3 \end{bmatrix};\ D = \begin{bmatrix} d_1 \\ d_2 \\ d_3 \end{bmatrix};\ A_a = \begin{bmatrix} a_1 & b_1 & c_1 & d_1 \\ a_2 & b_2 & c_2 & d_2 \\ a_3 & b_3 & c_3 & d_3 \end{bmatrix}$$

To solve the augmented matrix and the system of equations, use elementary row operations to form an identity matrix in the first 3×3 section. When this is complete, the values in the last column are the solutions to the system of equations:

$$\begin{bmatrix} 1 & 0 & 0 & x \\ 0 & 1 & 0 & y \\ 0 & 0 & 1 & z \end{bmatrix}$$

If an identity matrix is not possible, the system of equations has no unique solution. Sometimes only a partial solution will be possible. The following are partial solutions you may find:

$\begin{bmatrix} 1 & 0 & k_1 & x_0 \\ 0 & 1 & k_2 & y_0 \\ 0 & 0 & 0 & 0 \end{bmatrix}$ gives the non-unique solution $x = x_0 - k_1z;\ y = y_0 - k_2z$

$\begin{bmatrix} 1 & j_1 & k_1 & x_0 \\ 0 & 0 & 0 & 0 \\ 0 & 0 & 0 & 0 \end{bmatrix}$ gives the non-unique solution $x = x_0 - j_1y - k_1z$

This process can be used to solve systems of equations with any number of variables, but three is the upper limit for practical purposes. Anything more ought to be done with a graphing calculator.

Review Video: Matrices: Data Systems
Visit mometrix.com/academy and enter code: 579763

Functions

Algebraic Theorems

According to the **fundamental theorem of algebra**, every non-constant, single-variable polynomial has exactly as many roots as the polynomial's highest exponent. For example, if x^4 is the largest exponent of a term, the polynomial will have exactly 4 roots. However, some of these roots may have multiplicity or be complex numbers. For instance, in the polynomial function $f(x) = x^4 - 4x + 3$, the only real root is 1, though it has multiplicity of 2 – that is, it occurs twice. The other two roots, $(-1 - i\sqrt{2})$ and $(-1 + i\sqrt{2})$, are complex, consisting of both real and non-real components.

The **remainder theorem** is useful for determining the remainder when a polynomial is divided by a binomial. The remainder theorem states that if a polynomial function $f(x)$ is divided by a binomial $x - a$, where a is a real number, the remainder of the division will be the value of $f(a)$. If $f(a) = 0$, then a is a root of the polynomial.

The **factor theorem** is related to the remainder theorem and states that if $f(a) = 0$ then $(x - a)$ is a factor of the function.

According to the **rational root theorem,** any rational root of a polynomial function $f(x) = a_n x^n + a_{n-1}x^{n-1} + \cdots + a_1 x + a_0$ with integer coefficients will, when reduced to its lowest terms, be a positive or negative fraction such that the numerator is a factor of a_0 and the denominator is a factor of a_n. For instance, if the polynomial function $f(x) = x^3 + 3x^2 - 4$ has any rational roots, the numerators of those roots can only be factors of 4 (1, 2, 4), and the denominators can only be factors of 1 (1). The function in this example has roots of 1 (or $\frac{1}{1}$) and -2 (or $\frac{-2}{1}$).

Working with Functions

Manipulation of Functions

Translation occurs when values are added to or subtracted from the x- or y-values. If a constant is added to the y-portion of each point, the graph shifts up. If a constant is subtracted from the y-portion of each point, the graph shifts down. This is represented by the expression $f(x) \pm k$, where k is a constant. If a constant is added to the x-portion of each point, the graph shifts left. If a constant is subtracted from the x-portion of each point, the graph shifts right. This is represented by the expression $f(x \pm k)$, where k is a constant.

Stretching, compression, and reflection occur when different parts of a function are multiplied by different groups of constants. If the function as a whole is multiplied by a real number constant greater than 1, $(k \times f(x))$, the graph is stretched vertically. If k in the previous equation is greater than zero but less than 1, the graph is compressed vertically. If k is less than zero, the graph is reflected about the x-axis, in addition to being either stretched or compressed vertically if k is less than or greater than -1, respectively. If instead, just the x-term is multiplied by a constant greater than 1 $(f(k \times x))$, the graph is compressed horizontally. If k in the previous equation is greater than zero but less than 1, the graph is stretched horizontally. If k is less than zero, the graph is reflected about the y-axis, in addition to being either stretched or compressed horizontally if k is greater than or less than -1, respectively.

Review Video: Manipulation of Functions
Visit mometrix.com/academy and enter code: 669117

Applying the Basic Operations to Functions

For each of the basic operations, we will use these functions as examples: $f(x) = x^2$ and $g(x) = x$.

To find the sum of two functions f and g, assuming the domains are compatible, simply add the two functions together: $(f + g)(x) = f(x) + g(x) = x^2 + x$.

To find the difference of two functions f and g, assuming the domains are compatible, simply subtract the second function from the first: $(f - g)(x) = f(x) - g(x) = x^2 - x$.

To find the product of two functions f and g, assuming the domains are compatible, multiply the two functions together: $(f \times g)(x) = f(x) \times g(x) = x^2 \times x = x^3$.

To find the quotient of two functions f and g, assuming the domains are compatible, divide the first function by the second: $\frac{f}{g}(x) = \frac{f(x)}{g(x)} = \frac{x^2}{x} = x\,; x \neq 0$.

The example given in each case is fairly simple, but on a given problem, if you are looking only for the value of the sum, difference, product, or quotient of two functions at a particular x-value, it may be simpler to solve the functions individually and then perform the given operation using those values.

The composite of two functions f and g, written as $(f \circ g)(x)$ simply means that the output of the second function is used as the input of the first. This can also be written as $f(g(x))$. In general, this can be solved by substituting $g(x)$ for all instances of x in $f(x)$ and simplifying. Using the example functions $f(x) = x^2 - x + 2$ and $g(x) = x + 1$, we can find that $(f \circ g)(x)$ or $f(g(x))$ is equal to $f(x+1) = (x+1)^2 - (x+1) + 2$, which simplifies to $x^2 + x + 2$.

It is important to note that $(f \circ g)(x)$ is not necessarily the same as $(g \circ f)(x)$. The process is not always commutative like addition or multiplication expressions. It *can* be commutative, but most often this is not the case.

Evaluating Linear Functions

A **function** can be expressed as an equation that relates an input to an output where each input corresponds to exactly one output. The input of a function is defined by the x-variable, and the output is defined by the y-variable. For example, consider the function $y = 2x + 6$. The value of y, the output, is determined by the value of the x, the input. If the value of x is 3, the value of y is $y = 2(3) + 6 = 6 + 6 = 12$. This means that when $x = 3$, $y = 12$. This can be expressed as the ordered pair (3,12).

It is common for function equations to use the form $f(x) =$ instead of $y =$. However, $f(x)$ and y represent the same thing. We read $f(x)$ as "f of x." "f of x" implies that the value of f depends on the value of x. The function used in the example above could be expressed as $y = 2x + 6$ or $f(x) = 2x + 6$. Both functions represent the same line when graphed.

Functions that are expressed in the form $f(x) =$ are evaluated in the same way the equations are evaluated in the form $y =$. For example, when evaluating the function $f(x) = 3x - 2$ for $f(6)$, substitute 6 in for x, and simplify. $f(x) = 3x - 2$ becomes $f(6) = 3(6) - 2 = 18 - 2 = 16$. When x is 6, $f(x)$ is 16.

Find the value of $f(8)$.

$$f(x) = 3x - 2$$
$$f(8) = 3(8) - 2$$
$$f(8) = 22$$

Geometry

Polygons

A **polygon** is a closed, two-dimensional figure with three or more straight line segments called **sides**. The point at which two sides of a polygon intersect is called the **vertex**. In a polygon, the number of sides is always equal to the number of vertices. A polygon with all sides congruent and all angles equal is called a **regular polygon**. Common polygons are:

Triangle = 3 sides
Quadrilateral = 4 sides
Pentagon = 5 sides
Hexagon = 6 sides
Heptagon = 7 sides
Octagon = 8 sides
Nonagon = 9 sides
Decagon = 10 sides
Dodecagon = 12 sides

More generally, an n-gon is a polygon that has n angles and n sides.

Review Video: Intro to Polygons
Visit mometrix.com/academy and enter code: 271869

The sum of the interior angles of an n-sided polygon is $(n - 2) \times 180°$. For example, in a triangle $n = 3$. So the sum of the interior angles is $(3 - 2) \times 180° = 180°$. In a quadrilateral, $n = 4$, and the sum of the angles is $(4 - 2) \times 180° = 360°$.

Review Video: Sum of Interior Angles
Visit mometrix.com/academy and enter code: 984991

Convex and Concave Polygons

A **convex polygon** is a polygon whose diagonals all lie within the interior of the polygon. A **concave polygon** is a polygon with a least one diagonal that is outside the polygon. In the diagram below, quadrilateral $ABCD$ is concave because diagonal $\overline{AC}$ lies outside the polygon and quadrilateral $EFGH$ is convex because both diagonals lie inside the polygon.

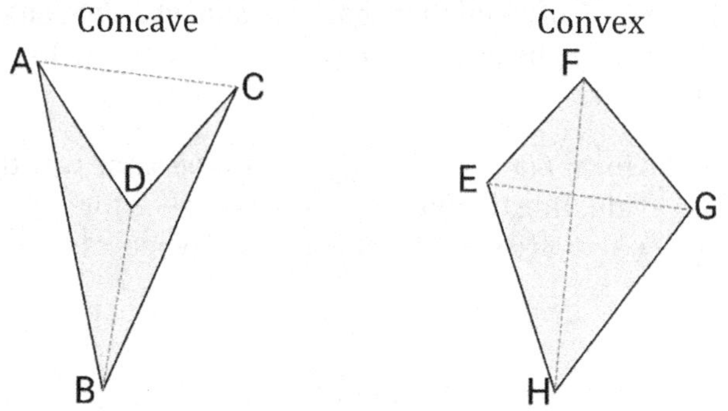

Apothem and Radius

A line segment from the center of a polygon that is perpendicular to a side of the polygon is called the **apothem**. A line segment from the center of a polygon to a vertex of the polygon is called a **radius**. In a regular polygon, the apothem can be used to find the area of the polygon using the formula $A = \frac{1}{2}ap$, where a is the apothem, and p is the perimeter.

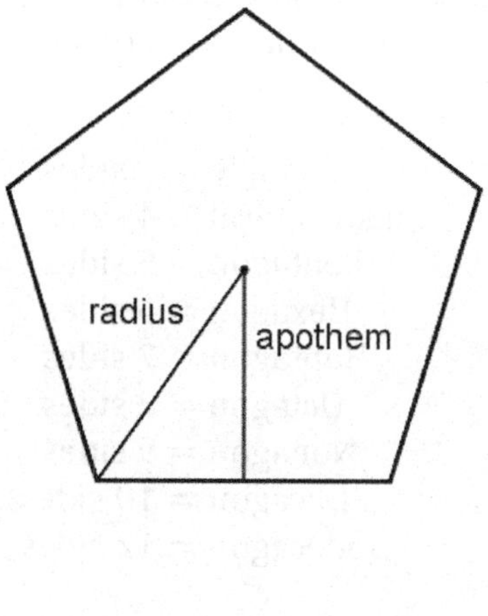

A **diagonal** is a line segment that joins two non-adjacent vertices of a polygon. The number of diagonals a polygon has can be found by using the formula:

$$\text{number of diagonals} = \frac{n(n-3)}{2}$$

Note that n is the number of sides in the polygon. This formula works for all polygons, not just regular polygons.

Congruence and Similarity

Congruent figures are geometric figures that have the same size and shape. All corresponding angles are equal, and all corresponding sides are equal. Congruence is indicated by the symbol $\cong$.

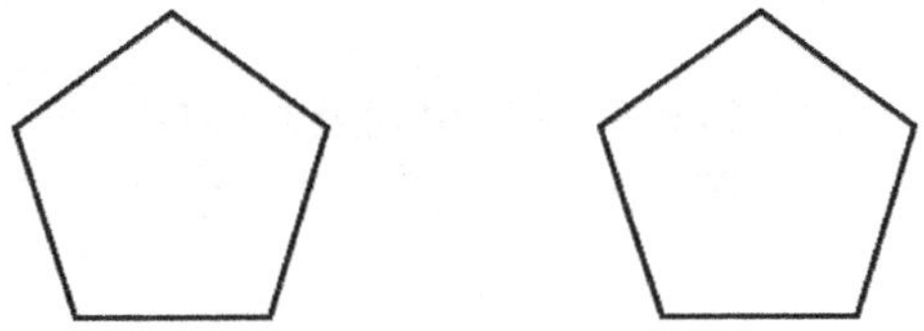

Congruent polygons

Similar figures are geometric figures that have the same shape, but do not necessarily have the same size. All corresponding angles are equal, and all corresponding sides are proportional, but they do not have to be equal. It is indicated by the symbol $\sim$.

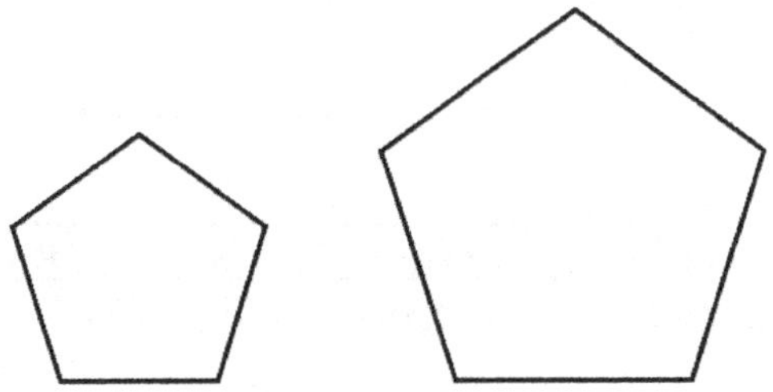

Similar polygons

Note that all congruent figures are also similar, but not all similar figures are congruent.

Review Video: Congruent Shapes
Visit mometrix.com/academy and enter code: 492281

LINE OF SYMMETRY

A line that divides a figure or object into congruent parts is called a **line of symmetry**. An object may have no lines of symmetry, one line of symmetry, or multiple (i.e., more than one) lines of symmetry.

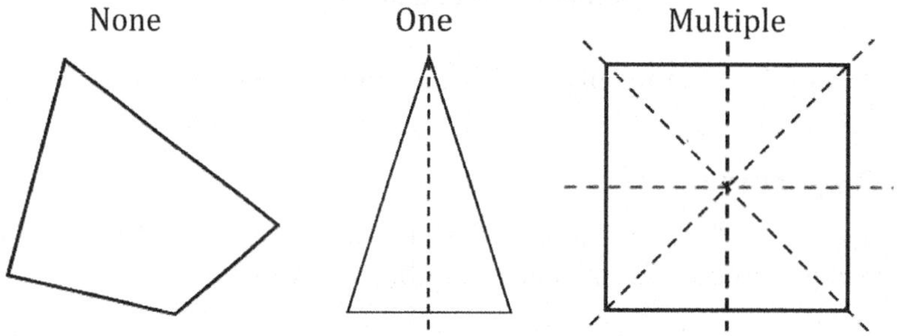

Review Video: Symmetry
Visit mometrix.com/academy and enter code: 528106

TRIANGLES

A triangle is a three-sided figure with the sum of its interior angles being 180°. The **perimeter of any triangle** is found by summing the three side lengths; $P = a + b + c$. For an equilateral triangle, this is the same as $P = 3a$, where a is any side length, since all three sides are the same length.

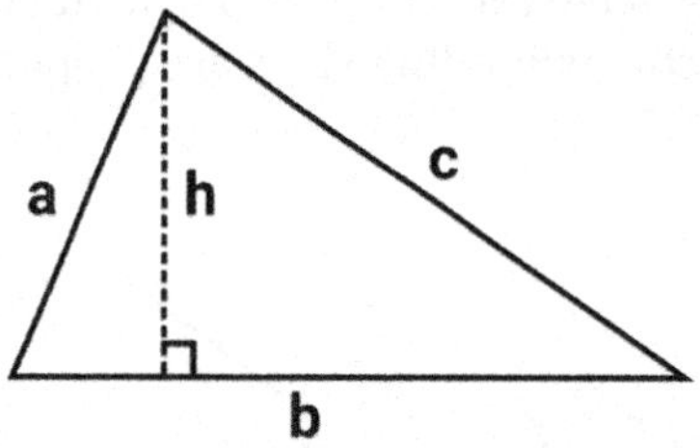

Review Video: Proof that a Triangle is 180 Degrees
Visit mometrix.com/academy and enter code: 687591

Review Video: Area and Perimeter of a Triangle
Visit mometrix.com/academy and enter code: 853779

The **area of any triangle** can be found by taking half the product of one side length referred to as the base, often given the variable b and the perpendicular distance from that side to the opposite vertex called the altitude or height and given the variable h. In equation form that is $A = \frac{1}{2}bh$. Another formula that works for any triangle is $A = \sqrt{s(s-a)(s-b)(s-c)}$, where s is the semiperimeter: $\frac{a+b+c}{2}$, and a, b, and c are the lengths of the three sides. Special cases include isosceles triangles, $A = \frac{1}{2}b\sqrt{a^2 - \frac{b^2}{4}}$, where b is the unique side and a is the length of one of the two congruent sides, and equilateral triangles, $A = \frac{\sqrt{3}}{4}a^2$, where a is the length of a side.

Review Video: Area of Any Triangle
Visit mometrix.com/academy and enter code: 138510

PARTS OF A TRIANGLE

An **altitude** of a triangle is a line segment drawn from one vertex perpendicular to the opposite side. In the diagram that follows, $\overline{BE}$, $\overline{AD}$, and $\overline{CF}$ are altitudes. The length of an altitude is also called the height of the triangle. The three altitudes in a triangle are always concurrent. The point of concurrency of the altitudes of a triangle, O, is called the **orthocenter**. Note that in an obtuse triangle, the orthocenter will be outside the triangle, and in a right triangle, the orthocenter is the vertex of the right angle.

A **median** of a triangle is a line segment drawn from one vertex to the midpoint of the opposite side. In the diagram that follows, $\overline{BH}$, $\overline{AG}$, and $\overline{CI}$ are medians. This is not the same as the altitude, except the altitude to the base of an isosceles triangle and all three altitudes of an equilateral triangle. The point of concurrency of the medians of a triangle, T, is called the **centroid**. This is the same point as the orthocenter only in an equilateral triangle. Unlike the orthocenter, the centroid is always inside the triangle. The centroid can also be considered the exact center of the triangle. Any shape triangle can be perfectly balanced on a tip placed at the centroid. The centroid is also the point that is two-thirds the distance from the vertex to the opposite side.

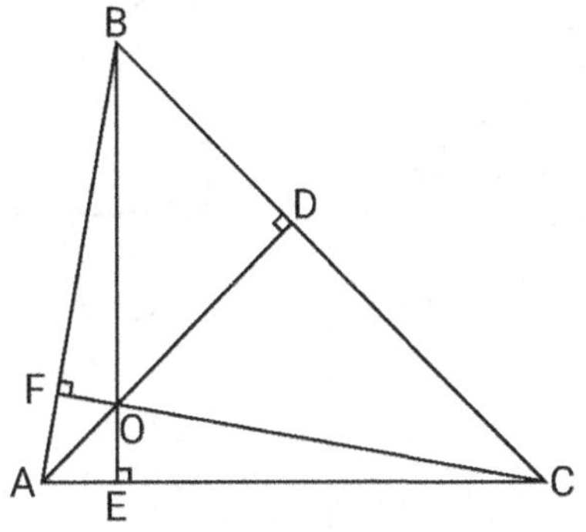

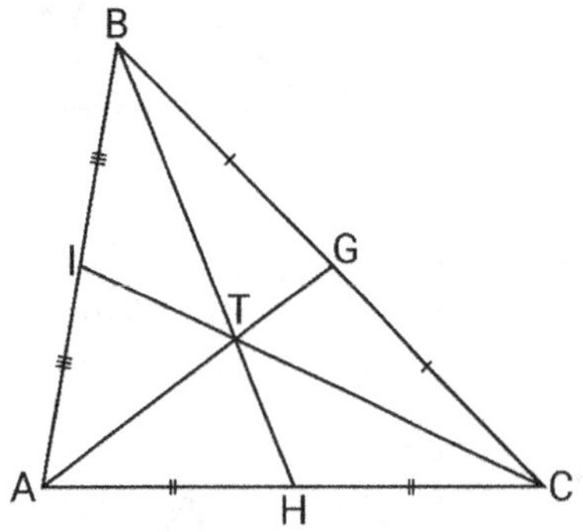

Review Video: Centroid, Incenter, Circumcenter, and Orthocenter
Visit mometrix.com/academy and enter code: 598260

TRIANGLE PROPERTIES

CLASSIFICATIONS OF TRIANGLES

A **scalene triangle** is a triangle with no congruent sides. A scalene triangle will also have three angles of different measures. The angle with the largest measure is opposite the longest side, and the angle with the smallest measure is opposite the shortest side. An **acute triangle** is a triangle whose three angles are all less than 90°. If two of the angles are equal, the acute triangle is also an **isosceles triangle**. An isosceles triangle will also have two congruent angles opposite the two congruent sides. If the three angles are all equal, the acute triangle is also an **equilateral triangle**. An equilateral triangle will also have three congruent angles, each 60°. All equilateral triangles are also acute triangles. An **obtuse triangle** is a triangle with exactly one angle greater than 90°. The other two angles may or may not be equal. If the two remaining angles are equal, the obtuse triangle is also an isosceles triangle. A **right triangle** is a triangle with exactly one angle equal to 90°. All right triangles follow the Pythagorean theorem. A right triangle can never be acute or obtuse.

The table below illustrates how each descriptor places a different restriction on the triangle:

Angles / Sides	Acute: All angles < 90°	Obtuse: One angle > 90°	Right: One angle = 90°
Scalene: No equal side lengths	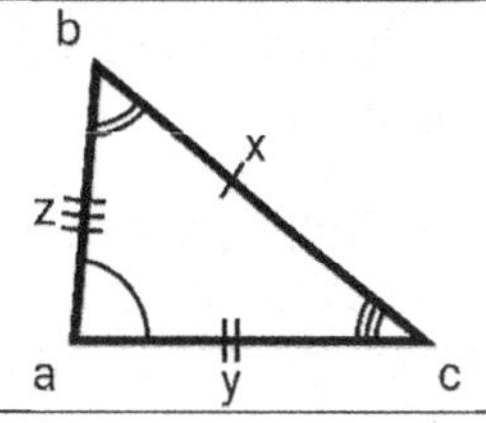	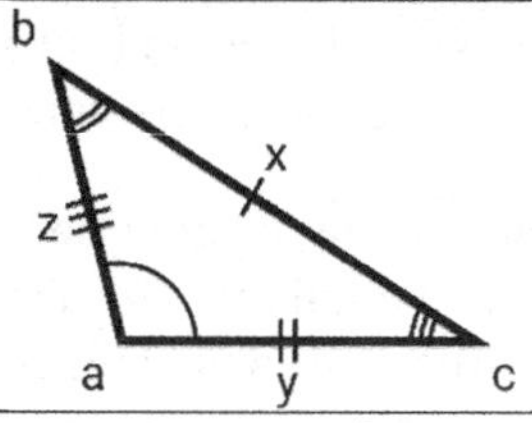	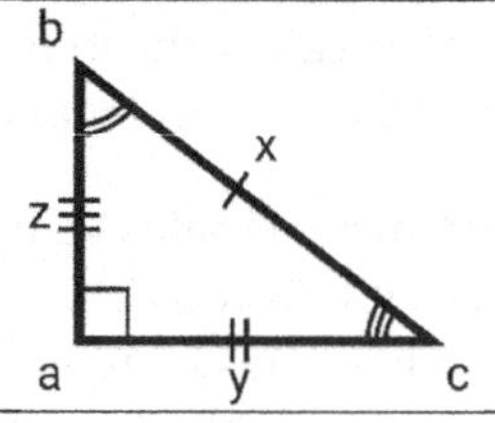
	$90° > \angle a > \angle b > \angle c$ $x > y > z$	$\angle a > 90° > \angle b > \angle c$ $x > y > z$	$90° = \angle a > \angle b > \angle c$ $x > y > z$
Isosceles: Two equal side lengths	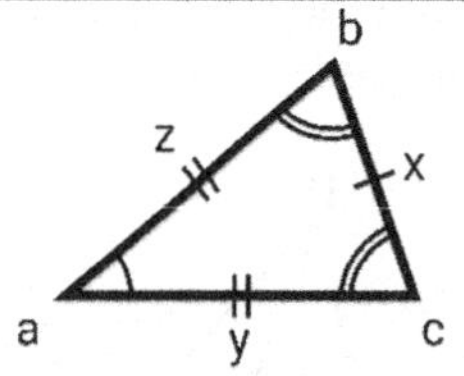	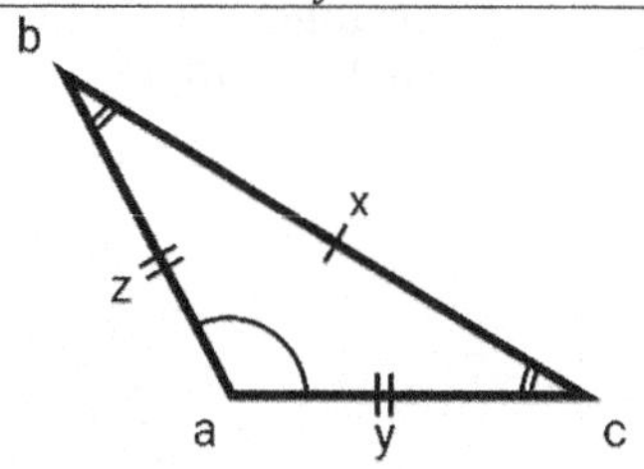	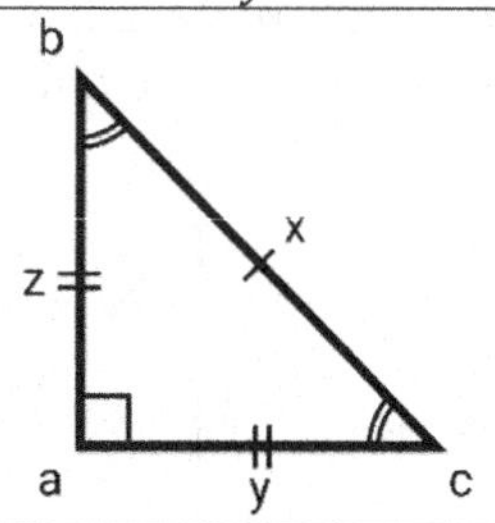
	$90° > \angle a, \angle b, or\ \angle c$ $\angle b = \angle c, \quad y = z$	$\angle a > 90° > \angle b = \angle c$ $x > y = z$	$\angle a = 90°$ $\angle b = \angle c = 45°$ $x > y = z$
Equilateral: Three equal side lengths	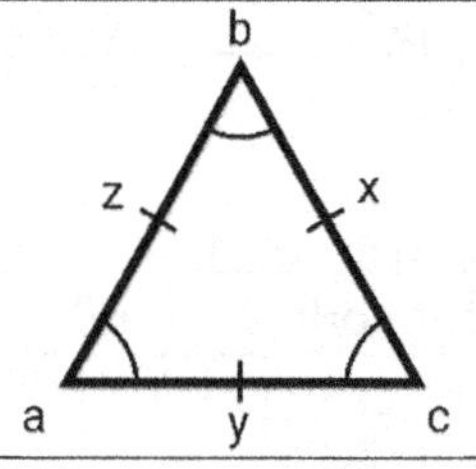		
	$60° = \angle a = \angle b = \angle c$ $x = y = z$		

Review Video: Introduction to Types of Triangles
Visit mometrix.com/academy and enter code: 511711

General Rules for Triangles

The **triangle inequality theorem** states that the sum of the measures of any two sides of a triangle is always greater than the measure of the third side. If the sum of the measures of two sides were equal to the third side, a triangle would be impossible because the two sides would lie flat across the third side and there would be no vertex. If the sum of the measures of two of the sides was less than the third side, a closed figure would be impossible because the two shortest sides would never meet. In other words, for a triangle with sides lengths A, B, and C: $A + B > C$, $B + C > A$, and $A + C > B$.

The sum of the measures of the interior angles of a triangle is always 180°. Therefore, a triangle can never have more than one angle greater than or equal to 90°.

In any triangle, the angles opposite congruent sides are congruent, and the sides opposite congruent angles are congruent. The largest angle is always opposite the longest side, and the smallest angle is always opposite the shortest side.

The line segment that joins the midpoints of any two sides of a triangle is always parallel to the third side and exactly half the length of the third side.

Review Video: General Rules (Triangle Inequality Theorem)
Visit mometrix.com/academy and enter code: 166488

Similarity and Congruence Rules

Similar triangles are triangles whose corresponding angles are equal and whose corresponding sides are proportional. Represented by AAA. Similar triangles whose corresponding sides are congruent are also congruent triangles.

Triangles can be shown to be **congruent** in 5 ways:

- **SSS**: Three sides of one triangle are congruent to the three corresponding sides of the second triangle.
- **SAS**: Two sides and the included angle (the angle formed by those two sides) of one triangle are congruent to the corresponding two sides and included angle of the second triangle.
- **ASA**: Two angles and the included side (the side that joins the two angles) of one triangle are congruent to the corresponding two angles and included side of the second triangle.
- **AAS**: Two angles and a non-included side of one triangle are congruent to the corresponding two angles and non-included side of the second triangle.
- **HL**: The hypotenuse and leg of one right triangle are congruent to the corresponding hypotenuse and leg of the second right triangle.

Review Video: Similar Triangles
Visit mometrix.com/academy and enter code: 398538

Pythagorean Theorem

The side of a triangle opposite the right angle is called the **hypotenuse**. The other two sides are called the legs. The Pythagorean theorem states a relationship among the legs and hypotenuse of a right triangle: $(a^2 + b^2 = c^2)$, where a and b are the lengths of the legs of a right triangle, and c is the length of the hypotenuse. Note that this formula will only work with right triangles.

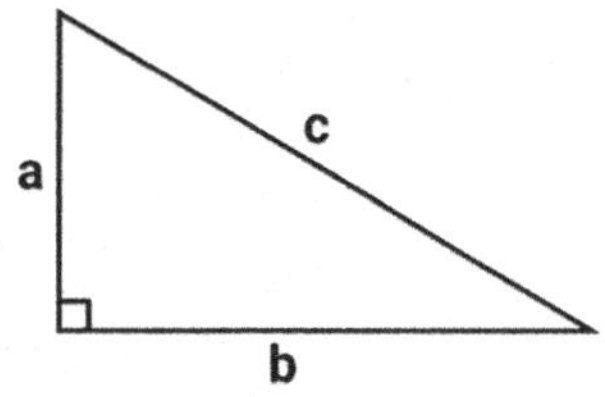

Review Video: Pythagorean Theorem
Visit mometrix.com/academy and enter code: 906576

Trigonometric Formulas

In the diagram below, angle C is the right angle, and side c is the hypotenuse. Side a is the side opposite to angle A and side b is the side opposite to angle B. Using ratios of side lengths as a means to calculate the sine, cosine, and tangent of an acute angle only works for right triangles.

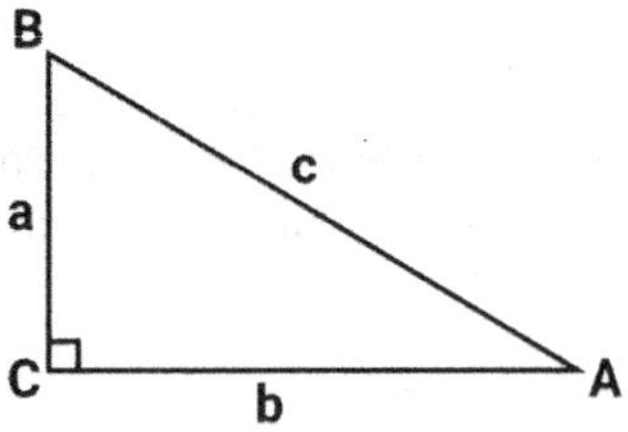

$$\sin A = \frac{\text{opposite side}}{\text{hypotenuse}} = \frac{a}{c} \qquad \csc A = \frac{1}{\sin A} = \frac{\text{hypotenuse}}{\text{opposite side}} = \frac{c}{a}$$

$$\cos A = \frac{\text{adjacent side}}{\text{hypotenuse}} = \frac{b}{c} \qquad \sec A = \frac{1}{\cos A} = \frac{\text{hypotenuse}}{\text{adjacent side}} = \frac{c}{b}$$

$$\tan A = \frac{\text{opposite side}}{\text{adjacent side}} = \frac{a}{b} \qquad \cot A = \frac{1}{\tan A} = \frac{\text{adjacent side}}{\text{opposite side}} = \frac{b}{a}$$

Laws of Sines and Cosines

The **law of sines** states that $\frac{\sin A}{a} = \frac{\sin B}{b} = \frac{\sin C}{c}$, where A, B, and C are the angles of a triangle, and a, b, and c are the sides opposite their respective angles. This formula will work with all triangles, not just right triangles.

The **law of cosines** is given by the formula $c^2 = a^2 + b^2 - 2ab(\cos C)$, where a, b, and c are the sides of a triangle, and C is the angle opposite side c. This is a generalized form of the Pythagorean theorem that can be used on any triangle.

Review Video: Upper Level Trig: Law of Sines
Visit mometrix.com/academy and enter code: 206844

Review Video: Upper Level Trig: Law of Cosines
Visit mometrix.com/academy and enter code: 158911

Quadrilaterals

A **quadrilateral** is a closed two-dimensional geometric figure that has four straight sides. The sum of the interior angles of any quadrilateral is 360°.

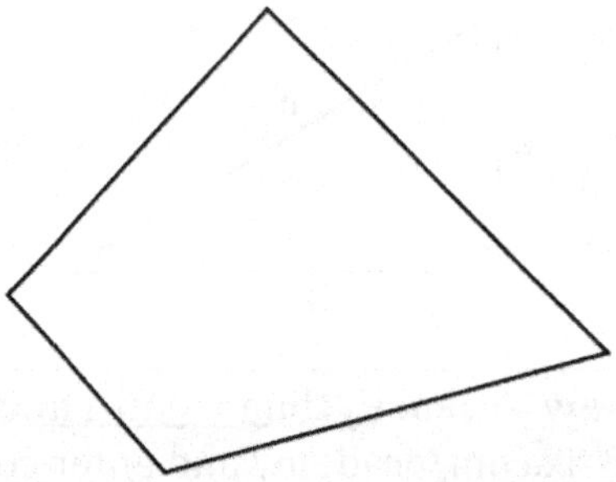

Review Video: Diagonals of Parallelograms, Rectangles, and Rhombi
Visit mometrix.com/academy and enter code: 320040

KITE

A **kite** is a quadrilateral with two pairs of adjacent sides that are congruent. A result of this is perpendicular diagonals. A kite can be concave or convex and has one line of symmetry.

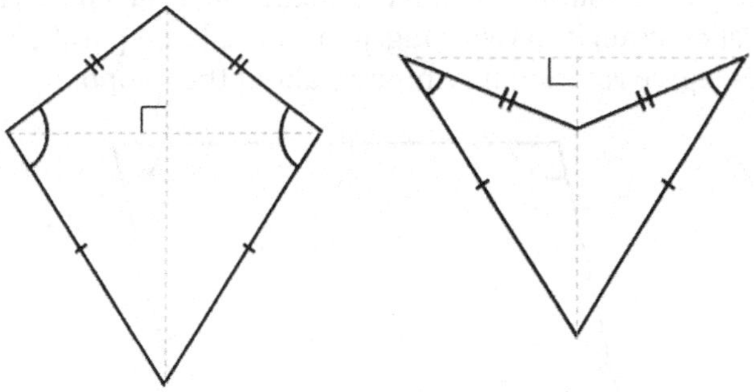

TRAPEZOID

Trapezoid: A trapezoid is defined as a quadrilateral that has at least one pair of parallel sides. There are no rules for the second pair of sides. So, there are no rules for the diagonals and no lines of symmetry for a trapezoid.

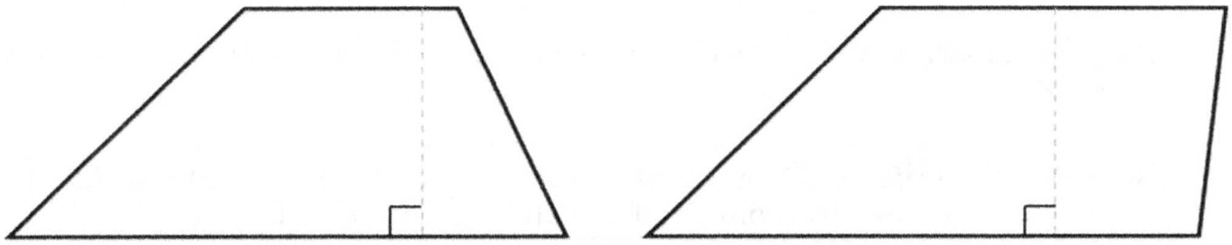

The **area of a trapezoid** is found by the formula $A = \frac{1}{2}h(b_1 + b_2)$, where h is the height (segment joining and perpendicular to the parallel bases), and b_1 and b_2 are the two parallel sides (bases). Do not use one of the other two sides as the height unless that side is also perpendicular to the parallel bases.

The **perimeter of a trapezoid** is found by the formula $P = a + b_1 + c + b_2$, where a, b_1, c, and b_2 are the four sides of the trapezoid.

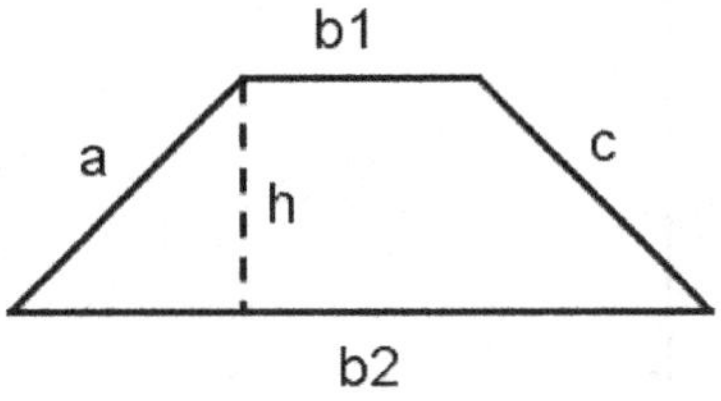

Review Video: Area and Perimeter of a Trapezoid
Visit mometrix.com/academy and enter code: 587523

Isosceles trapezoid: A trapezoid with equal base angles. This gives rise to other properties including: the two nonparallel sides have the same length, the two non-base angles are also equal, and there is one line of symmetry through the midpoints of the parallel sides.

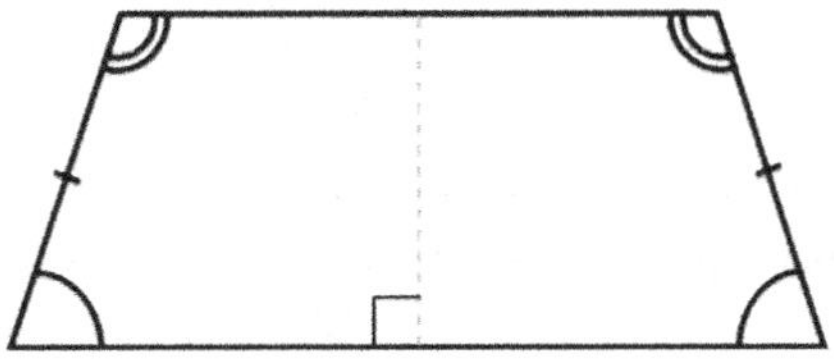

PARALLELOGRAM

A **parallelogram** is a quadrilateral that has two pairs of opposite parallel sides. As such it is a special type of trapezoid. The sides that are parallel are also congruent. The opposite interior angles are always congruent, and the consecutive interior angles are supplementary. The diagonals of a parallelogram divide each other. Each diagonal divides the parallelogram into two congruent triangles. A parallelogram has no line of symmetry, but does have 180-degree rotational symmetry about the midpoint.

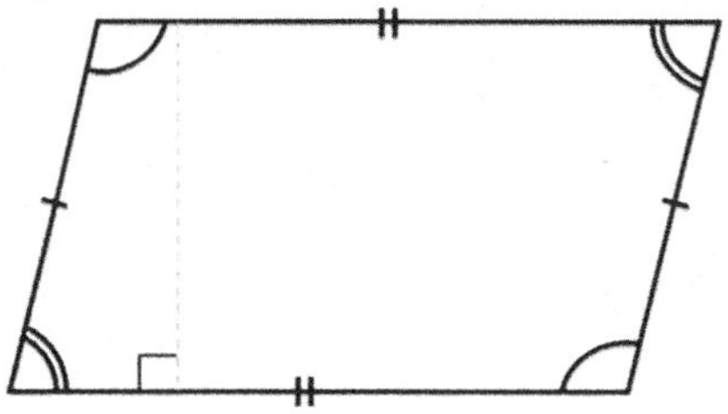

The **area of a parallelogram** is found by the formula $A = bh$, where b is the length of the base, and h is the height. Note that the base and height correspond to the length and width in a rectangle, so this formula would apply to rectangles as well. Do not confuse the height of a parallelogram with the length of the second side. The two are only the same measure in the case of a rectangle.

The **perimeter of a parallelogram** is found by the formula $P = 2a + 2b$ or $P = 2(a + b)$, where a and b are the lengths of the two sides.

Review Video: How to Find the Area and Perimeter of a Parallelogram
Visit mometrix.com/academy and enter code: 718313

RECTANGLE

A **rectangle** is a quadrilateral with four right angles. All rectangles are parallelograms and trapezoids, but not all parallelograms or trapezoids are rectangles. The diagonals of a rectangle are congruent. Rectangles have two lines of symmetry (through each pair of opposing midpoints) and 180-degree rotational symmetry about the midpoint.

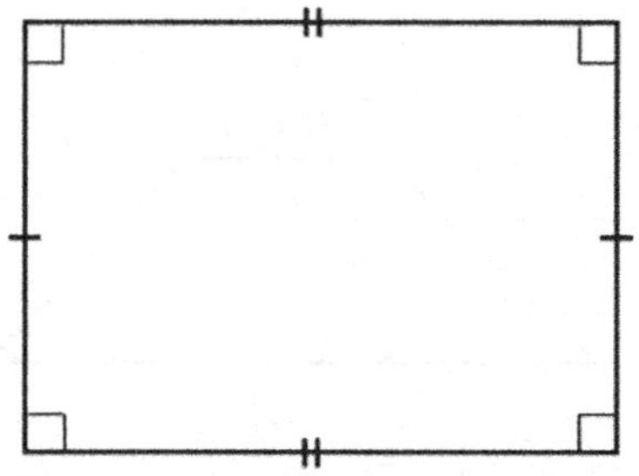

The **area of a rectangle** is found by the formula $A = lw$, where A is the area of the rectangle, l is the length (usually considered to be the longer side) and w is the width (usually considered to be the shorter side). The numbers for l and w are interchangeable.

The **perimeter of a rectangle** is found by the formula $P = 2l + 2w$ or $P = 2(l + w)$, where l is the length, and w is the width. It may be easier to add the length and width first and then double the result, as in the second formula.

RHOMBUS

A **rhombus** is a quadrilateral with four congruent sides. All rhombuses are parallelograms and kites; thus, they inherit all the properties of both types of quadrilaterals. The diagonals of a rhombus are perpendicular to each other. Rhombi have two lines of symmetry (along each of the diagonals) and 180° rotational symmetry. The

area of a rhombus is half the product of the diagonals: $A = \frac{d_1 d_2}{2}$ and the perimeter of a rhombus is: $P = 2\sqrt{(d_1)^2 + (d_2)^2}$.

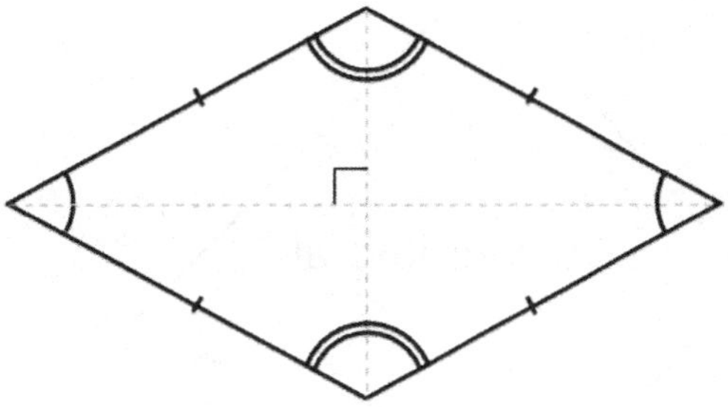

SQUARE

A **square** is a quadrilateral with four right angles and four congruent sides. Squares satisfy the criteria of all other types of quadrilaterals. The diagonals of a square are congruent and perpendicular to each other. Squares have four lines of symmetry (through each pair of opposing midpoints and along each of the diagonals) as well as 90° rotational symmetry about the midpoint.

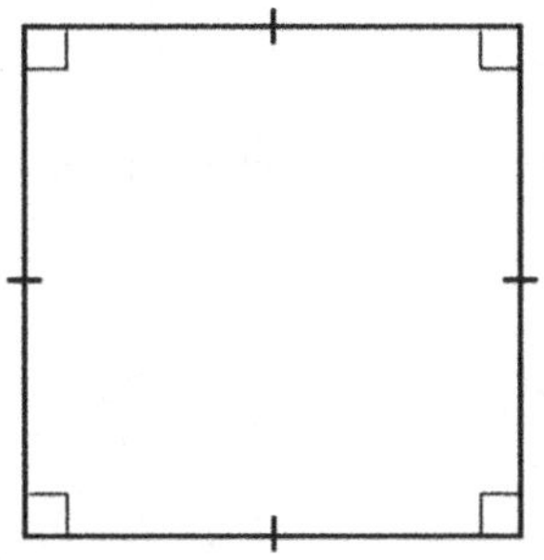

The **area of a square** is found by using the formula $A = s^2$, where s is the length of one side. The **perimeter of a square** is found by using the formula $P = 4s$, where s is the length of one side. Because all four sides are equal in a square, it is faster to multiply the length of one side by 4 than to add the same number four times. You could use the formulas for rectangles and get the same answer.

Review Video: Area and Perimeter of Rectangles and Squares
Visit mometrix.com/academy and enter code: 428109

Hierarchy of Quadrilaterals

The hierarchy of quadrilaterals is as follows:

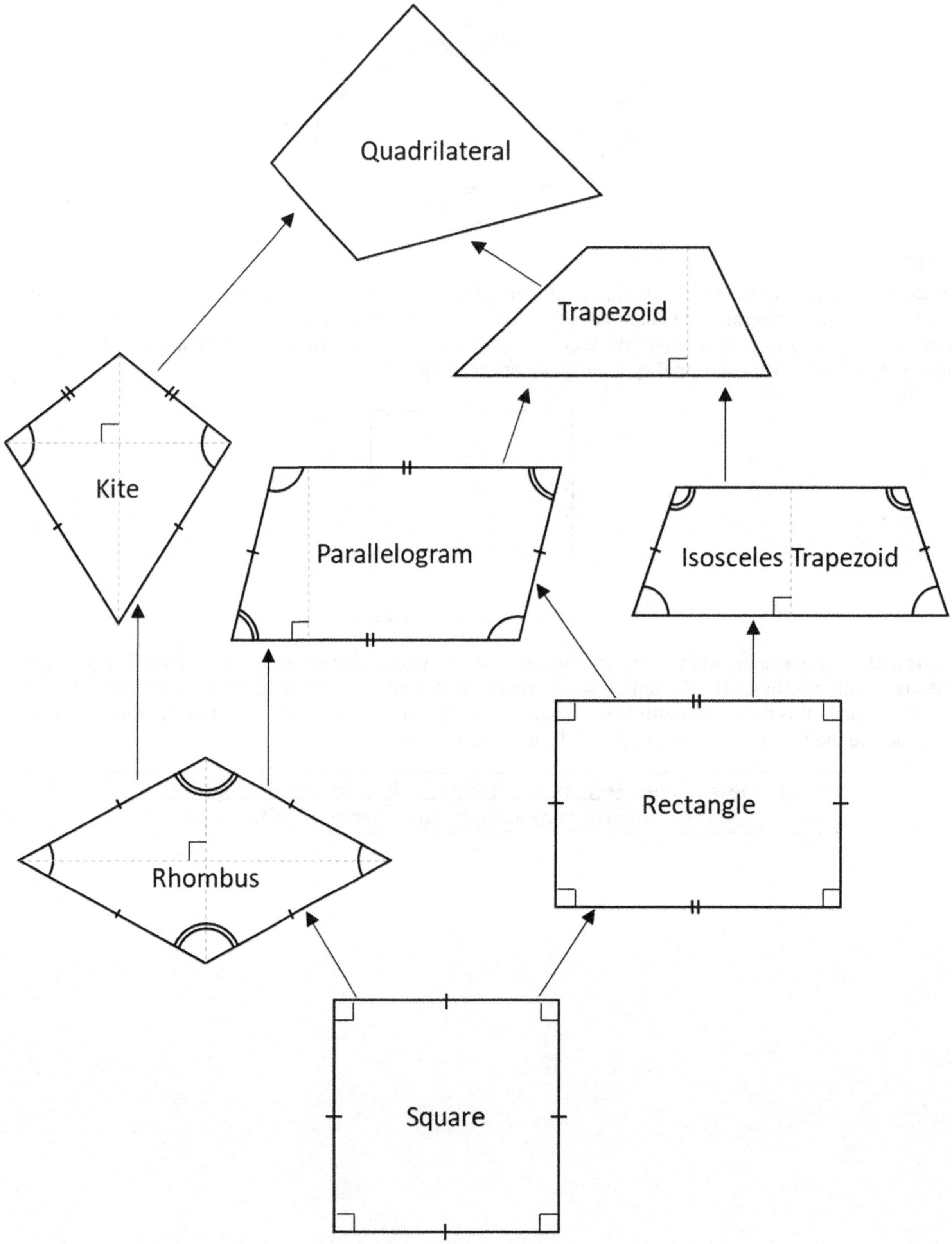

Circles

The **center** of a circle is the single point from which every point on the circle is **equidistant**. The **radius** is a line segment that joins the center of the circle and any one point on the circle. All radii of a circle are equal. Circles that have the same center but not the same length of radii are **concentric**. The **diameter** is a line segment that passes through the center of the circle and has both endpoints on the circle. The length of the diameter is exactly twice the length of the radius. Point O in the diagram below is the center of the circle, segments $\overline{OX}$, $\overline{OY}$, and $\overline{OZ}$ are radii; and segment $\overline{XZ}$ is a diameter.

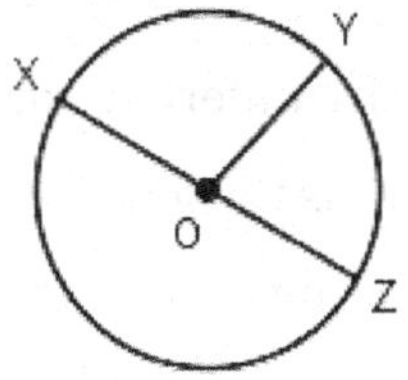

Review Video: Points of a Circle
Visit mometrix.com/academy and enter code: 420746

Review Video: The Diameter, Radius, and Circumference of Circles
Visit mometrix.com/academy and enter code: 448988

The **area of a circle** is found by the formula $A = \pi r^2$, where r is the length of the radius. If the diameter of the circle is given, remember to divide it in half to get the length of the radius before proceeding.

The **circumference** of a circle is found by the formula $C = 2\pi r$, where r is the radius. Again, remember to convert the diameter if you are given that measure rather than the radius.

Review Video: Area and Circumference of a Circle
Visit mometrix.com/academy and enter code: 243015

Inscribed and Circumscribed Figures

These terms can both be used to describe a given arrangement of figures, depending on perspective. If each of the vertices of figure A lie on figure B, then it can be said that figure A is **inscribed** in figure B, but it can also be said that figure B is **circumscribed** about figure A. The following table and examples help to illustrate the concept. Note that the figures cannot both be circles, as they would be completely overlapping and neither would be inscribed or circumscribed.

Given	Description	Equivalent Description	Figures
Each of the sides of a pentagon is tangent to a circle	The circle is inscribed in the pentagon	The pentagon is circumscribed about the circle	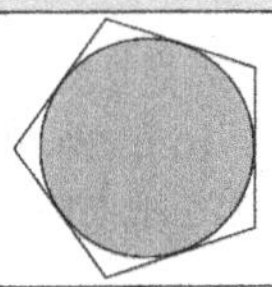
Each of the vertices of a pentagon lie on a circle	The pentagon is inscribed in the circle	The circle is circumscribed about the pentagon	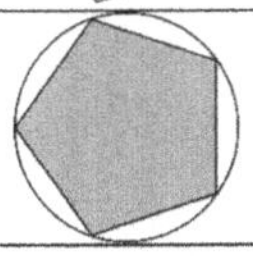

Circle Properties

Arcs

An **arc** is a portion of a circle. Specifically, an arc is the set of points between and including two points on a circle. An arc does not contain any points inside the circle. When a segment is drawn from the endpoints of an arc to the center of the circle, a sector is formed. A **minor arc** is an arc that has a measure less than 180°. A **major arc** is an arc that has a measure of at least 180°. Every minor arc has a corresponding major arc that can be found by subtracting the measure of the minor arc from 360°. A **semicircle** is an arc whose endpoints are the endpoints of the diameter of a circle. A semicircle is exactly half of a circle.

Arc length is the length of that portion of the circumference between two points on the circle. The formula for arc length is $s = \frac{\pi r \theta}{180°}$, where s is the arc length, r is the length of the radius, and θ is the angular measure of the arc in degrees, or $s = r\theta$, where θ is the angular measure of the arc in radians (2π radians $= 360$ degrees).

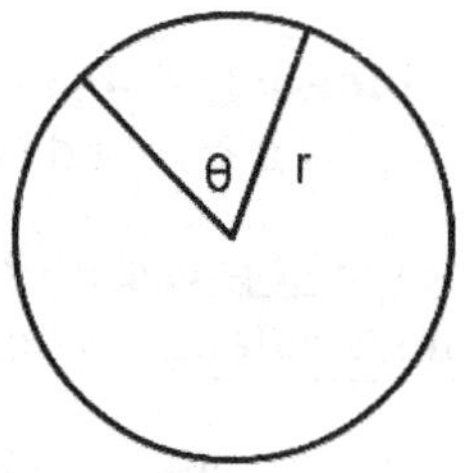

Angles of Circles

A **central angle** is an angle whose vertex is the center of a circle and whose legs intercept an arc of the circle. The measure of a central angle is equal to the measure of the minor arc it intercepts.

An **inscribed angle** is an angle whose vertex lies on a circle and whose legs contain chords of that circle. The portion of the circle intercepted by the legs of the angle is called the intercepted arc. The measure of the intercepted arc is exactly twice the measure of the inscribed angle. In the following diagram, angle ABC is an inscribed angle. $\widehat{AC} = 2(\text{m}\angle ABC)$.

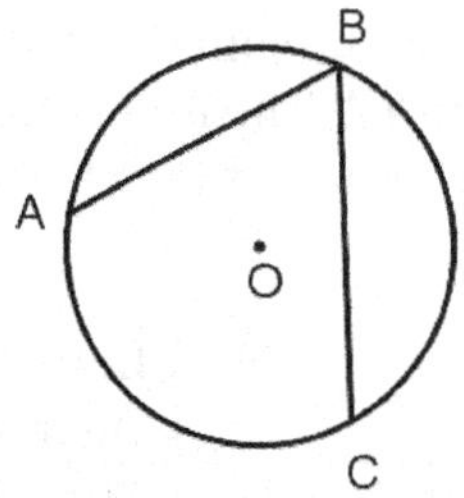

Any angle inscribed in a semicircle is a right angle. The intercepted arc is 180°, making the inscribed angle half that, or 90°. In the diagram below, angle ABC is inscribed in semicircle ABC, making angle ABC equal to 90°.

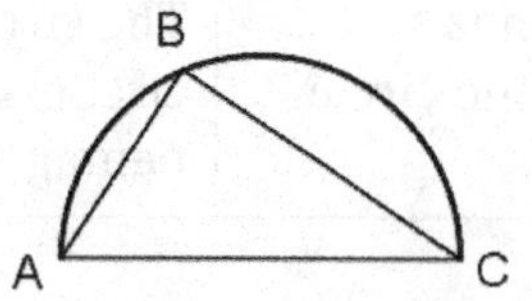

Review Video: Arcs and Angles of Circles
Visit mometrix.com/academy and enter code: 652838

Secants, Chords, and Tangents

A **secant** is a line that intersects a circle in two points. The segment of a secant line that is contained within the circle is called a **chord**. Two secants may intersect inside the circle, on the circle, or outside the circle. When the two secants intersect on the circle, an inscribed angle is formed. When two secants intersect inside a circle, the measure of each of two vertical angles is equal to half the sum of the two intercepted arcs. Consider the following diagram where $m\angle AEB = \frac{1}{2}(\widehat{AB} + \widehat{CD})$ and $m\angle BEC = \frac{1}{2}(\widehat{BC} + \widehat{AD})$.

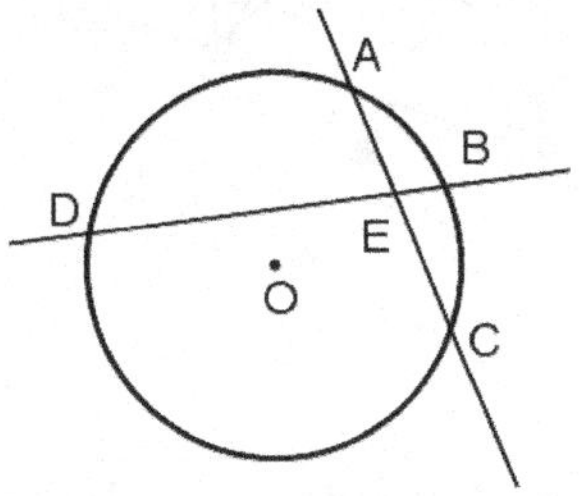

When two secants intersect outside a circle, the measure of the angle formed is equal to half the difference of the two arcs that lie between the two secants. In the diagram below, $m\angle AEB = \frac{1}{2}(\widehat{AB} - \widehat{CD})$.

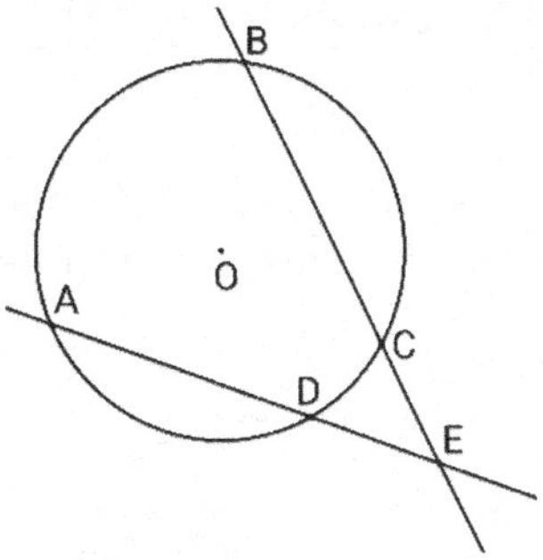

A **tangent** is a line in the same plane as a circle that touches the circle in exactly one point. The point at which a tangent touches a circle is called the **point of tangency**. While a line segment can be tangent to a circle as part of a line that is tangent, it is improper to say a tangent can be simply a line segment that touches the circle in exactly one point.

In the diagram below, $\overleftrightarrow{EB}$ is a secant and contains chord $\overline{EB}$, and $\overleftrightarrow{CD}$ is tangent to circle A. Notice that $\overline{FB}$ is not tangent to the circle. $\overline{FB}$ is a line segment that touches the circle in exactly one point, but if the segment were extended, it would touch the circle in a second point. In the diagram below, point B is the point of tangency.

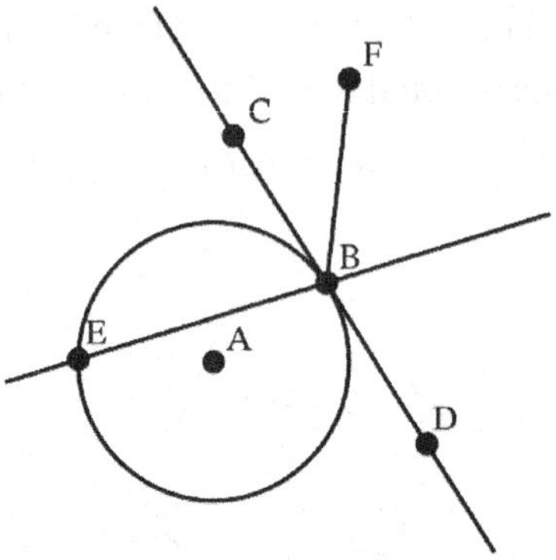

Review Video: Secants, Chords, and Tangents
Visit mometrix.com/academy and enter code: 258360

Review Video: Tangent Lines of a Circle
Visit mometrix.com/academy and enter code: 780167

Sectors

A **sector** is the portion of a circle formed by two radii and their intercepted arc. While the arc length is exclusively the points that are also on the circumference of the circle, the sector is the entire area bounded by the arc and the two radii.

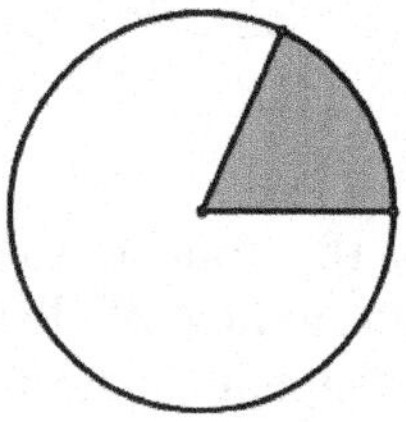

The **area of a sector** of a circle is found by the formula, $A = \frac{\theta r^2}{2}$, where A is the area, θ is the measure of the central angle in radians, and r is the radius. To find the area with the central angle in degrees, use the formula, $A = \frac{\theta \pi r^2}{360}$, where θ is the measure of the central angle and r is the radius.

3D Shapes

Solids

The **surface area of a solid object** is the area of all sides or exterior surfaces. For objects such as prisms and pyramids, a further distinction is made between base surface area (B) and lateral surface area (LA). For a prism, the total surface area (SA) is $SA = LA + 2B$. For a pyramid or cone, the total surface area is $SA = LA + B$.

The **surface area of a sphere** can be found by the formula $A = 4\pi r^2$, where r is the radius. The volume is given by the formula $V = \frac{4}{3}\pi r^3$, where r is the radius. Both quantities are generally given in terms of π.

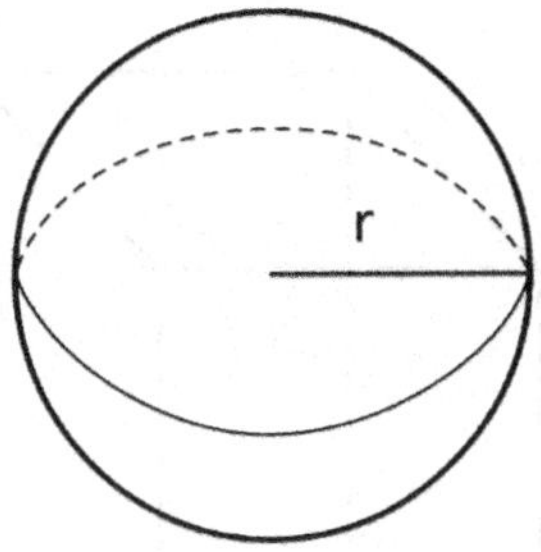

Review Video: Volume and Surface Area of a Sphere
Visit mometrix.com/academy and enter code: 786928

Review Video: How to Calculate the Volume of 3D Objects
Visit mometrix.com/academy and enter code: 163343

The **volume of any prism** is found by the formula $V = Bh$, where B is the area of the base, and h is the height (perpendicular distance between the bases). The surface area of any prism is the sum of the areas of both bases and all sides. It can be calculated as $SA = 2B + Ph$, where P is the perimeter of the base.

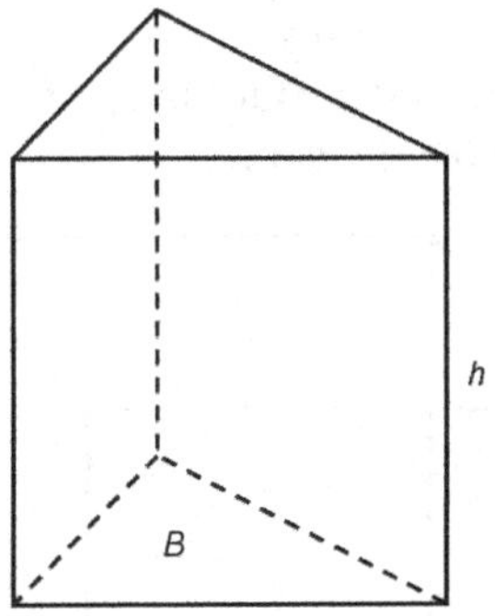

Review Video: Volume and Surface Area of a Prism
Visit mometrix.com/academy and enter code: 420158

For a **rectangular prism**, the volume can be found by the formula $V = lwh$, where V is the volume, l is the length, w is the width, and h is the height. The surface area can be calculated as $SA = 2lw + 2hl + 2wh$ or $SA = 2(lw + hl + wh)$.

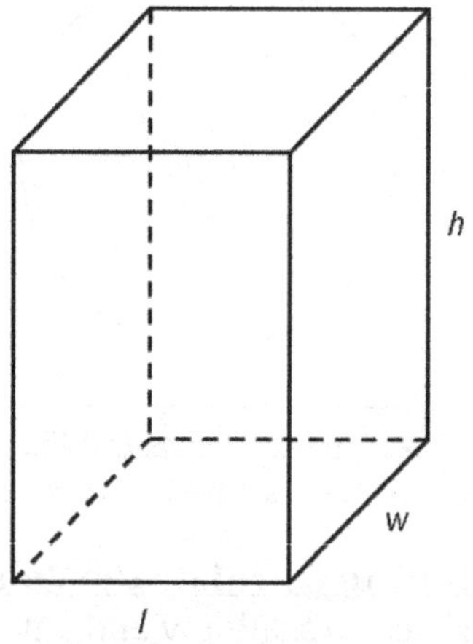

Review Video: Volume and Surface Area of a Rectangular Prism
Visit mometrix.com/academy and enter code: 282814

The **volume of a cube** can be found by the formula $V = s^3$, where s is the length of a side. The surface area of a cube is calculated as $SA = 6s^2$, where SA is the total surface area and s is the length of a side. These formulas are the same as the ones used for the volume and surface area of a rectangular prism, but simplified since all three quantities (length, width, and height) are the same.

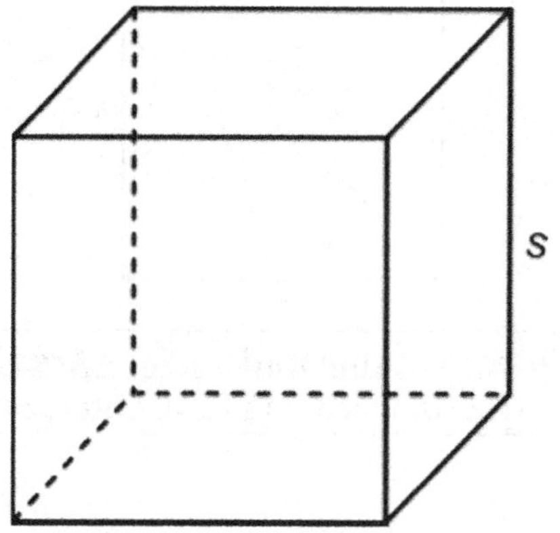

Review Video: Volume and Surface Area of a Cube
Visit mometrix.com/academy and enter code: 664455

The **volume of a cylinder** can be calculated by the formula $V = \pi r^2 h$, where r is the radius, and h is the height. The surface area of a cylinder can be found by the formula $SA = 2\pi r^2 + 2\pi rh$. The first term is the base area multiplied by two, and the second term is the perimeter of the base multiplied by the height.

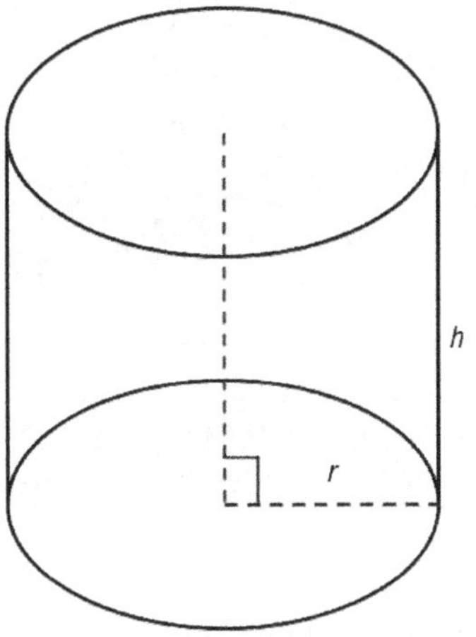

Review Video: Finding the Volume and Surface Area of a Right Circular Cylinder
Visit mometrix.com/academy and enter code: 226463

The **volume of a pyramid** is found by the formula $V = \frac{1}{3}Bh$, where B is the area of the base, and h is the height (perpendicular distance from the vertex to the base). Notice this formula is the same as $\frac{1}{3}$ times the volume of a prism. Like a prism, the base of a pyramid can be any shape.

Finding the **surface area of a pyramid** is not as simple as the other shapes we've looked at thus far. If the pyramid is a right pyramid, meaning the base is a regular polygon and the vertex is directly over the center of that polygon, the surface area can be calculated as $SA = B + \frac{1}{2}Ph_s$, where P is the perimeter of the base, and h_s is the slant height (distance from the vertex to the midpoint of one side of the base). If the pyramid is irregular, the area of each triangle side must be calculated individually and then summed, along with the base.

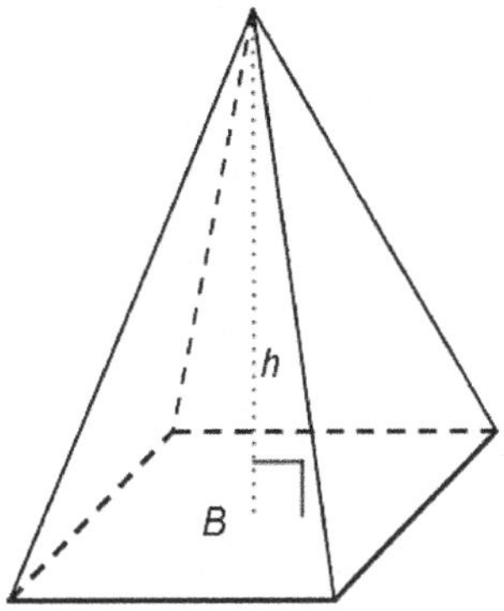

Review Video: Finding the Volume and Surface Area of a Pyramid
Visit mometrix.com/academy and enter code: 621932

The **volume of a cone** is found by the formula $V = \frac{1}{3}\pi r^2 h$, where r is the radius, and h is the height. Notice this is the same as $\frac{1}{3}$ times the volume of a cylinder. The surface area can be calculated as $SA = \pi r^2 + \pi rs$, where s

is the slant height. The slant height can be calculated using the Pythagorean theorem to be $\sqrt{r^2 + h^2}$, so the surface area formula can also be written as $SA = \pi r^2 + \pi r\sqrt{r^2 + h^2}$.

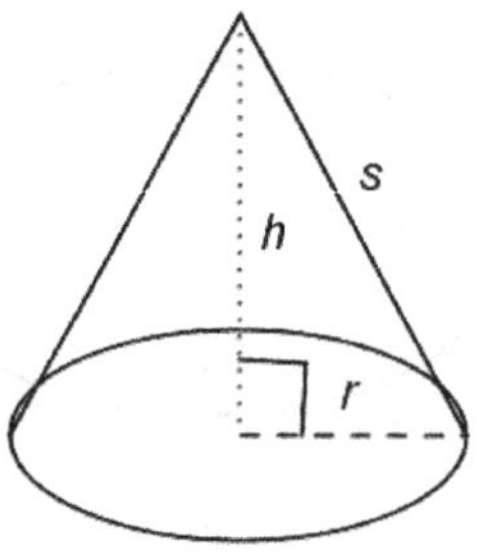

Review Video: Volume and Surface Area of a Right Circular Cone
Visit mometrix.com/academy and enter code: 573574

Conic Sections

Conic sections are a family of shapes that can be thought of as cross sections of a pair of infinite right cones stacked vertex to vertex. This is easiest to see with a visual representation:

A three-dimensional look at representative conic sections. (Note that a hyperbola intersects both cones.)

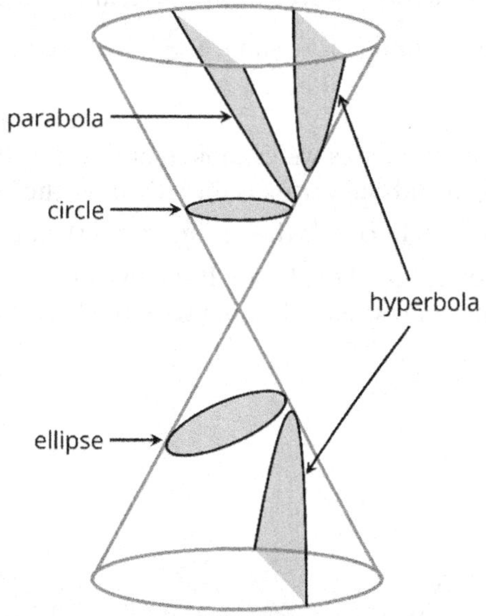

A side-on look at representative conic sections. (Note that the parabola is parallel to the slant of the cones.)

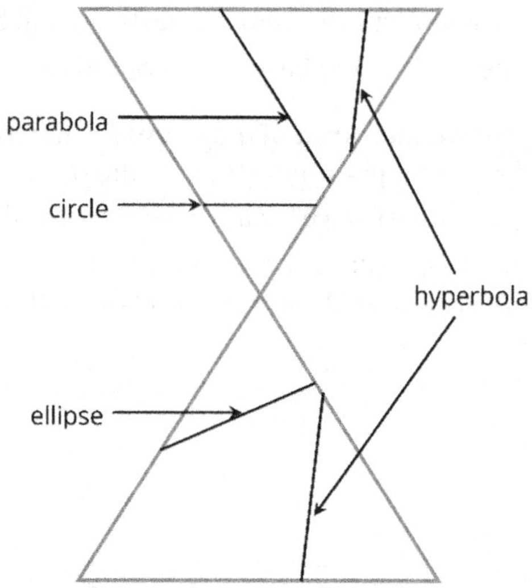

In short, a circle is a horizontal cross section, a parabola is a cross section parallel to the slant of the cone, an ellipse is a cross section at an angle *less than* the slant of the cone, and a hyperbola is a cross section at an angle *greater than* the slant of the cone.

Statistics and Probability

Probability

Probability is the likelihood of a certain outcome occurring for a given event. An **event** is any situation that produces a result. It could be something as simple as flipping a coin or as complex as launching a rocket.

Determining the probability of an outcome for an event can be equally simple or complex. As such, there are specific terms used in the study of probability that need to be understood:

- **Compound event**—an event that involves two or more independent events (rolling a pair of dice and taking the sum)
- **Desired outcome** (or success)—an outcome that meets a particular set of criteria (a roll of 1 or 2 if we are looking for numbers less than 3)
- **Independent events**—two or more events whose outcomes do not affect one another (two coins tossed at the same time)
- **Dependent events**—two or more events whose outcomes affect one another (two cards drawn consecutively from the same deck)
- **Certain outcome**—probability of outcome is 100% or 1
- **Impossible outcome**—probability of outcome is 0% or 0
- **Mutually exclusive outcomes**—two or more outcomes whose criteria cannot all be satisfied in a single event (a coin coming up heads and tails on the same toss)
- **Random variable**—refers to all possible outcomes of a single event which may be discrete or continuous.

Review Video: Intro to Probability
Visit mometrix.com/academy and enter code: 212374

Sample Space

The total set of all possible results of a test or experiment is called a **sample space**, or sometimes a universal sample space. The sample space, represented by one of the variables S, Ω, or U (for universal sample space) has individual elements called outcomes. Other terms for outcome that may be used interchangeably include elementary outcome, simple event, or sample point. The number of outcomes in a given sample space could be infinite or finite, and some tests may yield multiple unique sample sets. For example, tests conducted by drawing playing cards from a standard deck would have one sample space of the card values, another sample space of the card suits, and a third sample space of suit-denomination combinations. For most tests, the sample spaces considered will be finite.

An **event**, represented by the variable E, is a portion of a sample space. It may be one outcome or a group of outcomes from the same sample space. If an event occurs, then the test or experiment will generate an outcome that satisfies the requirement of that event. For example, given a standard deck of 52 playing cards as the sample space, and defining the event as the collection of face cards, then the event will occur if the card drawn is a J, Q, or K. If any other card is drawn, the event is said to have not occurred.

For every sample space, each possible outcome has a specific likelihood, or probability, that it will occur. The probability measure, also called the **distribution**, is a function that assigns a real number probability, from zero to one, to each outcome. For a probability measure to be accurate, every outcome must have a real number probability measure that is greater than or equal to zero and less than or equal to one. Also, the probability measure of the sample space must equal one, and the probability measure of the union of multiple outcomes must equal the sum of the individual probability measures.

Probabilities of events are expressed as real numbers from zero to one. They give a numerical value to the chance that a particular event will occur. The probability of an event occurring is the sum of the probabilities of the individual elements of that event. For example, in a standard deck of 52 playing cards as the sample space and the collection of face cards as the event, the probability of drawing a specific face card is $\frac{1}{52} = 0.019$, but the probability of drawing any one of the twelve face cards is $12(0.019) = 0.228$. Note that rounding of numbers can generate different results. If you multiplied 12 by the fraction $\frac{1}{52}$ before converting to a decimal, you would get the answer $\frac{12}{52} = 0.231$.

Theoretical and Experimental Probability

Theoretical probability can usually be determined without actually performing the event. The likelihood of an outcome occurring, or the probability of an outcome occurring, is given by the formula:

$$P(A) = \frac{\text{Number of acceptable outcomes}}{\text{Number of possible outcomes}}$$

Note that $P(A)$ is the probability of an outcome A occurring, and each outcome is just as likely to occur as any other outcome. If each outcome has the same probability of occurring as every other possible outcome, the outcomes are said to be equally likely to occur. The total number of acceptable outcomes must be less than or equal to the total number of possible outcomes. If the two are equal, then the outcome is certain to occur and the probability is 1. If the number of acceptable outcomes is zero, then the outcome is impossible and the probability is 0. For example, if there are 20 marbles in a bag and 5 are red, then the theoretical probability of randomly selecting a red marble is 5 out of 20, $\left(\frac{5}{20} = \frac{1}{4}, 0.25, \text{or } 25\%\right)$.

If the theoretical probability is unknown or too complicated to calculate, it can be estimated by an experimental probability. **Experimental probability**, also called empirical probability, is an estimate of the likelihood of a certain outcome based on repeated experiments or collected data. In other words, while theoretical probability is based on what *should* happen, experimental probability is based on what *has* happened. Experimental probability is calculated in the same way as theoretical probability, except that actual outcomes are used instead of possible outcomes. The more experiments performed or datapoints gathered, the better the estimate should be.

Theoretical and experimental probability do not always line up with one another. Theoretical probability says that out of 20 coin-tosses, 10 should be heads. However, if we were actually to toss 20 coins, we might record just 5 heads. This doesn't mean that our theoretical probability is incorrect; it just means that this particular experiment had results that were different from what was predicted. A practical application of empirical probability is the insurance industry. There are no set functions that define lifespan, health, or safety. Insurance companies look at factors from hundreds of thousands of individuals to find patterns that they then use to set the formulas for insurance premiums.

Review Video: Empirical Probability
Visit mometrix.com/academy and enter code: 513468

Objective and Subjective Probability

Objective probability is based on mathematical formulas and documented evidence. Examples of objective probability include raffles or lottery drawings where there is a pre-determined number of possible outcomes and a predetermined number of outcomes that correspond to an event. Other cases of objective probability include probabilities of rolling dice, flipping coins, or drawing cards. Most gambling games are based on objective probability.

In contrast, **subjective probability** is based on personal or professional feelings and judgments. Often, there is a lot of guesswork following extensive research. Areas where subjective probability is applicable include sales trends and business expenses. Attractions set admission prices based on subjective probabilities of attendance based on varying admission rates in an effort to maximize their profit.

Complement of an Event

Sometimes it may be easier to calculate the possibility of something not happening, or the **complement of an event**. Represented by the symbol $\bar{A}$, the complement of A is the probability that event A does not happen. When you know the probability of event A occurring, you can use the formula $P(\bar{A}) = 1 - P(A)$, where $P(\bar{A})$ is the probability of event A not occurring, and $P(A)$ is the probability of event A occurring.

ADDITION RULE

The **addition rule** for probability is used for finding the probability of a compound event. Use the formula $P(A \cup B) = P(A) + P(B) - P(A \cap B)$, where $P(A \cap B)$ is the probability of both events occurring to find the probability of a compound event. The probability of both events occurring at the same time must be subtracted to eliminate any overlap in the first two probabilities.

CONDITIONAL PROBABILITY

Given two events A and B, the **conditional probability** $P(A|B)$ is the probability that event A will occur, given that event B has occurred. The conditional probability cannot be calculated simply from $P(A)$ and $P(B)$; these probabilities alone do not give sufficient information to determine the conditional probability. It can, however, be determined if you are also given the probability of the intersection of events A and B, $P(A \cap B)$, the probability that events A and B both occur. Specifically, $P(A|B) = \frac{P(A \cap B)}{P(B)}$. For instance, suppose you have a jar containing two red marbles and two blue marbles, and you draw two marbles at random. Consider event A being the event that the first marble drawn is red, and event B being the event that the second marble drawn is blue. If we want to find the probability that B occurs given that A occurred, $P(B|A)$, then we can compute it using the fact that $P(A)$ is $\frac{1}{2}$, and $P(A \cap B)$ is $\frac{1}{3}$. (The latter may not be obvious, but may be determined by finding the product of $\frac{1}{2}$ and $\frac{2}{3}$). Therefore $P(B|A) = \frac{P(A \cap B)}{P(A)} = \frac{1/3}{1/2} = \frac{2}{3}$.

CONDITIONAL PROBABILITY IN EVERYDAY SITUATIONS

Conditional probability often arises in everyday situations in, for example, estimating the risk or benefit of certain activities. The conditional probability of having a heart attack given that you exercise daily may be smaller than the overall probability of having a heart attack. The conditional probability of having lung cancer given that you are a smoker is larger than the overall probability of having lung cancer. Note that changing the order of the conditional probability changes the meaning: the conditional probability of having lung cancer given that you are a smoker is a very different thing from the probability of being a smoker given that you have lung cancer. In an extreme case, suppose that a certain rare disease is caused only by eating a certain food, but even then, it is unlikely. Then the conditional probability of having that disease given that you eat the dangerous food is nonzero but low, but the conditional probability of having eaten that food given that you have the disease is 100%!

Review Video: Conditional Probability
Visit mometrix.com/academy and enter code: 397924

INDEPENDENCE

The conditional probability $P(A|B)$ is the probability that event A will occur given that event B occurs. If the two events are independent, we do not expect that whether or not event B occurs should have any effect on whether or not event A occurs. In other words, we expect $P(A|B) = P(A)$.

This can be proven using the usual equations for conditional probability and the joint probability of independent events. The conditional probability $P(A|B) = \frac{P(A \cap B)}{P(B)}$. If A and B are independent, then $P(A \cap B) = P(A)P(B)$. So $P(A|B) = \frac{P(A)P(B)}{P(B)} = P(A)$. By similar reasoning, if A and B are independent then $P(B|A) = P(B)$.

MULTIPLICATION RULE

The **multiplication rule** can be used to find the probability of two independent events occurring using the formula $P(A \cap B) = P(A) \times P(B)$, where $P(A \cap B)$ is the probability of two independent events occurring, $P(A)$ is the probability of the first event occurring, and $P(B)$ is the probability of the second event occurring.

The multiplication rule can also be used to find the probability of two dependent events occurring using the formula $P(A \cap B) = P(A) \times P(B|A)$, where $P(A \cap B)$ is the probability of two dependent events occurring and $P(B|A)$ is the probability of the second event occurring after the first event has already occurred.

Use a **combination of the multiplication** rule and the rule of complements to find the probability that at least one outcome of the element will occur. This is given by the general formula $P(\text{at least one event occurring}) = 1 - P(\text{no outcomes occurring})$. For example, to find the probability that at least one even number will show when a pair of dice is rolled, find the probability that two odd numbers will be rolled (no even numbers) and subtract from one. You can always use a tree diagram or make a chart to list the possible outcomes when the sample space is small, such as in the dice-rolling example, but in most cases it will be much faster to use the multiplication and complement formulas.

Review Video: Multiplication Rule
Visit mometrix.com/academy and enter code: 782598

Union and Intersection of Two Sets of Outcomes

If A and B are each a set of elements or outcomes from an experiment, then the **union** (symbol ∪) of the two sets is the set of elements found in set A or set B. For example, if $A = \{2, 3, 4\}$ and $B = \{3, 4, 5\}$, $A \cup B = \{2, 3, 4, 5\}$. Note that the outcomes 3 and 4 appear only once in the union. For statistical events, the union is equivalent to "or"; $P(A \cup B)$ is the same thing as $P(A \text{ or } B)$. The **intersection** (symbol ∩) of two sets is the set of outcomes common to both sets. For the above sets A and B, $A \cap B = \{3, 4\}$. For statistical events, the intersection is equivalent to "and"; $P(A \cap B)$ is the same thing as $P(A \text{ and } B)$. It is important to note that union and intersection operations commute. That is:

$$A \cup B = B \cup A \text{ and } A \cap B = B \cap A$$

Two-Way Frequency Tables

If we have a two-way frequency table, it is generally a straightforward matter to read off the probabilities of any two events A and B, as well as the joint probability of both events occurring, $P(A \cap B)$. We can then find the conditional probability $P(A|B)$ by calculating $P(A|B) = \frac{P(A \cap B)}{P(B)}$. We could also check whether or not events are independent by verifying whether $P(A)P(B) = P(A \cap B)$.

For example, a certain store's recent T-shirt sales:

	Small	Medium	Large	Total
Blue	25	40	35	100
White	27	25	22	74
Black	8	23	15	46
Total	60	88	72	220

Suppose we want to find the conditional probability that a customer buys a black shirt (event A), given that the shirt he buys is size small (event B). From the table, the probability $P(B)$ that a customer buys a small shirt is $\frac{60}{220} = \frac{3}{11}$. The probability $P(A \cap B)$ that he buys a small, black shirt is $\frac{8}{220} = \frac{2}{55}$. The conditional probability $P(A|B)$ that he buys a black shirt, given that he buys a small shirt, is therefore $P(A|B) = \frac{2/55}{3/11} = \frac{2}{15}$.

Similarly, if we want to check whether the event a customer buys a blue shirt, A, is independent of the event that a customer buys a medium shirt, B. From the table, $P(A) = \frac{100}{220} = \frac{5}{11}$ and $P(B) = \frac{88}{220} = \frac{4}{10}$. Also, $P(A \cap B) = \frac{40}{220} = \frac{2}{11}$. Since $\left(\frac{5}{11}\right)\left(\frac{4}{10}\right) = \frac{20}{110} = \frac{2}{11}$, $P(A)P(B) = P(A \cap B)$ and these two events are indeed independent.

Introduction to Statistics

Statistics is the branch of mathematics that deals with collecting, recording, interpreting, illustrating, and analyzing large amounts of **data**. The following terms are often used in the discussion of data and **statistics**:

- **Data** – the collective name for pieces of information (singular is datum)
- **Quantitative data** – measurements (such as length, mass, and speed) that provide information about quantities in numbers
- **Qualitative data** – information (such as colors, scents, tastes, and shapes) that cannot be measured using numbers
- **Discrete data** – information that can be expressed only by a specific value, such as whole or half numbers. (e.g., since people can be counted only in whole numbers, a population count would be discrete data.)
- **Continuous data** – information (such as time and temperature) that can be expressed by any value within a given range
- **Primary data** – information that has been collected directly from a survey, investigation, or experiment, such as a questionnaire or the recording of daily temperatures. (Primary data that has not yet been organized or analyzed is called **raw data**.)
- **Secondary data** – information that has been collected, sorted, and processed by the researcher
- **Ordinal data** – information that can be placed in numerical order, such as age or weight
- **Nominal data** – information that *cannot* be placed in numerical order, such as names or places

Data Collection

Population

In statistics, the **population** is the entire collection of people, plants, etc., that data can be collected from. For example, a study to determine how well students in local schools perform on a standardized test would have a population of all the students enrolled in those schools, although a study may include just a small sample of students from each school. A **parameter** is a numerical value that gives information about the population, such as the mean, median, mode, or standard deviation. Remember that the symbol for the mean of a population is μ and the symbol for the standard deviation of a population is σ.

Sample

A **sample** is a portion of the entire population. Whereas a parameter helped describe the population, a **statistic** is a numerical value that gives information about the sample, such as mean, median, mode, or standard deviation. Keep in mind that the symbols for mean and standard deviation are different when they are referring to a sample rather than the entire population. For a sample, the symbol for mean is $\bar{x}$ and the symbol for standard deviation is s. The mean and standard deviation of a sample may or may not be identical to that of the entire population due to a sample only being a subset of the population. However, if the sample is random and large enough, statistically significant values can be attained. Samples are generally used when the population is too large to justify including every element or when acquiring data for the entire population is impossible.

Inferential Statistics

Inferential statistics is the branch of statistics that uses samples to make predictions about an entire population. This type of statistic is often seen in political polls, where a sample of the population is questioned about a particular topic or politician to gain an understanding of the attitudes of the entire population of the country. Often, exit polls are conducted on election days using this method. Inferential statistics can have a large margin of error if you do not have a valid sample.

Sampling Distribution

Statistical values calculated from various samples of the same size make up the **sampling distribution**. For example, if several samples of identical size are randomly selected from a large population and then the mean of each sample is calculated, the distribution of values of the means would be a sampling distribution.

The **sampling distribution of the mean** is the distribution of the sample mean, $\bar{x}$, derived from random samples of a given size. It has three important characteristics. First, the mean of the sampling distribution of the mean is equal to the mean of the population that was sampled. Second, assuming the standard deviation is non-zero, the standard deviation of the sampling distribution of the mean equals the standard deviation of the sampled population divided by the square root of the sample size. This is sometimes called the standard error. Finally, as the sample size gets larger, the sampling distribution of the mean gets closer to a normal distribution via the central limit theorem.

SURVEY STUDY

A **survey study** is a method of gathering information from a small group in an attempt to gain enough information to make accurate general assumptions about the population. Once a survey study is completed, the results are then put into a summary report.

Survey studies are generally in the format of surveys, interviews, or questionnaires as part of an effort to find opinions of a particular group or to find facts about a group.

It is important to note that the findings from a survey study are only as accurate as the sample chosen from the population.

CORRELATIONAL STUDIES

Correlational studies seek to determine how much one variable is affected by changes in a second variable. For example, correlational studies may look for a relationship between the amount of time a student spends studying for a test and the grade that student earned on the test or between student scores on college admissions tests and student grades in college.

It is important to note that correlational studies cannot show a cause and effect, but rather can show only that two variables are or are not potentially correlated.

EXPERIMENTAL STUDIES

Experimental studies take correlational studies one step farther, in that they attempt to prove or disprove a cause-and-effect relationship. These studies are performed by conducting a series of experiments to test the hypothesis. For a study to be scientifically accurate, it must have both an experimental group that receives the specified treatment and a control group that does not get the treatment. This is the type of study pharmaceutical companies do as part of drug trials for new medications. Experimental studies are only valid when the proper scientific method has been followed. In other words, the experiment must be well-planned and executed without bias in the testing process, all subjects must be selected at random, and the process of determining which subject is in which of the two groups must also be completely random.

OBSERVATIONAL STUDIES

Observational studies are the opposite of experimental studies. In observational studies, the tester cannot change or in any way control all of the variables in the test. For example, a study to determine which gender does better in math classes in school is strictly observational. You cannot change a person's gender, and you cannot change the subject being studied. The big downfall of observational studies is that you have no way of proving a cause-and-effect relationship because you cannot control outside influences. Events outside of school can influence a student's performance in school, and observational studies cannot take that into consideration.

RANDOM SAMPLES

For most studies, a **random sample** is necessary to produce valid results. Random samples should not have any particular influence to cause sampled subjects to behave one way or another. The goal is for the random sample to be a **representative sample**, or a sample whose characteristics give an accurate picture of the characteristics of the entire population. To accomplish this, you must make sure you have a proper **sample size**, or an appropriate number of elements in the sample.

Biases

In statistical studies, biases must be avoided. **Bias** is an error that causes the study to favor one set of results over another. For example, if a survey to determine how the country views the president's job performance only speaks to registered voters in the president's party, the results will be skewed because a disproportionately large number of responders would tend to show approval, while a disproportionately large number of people in the opposite party would tend to express disapproval. **Extraneous variables** are, as the name implies, outside influences that can affect the outcome of a study. They are not always avoidable but could trigger bias in the result.

Data Analysis

Dispersion

A **measure of dispersion** is a single value that helps to "interpret" the measure of central tendency by providing more information about how the data values in the set are distributed about the measure of central tendency. The measure of dispersion helps to eliminate or reduce the disadvantages of using the mean, median, or mode as a single measure of central tendency, and give a more accurate picture of the dataset as a whole. To have a measure of dispersion, you must know or calculate the range, standard deviation, or variance of the data set.

Range

The **range** of a set of data is the difference between the greatest and lowest values of the data in the set. To calculate the range, you must first make sure the units for all data values are the same, and then identify the greatest and lowest values. If there are multiple data values that are equal for the highest or lowest, just use one of the values in the formula. Write the answer with the same units as the data values you used to do the calculations.

Review Video: Statistical Range
Visit mometrix.com/academy and enter code: 778541

Sample Standard Deviation

Standard deviation is a measure of dispersion that compares all the data values in the set to the mean of the set to give a more accurate picture. To find the **standard deviation of a sample**, use the formula

$$s = \sqrt{\frac{\sum_{i=1}^{n}(x_i - \bar{x})^2}{n-1}}$$

Note that s is the standard deviation of a sample, x_i represents the individual values in the data set, $\bar{x}$ is the mean of the data values in the set, and n is the number of data values in the set. The higher the value of the standard deviation is, the greater the variance of the data values from the mean. The units associated with the standard deviation are the same as the units of the data values.

Review Video: Standard Deviation
Visit mometrix.com/academy and enter code: 419469

Sample Variance

The **variance of a sample** is the square of the sample standard deviation (denoted s^2). While the mean of a set of data gives the average of the set and gives information about where a specific data value lies in relation to the average, the variance of the sample gives information about the degree to which the data values are spread out and tells you how close an individual value is to the average compared to the other values. The units associated with variance are the same as the units of the data values squared.

Percentile

Percentiles and quartiles are other methods of describing data within a set. **Percentiles** tell what percentage of the data in the set fall below a specific point. For example, achievement test scores are often given in percentiles. A score at the 80th percentile is one which is equal to or higher than 80 percent of the scores in the set. In other words, 80 percent of the scores were lower than that score.

Quartiles are percentile groups that make up quarter sections of the data set. The first quartile is the 25th percentile. The second quartile is the 50th percentile; this is also the median of the dataset. The third quartile is the 75th percentile.

Skewness

Skewness is a way to describe the symmetry or asymmetry of the distribution of values in a dataset. If the distribution of values is symmetrical, there is no skew. In general the closer the mean of a data set is to the median of the data set, the less skew there is. Generally, if the mean is to the right of the median, the data set is *positively skewed*, or right-skewed, and if the mean is to the left of the median, the data set is *negatively skewed*, or left-skewed. However, this rule of thumb is not infallible. When the data values are graphed on a curve, a set with no skew will be a perfect bell curve.

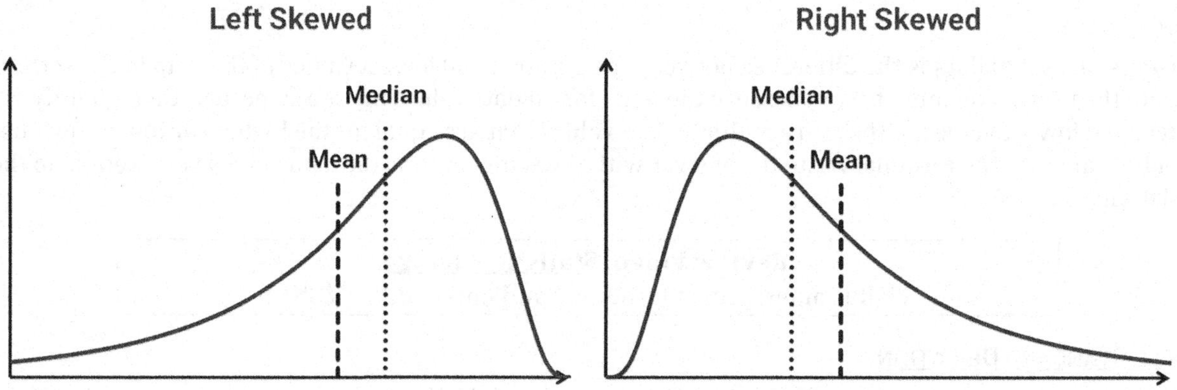

To estimate skew, use the formula:

$$\text{skew} = \frac{\sqrt{n(n-1)}}{n-2}\left(\frac{\frac{1}{n}\sum_{i=1}^{n}(x_i-\bar{x})^3}{\left(\frac{1}{n}\sum_{i=1}^{n}(x_i-\bar{x})^2\right)^{\frac{3}{2}}}\right)$$

Note that n is the datapoints in the set, x_i is the ith value in the set, and $\bar{x}$ is the mean of the set.

Review Video: Skew
Visit mometrix.com/academy and enter code: 661486

Unimodal vs. Bimodal

If a distribution has a single peak, it would be considered **unimodal**. If it has two discernible peaks it would be considered **bimodal**. Bimodal distributions may be an indication that the set of data being considered is actually the combination of two sets of data with significant differences. A **uniform distribution** is a distribution in which there is *no distinct peak or variation* in the data. No values or ranges are particularly more common than any other values or ranges.

Outlier

An outlier is an extremely high or extremely low value in the data set. It may be the result of measurement error, in which case, the outlier is not a valid member of the data set. However, it may also be a valid member of the distribution. Unless a measurement error is identified, the experimenter cannot know for certain if an outlier is or is not a member of the distribution. There are arbitrary methods that can be employed to designate an extreme value as an outlier. One method designates an outlier (or possible outlier) to be any value less than $Q_1 - 1.5(IQR)$ or any value greater than $Q_3 + 1.5(IQR)$.

Data Analysis

Simple Regression

In statistics, **simple regression** is using an equation to represent a relation between independent and dependent variables. The independent variable is also referred to as the explanatory variable or the predictor and is generally represented by the variable x in the equation. The dependent variable, usually represented by the variable y, is also referred to as the response variable. The equation may be any type of function – linear, quadratic, exponential, etc. The best way to handle this task is to use the regression feature of your graphing calculator. This will easily give you the curve of best fit and provide you with the coefficients and other information you need to derive an equation.

Line of Best Fit

In a scatter plot, the **line of best fit** is the line that best shows the trends of the data. The line of best fit is given by the equation $\hat{y} = ax + b$, where a and b are the regression coefficients. The regression coefficient a is also the slope of the line of best fit, and b is also the y-coordinate of the point at which the line of best fit crosses the y-axis. Not every point on the scatter plot will be on the line of best fit. The differences between the y-values of the points in the scatter plot and the corresponding y-values according to the equation of the line of best fit are the residuals. The line of best fit is also called the least-squares regression line because it is also the line that has the lowest sum of the squares of the residuals.

Correlation Coefficient

The **correlation coefficient** is the numerical value that indicates how strong the relationship is between the two variables of a linear regression equation. A correlation coefficient of −1 is a perfect negative correlation. A correlation coefficient of +1 is a perfect positive correlation. Correlation coefficients close to −1 or +1 are very strong correlations. A correlation coefficient equal to zero indicates there is no correlation between the two variables. This test is a good indicator of whether or not the equation for the line of best fit is accurate. The formula for the correlation coefficient is

$$r = \frac{\sum_{i=1}^{n}(x_i - \bar{x})(y_i - \bar{y})}{\sqrt{\sum_{i=1}^{n}(x_i - \bar{x})^2}\sqrt{\sum_{i=1}^{n}(y_i - \bar{y})^2}}$$

where r is the correlation coefficient, n is the number of data values in the set, (x_i, y_i) is a point in the set, and $\bar{x}$ and $\bar{y}$ are the means.

Z-Score

A **z-score** is an indication of how many standard deviations a given value falls from the sample mean. To calculate a z-score, use the formula:

$$\frac{x - \bar{x}}{\sigma}$$

In this formula x is the data value, $\bar{x}$ is the mean of the sample data, and σ is the standard deviation of the population. If the z-score is positive, the data value lies above the mean. If the z-score is negative, the data value falls below the mean. These scores are useful in interpreting data such as standardized test scores, where every piece of data in the set has been counted, rather than just a small random sample. In cases where standard deviations are calculated from a random sample of the set, the z-scores will not be as accurate.

Central Limit Theorem

According to the **central limit theorem**, regardless of what the original distribution of a sample is, the distribution of the means tends to get closer and closer to a normal distribution as the sample size gets larger and larger (this is necessary because the sample is becoming more all-encompassing of the elements of the population). As the sample size gets larger, the distribution of the sample mean will approach a normal distribution with a mean of the population mean and a variance of the population variance divided by the sample size.

Measures of Central Tendency

A **measure of central tendency** is a statistical value that gives a reasonable estimate for the center of a group of data. There are several different ways of describing the measure of central tendency. Each one has a unique way it is calculated, and each one gives a slightly different perspective on the data set. Whenever you give a measure of central tendency, always make sure the units are the same. If the data has different units, such as hours, minutes, and seconds, convert all the data to the same unit, and use the same unit in the measure of central tendency. If no units are given in the data, do not give units for the measure of central tendency.

Mean

The **statistical mean** of a group of data is the same as the arithmetic average of that group. To find the mean of a set of data, first convert each value to the same units, if necessary. Then find the sum of all the values, and count the total number of data values, making sure you take into consideration each individual value. If a value appears more than once, count it more than once. Divide the sum of the values by the total number of values and apply the units, if any. Note that the mean does not have to be one of the data values in the set, and may not divide evenly.

$$\text{mean} = \frac{\text{sum of the data values}}{\text{quantity of data values}}$$

For instance, the mean of the data set {88, 72, 61, 90, 97, 68, 88, 79, 86, 93, 97, 71, 80, 84, 89} would be the sum of the fifteen numbers divided by 15:

$$\frac{88 + 72 + 61 + 90 + 97 + 68 + 88 + 79 + 86 + 93 + 97 + 71 + 80 + 84 + 89}{15} = \frac{1242}{15} = 82.8$$

While the mean is relatively easy to calculate and averages are understood by most people, the mean can be very misleading if it is used as the sole measure of central tendency. If the data set has outliers (data values that are unusually high or unusually low compared to the rest of the data values), the mean can be very distorted, especially if the data set has a small number of values. If unusually high values are countered with unusually low values, the mean is not affected as much. For example, if five of twenty students in a class get a 100 on a test, but the other 15 students have an average of 60 on the same test, the class average would appear as 70. Whenever the mean is skewed by outliers, it is always a good idea to include the median as an alternate measure of central tendency.

A **weighted mean**, or weighted average, is a mean that uses "weighted" values. The formula is weighted mean $= \frac{w_1x_1 + w_2x_2 + w_3x_3 ... + w_nx_n}{w_1 + w_2 + w_3 + \cdots + w_n}$. Weighted values, such as $w_1, w_2, w_3, ... w_n$ are assigned to each member of the set $x_1, x_2, x_3, \ldots x_n$. When calculating the weighted mean, make sure a weight value for each member of the set is used.

> **Review Video: All About Averages**
> Visit mometrix.com/academy and enter code: 176521

Median

The **statistical median** is the value in the middle of the set of data. To find the median, list all data values in order from smallest to largest or from largest to smallest. Any value that is repeated in the set must be listed the number of times it appears. If there are an odd number of data values, the median is the value in the middle of the list. If there is an even number of data values, the median is the arithmetic mean of the two middle values.

For example, the median of the data set {88, 72, 61, 90, 97, 68, 88, 79, 86, 93, 97, 71, 80, 84, 88} is 86 since the ordered set is {61, 68, 71, 72, 79, 80, 84, **86**, 88, 88, 88, 90, 93, 97, 97}.

The big disadvantage of using the median as a measure of central tendency is that is relies solely on a value's relative size as compared to the other values in the set. When the individual values in a set of data are evenly dispersed, the median can be an accurate tool. However, if there is a group of rather large values or a group of rather small values that are not offset by a different group of values, the information that can be inferred from the median may not be accurate because the distribution of values is skewed.

Mode

The **statistical mode** is the data value that occurs the greatest number of times in the data set. It is possible to have exactly one mode, more than one mode, or no mode. To find the mode of a set of data, arrange the data like you do to find the median (all values in order, listing all multiples of data values). Count the number of times each value appears in the data set. If all values appear an equal number of times, there is no mode. If one value appears more than any other value, that value is the mode. If two or more values appear the same number of times, but there are other values that appear fewer times and no values that appear more times, all of those values are the modes.

For example, the mode of the data set {**88**, 72, 61, 90, 97, 68, **88**, 79, 86, 93, 97, 71, 80, 84, **88**} is 88.

The main disadvantage of the mode is that the values of the other data in the set have no bearing on the mode. The mode may be the largest value, the smallest value, or a value anywhere in between in the set. The mode only tells which value or values, if any, occurred the greatest number of times. It does not give any suggestions about the remaining values in the set.

> **Review Video: Mean, Median, and Mode**
> Visit mometrix.com/academy and enter code: 286207

Scatter Plots

Bivariate Data

Bivariate data is simply data from two different variables. (The prefix *bi-* means *two.*) In a *scatter plot,* each value in the set of data is plotted on a grid similar to a Cartesian plane, where each axis represents one of the two variables. By looking at the pattern formed by the points on the grid, you can often determine whether or not there is a relationship between the two variables, and what that relationship is, if it exists. The variables may be directly proportionate, inversely proportionate, or show no proportion at all. It may also be possible to determine if the data is linear, and if so, to find an equation to relate the two variables. The following scatter plot shows the relationship between preference for brand "A" and the age of the consumers surveyed.

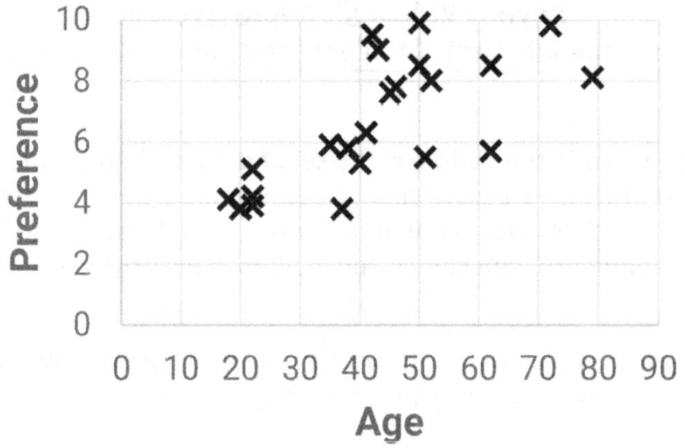

Scatter Plots

Scatter plots are also useful in determining the type of function represented by the data and finding the simple regression. Linear scatter plots may be positive or negative. Nonlinear scatter plots are generally exponential or quadratic. Below are some common types of scatter plots:

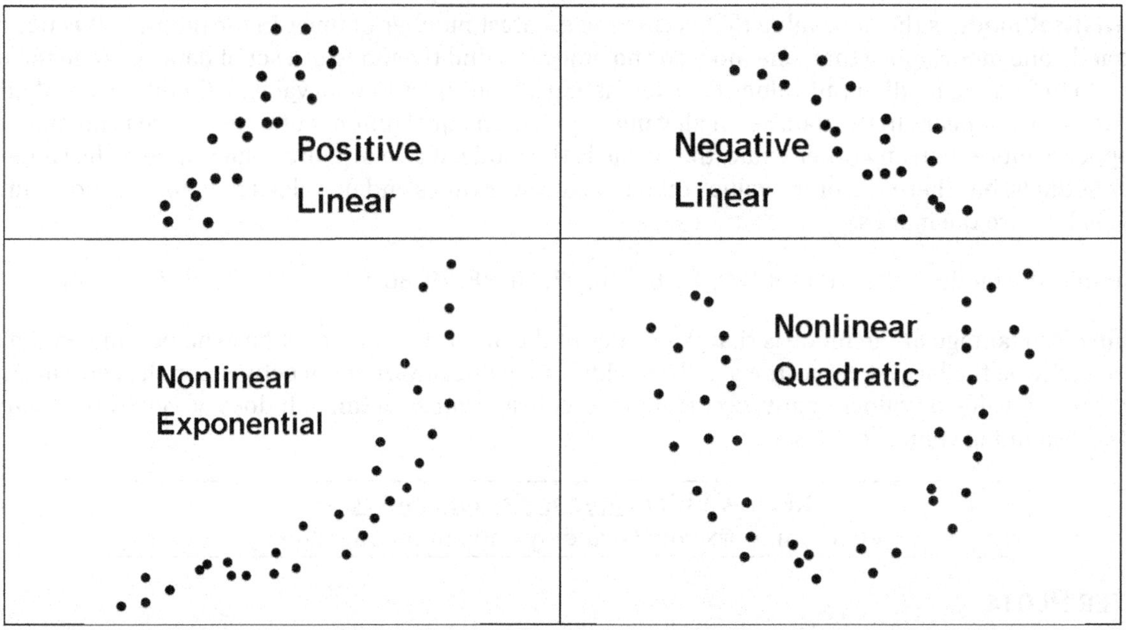

Review Video: What is a Scatter Plot?
Visit mometrix.com/academy and enter code: 596526

Integrating Essential Skills

Proportions and Ratios

Proportions

A proportion is a relationship between two quantities that dictates how one changes when the other changes. A **direct proportion** describes a relationship in which a quantity increases by a set amount for every increase in the other quantity, or decreases by that same amount for every decrease in the other quantity. Example: Assuming a constant driving speed, the time required for a car trip increases as the distance of the trip increases. The distance to be traveled and the time required to travel are directly proportional.

An **inverse proportion** is a relationship in which an increase in one quantity is accompanied by a decrease in the other, or vice versa. Example: the time required for a car trip decreases as the speed increases and increases as the speed decreases, so the time required is inversely proportional to the speed of the car.

Review Video: Proportions
Visit mometrix.com/academy and enter code: 505355

Ratios

A **ratio** is a comparison of two quantities in a particular order. Example: If there are 14 computers in a lab, and the class has 20 students, there is a student to computer ratio of 20 to 14, commonly written as 20: 14. Ratios are normally reduced to their smallest whole number representation, so 20: 14 would be reduced to 10: 7 by dividing both sides by 2.

Review Video: Ratios
Visit mometrix.com/academy and enter code: 996914

Constant of Proportionality

When two quantities have a proportional relationship, there exists a **constant of proportionality** between the quantities. The product of this constant and one of the quantities is equal to the other quantity. For example, if one lemon costs $0.25, two lemons cost $0.50, and three lemons cost $0.75, there is a proportional relationship between the total cost of lemons and the number of lemons purchased. The constant of proportionality is the **unit price**, namely $0.25/lemon. Notice that the total price of lemons, t, can be found by multiplying the unit price of lemons, p, and the number of lemons, n: $t = pn$.

Work/Unit Rate

Unit rate expresses a quantity of one thing in terms of one unit of another. For example, if you travel 30 miles every two hours, a unit rate expresses this comparison in terms of one hour: in one hour you travel 15 miles, so your unit rate is 15 miles per hour. Other examples are how much one ounce of food costs (price per ounce) or figuring out how much one egg costs out of the dozen (price per 1 egg, instead of price per 12 eggs). The denominator of a unit rate is always 1. Unit rates are used to compare different situations to solve problems. For example, to make sure you get the best deal when deciding which kind of soda to buy, you can find the unit rate of each. If soda #1 costs $1.50 for a 1-liter bottle, and soda #2 costs $2.75 for a 2-liter bottle, it would be a better deal to buy soda #2, because its unit rate is only $1.375 per 1-liter, which is cheaper than soda #1. Unit rates can also help determine the length of time a given event will take. For example, if you can paint 2 rooms in 4.5 hours, you can determine how long it will take you to paint 5 rooms by solving for the unit rate per room and then multiplying that by 5.

Review Video: Rates and Unit Rates
Visit mometrix.com/academy and enter code: 185363

SLOPE

On a graph with two points, (x_1, y_1) and (x_2, y_2), the **slope** is found with the formula $m = \frac{y_2 - y_1}{x_2 - x_1}$; where $x_1 \neq x_2$ and m stands for slope. If the value of the slope is **positive**, the line has an *upward direction* from left to right. If the value of the slope is **negative**, the line has a *downward direction* from left to right. Consider the following example:

A new book goes on sale in bookstores and online stores. In the first month, 5,000 copies of the book are sold. Over time, the book continues to grow in popularity. The data for the number of copies sold is in the table below.

# of Months on Sale	1	2	3	4	5
# of Copies Sold (In Thousands)	5	10	15	20	25

So, the number of copies that are sold and the time that the book is on sale is a proportional relationship. In this example, an equation can be used to show the data: $y = 5x$, where x is the number of months that the book is on sale. Also, y is the number of copies sold. So, the slope of the corresponding line is $\frac{\text{rise}}{\text{run}} = \frac{5}{1} = 5$.

Review Video: Finding the Slope of a Line
Visit mometrix.com/academy and enter code: 766664

CROSS MULTIPLICATION

FINDING AN UNKNOWN IN EQUIVALENT EXPRESSIONS

It is often necessary to apply information given about a rate or proportion to a new scenario. For example, if you know that Jedha can run a marathon (26.2 miles) in 3 hours, how long would it take her to run 10 miles at the same pace? Start by setting up equivalent expressions:

$$\frac{26.2 \text{ mi}}{3 \text{ hr}} = \frac{10 \text{ mi}}{x \text{ hr}}$$

Now, cross multiply and solve for x:

$$26.2x = 30$$
$$x = \frac{30}{26.2} = \frac{15}{13.1}$$
$$x \approx 1.15 \text{ hrs } or \text{ 1 hr 9 min}$$

So, at this pace, Jedha could run 10 miles in about 1.15 hours or about 1 hour and 9 minutes.

Review Video: Cross Multiplying Fractions
Visit mometrix.com/academy and enter code: 893904

BASIC FUNCTIONS

FUNCTION AND RELATION

When expressing functional relationships, the **variables** x and y are typically used. These values are often written as the **coordinates** (x, y). The x-value is the independent variable and the y-value is the dependent variable. A **relation** is a set of data in which there is not a unique y-value for each x-value in the dataset. This means that there can be two of the same x-values assigned to different y-values. A relation is simply a relationship between the x- and y-values in each coordinate but does not apply to the relationship between the values of x and y in the data set. A **function** is a relation where one quantity depends on the other. For example, the amount of money that you make depends on the number of hours that you work. In a function, each x-value in the data set has one unique y-value because the y-value depends on the x-value.

Functions

A function has exactly one value of **output variable** (dependent variable) for each value of the **input variable** (independent variable). The set of all values for the input variable (here assumed to be x) is the domain of the function, and the set of all corresponding values of the output variable (here assumed to be y) is the range of the function. When looking at a graph of an equation, the easiest way to determine if the equation is a function or not is to conduct the vertical line test. If a vertical line drawn through any value of x crosses the graph in more than one place, the equation is not a function.

Determining a Function

You can determine whether an equation is a **function** by substituting different values into the equation for x. You can display and organize these numbers in a data table. A **data table** contains the values for x and y, which you can also list as coordinates. In order for a function to exist, the table cannot contain any repeating x-values that correspond with different y-values. If each x-coordinate has a unique y-coordinate, the table contains a function. However, there can be repeating y-values that correspond with different x-values. An example of this is when the function contains an exponent. Example: if $x^2 = y$, $2^2 = 4$, and $(-2)^2 = 4$.

Review Video: Definition of a Function
Visit mometrix.com/academy and enter code: 784611

Finding the Domain and Range of a Function

The **domain** of a function $f(x)$ is the set of all input values for which the function is defined. The **range** of a function $f(x)$ is the set of all possible output values of the function—that is, of every possible value of $f(x)$, for any value of x in the function's domain. For a function expressed in a table, every input-output pair is given explicitly. To find the domain, we just list all the x-values and to find the range, we just list all the values of $f(x)$. Consider the following example:

x	-1	4	2	1	0	3	8	6
$f(x)$	3	0	3	-1	-1	2	4	6

In this case, the domain would be $\{-1, 4, 2, 1, 0, 3, 8, 6\}$ or, putting them in ascending order, $\{-1, 0, 1, 2, 3, 4, 6, 8\}$. (Putting the values in ascending order isn't strictly necessary, but generally makes the set easier to read.) The range would be $\{3, 0, 3, -1, -1, 2, 4, 6\}$. Note that some of these values appear more than once. This is entirely permissible for a function; while each value of x must be matched to a unique value of $f(x)$, the converse is not true. We don't need to list each value more than once, so eliminating duplicates, the range is $\{3, 0, -1, 2, 4, 6\}$, or, putting them in ascending order, $\{-1, 0, 2, 3, 4, 6\}$.

Note that by definition of a function, no input value can be matched to more than one output value. It is good to double-check to make sure that the data given follows this and is therefore actually a function.

Review Video: Domain and Range
Visit mometrix.com/academy and enter code: 778133

Review Video: Domain and Range of Quadratic Functions
Visit mometrix.com/academy and enter code: 331768

Writing a Function Rule Using a Table

If given a set of data, place the corresponding x- and y-values into a table and analyze the relationship between them. Consider what you can do to each x-value to obtain the corresponding y-value. Try adding or subtracting different numbers to and from x and then try multiplying or dividing different numbers to and from x. If none of these **operations** give you the y-value, try combining the operations. Once you find a rule that works for one pair, make sure to try it with each additional set of ordered pairs in the table. If the same operation or combination of operations satisfies each set of coordinates, then the table contains a function. The rule is then used to write the equation of the function in "$y = f(x)$" form.

DIRECT AND INVERSE VARIATIONS OF VARIABLES

Variables that vary directly are those that either both increase at the same rate or both decrease at the same rate. For example, in the functions $y = kx$ or $y = kx^n$, where k and n are positive, the value of y increases as the value of x increases and decreases as the value of x decreases.

Variables that vary inversely are those where one increases while the other decreases. For example, in the functions $y = \frac{k}{x}$ or $y = \frac{k}{x^n}$ where k and n are positive, the value of y increases as the value of x decreases and decreases as the value of x increases.

In both cases, k is the constant of variation.

PROPERTIES OF FUNCTIONS

There are many different ways to classify functions based on their structure or behavior. Important features of functions include:

- **End behavior**: the behavior of the function at extreme values ($f(x)$ as $x \to \pm\infty$)
- **y-intercept**: the value of the function at $f(0)$
- **Roots**: the values of x where the function equals zero ($f(x) = 0$)
- **Extrema**: minimum or maximum values of the function or where the function changes direction ($f(x) \geq k$ or $f(x) \leq k$)

CLASSIFICATION OF FUNCTIONS

An **invertible function** is defined as a function, $f(x)$, for which there is another function, $f^{-1}(x)$, such that $f^{-1}(f(x)) = x$. For example, if $f(x) = 3x - 2$ the inverse function, $f^{-1}(x)$, can be found:

$$x = 3\left(f^{-1}(x)\right) - 2$$
$$\frac{x+2}{3} = f^{-1}(x)$$

$$f^{-1}(f(x)) = \frac{3x - 2 + 2}{3} = \frac{3x}{3} = x$$

Note that $f^{-1}(x)$ is a valid function over all values of x.

In a **one-to-one function**, each value of x has exactly one value for y on the coordinate plane (this is the definition of a function) and each value of y has exactly one value for x. While the vertical line test will determine if a graph is that of a function, the horizontal line test will determine if a function is a one-to-one function. If a horizontal line drawn at any value of y intersects the graph in more than one place, the graph is not that of a one-to-one function. Do not make the mistake of using the horizontal line test exclusively in determining if a graph is that of a one-to-one function. A one-to-one function must pass both the vertical line test and the horizontal line test. As such, one-to-one functions are invertible functions.

A **many-to-one function** is a function whereby the relation is a function, but the inverse of the function is not a function. In other words, each element in the domain is mapped to one and only one element in the range. However, one or more elements in the range may be mapped to the same element in the domain. A graph of a many-to-one function would pass the vertical line test, but not the horizontal line test. This is why many-to-one functions are not invertible.

A **monotone function** is a function whose graph either constantly increases or constantly decreases. Examples include the functions $f(x) = x$, $f(x) = -x$, or $f(x) = x^3$.

An **even function** has a graph that is symmetric with respect to the y-axis and satisfies the equation $f(x) = f(-x)$. Examples include the functions $f(x) = x^2$ and $f(x) = ax^n$, where a is any real number and n is a positive even integer.

An **odd function** has a graph that is symmetric with respect to the origin and satisfies the equation $f(x) = -f(-x)$. Examples include the functions $f(x) = x^3$ and $f(x) = ax^n$, where a is any real number and n is a positive odd integer.

Review Video: Even and Odd Functions
Visit mometrix.com/academy and enter code: 278985

Constant functions are given by the equation $f(x) = b$, where b is a real number. There is no independent variable present in the equation, so the function has a constant value for all x. The graph of a constant function is a horizontal line of slope 0 that is positioned b units from the x-axis. If b is positive, the line is above the x-axis; if b is negative, the line is below the x-axis.

Identity functions are identified by the equation $f(x) = x$, where every value of the function is equal to its corresponding value of x. The only zero is the point (0,0). The graph is a line with a slope of 1.

In **linear functions**, the value of the function changes in direct proportion to x. The rate of change, represented by the slope on its graph, is constant throughout. The standard form of a linear equation is $ax + cy = d$, where a, c, and d are real numbers. As a function, this equation is commonly in the form $y = mx + b$ or $f(x) = mx + b$ where $m = -\frac{a}{c}$ and $b = \frac{d}{c}$. This is known as the slope-intercept form, because the coefficients give the slope of the graphed function (m) and its y-intercept (b). Solve the equation $mx + b = 0$ for x to get $x = -\frac{b}{m}$, which is the only zero of the function. The domain and range are both the set of all real numbers.

Review Video: Graphing Linear Functions
Visit mometrix.com/academy and enter code: 699478

Algebraic functions are those that exclusively use polynomials and roots. These would include polynomial functions, rational functions, square root functions, and all combinations of these functions, such as polynomials as the radicand. These combinations may be joined by addition, subtraction, multiplication, or division, but may not include variables as exponents.

Review Video: Common Functions
Visit mometrix.com/academy and enter code: 629798

Absolute Value Functions

An **absolute value function** is in the format $f(x) = |ax + b|$. Like other functions, the domain is the set of all real numbers. However, because absolute value indicates positive numbers, the range is limited to positive real numbers. To find the zero of an absolute value function, set the portion inside the absolute value sign equal to zero and solve for x. An absolute value function is also known as a piecewise function because it must be solved in pieces—one for if the value inside the absolute value sign is positive, and one for if the value is negative. The function can be expressed as:

$$f(x) = \begin{cases} ax + b \text{ if } ax + b \geq 0 \\ -(ax + b) \text{ if } ax + b < 0 \end{cases}$$

This will allow for an accurate statement of the range. The graph of an example absolute value function, $f(x) = |2x - 1|$, is below:

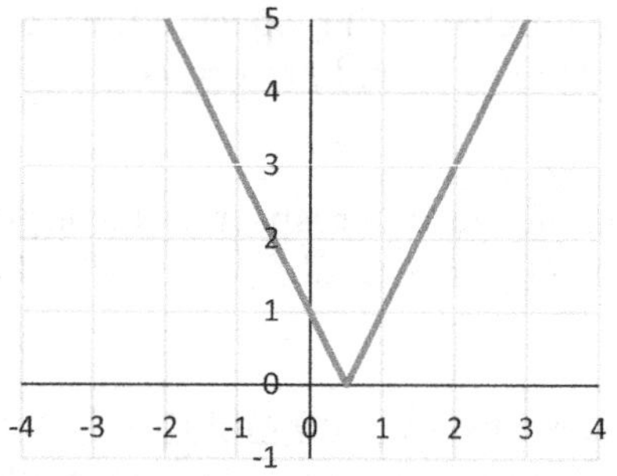

Piecewise Functions

A **piecewise function** is a function that has different definitions on two or more different intervals. The following, for instance, is one example of a piecewise-defined function:

$$f(x) = \begin{cases} x^2, & x < 0 \\ x, & 0 \leq x \leq 2 \\ (x-2)^2, & x > 2 \end{cases}$$

To graph this function, you would simply graph each part separately in the appropriate domain. The final graph would look like this:

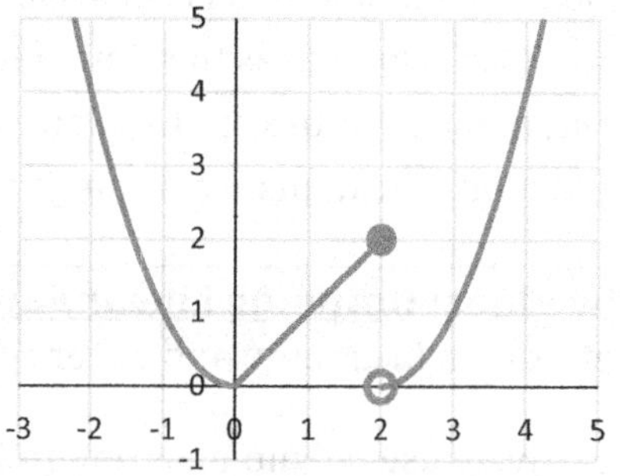

Note the filled and hollow dots at the discontinuity at $x = 2$. This is important to show which side of the graph that point corresponds to. Because $f(x) = x$ on the closed interval $0 \leq x \leq 2$, $f(2) = 2$. The point $(2, 2)$ is therefore marked with a filled circle, and the point (2,0), which is the endpoint of the rightmost $(x-2)^2$ part of the graph but *not actually part of the function*, is marked with a hollow dot to indicate this.

Review Video: Piecewise Functions
Visit mometrix.com/academy and enter code: 707921

Quadratic Functions

A **quadratic function** is a function in the form $y = ax^2 + bx + c$, where a does not equal 0. While a linear function forms a line, a quadratic function forms a **parabola**, which is a u-shaped figure that either opens upward or downward. A parabola that opens upward is said to be a **positive quadratic function,** and a parabola that opens downward is said to be a **negative quadratic function**. The shape of a parabola can differ, depending on the values of a, b, and c. All parabolas contain a **vertex**, which is the highest possible point, the **maximum**, or the lowest possible point, the **minimum**. This is the point where the graph begins moving in the opposite direction. A quadratic function can have zero, one, or two solutions, and therefore zero, one, or two x-intercepts. Recall that the x-intercepts are referred to as the zeros, or roots, of a function. A quadratic function will have only one y-intercept. Understanding the basic components of a quadratic function can give you an idea of the shape of its graph.

Example graph of a positive quadratic function, $x^2 + 2x - 3$:

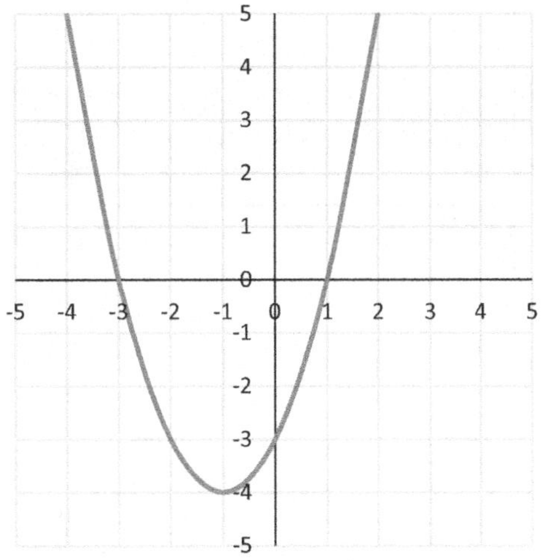

POLYNOMIAL FUNCTIONS

A **polynomial function** is a function with multiple terms and multiple powers of x, such as:

$$f(x) = a_n x^n + a_{n-1}x^{n-1} + a_{n-2}x^{n-2} + \cdots + a_1 x + a_0$$

where n is a non-negative integer that is the highest exponent in the polynomial and $a_n \neq 0$. The domain of a polynomial function is the set of all real numbers. If the greatest exponent in the polynomial is even, the polynomial is said to be of even degree and the range is the set of real numbers that satisfy the function. If the greatest exponent in the polynomial is odd, the polynomial is said to be odd and the range, like the domain, is the set of all real numbers.

RATIONAL FUNCTIONS

A **rational function** is a function that can be constructed as a ratio of two polynomial expressions: $f(x) = \frac{p(x)}{q(x)}$, where $p(x)$ and $q(x)$ are both polynomial expressions and $q(x) \neq 0$. The domain is the set of all real numbers, except any values for which $q(x) = 0$. The range is the set of real numbers that satisfies the function when the domain is applied. When you graph a rational function, you will have vertical asymptotes wherever $q(x) = 0$. If the polynomial in the numerator is of lesser degree than the polynomial in the denominator, the x-axis will also be a horizontal asymptote. If the numerator and denominator have equal degrees, there will be a horizontal asymptote not on the x-axis. If the degree of the numerator is exactly one greater than the degree of the denominator, the graph will have an oblique, or diagonal, asymptote. The asymptote will be along the line $y = \frac{p_n}{q_{n-1}}x + \frac{p_{n-1}}{q_{n-1}}$, where p_n and q_{n-1} are the coefficients of the highest degree terms in their respective polynomials.

SQUARE ROOT FUNCTIONS

A **square root function** is a function that contains a radical and is in the format $f(x) = \sqrt{ax + b}$. The domain is the set of all real numbers that yields a positive radicand or a radicand equal to zero. Because square root values are assumed to be positive unless otherwise identified, the range is all real numbers from zero to infinity. To find the zero of a square root function, set the radicand equal to zero and solve for x. The graph of a square root function is always to the right of the zero and always above the x-axis.

Example graph of a square root function, $f(x) = \sqrt{2x + 1}$:

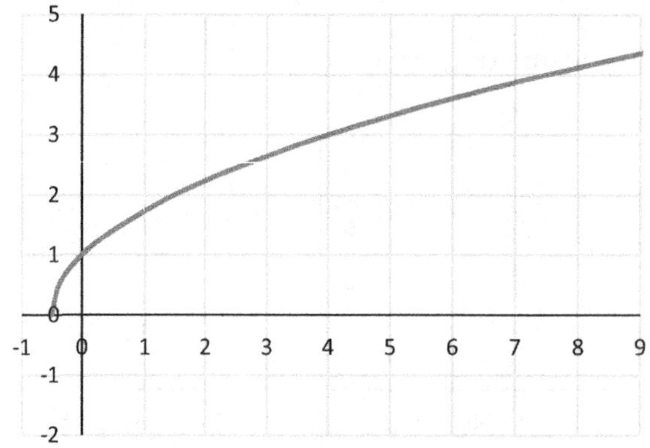

Reading

Transform passive reading into active learning! After immersing yourself in this chapter, put your comprehension to the test by taking a quiz. The insights you gained will stay with you longer this way. Scan the QR code to go directly to the chapter quiz interface for this study guide. If you're using a computer, simply visit the bonus page at **mometrix.com/bonus948/act** and click the Chapter Quizzes link.

Reading Overview

The 35-minute ACT reading test consists of four reading selections, followed by 10 questions each for a total of 40 questions. One of the four selections is drawn from the humanities, one from social studies, one from the natural sciences, and one from prose fiction.

In each of the passages, you will be asked a variety of questions requiring you to:

- determine main ideas
- locate and interpret significant details
- understand sequences of events
- make comparisons
- comprehend cause-effect relationships
- determine the meaning of context-dependent words,
- phrases, and statements
- draw generalizations
- analyze the author's or narrator's voice and method
- analyze claims and evidence in arguments
- integrate information from multiple texts

Some of these question types may require you to find and identify information directly presented in the text, whereas others may have you interpret or draw inferences that must be synthesized from the information given in the passage.

Key Ideas and Details

Main Ideas and Supporting Details

Identifying Topics and Main Ideas

One of the most important skills in reading comprehension is the identification of **topics** and **main ideas**. There is a subtle difference between these two features. The topic is the subject of a text (i.e., what the text is all about). The main idea, on the other hand, is the most important point being made by the author. The topic is usually expressed in a few words at the most while the main idea often needs a full sentence to be completely defined. As an example, a short passage might be written on the topic of penguins, and the main idea could be written as *Penguins are different from other birds in many ways.* In most nonfiction writing, the topic and the main idea will be **stated directly** and often appear in a sentence at the very beginning or end of the text. When being tested on an understanding of the author's topic, you may be able to skim the passage for the general idea by reading only the first sentence of each paragraph. A body paragraph's first sentence is often—but not always—the main **topic sentence** which gives you a summary of the content in the paragraph.

However, there are cases in which the reader must figure out an **unstated** topic or main idea. In these instances, you must read every sentence of the text and try to come up with an overarching idea that is supported by each of those sentences.

Note: The main idea should not be confused with the thesis statement. While the main idea gives a brief, general summary of a text, the thesis statement provides a **specific perspective** on an issue that the author supports with evidence.

Review Video: Topics and Main Ideas
Visit mometrix.com/academy and enter code: 407801

Supporting Details

Supporting details are smaller pieces of evidence that provide backing for the main point. In order to show that a main idea is correct or valid, an author must add details that prove their point. All texts contain details, but they are only classified as supporting details when they serve to reinforce some larger point. Supporting details are most commonly found in informative and persuasive texts. In some cases, they will be clearly indicated with terms like *for example* or *for instance*, or they will be enumerated with terms like *first, second*, and *last*. However, you need to be prepared for texts that do not contain those indicators. As a reader, you should consider whether the author's supporting details really back up his or her main point. Details can be factual and correct, yet they may not be **relevant** to the author's point. Conversely, details can be relevant, but be ineffective because they are based on opinion or assertions that cannot be proven.

Review Video: Supporting Details
Visit mometrix.com/academy and enter code: 396297

Common Organizations of Texts

Organization of the Text

The way a text is organized can help readers understand the author's intent and his or her conclusions. There are various ways to organize a text, and each one has a purpose and use. Usually, authors will organize information logically in a passage so the reader can follow and locate the information within the text. However, since not all passages are written with the same logical structure, you need to be familiar with several different types of passage structure.

Review Video: Organizational Methods to Structure Text
Visit mometrix.com/academy and enter code: 606263

Review Video: Sequence of Events in a Story
Visit mometrix.com/academy and enter code: 807512

Chronological

When using **chronological** order, the author presents information in the order that it happened. For example, biographies are typically written in chronological order. The subject's birth and childhood are presented first, followed by their adult life, and lastly the events leading up to the person's death.

Cause and Effect

One of the most common text structures is **cause and effect**. A **cause** is an act or event that makes something happen, and an **effect** is the thing that happens as a result of the cause. A cause-and-effect relationship is not always explicit, but there are some terms in English that signal causes, such as *since, because*, and *due to*. Furthermore, terms that signal effects include *consequently, therefore, this leads to*. As an example, consider the sentence *Because the sky was clear, Ron did not bring an umbrella*. The cause is the clear sky, and the effect is that Ron did not bring an umbrella. However, readers may find that sometimes the cause-and-effect relationship will not be clearly noted. For instance, the sentence *He was late and missed the meeting* does not contain any signaling words, but the sentence still contains a cause (he was late) and an effect (he missed the meeting).

Review Video: Cause and Effect
Visit mometrix.com/academy and enter code: 868099

Review Video: Rhetorical Strategy of Cause and Effect Analysis
Visit mometrix.com/academy and enter code: 725944

Multiple Effects

Be aware of the possibility for a single cause to have **multiple effects.** (e.g., *Single cause*: Because you left your homework on the table, your dog engulfed the assignment. *Multiple effects*: As a result, you receive a failing grade, your parents do not allow you to go out with your friends, you miss out on the new movie, and one of your classmates spoils it for you before you have another chance to watch it).

Multiple Causes

Also, there is the possibility for a single effect to have **multiple causes.** (e.g., *Single effect*: Alan has a fever. *Multiple causes*: An unexpected cold front came through the area, and Alan forgot to take his multi-vitamin to avoid getting sick.) Additionally, an effect can in turn be the cause of another effect, in what is known as a cause-and-effect chain. (e.g., As a result of her disdain for procrastination, Lynn prepared for her exam. This led to her passing her test with high marks. Hence, her resume was accepted and her application was approved.)

Cause and Effect in Persuasive Essays

Persuasive essays, in which an author tries to make a convincing argument and change the minds of readers, usually include cause-and-effect relationships. However, these relationships should not always be taken at face value. Frequently, an author will assume a cause or take an effect for granted. To read a persuasive essay effectively, readers need to judge the cause-and-effect relationships that the author is presenting. For instance, imagine an author wrote the following: *The parking deck has been unprofitable because people would prefer to ride their bikes.* The relationship is clear: the cause is that people prefer to ride their bikes, and the effect is that the parking deck has been unprofitable. However, readers should consider whether this argument is conclusive. Perhaps there are other reasons for the failure of the parking deck: a down economy, excessive fees, etc. Too often, authors present causal relationships as if they are fact rather than opinion. Readers should be on the alert for these dubious claims.

Problem-Solution

Some nonfiction texts are organized to **present a problem** followed by a solution. For this type of text, the problem is often explained before the solution is offered. In some cases, as when the problem is well known, the solution may be introduced briefly at the beginning. Other passages may focus on the solution, and the problem will be referenced only occasionally. Some texts will outline multiple solutions to a problem, leaving readers to choose among them. If the author has an interest or an allegiance to one solution, he or she may fail to mention or describe accurately some of the other solutions. Readers should be careful of the author's agenda when reading a problem-solution text. Only by understanding the author's perspective and interests can one develop a proper judgment of the proposed solution.

Compare and Contrast

Many texts follow the **compare-and-contrast** model in which the similarities and differences between two ideas or things are explored. Analysis of the similarities between ideas is called **comparison**. In an ideal comparison, the author places ideas or things in an equivalent structure, i.e., the author presents the ideas in the same way. If an author wants to show the similarities between cricket and baseball, then he or she may do so by summarizing the equipment and rules for each game. Be mindful of the similarities as they appear in the passage and take note of any differences that are mentioned. Often, these small differences will only reinforce the more general similarity.

Review Video: Compare and Contrast
Visit mometrix.com/academy and enter code: 798319

Thinking critically about ideas and conclusions can seem like a daunting task. One way to ease this task is to understand the basic elements of ideas and writing techniques. Looking at the ways different ideas relate to each other can be a good way for readers to begin their analysis. For instance, sometimes authors will write about two ideas that are in opposition to each other. Or, one author will provide his or her ideas on a topic, and another author may respond in opposition. The analysis of these opposing ideas is known as **contrast**. Contrast is often marred by the author's obvious partiality to one of the ideas. A discerning reader will be put off by an author who does not engage in a fair fight. In an analysis of opposing ideas, both ideas should be presented in clear and reasonable terms. If the author does prefer a side, you need to read carefully to determine the areas where the author shows or avoids this preference. In an analysis of opposing ideas, you should proceed through the passage by marking the major differences point by point with an eye that is looking for an explanation of each side's view. For instance, in an analysis of capitalism and communism, there is an importance in outlining each side's view on labor, markets, prices, personal responsibility, etc. Additionally, as you read through the passages, you should note whether the opposing views present each side in a similar manner.

SEQUENCE

Readers must be able to identify a text's **sequence**, or the order in which things happen. Often, when the sequence is very important to the author, the text is indicated with signal words like *first, then, next,* and *last*. However, a sequence can be merely implied and must be noted by the reader. Consider the sentence *He walked through the garden and gave water and fertilizer to the plants.* Clearly, the man did not walk through the garden before he collected water and fertilizer for the plants. So, the implied sequence is that he first collected water, then he collected fertilizer, next he walked through the garden, and last he gave water or fertilizer as necessary to the plants. Texts do not always proceed in an orderly sequence from first to last. Sometimes they begin at the end and start over at the beginning. As a reader, you can enhance your understanding of the passage by taking brief notes to clarify the sequence.

Review Video: Sequence
Visit mometrix.com/academy and enter code: 489027

MAKING AND EVALUATING PREDICTIONS

MAKING PREDICTIONS

When we read literature, **making predictions** about what will happen in the writing reinforces our purpose for reading and prepares us mentally. A **prediction** is a guess about what will happen next. Readers constantly make predictions based on what they have read and what they already know. We can make predictions before we begin reading and during our reading. Consider the following sentence: *Staring at the computer screen in shock, Kim blindly reached over for the brimming glass of water on the shelf to her side.* The sentence suggests that Kim is distracted, and that she is not looking at the glass that she is going to pick up. So, a reader might predict that Kim is going to knock over the glass. Of course, not every prediction will be accurate: perhaps Kim will pick the glass up cleanly. Nevertheless, the author has certainly created the expectation that the water might be spilled.

As we read on, we can test the accuracy of our predictions, revise them in light of additional reading, and confirm or refute our predictions. Predictions are always subject to revision as the reader acquires more information. A reader can make predictions by observing the title and illustrations; noting the structure, characters, and subject; drawing on existing knowledge relative to the subject; and asking "why" and "who" questions. Connecting reading to what we already know enables us to learn new information and construct meaning. For example, before third-graders read a book about Johnny Appleseed, they may start a KWL chart—a list of what they *Know*, what they *Want* to know or learn, and what they have *Learned* after reading. Activating existing background knowledge and thinking about the text before reading improves comprehension.

Review Video: Predictive Reading
Visit mometrix.com/academy and enter code: 437248

Test-taking tip: To respond to questions requiring future predictions, your answers should be based on evidence of past or present behavior and events.

EVALUATING PREDICTIONS

When making predictions, readers should be able to explain how they developed their prediction. One way readers can defend their thought process is by citing textual evidence. Textual evidence to evaluate reader predictions about literature includes specific synopses of the work, paraphrases of the work or parts of it, and direct quotations from the work. These references to the text must support the prediction by indicating, clearly or unclearly, what will happen later in the story. A text may provide these indications through literary devices such as foreshadowing. Foreshadowing is anything in a text that gives the reader a hint about what is to come by emphasizing the likelihood of an event or development. Foreshadowing can occur through descriptions, exposition, and dialogue. Foreshadowing in dialogue usually occurs when a character gives a warning or expresses a strong feeling that a certain event will occur. Foreshadowing can also occur through irony. However, unlike other forms of foreshadowing, the events that seem the most likely are the opposite of what actually happens. Instances of foreshadowing and irony can be summarized, paraphrased, or quoted to defend a reader's prediction.

Review Video: Textual Evidence for Predictions
Visit mometrix.com/academy and enter code: 261070

MAKING INFERENCES AND DRAWING CONCLUSIONS

Inferences are logical conclusions that readers make based on their observations and previous knowledge. An inference is based on both what is found in a passage or a story and what is known from personal experience. For instance, a story may say that a character is frightened and can hear howling in the distance. Based on both what is in the text and personal knowledge, it is a logical conclusion that the character is frightened because he hears the sound of wolves. A good inference is supported by the information in a passage.

IMPLICIT AND EXPLICIT INFORMATION

By inferring, readers construct meanings from text that are personally relevant. By combining their own schemas or concepts and their background information pertinent to the text with what they read, readers interpret it according to both what the author has conveyed and their own unique perspectives. Inferences are different from **explicit information**, which is clearly stated in a passage. Authors do not always explicitly spell out every meaning in what they write; many meanings are implicit. Through inference, readers can comprehend implied meanings in the text, and also derive personal significance from it, making the text meaningful and memorable to them. Inference is a natural process in everyday life. When readers infer, they can draw conclusions about what the author is saying, predict what may reasonably follow, amend these predictions as they continue to read, interpret the import of themes, and analyze the characters' feelings and motivations through their actions.

EXAMPLE OF DRAWING CONCLUSIONS FROM INFERENCES

Read the excerpt and decide why Jana finally relaxed.

> Jana loved her job, but the work was very demanding. She had trouble relaxing. She called a friend, but she still thought about work. She ordered a pizza, but eating it did not help. Then,

her kitten jumped on her lap and began to purr. Jana leaned back and began to hum a little tune. She felt better.

You can draw the conclusion that Jana relaxed because her kitten jumped on her lap. The kitten purred, and Jana leaned back and hummed a tune. Then she felt better. The excerpt does not explicitly say that this is the reason why she was able to relax. The text leaves the matter unclear, but the reader can infer or make a "best guess" that this is the reason she is relaxing. This is a logical conclusion based on the information in the passage. It is the best conclusion a reader can make based on the information he or she has read. Inferences are based on the information in a passage, but they are not directly stated in the passage.

Test-taking tip: While being tested on your ability to make correct inferences, you must look for **contextual clues**. An answer can be true, but not the best or most correct answer. The contextual clues will help you find the answer that is the **best answer** out of the given choices. Be careful in your reading to understand the context in which a phrase is stated. When asked for the implied meaning of a statement made in the passage, you should immediately locate the statement and read the **context** in which the statement was made. Also, look for an answer choice that has a similar phrase to the statement in question.

Review Video: Inference
Visit mometrix.com/academy and enter code: 379203

Review Video: How to Support a Conclusion
Visit mometrix.com/academy and enter code: 281653

Reading Informational Texts

Language Use

Literal and Figurative Language

As in fictional literature, informational text also uses both **literal language**, which means just what it says, and **figurative language**, which imparts more than literal meaning. For example, an informational text author might use a simile or direct comparison, such as writing that a racehorse "ran like the wind." Informational text authors also use metaphors or implied comparisons, such as "the cloud of the Great Depression." Imagery may also appear in informational texts to increase the reader's understanding of ideas and concepts discussed in the text.

Explicit and Implicit Information

When informational text states something explicitly, the reader is told by the author exactly what is meant, which can include the author's interpretation or perspective of events. For example, a professor writes, "I have seen students go into an absolute panic just because they weren't able to complete the exam in the time they were allotted." This explicitly tells the reader that the students were afraid, and by using the words "just because," the writer indicates their fear was exaggerated out of proportion relative to what happened. However, another professor writes, "I have had students come to me, their faces drained of all color, saying 'We weren't able to finish the exam.'" This is an example of implicit meaning: the second writer did not state explicitly that the students were panicked. Instead, he wrote a description of their faces being "drained of all color." From this description, the reader can infer that the students were so frightened that their faces paled.

Review Video: Explicit and Implicit Information
Visit mometrix.com/academy and enter code: 735771

Making Inferences About Informational Text

With informational text, reader comprehension depends not only on recalling important statements and details, but also on reader inferences based on examples and details. Readers add information from the text to what they already know to draw inferences about the text. These inferences help the readers to fill in the information that the text does not explicitly state, enabling them to understand the text better. When reading a nonfictional autobiography or biography, for example, the most appropriate inferences might concern the events in the book, the actions of the subject of the autobiography or biography, and the message the author means to convey. When reading a nonfictional expository (informational) text, the reader would best draw inferences about problems and their solutions, and causes and their effects. When reading a nonfictional persuasive text, the reader will want to infer ideas supporting the author's message and intent.

Structures or Organizational Patterns in Informational Texts

Informational text can be **descriptive**, appealing to the five senses and answering the questions what, who, when, where, and why. Another method of structuring informational text is sequence and order. **Chronological** texts relate events in the sequence that they occurred, from start to finish, while how-to texts organize information into a series of instructions in the sequence in which the steps should be followed. **Comparison-contrast** structures of informational text describe various ideas to their readers by pointing out how things or ideas are similar and how they are different. **Cause and effect** structures of informational text describe events that occurred and identify the causes or reasons that those events occurred. **Problem and solution** structures of informational texts introduce and describe problems and offer one or more solutions for each problem described.

Determining an Informational Author's Purpose

Informational authors' purposes are why they write texts. Readers must determine authors' motivations and goals. Readers gain greater insight into a text by considering the author's motivation. This develops critical reading skills. Readers perceive writing as a person's voice, not simply printed words. Uncovering author motivations and purposes empowers readers to know what to expect from the text, read for relevant details, evaluate authors and their work critically, and respond effectively to the motivations and persuasions of the text. The main idea of a text is what the reader is supposed to understand from reading it; the purpose of the text is why the author has written it and what the author wants readers to do with its information. Authors state some purposes clearly, while other purposes may be unstated but equally significant. When stated purposes contradict other parts of a text, the author may have a hidden agenda. Readers can better evaluate a text's effectiveness, whether they agree or disagree with it, and why they agree or disagree through identifying unstated author purposes.

Identifying Author's Point of View or Purpose

In some informational texts, readers find it easy to identify the author's point of view and purpose, such as when the author explicitly states his or her position and reason for writing. But other texts are more difficult, either because of the content or because the authors give neutral or balanced viewpoints. This is particularly true in scientific texts, in which authors may state the purpose of their research in the report, but never state their point of view except by interpreting evidence or data.

To analyze text and identify point of view or purpose, readers should ask themselves the following four questions:

1. With what main point or idea does this author want to persuade readers to agree?
2. How does this author's word choice affect the way that readers consider this subject?
3. How do this author's choices of examples and facts affect the way that readers consider this subject?
4. What is it that this author wants to accomplish by writing this text?

Review Video: Understanding the Author's Intent
Visit mometrix.com/academy and enter code: 511819

Review Video: Author's Position
Visit mometrix.com/academy and enter code: 827954

Evaluating Arguments Made by Informational Text Writers

When evaluating an informational text, the first step is to identify the argument's conclusion. Then identify the author's premises that support the conclusion. Try to paraphrase premises for clarification and make the conclusion and premises fit. List all premises first, sequentially numbered, then finish with the conclusion. Identify any premises or assumptions not stated by the author but required for the stated premises to support the conclusion. Read word assumptions sympathetically, as the author might. Evaluate whether premises reasonably support the conclusion. For inductive reasoning, the reader should ask if the premises are true, if they support the conclusion, and if so, how strongly. For deductive reasoning, the reader should ask if the argument is valid or invalid. If all premises are true, then the argument is valid unless the conclusion can be false. If it can, then the argument is invalid. An invalid argument can be made valid through alterations such as the addition of needed premises.

Use of Rhetoric in Informational Texts

There are many ways authors can support their claims, arguments, beliefs, ideas, and reasons for writing in informational texts. For example, authors can appeal to readers' sense of **logic** by communicating their reasoning through a carefully sequenced series of logical steps to help "prove" the points made. Authors can appeal to readers' **emotions** by using descriptions and words that evoke feelings of sympathy, sadness, anger, righteous indignation, hope, happiness, or any other emotion to reinforce what they express and share with their audience. Authors may appeal to the **moral** or **ethical values** of readers by using words and descriptions that can convince readers that something is right or wrong. By relating personal anecdotes, authors can supply readers with more accessible, realistic examples of points they make, as well as appealing to their emotions. They can provide supporting evidence by reporting case studies. They can also illustrate their points by making analogies to which readers can better relate.

Organizational Features in Texts

Text Features in Informational Texts

- The **title of a text** gives readers some idea of its content.
- The **table of contents** is a list near the beginning of a text, showing the book's sections and chapters and their coinciding page numbers. This gives readers an overview of the whole text and helps them find specific chapters easily.
- An **appendix**, at the back of the book or document, includes important information that is not present in the main text.
- Also at the back, an **index** lists the book's important topics alphabetically with their page numbers to help readers find them easily.
- **Glossaries**, usually found at the backs of books, list technical terms alphabetically with their definitions to aid vocabulary learning and comprehension. Boldface print is used to emphasize certain words, often identifying words included in the text's glossary where readers can look up their definitions.
- **Headings** separate sections of text and show the topic of each.
- **Subheadings** divide subject headings into smaller, more specific categories to help readers organize information.
- **Footnotes**, at the bottom of the page, give readers more information, such as citations or links.
- **Bullet points** list items separately, making facts and ideas easier to see and understand.
- A **sidebar** is a box of information to one side of the main text giving additional information, often on a more focused or in-depth example of a topic.

Visual Features in Texts

- **Illustrations** and **photographs** are pictures that visually emphasize important points in text.
- The **captions** below the illustrations explain what those images show.
- **Charts** and **tables** are visual forms of information that make something easier to understand quickly.
- **Diagrams** are drawings that show relationships or explain a process.

- **Graphs** visually show the relationships among multiple sets of information plotted along vertical and horizontal axes.
- **Maps** show geographical information visually to help readers understand the relative locations of places covered in the text.
- **Timelines** are visual graphics that show historical events in chronological order to help readers see their sequence.

Review Video: Informational Text
Visit mometrix.com/academy and enter code: 924964

TECHNICAL LANGUAGE

TECHNICAL LANGUAGE

Technical language is more impersonal than literary and vernacular language. Passive voice makes the tone impersonal. For example, instead of writing, "We found this a central component of protein metabolism," scientists write, "This was found a central component of protein metabolism." While science professors have traditionally instructed students to avoid active voice because it leads to first-person ("I" and "we") usage, science editors today find passive voice dull and weak. Many journal articles combine both. Tone in technical science writing should be detached, concise, and professional. While one may normally write, "This chemical has to be available for proteins to be digested," professionals write technically, "The presence of this chemical is required for the enzyme to break the covalent bonds of proteins." The use of technical language appeals to both technical and non-technical audiences by displaying the author or speaker's understanding of the subject and suggesting their credibility regarding the message they are communicating.

TECHNICAL MATERIAL FOR NON-TECHNICAL READERS

Writing about **technical subjects** for **non-technical readers** differs from writing for colleagues because authors place more importance on delivering a critical message than on imparting the maximum technical content possible. Technical authors also must assume that non-technical audiences do not have the expertise to comprehend extremely scientific or technical messages, concepts, and terminology. They must resist the temptation to impress audiences with their scientific knowledge and expertise and remember that their primary purpose is to communicate a message that non-technical readers will understand, feel, and respond to. Non-technical and technical styles include similarities. Both should formally cite any references or other authors' work utilized in the text. Both must follow intellectual property and copyright regulations. This includes the author's protecting his or her own rights, or a public domain statement, as he or she chooses.

Review Video: Technical Passages
Visit mometrix.com/academy and enter code: 478923

NON-TECHNICAL AUDIENCES

Writers of technical or scientific material may need to write for many non-technical audiences. Some readers have no technical or scientific background, and those who do may not be in the same field as the authors. Government and corporate policymakers and budget managers need technical information they can understand for decision-making. Citizens affected by technology or science are a different audience. Non-governmental organizations can encompass many of the preceding groups. Elementary and secondary school programs also need non-technical language for presenting technical subject matter. Additionally, technical authors will need to use non-technical language when collecting consumer responses to surveys, presenting scientific or para-scientific material to the public, writing about the history of science, and writing about science and technology in developing countries.

USE OF EVERYDAY LANGUAGE

Authors of technical information sometimes must write using non-technical language that readers outside their disciplinary fields can comprehend. They should use not only non-technical terms, but also normal, everyday language to accommodate readers whose native language is different than the language the text is written in. For example, instead of writing that "eustatic changes like thermal expansion are causing hazardous conditions in the littoral zone," an author would do better to write that "a rising sea level is threatening the coast." When technical terms cannot be avoided, authors should also define or explain them using non-technical language. Although authors must cite references and acknowledge their use of others' work, they should avoid the kinds of references or citations that they would use in scientific journals—unless they reinforce author messages. They should not use endnotes, footnotes, or any other complicated referential techniques because non-technical journal publishers usually do not accept them. Including high-resolution illustrations, photos, maps, or satellite images and incorporating multimedia into digital publications will enhance non-technical writing about technical subjects. Technical authors may publish using non-technical language in e-journals, trade journals, specialty newsletters, and daily newspapers.

Types of Technical Writing

Types of Printed Communication

Memo

A memo (short for *memorandum*) is a common form of written communication. There is a standard format for these documents. It is typical for there to be a **heading** at the top indicating the author, date, and recipient. In some cases, this heading will also include the author's title and the name of his or her institution. Below this information will be the **body** of the memo. These documents are typically written by and for members of the same organization. They usually contain a plan of action, a request for information on a specific topic, or a response to such a request. Memos are considered to be official documents, so they are usually written in a **formal** style. Many memos are organized with numbers or bullet points, which make it easier for the reader to identify key ideas.

Posted Announcement

People post **announcements** for all sorts of occasions. Many people are familiar with notices for lost pets, yard sales, and landscaping services. In order to be effective, these announcements need to *contain all of the information* the reader requires to act on the message. For instance, a lost pet announcement needs to include a good description of the animal and a contact number for the owner. A yard sale notice should include the address, date, and hours of the sale, as well as a brief description of the products that will be available there. When composing an announcement, it is important to consider the perspective of the **audience**—what will they need to know in order to respond to the message? Although a posted announcement can have color and decoration to attract the eye of the passerby, it must also convey the necessary information clearly.

Classified Advertisement

Classified advertisements, or **ads**, are used to sell or buy goods, to attract business, to make romantic connections, and to do countless other things. They are an inexpensive, and sometimes free, way to make a brief **pitch**. Classified ads used to be found only in newspapers or special advertising circulars, but there are now online listings as well. The style of these ads has remained basically the same. An ad usually begins with a word or phrase indicating what is being **sold** or **sought**. Then, the listing will give a brief **description** of the product or service. Because space is limited and costly in newspapers, classified ads there will often contain abbreviations for common attributes. For instance, two common abbreviations are *bk* for *black*, and *obo* for *or best offer*. Classified ads will then usually conclude by listing the **price** (or the amount the seeker is willing to pay), followed by **contact information** like a telephone number or email address.

Scale Readings of Standard Measurement Instruments

The scales used on **standard measurement instruments** are fairly easy to read with a little practice. Take the **ruler** as an example. A typical ruler has different units along each long edge. One side measures inches, and the other measures centimeters. The units are specified close to the zero reading for the ruler. Note that the ruler does not begin measuring from its outermost edge. The zero reading is a black line a tiny distance inside of the edge. On the inches side, each inch is indicated with a long black line and a number. Each half-inch is noted with a slightly shorter line. Quarter-inches are noted with still shorter lines, eighth-inches are noted with even shorter lines, and sixteenth-inches are noted with the shortest lines of all. On the centimeter side, the second-largest black lines indicate half-centimeters, and the smaller lines indicate tenths of centimeters, otherwise known as millimeters.

Visual Information in Informational Texts

Charts, Graphs, and Visuals

Pie Chart

A pie chart, also known as a circle graph, is useful for depicting how a single unit or category is divided. The standard pie chart is a circle with designated wedges. Each wedge is **proportional** in size to a part of the whole. For instance, consider Shawna, a student at City College, who uses a pie chart to represent her budget. If she spends half of her money on rent, then the pie chart will represent that amount with a line through the center of the pie. If she spends a quarter of her money on food, there will be a line extending from the edge of the circle to the center at a right angle to the line depicting rent. This illustration would make it clear that the student spends twice the amount of money on rent as she does on food.

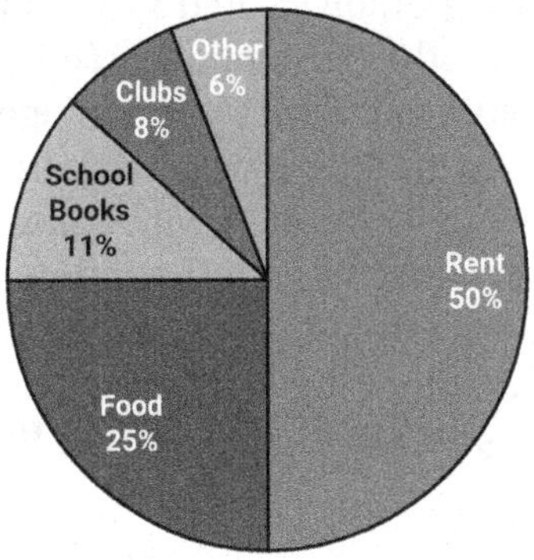

A pie chart is effective at showing how a single entity is divided into parts. They are not effective at demonstrating the relationships between parts of different wholes. For example, an unhelpful use of a pie chart would be to compare the respective amounts of state and federal spending devoted to infrastructure since these values are only meaningful in the context of the entire budget.

Bar Graph

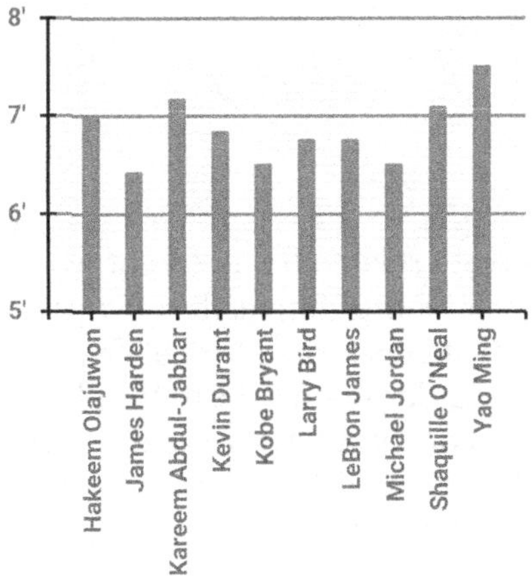

The bar graph is one of the most common visual representations of information. **Bar graphs** are used to illustrate sets of numerical **data**. The graph has a vertical axis (along which numbers are listed) and a horizontal axis (along which categories, words, or some other indicators are placed). One example of a bar graph is a depiction of the respective heights of famous basketball players: the vertical axis would contain numbers ranging from five to eight feet, and the horizontal axis would contain the names of the players. The length of the bar above the player's name would illustrate his height, and the top of the bar would stop perpendicular to the height listed along the left side. In this representation, one would see that Yao Ming is taller than Michael Jordan because Yao's bar would be higher.

LINE GRAPH

A line graph is a type of graph that is typically used for measuring trends over time. The graph is set up along a vertical and a horizontal **axis**. The variables being measured are listed along the left side and the bottom side of the axes. Points are then plotted along the graph as they correspond with their values for each variable. For instance, consider a line graph measuring a person's income for each month of the year. If the person earned $1500 in January, there should be a point directly above January (perpendicular to the horizontal axis) and directly to the right of $1500 (perpendicular to the vertical axis). Once all of the lines are plotted, they are connected with a line from left to right. This line provides a nice visual illustration of the general **trends** of the data, if they exist. For instance, using the earlier example, if the line sloped up, then one would see that the person's income had increased over the course of the year.

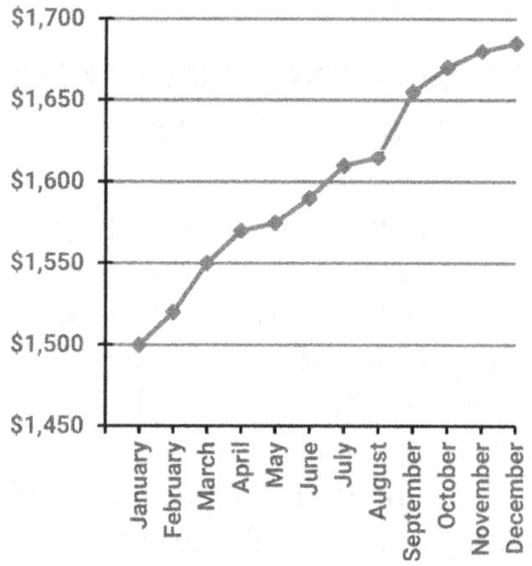

PICTOGRAPHS

A **pictograph** is a graph, generally in the horizontal orientation, that uses pictures or symbols to represent the data. Each pictograph must have a key that defines the picture or symbol and gives the quantity each picture or symbol represents. Pictures or symbols on a pictograph are not always shown as whole elements. In this case, the fraction of the picture or symbol shown represents the same fraction of the quantity a whole picture or symbol stands for.

Review Video: Pictographs
Visit mometrix.com/academy and enter code: 147860

Craft and Structure

WORD ROOTS AND PREFIXES AND SUFFIXES

AFFIXES

Affixes in the English language are morphemes that are added to words to create related but different words. Derivational affixes form new words based on and related to the original words. For example, the affix *-ness* added to the end of the adjective *happy* forms the noun *happiness.* Inflectional affixes form different grammatical versions of words. For example, the plural affix *-s* changes the singular noun *book* to the plural noun *books*, and the past tense affix *-ed* changes the present tense verb *look* to the past tense *looked.* Prefixes are affixes placed in front of words. For example, *heat* means to make hot; *preheat* means to heat in advance. Suffixes are affixes placed at the ends of words. The *happiness* example above contains the suffix *-ness.* Circumfixes add parts both before and after words, such as how *light* becomes *enlighten* with the prefix *en-* and the suffix *-en.* Interfixes create compound words via central affixes: *speed* and *meter* become *speedometer* via the interfix *-o-*.

Review Video: Affixes
Visit mometrix.com/academy and enter code: 782422

WORD ROOTS, PREFIXES, AND SUFFIXES TO HELP DETERMINE MEANINGS OF WORDS

Many English words were formed from combining multiple sources. For example, the Latin *habēre* means "to have," and the prefixes *in-* and *im-* mean a lack or prevention of something, as in *insufficient* and *imperfect.* Latin combined *in-* with *habēre* to form *inhibēre,* whose past participle was *inhibitus.* This is the origin of the

English word *inhibit,* meaning to prevent from having. Hence by knowing the meanings of both the prefix and the root, one can decipher the word meaning. In Greek, the root *enkephalo-* refers to the brain. Many medical terms are based on this root, such as encephalitis and hydrocephalus. Understanding the prefix and suffix meanings (*-itis* means inflammation; *hydro-* means water) allows a person to deduce that encephalitis refers to brain inflammation and hydrocephalus refers to water (or other fluid) in the brain.

Review Video: Determining Word Meanings
Visit mometrix.com/academy and enter code: 894894

PREFIXES

Knowing common prefixes is helpful for all readers as they try to determining meanings or definitions of unfamiliar words. For example, a common word used when cooking is *preheat.* Knowing that *pre-* means in advance can also inform them that *presume* means to assume in advance, that *prejudice* means advance judgment, and that this understanding can be applied to many other words beginning with *pre-*. Knowing that the prefix *dis-* indicates opposition informs the meanings of words like *disbar, disagree, disestablish,* and many more. Knowing *dys-* means bad, impaired, abnormal, or difficult informs *dyslogistic, dysfunctional, dysphagia,* and *dysplasia.*

SUFFIXES

In English, certain suffixes generally indicate both that a word is a noun, and that the noun represents a state of being or quality. For example, *-ness* is commonly used to change an adjective into its noun form, as with *happy* and *happiness, nice* and *niceness,* and so on. The suffix *–tion* is commonly used to transform a verb into its noun form, as with *converse* and *conversation or move* and *motion*. Thus, if readers are unfamiliar with the second form of a word, knowing the meaning of the transforming suffix can help them determine meaning.

PREFIXES FOR NUMBERS

Prefix	Definition	Examples
bi-	two	bisect, biennial
mono-	one, single	monogamy, monologue
poly-	many	polymorphous, polygamous
semi-	half, partly	semicircle, semicolon
uni-	one	uniform, unity

Prefixes for Time, Direction, and Space

Prefix	Definition	Examples
a-	in, on, of, up, to	abed, afoot
ab-	from, away, off	abdicate, abjure
ad-	to, toward	advance, adventure
ante-	before, previous	antecedent, antedate
anti-	against, opposing	antipathy, antidote
cata-	down, away, thoroughly	catastrophe, cataclysm
circum-	around	circumspect, circumference
com-	with, together, very	commotion, complicate
contra-	against, opposing	contradict, contravene
de-	from	depart
dia-	through, across, apart	diameter, diagnose
dis-	away, off, down, not	dissent, disappear
epi-	upon	epilogue
ex-	out	extract, excerpt
hypo-	under, beneath	hypodermic, hypothesis
inter-	among, between	intercede, interrupt
intra-	within	intramural, intrastate
ob-	against, opposing	objection
per-	through	perceive, permit
peri-	around	periscope, perimeter
post-	after, following	postpone, postscript
pre-	before, previous	prevent, preclude
pro-	forward, in place of	propel, pronoun
retro-	back, backward	retrospect, retrograde
sub-	under, beneath	subjugate, substitute
super-	above, extra	supersede, supernumerary
trans-	across, beyond, over	transact, transport
ultra-	beyond, excessively	ultramodern, ultrasonic

Negative Prefixes

Prefix	Definition	Examples
a-	without, lacking	atheist, agnostic
in-	not, opposing	incapable, ineligible
non-	not	nonentity, nonsense
un-	not, reverse of	unhappy, unlock

Extra Prefixes

Prefix	Definition	Examples
for-	away, off, from	forget, forswear
fore-	previous	foretell, forefathers
homo-	same, equal	homogenized, homonym
hyper-	excessive, over	hypercritical, hypertension
in-	in, into	intrude, invade
mal-	bad, poorly, not	malfunction, malpractice
mis-	bad, poorly, not	misspell, misfire
neo-	new	Neolithic, neoconservative
omni-	all, everywhere	omniscient, omnivore
ortho-	right, straight	orthogonal, orthodox
over-	above	overbearing, oversight
pan-	all, entire	panorama, pandemonium
para-	beside, beyond	parallel, paradox
re-	backward, again	revoke, recur
sym-	with, together	sympathy, symphony

Below is a list of common suffixes and their meanings:

Adjective Suffixes

Suffix	Definition	Examples
-able (-ible)	capable of being	toler*able*, ed*ible*
-esque	in the style of, like	picturesque, grotesque
-ful	filled with, marked by	thankful, zestful
-ific	make, cause	terrific, beatific
-ish	suggesting, like	churlish, childish
-less	lacking, without	hopeless, countless
-ous	marked by, given to	religious, riotous

Noun Suffixes

Suffix	Definition	Examples
-acy	state, condition	accuracy, privacy
-ance	act, condition, fact	acceptance, vigilance
-ard	one that does excessively	drunkard, sluggard
-ation	action, state, result	occupation, starvation
-dom	state, rank, condition	serfdom, wisdom
-er (-or)	office, action	teach*er*, elevat*or*, hon*or*
-ess	feminine	waitress, duchess
-hood	state, condition	manhood, statehood
-ion	action, result, state	union, fusion
-ism	act, manner, doctrine	barbarism, socialism
-ist	worker, follower	monopolist, socialist
-ity (-ty)	state, quality, condition	acid*ity*, civil*ity*, twen*ty*
-ment	result, action	Refreshment
-ness	quality, state	greatness, tallness
-ship	position	internship, statesmanship
-sion (-tion)	state, result	rev*ision*, expedi*tion*
-th	act, state, quality	warmth, width
-tude	quality, state, result	magnitude, fortitude

Verb Suffixes

Suffix	Definition	Examples
-ate	having, showing	separate, desolate
-en	cause to be, become	deepen, strengthen
-fy	make, cause to have	glorify, fortify
-ize	cause to be, treat with	sterilize, mechanize

Nuance and Word Meanings

Synonyms and Antonyms

When you understand how words relate to each other, you will discover more in a passage. This is explained by understanding **synonyms** (e.g., words that mean the same thing) and **antonyms** (e.g., words that mean the opposite of one another). As an example, *dry* and *arid* are synonyms, and *dry* and *wet* are antonyms.

There are many pairs of words in English that can be considered synonyms, despite having slightly different definitions. For instance, the words *friendly* and *collegial* can both be used to describe a warm interpersonal relationship, and one would be correct to call them synonyms. However, *collegial* (kin to *colleague*) is often used in reference to professional or academic relationships, and *friendly* has no such connotation.

If the difference between the two words is too great, then they should not be called synonyms. *Hot* and *warm* are not synonyms because their meanings are too distinct. A good way to determine whether two words are synonyms is to substitute one word for the other word and verify that the meaning of the sentence has not changed. Substituting *warm* for *hot* in a sentence would convey a different meaning. Although warm and hot may seem close in meaning, warm generally means that the temperature is moderate, and hot generally means that the temperature is excessively high.

Antonyms are words with opposite meanings. *Light* and *dark*, *up* and *down*, *right* and *left*, *good* and *bad*: these are all sets of antonyms. Be careful to distinguish between antonyms and pairs of words that are simply different. *Black* and *gray*, for instance, are not antonyms because gray is not the opposite of black. *Black* and *white*, on the other hand, are antonyms.

Not every word has an antonym. For instance, many nouns do not. What would be the antonym of *chair*? During your exam, the questions related to antonyms are more likely to concern adjectives. You will recall that adjectives are words that describe a noun. Some common adjectives include *purple*, *fast*, *skinny*, and *sweet*. From those four adjectives, *purple* is the item that lacks a group of obvious antonyms.

Review Video: What Are Synonyms and Antonyms?
Visit mometrix.com/academy and enter code: 105612

Denotative vs. Connotative Meaning

The **denotative** meaning of a word is the literal meaning. The **connotative** meaning goes beyond the denotative meaning to include the emotional reaction that a word may invoke. The connotative meaning often takes the denotative meaning a step further due to associations the reader makes with the denotative meaning. Readers can differentiate between the denotative and connotative meanings by first recognizing how authors use each meaning. Most non-fiction, for example, is fact-based and authors do not use flowery, figurative language. The reader can assume that the writer is using the denotative meaning of words. In fiction, the author may use the connotative meaning. Readers can determine whether the author is using the denotative or connotative meaning of a word by implementing context clues.

Review Video: Connotation and Denotation
Visit mometrix.com/academy and enter code: 310092

Nuances of Word Meaning Relative to Connotation, Denotation, Diction, and Usage

A word's denotation is simply its objective dictionary definition. However, its connotation refers to the subjective associations, often emotional, that specific words evoke in listeners and readers. Two or more words can have the same dictionary meaning, but very different connotations. Writers use diction (word choice) to convey various nuances of thought and emotion by selecting synonyms for other words that best communicate the associations they want to trigger for readers. For example, a car engine is naturally greasy; in this sense, "greasy" is a neutral term. But when a person's smile, appearance, or clothing is described as "greasy," it has a negative connotation. Some words have even gained additional or different meanings over time. For example, *awful* used to be used to describe things that evoked a sense of awe. When *awful* is separated into its root word, awe, and suffix, -ful, it can be understood to mean "full of awe." However, the word is now commonly used to describe things that evoke repulsion, terror, or another intense, negative reaction.

Review Video: Word Usage in Sentences
Visit mometrix.com/academy and enter code: 197863

Using Context to Determine Meaning

Context Clues

Readers of all levels will encounter words that they have either never seen or have encountered only on a limited basis. The best way to define a word in **context** is to look for nearby words that can assist in revealing the meaning of the word. For instance, unfamiliar nouns are often accompanied by examples that provide a definition. Consider the following sentence: *Dave arrived at the party in hilarious garb: a leopard-print shirt, buckskin trousers, and bright green sneakers.* If a reader was unfamiliar with the meaning of garb, he or she could read the examples (i.e., a leopard-print shirt, buckskin trousers, and high heels) and quickly determine that the word means *clothing*. Examples will not always be this obvious. Consider this sentence: *Parsley, lemon, and flowers were just a few of the items he used as garnishes.* Here, the word *garnishes* is exemplified by parsley, lemon, and flowers. Readers who have eaten in a variety of restaurants will probably be able to identify a garnish as something used to decorate a plate.

Review Video: Reading Comprehension: Using Context Clues
Visit mometrix.com/academy and enter code: 613660

Using Contrast in Context Clues

In addition to looking at the context of a passage, readers can use contrast to define an unfamiliar word in context. In many sentences, the author will not describe the unfamiliar word directly; instead, he or she will describe the opposite of the unfamiliar word. Thus, you are provided with some information that will bring you closer to defining the word. Consider the following example: *Despite his intelligence, Hector's low brow and bad posture made him look obtuse.* The author writes that Hector's appearance does not convey intelligence. Therefore, *obtuse* must mean unintelligent. Here is another example: *Despite the horrible weather, we were beatific about our trip to Alaska*. The word *despite* indicates that the speaker's feelings were at odds with the weather. Since the weather is described as *horrible*, then *beatific* must mean something positive.

Substitution to Find Meaning

In some cases, there will be very few contextual clues to help a reader define the meaning of an unfamiliar word. When this happens, one strategy that readers may employ is **substitution**. A good reader will brainstorm some possible synonyms for the given word, and he or she will substitute these words into the sentence. If the sentence and the surrounding passage continue to make sense, then the substitution has revealed at least some information about the unfamiliar word. Consider the sentence: *Frank's admonition rang in her ears as she climbed the mountain.* A reader unfamiliar with *admonition* might come up with some substitutions like *vow, promise, advice, complaint,* or *compliment.* All of these words make general sense of the sentence, though their meanings are diverse. However, this process has suggested that an admonition is some sort of message. The substitution strategy is rarely able to pinpoint a precise definition, but this process can be effective as a last resort.

Occasionally, you will be able to define an unfamiliar word by looking at the descriptive words in the context. Consider the following sentence: *Fred dragged the recalcitrant boy kicking and screaming up the stairs.* The words *dragged, kicking,* and *screaming* all suggest that the boy does not want to go up the stairs. The reader may assume that *recalcitrant* means something like unwilling or protesting. In this example, an unfamiliar adjective was identified.

Additionally, using description to define an unfamiliar noun is a common practice compared to unfamiliar adjectives, as in this sentence: *Don's wrinkled frown and constantly shaking fist identified him as a curmudgeon of the first order.* Don is described as having a *wrinkled frown and constantly shaking fist,* suggesting that a *curmudgeon* must be a grumpy person. Contrasts do not always provide detailed information about the unfamiliar word, but they at least give the reader some clues.

Words with Multiple Meanings

When a word has more than one meaning, readers can have difficulty determining how the word is being used in a given sentence. For instance, the verb *cleave,* can mean either *join* or *separate.* When readers come upon this word, they will have to select the definition that makes the most sense. Consider the following sentence: *Hermione's knife cleaved the bread cleanly.* Since a knife cannot join bread together, the word must indicate separation. A slightly more difficult example would be the sentence: *The birds cleaved to one another as they flew from the oak tree.* Immediately, the presence of the words *to one another* should suggest that in this sentence *cleave* is being used to mean *join.* Discovering the intent of a word with multiple meanings requires the same tricks as defining an unknown word: look for contextual clues and evaluate the substituted words.

Context Clues to Help Determine Meanings of Words

If readers simply bypass unknown words, they can reach unclear conclusions about what they read. However, looking for the definition of every unfamiliar word in the dictionary can slow their reading progress. Moreover, the dictionary may list multiple definitions for a word, so readers must search the word's context for meaning. Hence context is important to new vocabulary regardless of reader methods. Four types of context clues are examples, definitions, descriptive words, and opposites. Authors may use a certain word, and then follow it with several different examples of what it describes. Sometimes authors actually supply a definition of a word they use, which is especially true in informational and technical texts. Authors may use descriptive words that elaborate upon a vocabulary word they just used. Authors may also use opposites with negation that help define meaning.

Examples and Definitions

An author may use a word and then give examples that illustrate its meaning. Consider this text: "Teachers who do not know how to use sign language can help students who are deaf or hard of hearing understand certain instructions by using gestures instead, like pointing their fingers to indicate which direction to look or go; holding up a hand, palm outward, to indicate stopping; holding the hands flat, palms up, curling a finger toward oneself in a beckoning motion to indicate 'come here'; or curling all fingers toward oneself repeatedly to indicate 'come on', 'more', or 'continue.'" The author of this text has used the word "gestures" and then followed it with examples, so a reader unfamiliar with the word could deduce from the examples that "gestures" means "hand motions." Readers can find examples by looking for signal words "for example," "for instance," "like," "such as," and "e.g."

While readers sometimes have to look for definitions of unfamiliar words in a dictionary or do some work to determine a word's meaning from its surrounding context, at other times an author may make it easier for readers by defining certain words. For example, an author may write, "The company did not have sufficient capital, that is, available money, to continue operations." The author defined "capital" as "available money," and heralded the definition with the phrase "that is." Another way that authors supply word definitions is with appositives. Rather than being introduced by a signal phrase like "that is," "namely," or "meaning," an appositive comes after the vocabulary word it defines and is enclosed within two commas. For example, an author may write, "The Indians introduced the Pilgrims to pemmican, cakes they made of lean meat dried and mixed with fat, which proved greatly beneficial to keep settlers from starving while trapping." In this example, the appositive phrase following "pemmican" and preceding "which" defines the word "pemmican."

Descriptions

When readers encounter a word they do not recognize in a text, the author may expand on that word to illustrate it better. While the author may do this to make the prose more picturesque and vivid, the reader can also take advantage of this description to provide context clues to the meaning of the unfamiliar word. For example, an author may write, "The man sitting next to me on the airplane was obese. His shirt stretched across his vast expanse of flesh, strained almost to bursting." The descriptive second sentence elaborates on and helps to define the previous sentence's word "obese" to mean extremely fat. A reader unfamiliar with the word "repugnant" can decipher its meaning through an author's accompanying description: "The way the child grimaced and shuddered as he swallowed the medicine showed that its taste was particularly repugnant."

Opposites

Text authors sometimes introduce a contrasting or opposing idea before or after a concept they present. They may do this to emphasize or heighten the idea they present by contrasting it with something that is the reverse. However, readers can also use these context clues to understand familiar words. For example, an author may write, "Our conversation was not cheery. We sat and talked very solemnly about his experience and a number of similar events." The reader who is not familiar with the word "solemnly" can deduce by the author's preceding use of "not cheery" that "solemn" means the opposite of cheery or happy, so it must mean serious or sad. Or if someone writes, "Don't condemn his entire project because you couldn't find anything good to say about it," readers unfamiliar with "condemn" can understand from the sentence structure that it means the opposite of saying anything good, so it must mean reject, dismiss, or disapprove. "Entire" adds another context clue, meaning total or complete rejection.

Syntax to Determine Part of Speech and Meanings of Words

Syntax refers to sentence structure and word order. Suppose that a reader encounters an unfamiliar word when reading a text. To illustrate, consider an invented word like "splunch." If this word is used in a sentence like "Please splunch that ball to me," the reader can assume from syntactic context that "splunch" is a verb. We would not use a noun, adjective, adverb, or preposition with the object "that ball," and the prepositional phrase "to me" further indicates "splunch" represents an action. However, in the sentence, "Please hand that splunch to me," the reader can assume that "splunch" is a noun. Demonstrative adjectives like "that" modify nouns. Also, we hand someone some*thing*—a thing being a noun; we do not hand someone a verb, adjective, or adverb. Some sentences contain further clues. For example, from the sentence, "The princess wore the glittering splunch on her head," the reader can deduce that it is a crown, tiara, or something similar from the syntactic context, without knowing the word.

Syntax to Indicate Different Meanings of Similar Sentences

The syntax, or structure, of a sentence affords grammatical cues that aid readers in comprehending the meanings of words, phrases, and sentences in the texts that they read. Seemingly minor differences in how the words or phrases in a sentence are ordered can make major differences in meaning. For example, two sentences can use exactly the same words but have different meanings based on the word order:

- "The man with a broken arm sat in a chair."
- "The man sat in a chair with a broken arm."

While both sentences indicate that a man sat in a chair, differing syntax indicates whether the man's or chair's arm was broken.

Determining Meaning of Phrases and Paragraphs

Like unknown words, the meanings of phrases, paragraphs, and entire works can also be difficult to discern. Each of these can be better understood with added context. However, for larger groups of words, more context is needed. Unclear phrases are similar to unclear words, and the same methods can be used to understand their meaning. However, it is also important to consider how the individual words in the phrase work together. Paragraphs are a bit more complicated. Just as words must be compared to other words in a sentence, paragraphs must be compared to other paragraphs in a composition or a section.

Determining Meaning in Various Types of Compositions

To understand the meaning of an entire composition, the type of composition must be considered. **Expository writing** is generally organized so that each paragraph focuses on explaining one idea, or part of an idea, and its relevance. **Persuasive writing** uses paragraphs for different purposes to organize the parts of the argument. **Unclear paragraphs** must be read in the context of the paragraphs around them for their meaning to be fully understood. The meaning of full texts can also be unclear at times. The purpose of composition is also important for understanding the meaning of a text. To quickly understand the broad meaning of a text, look to the introductory and concluding paragraphs. Fictional texts are different. Some fictional works have implicit meanings, but some do not. The target audience must be considered for understanding texts that do have an implicit meaning, as most children's fiction will clearly state any lessons or morals. For other fiction, the application of literary theories and criticism may be helpful for understanding the text.

Resources for Determining Word Meaning and Usage

While these strategies are useful for determining the meaning of unknown words and phrases, sometimes additional resources are needed to properly use the terms in different contexts. Some words have multiple definitions, and some words are inappropriate in particular contexts or modes of writing. The following tools are helpful for understanding all meanings and proper uses for words and phrases.

- **Dictionaries** provide the meaning of a multitude of words in a language. Many dictionaries include additional information about each word, such as its etymology, its synonyms, or variations of the word.
- **Glossaries** are similar to dictionaries, as they provide the meanings of a variety of terms. However, while dictionaries typically feature an extensive list of words and comprise an entire publication, glossaries are often included at the end of a text and only include terms and definitions that are relevant to the text they follow.
- **Spell Checkers** are used to detect spelling errors in typed text. Some spell checkers may also detect the misuse of plural or singular nouns, verb tenses, or capitalization. While spell checkers are a helpful tool, they are not always reliable or attuned to the author's intent, so it is important to review the spell checker's suggestions before accepting them.
- **Style Manuals** are guidelines on the preferred punctuation, format, and grammar usage according to different fields or organizations. For example, the Associated Press Stylebook is a style guide often used for media writing. The guidelines within a style guide are not always applicable across different contexts and usages, as the guidelines often cover grammatical or formatting situations that are not objectively correct or incorrect.

Persuasion and Rhetoric

Persuasive Techniques

To **appeal using reason**, writers present logical arguments, such as using "If... then... because" statements. To **appeal to emotions**, authors may ask readers how they would feel about something or to put themselves in another's place, present their argument as one that will make the audience feel good, or tell readers how they should feel. To **appeal to character**, **morality**, or **ethics**, authors present their points to readers as the right or most moral choices. Authors cite expert opinions to show readers that someone very knowledgeable about the subject or viewpoint agrees with the author's claims. **Testimonials**, usually via anecdotes or quotations regarding the author's subject, help build the audience's trust in an author's message through positive support from ordinary people. **Bandwagon appeals** claim that everybody else agrees with the author's argument and persuade readers to conform and agree, also. Authors **appeal to greed** by presenting their choice as cheaper, free, or more valuable for less cost. They **appeal to laziness** by presenting their views as more convenient, easy, or relaxing. Authors also anticipate potential objections and argue against them before audiences think of them, thereby depicting those objections as weak.

Authors can use **comparisons** like analogies, similes, and metaphors to persuade audiences. For example, a writer might represent excessive expenses as "hemorrhaging" money, which the author's recommended solution will stop. Authors can use negative word connotations to make some choices unappealing to readers, and positive word connotations to make others more appealing. Using **humor** can relax readers and garner their agreement. However, writers must take care: ridiculing opponents can be a successful strategy for appealing to readers who already agree with the author, but can backfire by angering other readers. **Rhetorical questions** need no answer, but create effect that can force agreement, such as asking the question, "Wouldn't you rather be paid more than less?" **Generalizations** persuade readers by being impossible to disagree with. Writers can easily make generalizations that appear to support their viewpoints, like saying, "We all want peace, not war" regarding more specific political arguments. **Transfer** and **association** persuade by example: if advertisements show attractive actors enjoying their products, audiences imagine they will experience the same. **Repetition** can also sometimes effectively persuade audiences.

Review Video: Using Rhetorical Strategies for Persuasion
Visit mometrix.com/academy and enter code: 302658

Classical Author Appeals

In his *On Rhetoric,* ancient Greek philosopher Aristotle defined three basic types of appeal used in writing, which he called *pathos, ethos,* and *logos.* ***Pathos*** means suffering or experience and refers to appeals to the emotions (the English word *pathetic* comes from this root). Writing that is meant to entertain audiences, by making them either happy, as with comedy, or sad, as with tragedy, uses *pathos.* Aristotle's *Poetics* states that evoking the emotions of terror and pity is one of the criteria for writing tragedy. ***Ethos*** means character and connotes ideology (the English word *ethics* comes from this root). Writing that appeals to credibility, based on academic, professional, or personal merit, uses *ethos.* ***Logos*** means "I say" and refers to a plea, opinion, expectation, word or speech, account, opinion, or reason (the English word *logic* comes from this root.) Aristotle used it to mean persuasion that appeals to the audience through reasoning and logic to influence their opinions.

Rhetorical Devices

- An **anecdote** is a brief story authors may relate to their argument, which can illustrate their points in a more real and relatable way.
- **Aphorisms** concisely state common beliefs and may rhyme. For example, Benjamin Franklin's "Early to bed and early to rise / Makes a man healthy, wealthy, and wise" is an aphorism.
- **Allusions** refer to literary or historical figures to impart symbolism to a thing or person and to create reader resonance. In John Steinbeck's *Of Mice and Men,* protagonist George's last name is Milton. This alludes to John Milton, who wrote *Paradise Lost*, and symbolizes George's eventual loss of his dream.
- **Satire** exaggerates, ridicules, or pokes fun at human flaws or ideas, as in the works of Jonathan Swift and Mark Twain.
- A **parody** is a form of satire that imitates another work to ridicule its topic or style.
- A **paradox** is a statement that is true despite appearing contradictory.
- **Hyperbole** is overstatement using exaggerated language.
- An **oxymoron** combines seeming contradictions, such as "deafening silence."
- **Analogies** compare two things that share common elements.
- **Similes** (stated comparisons using the words *like* or *as*) and **metaphors** (stated comparisons that do not use *like* or *as*) are considered forms of analogy.
- When using logic to reason with audiences, **syllogism** refers either to deductive reasoning or a deceptive, very sophisticated, or subtle argument.
- **Deductive reasoning** moves from general to specific, **inductive reasoning** from specific to general.
- **Diction** is author word choice that establishes tone and effect.
- **Understatement** achieves effects like contrast or irony by downplaying or describing something more subtly than warranted.
- **Chiasmus** uses parallel clauses, the second reversing the order of the first. Examples include T. S. Eliot's "Has the Church failed mankind, or has mankind failed the Church?" and John F. Kennedy's "Ask not what your country can do for you; ask what you can do for your country."
- **Anaphora** regularly repeats a word or phrase at the beginnings of consecutive clauses or phrases to add emphasis to an idea. A classic example of anaphora was Winston Churchill's emphasis of determination: "[W]e shall fight on the beaches, we shall fight on the landing grounds, we shall fight in the fields and in the streets, we shall fight in the hills; we shall never surrender..."

Plot and Story Structure

Plot and Story Structure

The **plot** includes the events that happen in a story and the order in which they are told to the reader. There are several types of plot structures, as stories can be told in many ways. The most common plot structure is the chronological plot, which presents the events to the reader in the same order they occur for the characters in the story. Chronological plots usually have five main parts, the **exposition**, **rising action**, the **climax**, **falling action**, and the **resolution**. This type of plot structure guides the reader through the story's events as the characters experience them and is the easiest structure to understand and identify. While this is the most common plot structure, many stories are nonlinear, which means the plot does not sequence events in the same order the characters experience them. Such stories might include elements like flashbacks that cause the story to be nonlinear.

Review Video: How to Make a Story Map
Visit mometrix.com/academy and enter code: 261719

Exposition

The **exposition** is at the beginning of the story and generally takes place before the rising action begins. The purpose of the exposition is to give the reader context for the story, which the author may do by introducing one or more characters, describing the setting or world, or explaining the events leading up to the point where the story begins. The exposition may still include events that contribute to the plot, but the **rising action** and main conflict of the story are not part of the exposition. Some narratives skip the exposition and begin the story with the beginning of the rising action, which causes the reader to learn the context as the story intensifies.

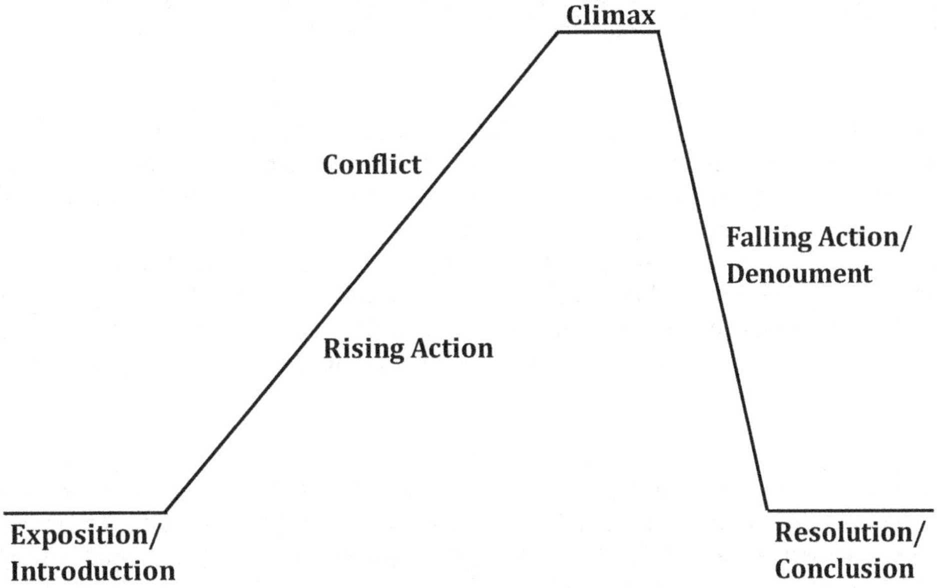

Review Video: Plot Line
Visit mometrix.com/academy and enter code: 944011

Conflict

A **conflict** is a problem to be solved. Literary plots typically include one conflict or more. Characters' attempts to resolve conflicts drive the narrative's forward movement. **Conflict resolution** is often the protagonist's primary occupation. Physical conflicts like exploring, wars, and escapes tend to make plots most suspenseful and exciting. Emotional, mental, or moral conflicts tend to make stories more personally gratifying or rewarding for many audiences. Conflicts can be external or internal. A major type of internal conflict is some inner personal battle, or **man versus self**. Major types of external conflicts include **man versus nature**, **man versus man**, and **man versus society**. Readers can identify conflicts in literary plots by identifying the protagonist and antagonist and asking why they conflict, what events develop the conflict, where the climax occurs, and how they identify with the characters.

Read the following paragraph and discuss the type of conflict present:

> Timothy was shocked out of sleep by the appearance of a bear just outside his tent. After panicking for a moment, he remembered some advice he had read in preparation for this trip: he should make noise so the bear would not be startled. As Timothy started to hum and sing, the bear wandered away.

There are three main types of conflict in literature: **man versus man**, **man versus nature**, and **man versus self**. This paragraph is an example of man versus nature. Timothy is in conflict with the bear. Even though no physical conflict like an attack exists, Timothy is pitted against the bear. Timothy uses his knowledge to "defeat" the bear and keep himself safe. The solution to the conflict is that Timothy makes noise, the bear wanders away, and Timothy is safe.

Review Video: Conflict
Visit mometrix.com/academy and enter code: 559550

Review Video: Determining Relationships in a Story
Visit mometrix.com/academy and enter code: 929925

Rising Action

The **rising action** is the part of the story where conflict **intensifies**. The rising action begins with an event that prompts the main conflict of the story. This may also be called the **inciting incident**. The main conflict generally occurs between the protagonist and an antagonist, but this is not the only type of conflict that may occur in a narrative. After this event, the protagonist works to resolve the main conflict by preparing for an altercation, pursuing a goal, fleeing an antagonist, or doing some other action that will end the conflict. The rising action is composed of several additional events that increase the story's tension. Most often, other developments will occur alongside the growth of the main conflict, such as character development or the development of minor conflicts. The rising action ends with the **climax**, which is the point of highest tension in the story.

Climax

The **climax** is the event in the narrative that marks the height of the story's conflict or tension. The event that takes place at the story's climax will end the rising action and bring about the results of the main conflict. If the conflict was between a good protagonist and an evil antagonist, the climax may be a final battle between the two characters. If the conflict is an adventurer looking for heavily guarded treasure, the climax may be the adventurer's encounter with the final obstacle that protects the treasure. The climax may be made of multiple scenes, but can usually be summarized as one event. Once the conflict and climax are complete, the **falling action** begins.

Falling Action

The **falling action** shows what happens in the story between the climax and the resolution. The falling action often composes a much smaller portion of the story than the rising action does. While the climax includes the end of the main conflict, the falling action may show the results of any minor conflicts in the story. For example, if the protagonist encountered a troll on the way to find some treasure, and the troll demanded the protagonist share the treasure after retrieving it, the falling action would include the protagonist returning to share the treasure with the troll. Similarly, any unexplained major events are usually made clear during the falling action. Once all significant elements of the story are resolved or addressed, the story's resolution will occur. The **resolution** is the end of the story, which shows the final result of the plot's events and shows what life is like for the main characters once they are no longer experiencing the story's conflicts.

Resolution

The way the conflict is **resolved** depends on the type of conflict. The plot of any book starts with the lead up to the conflict, then the conflict itself, and finally the solution, or **resolution**, to the conflict. In **man versus man** conflicts, the conflict is often resolved by two parties coming to some sort of agreement or by one party triumphing over the other party. In **man versus nature** conflicts, the conflict is often resolved by man coming to some realization about some aspect of nature. In **man versus self** conflicts, the conflict is often resolved by the character growing or coming to an understanding about part of himself.

THEME

A **theme** is a central idea demonstrated by a passage. Often, a theme is a lesson or moral contained in the text, but it does not have to be. It also is a unifying idea that is used throughout the text; it can take the form of a common setting, idea, symbol, design, or recurring event. A passage can have two or more themes that convey its overall idea. The theme or themes of a passage are often based on **universal themes**. They can frequently be expressed using well-known sayings about life, society, or human nature, such as "Hard work pays off" or "Good triumphs over evil." Themes are not usually stated **explicitly**. The reader must figure them out by carefully reading the passage. Themes are created through descriptive language or events in the plot. The events of a story help shape the themes of a passage.

EXAMPLE

Explain why "if you care about something, you need to take care of it" accurately describes the theme of the following excerpt.

> Luca collected baseball cards, but he wasn't very careful with them. He left them around the house. His dog liked to chew. One day, Luca and his friend Bart were looking at his collection. Then they went outside. When Luca got home, he saw his dog chewing on his cards. They were ruined.

This excerpt tells the story of a boy who is careless with his baseball cards and leaves them lying around. His dog ends up chewing them and ruining them. The lesson is that if you care about something, you need to take care of it. This is the theme, or point, of the story. Some stories have more than one theme, but this is not really true of this excerpt. The reader needs to figure out the theme based on what happens in the story. Sometimes, as in the case of fables, the theme is stated directly in the text. However, this is not usually the case.

Review Video: Themes in Literature
Visit mometrix.com/academy and enter code: 732074

NARRATOR'S POINT OF VIEW

POINT OF VIEW

Another element that impacts a text is the author's point of view. The **point of view** of a text is the perspective from which a passage is told. An author will always have a point of view about a story before he or she draws up a plot line. The author will know what events they want to take place, how they want the characters to interact, and how they want the story to resolve. An author will also have an opinion on the topic or series of events which is presented in the story that is based on their prior experience and beliefs.

The two main points of view that authors use, especially in a work of fiction, are first person and third person. If the narrator of the story is also the main character, or *protagonist*, the text is written in first-person point of view. In first person, the author writes from the perspective of *I*. Third-person point of view is probably the most common that authors use in their passages. Using third person, authors refer to each character by using *he* or *she*. In third-person omniscient, the narrator is not a character in the story and tells the story of all of the characters at the same time.

Review Video: Point of View
Visit mometrix.com/academy and enter code: 383336

First-Person Narration

First-person narratives let narrators express inner feelings and thoughts, especially when the narrator is the protagonist as Lemuel Gulliver is in Jonathan Swift's *Gulliver's Travels.* The narrator may be a close friend of the protagonist, like Dr. Watson in Sir Arthur Conan Doyle's *Sherlock Holmes.* Or, the narrator can be less involved with the main characters and plot, like Nick Carraway in F. Scott Fitzgerald's *The Great Gatsby.* When a narrator reports others' narratives, she or he is a "**frame narrator**," like the nameless narrator of Joseph Conrad's *Heart of Darkness* or Mr. Lockwood in Emily Brontë's *Wuthering Heights.* **First-person plural** is unusual but can be effective. Isaac Asimov's *I, Robot,* William Faulkner's *A Rose for Emily,* Maxim Gorky's *Twenty-Six Men and a Girl,* and Jeffrey Eugenides' *The Virgin Suicides* all use first-person plural narration. Author Kurt Vonnegut is the first-person narrator in his semi-autobiographical novel *Timequake.* Also unusual, but effective, is a **first-person omniscient** (rather than the more common third-person omniscient) narrator, like Death in Markus Zusak's *The Book Thief* and the ghost in Alice Sebold's *The Lovely Bones.*

Second-Person Narration

While **second-person** address is very commonplace in popular song lyrics, it is the least used form of narrative voice in literary works. Popular serial books of the 1980s like *Fighting Fantasy* or *Choose Your Own Adventure* employed second-person narratives. In some cases, a narrative combines both second-person and first-person voices, using the pronouns *you* and *I.* This can draw readers into the story, and it can also enable the authors to compare directly "your" and "my" feelings, thoughts, and actions. When the narrator is also a character in the story, as in Edgar Allan Poe's short story "The Tell-Tale Heart" or Jay McInerney's novel *Bright Lights, Big City,* the narrative is better defined as first-person despite it also addressing "you."

Third-Person Narration

Narration in the third person is the most prevalent type, as it allows authors the most flexibility. It is so common that readers simply assume without needing to be informed that the narrator is not a character in the story, or involved in its events. **Third-person singular** is used more frequently than **third-person plural**, though some authors have also effectively used plural. However, both singular and plural are most often included in stories according to which characters are being described. The third-person narrator may be either objective or subjective, and either omniscient or limited. **Objective third-person** narration does not include what the characters described are thinking or feeling, while **subjective third-person** narration does. The **third-person omniscient** narrator knows everything about all characters, including their thoughts and emotions, and all related places, times, and events. However, the **third-person limited** narrator may know everything about a particular character, but is limited to that character. In other words, the narrator cannot speak about anything that character does not know.

Alternating-Person Narration

Although authors more commonly write stories from one point of view, there are also instances wherein they alternate the narrative voice within the same book. For example, they may sometimes use an omniscient third-person narrator and a more intimate first-person narrator at other times. In J. K. Rowling's series of *Harry Potter* novels, she often writes in a third-person limited narrative, but sometimes changes to narration by characters other than the protagonist. George R. R. Martin's series *A Song of Ice and Fire* changes the point of view to coincide with divisions between chapters. The same technique is used by Erin Hunter (a pseudonym for several authors of the *Warriors, Seekers,* and *Survivors* book series). Authors using first-person narrative sometimes switch to third-person to describe significant action scenes, especially those where the narrator was absent or uninvolved, as Barbara Kingsolver does in her novel *The Poisonwood Bible.*

Setting, Mood, and Tone

Setting and Time Frame

A literary text has both a setting and time frame. A **setting** is the place in which the story as a whole is set. The **time frame** is the period in which the story is set. This may refer to the historical period the story takes place in or if the story takes place over a single day. Both setting and time frame are relevant to a text's meaning because they help the reader place the story in time and space. An author uses setting and time frame to anchor a text, create a mood, and enhance its meaning. This helps a reader understand why a character acts the way he does, or why certain events in the story are important. The setting impacts the **plot** and character **motivations**, while the time frame helps place the story in **chronological context**.

EXAMPLE

Read the following excerpt from The Adventures of Huckleberry Finn by Mark Twain and analyze the relevance of setting to the text's meaning:

> We said there warn't no home like a raft, after all. Other places do seem so cramped up and smothery, but a raft don't. You feel mighty free and easy and comfortable on a raft.

This excerpt from *The Adventures of Huckleberry Finn* by Mark Twain reveals information about the **setting** of the book. By understanding that the main character, Huckleberry Finn, lives on a raft, the reader can place the story on a river, in this case, the Mississippi River in the South before the Civil War. The information about the setting also gives the reader clues about the **character** of Huck Finn: he clearly values independence and freedom, and he likes the outdoors. The information about the setting in the quote helps the reader to better understand the rest of the text.

SYNTAX AND WORD CHOICE

Authors use words and **syntax**, or sentence structure, to make their texts unique, convey their own writing style, and sometimes to make a point or emphasis. They know that word choice and syntax contribute to the reader's understanding of the text as well as to the tone and mood of a text.

Review Video: What is Syntax?
Visit mometrix.com/academy and enter code: 242280

MOOD AND TONE

Mood is a story's atmosphere, or the feelings the reader gets from reading it. The way authors set the mood in writing is comparable to the way filmmakers use music to set the mood in movies. Instead of music, though, writers judiciously select descriptive words to evoke certain **moods**. The mood of a work may convey joy, anger, bitterness, hope, gloom, fear, apprehension, or any other emotion the author wants the reader to feel. In addition to vocabulary choices, authors also use figurative expressions, particular sentence structures, and choices of diction that project and reinforce the moods they want to create. Whereas mood is the reader's emotions evoked by reading what is written, **tone** is the emotions and attitudes of the writer that she or he expresses in the writing. Authors use the same literary techniques to establish tone as they do to establish mood. An author may use a humorous tone, an angry or sad tone, a sentimental or unsentimental tone, or something else entirely.

MOOD AND TONE IN THE GREAT GATSBY

To understand the difference between mood and tone, look at this excerpt from F. Scott Fitzgerald's *The Great Gatsby*. In this passage, Nick Caraway, the novel's narrator, is describing his affordable house, which sits in a neighborhood full of expensive mansions.

> "I lived at West Egg, the—well the less fashionable of the two, though this is a most superficial tag to express the bizarre and not a little sinister contrast between them. My house was at the very tip of the egg, only fifty yard from the Sound, and squeezed between two huge places that rented for twelve or fifteen thousand a season ... My own house was an eyesore, but it was a small eyesore, and it had been overlooked, so I had a view of the water, a partial view of my neighbor's lawn, and the consoling proximity of millionaires—all for eighty dollars a month."

In this description, the mood created for the reader does not match the tone created through the narrator. The mood in this passage is one of dissatisfaction and inferiority. Nick compares his home to his neighbors', saying he lives in the "less fashionable" neighborhood and that his house is "overlooked," an "eyesore," and "squeezed between two huge" mansions. He also adds that his placement allows him the "consoling proximity of millionaires." A literal reading of these details leads the reader to have negative feelings toward Nick's house and his economic inferiority to his neighbors, creating the mood.

However, Fitzgerald also conveys an opposing attitude, or tone, through Nick's description. Nick calls the distinction between the neighborhoods "superficial," showing a suspicion of the value suggested by the neighborhoods' titles, properties, and residents. Nick also undermines his critique of his own home by calling it "a small eyesore" and claiming it has "been overlooked." However, he follows these statements with a description of his surroundings, claiming that he has "a view of the water" and can see some of his wealthy neighbor's property from his home, and a comparison between the properties' rent. While the mental image created for the reader depicts a small house shoved between looming mansions, the tone suggests that Nick enjoys these qualities about his home, or at least finds it charming. He acknowledges its shortcomings, but includes the benefits of his home's unassuming appearance.

Review Video: Style, Tone, and Mood
Visit mometrix.com/academy and enter code: 416961

Historical and Social Context

Fiction that is heavily influenced by a historical or social context cannot be comprehended as the author intended if the reader does not keep this context in mind. Many important elements of the text will be influenced by any context, including symbols, allusions, settings, and plot events. These contexts, as well as the identity of the work's author, can help to inform the reader about the author's concerns and intended meanings. For example, George Orwell published his novel *1984* in the year 1949, soon after the end of World War II. At that time, following the defeat of the Nazis, the Cold War began between the Western Allied nations and the Eastern Soviet Communists. People were therefore concerned about the conflict between the freedoms afforded by Western democracies versus the oppression represented by Communism. Orwell had also previously fought in the Spanish Civil War against a Spanish regime that he and his fellows viewed as oppressive. From this information, readers can infer that Orwell was concerned about oppression by totalitarian governments. This informs *1984*'s story of Winston Smith's rebellion against the oppressive "Big Brother" government, of the fictional dictatorial state of Oceania, and his capture, torture, and ultimate conversion by that government. Some literary theories also seek to use historical and social contexts to reveal deeper meanings and implications in a text.

Character Development and Dialogue

Character Development

When depicting characters or figures in a written text, authors generally use actions, dialogue, and descriptions as characterization techniques. Characterization can occur in both fiction and nonfiction and is used to show a character or figure's personality, demeanor, and thoughts. This helps create a more engaging experience for the reader by providing a more concrete picture of a character or figure's tendencies and features. Characterizations also gives authors the opportunity to integrate elements such as dialects, activities, attire, and attitudes into their writing.

To understand the meaning of a story, it is vital to understand the characters as the author describes them. We can look for contradictions in what a character thinks, says, and does. We can notice whether the author's observations about a character differ from what other characters in the story say about that character. A character may be dynamic, meaning they change significantly during the story, or static, meaning they remain the same from beginning to end. Characters may be two-dimensional, not fully developed, or may be well developed with characteristics that stand out vividly. Characters may also symbolize universal properties. Additionally, readers can compare and contrast characters to analyze how each one developed.

A well-known example of character development can be found in Charles Dickens's *Great Expectations*. The novel's main character, Pip, is introduced as a young boy, and he is depicted as innocent, kind, and humble. However, as Pip grows up and is confronted with the social hierarchy of Victorian England, he becomes arrogant and rejects his loved ones in pursuit of his own social advancement. Once he achieves his social goals, he realizes the merits of his former lifestyle, and lives with the wisdom he gained in both environments and life stages. Dickens shows Pip's ever-changing character through his interactions with others and his inner thoughts, which evolve as his personal values and personality shift.

Review Video: Character Changes
Visit mometrix.com/academy and enter code: 408719

Dialogue

Effectively written dialogue serves at least one, but usually several, purposes. It advances the story and moves the plot, develops the characters, sheds light on the work's theme or meaning, and can, often subtly, account for the passage of time not otherwise indicated. It can alter the direction that the plot is taking, typically by introducing some new conflict or changing existing ones. **Dialogue** can establish a work's narrative voice and the characters' voices and set the tone of the story or of particular characters. When fictional characters display enlightenment or realization, dialogue can give readers an understanding of what those characters have discovered and how. Dialogue can illuminate the motivations and wishes of the story's characters. By using consistent thoughts and syntax, dialogue can support character development. Skillfully created, it can also represent real-life speech rhythms in written form. Via conflicts and ensuing action, dialogue also provides drama.

Dialogue in Fiction

In fictional works, effectively written dialogue does more than just break up or interrupt sections of narrative. While **dialogue** may supply exposition for readers, it must nonetheless be believable. Dialogue should be dynamic, not static, and it should not resemble regular prose. Authors should not use dialogue to write clever similes or metaphors, or to inject their own opinions. Nor should they use dialogue at all when narrative would be better. Most importantly, dialogue should not slow the plot movement. Dialogue must seem natural, which means careful construction of phrases rather than actually duplicating natural speech, which does not necessarily translate well to the written word. Finally, all dialogue must be pertinent to the story, rather than just added conversation.

Figurative Language

Literal and Figurative Meaning

When language is used **literally**, the words mean exactly what they say and nothing more. When language is used **figuratively**, the words mean something beyond their literal meaning. For example, "The weeping willow tree has long, trailing branches and leaves" is a literal description. But "The weeping willow tree looks as if it is bending over and crying" is a figurative description—specifically, a **simile** or stated comparison. Another figurative language form is **metaphor**, or an implied comparison. A good example is the metaphor of a city, state, or city-state as a ship, and its governance as sailing that ship. Ancient Greek lyrical poet Alcaeus is credited with first using this metaphor, and ancient Greek tragedian Aeschylus then used it in *Seven Against Thebes*, and then Plato used it in the *Republic*.

Figures of Speech

A **figure of speech** is a verbal expression whose meaning is figurative rather than literal. For example, the phrase "butterflies in the stomach" does not refer to actual butterflies in a person's stomach. It is a metaphor representing the fluttery feelings experienced when a person is nervous or excited—or when one "falls in love," which does not mean physically falling. "Hitting a sales target" does not mean physically hitting a target with arrows as in archery; it is a metaphor for meeting a sales quota. "Climbing the ladder of success" metaphorically likens advancing in one's career to ascending ladder rungs. Similes, such as "light as a feather" (meaning very light, not a feather's actual weight), and hyperbole, like "I'm starving/freezing/roasting," are also figures of speech. Figures of speech are often used and crafted for emphasis, freshness of expression, or clarity.

Review Video: Figures of Speech
Visit mometrix.com/academy and enter code: 111295

Figurative Language

Figurative language extends past the literal meanings of words. It offers readers new insight into the people, things, events, and subjects covered in a work of literature. Figurative language also enables readers to feel they are sharing the authors' experiences. It can stimulate the reader's senses, make comparisons that readers find intriguing or even startling, and enable readers to view the world in different ways. When looking for figurative language, it is important to consider the context of the sentence or situation. Phrases that appear out of place or make little sense when read literally are likely instances of figurative language. Once figurative language has been recognized, context is also important to determining the type of figurative language being used and its function. For example, when a comparison is being made, a metaphor or simile is likely being used. This means the comparison may emphasize or create irony through the things being compared. Seven specific types of figurative language include: alliteration, onomatopoeia, personification, imagery, similes, metaphors, and hyperbole.

Review Video: Figurative Language
Visit mometrix.com/academy and enter code: 584902

Alliteration and Onomatopoeia

Alliteration describes a series of words beginning with the same sounds. **Onomatopoeia** uses words imitating the sounds of things they name or describe. For example, in his poem "Come Down, O Maid," Alfred Tennyson writes of "The moan of doves in immemorial elms, / And murmuring of innumerable bees." The word "moan" sounds like some sounds doves make, "murmuring" represents the sounds of bees buzzing. Onomatopoeia also includes words that are simply meant to represent sounds, such as "meow," "kaboom," and "whoosh."

Review Video: Alliteration in Everyday Expressions
Visit mometrix.com/academy and enter code: 462837

Personification

Another type of figurative language is **personification**. This is describing a non-human thing, like an animal or an object, as if it were human. The general intent of personification is to describe things in a manner that will be comprehensible to readers. When an author states that a tree *groans* in the wind, he or she does not mean that the tree is emitting a low, pained sound from a mouth. Instead, the author means that the tree is making a noise similar to a human groan. Of course, this personification establishes a tone of sadness or suffering. A different tone would be established if the author said that the tree was *swaying* or *dancing*. Alfred Tennyson's poem "The Eagle" uses all of these types of figurative language: "He clasps the crag with crooked hands." Tennyson used alliteration, repeating /k/ and /kr/ sounds. These hard-sounding consonants reinforce the imagery, giving visual and tactile impressions of the eagle.

Review Video: Personification
Visit mometrix.com/academy and enter code: 260066

SIMILES AND METAPHORS

Similes are stated comparisons using "like" or "as." Similes can be used to stimulate readers' imaginations and appeal to their senses. Because a simile includes *like* or *as,* the device creates more space between the description and the thing being described than a metaphor does. If an author says that *a house was like a shoebox*, then the tone is different than the author saying that the house *was* a shoebox. Authors will choose between a metaphor and a simile depending on their intended tone.

Similes also help compare fictional characters to well-known objects or experiences, so the reader can better relate to them. William Wordsworth's poem about "Daffodils" begins, "I wandered lonely as a cloud." This simile compares his loneliness to that of a cloud. It is also personification, giving a cloud the human quality loneliness. In his novel *Lord Jim* (1900), Joseph Conrad writes in Chapter 33, "I would have given anything for the power to soothe her frail soul, tormenting itself in its invincible ignorance like a small bird beating about the cruel wires of a cage." Conrad uses the word "like" to compare the girl's soul to a small bird. His description of the bird beating at the cage shows the similar helplessness of the girl's soul to gain freedom.

Review Video: Similes
Visit mometrix.com/academy and enter code: 642949

A **metaphor** is a type of figurative language in which the writer equates something with another thing that is not particularly similar, instead of using *like* or *as*. For instance, *the bird was an arrow arcing through the sky*. In this sentence, the arrow is serving as a metaphor for the bird. The point of a metaphor is to encourage the reader to consider the item being described in a *different way*. Let's continue with this metaphor for a flying bird. You are asked to envision the bird's flight as being similar to the arc of an arrow. So, you imagine the flight to be swift and bending. Metaphors are a way for the author to describe an item *without being direct and obvious*. This literary device is a lyrical and suggestive way of providing information. Note that the reference for a metaphor will not always be mentioned explicitly by the author. Consider the following description of a forest in winter: *Swaying skeletons reached for the sky and groaned as the wind blew through them.* In this example, the author is using *skeletons* as a metaphor for leafless trees. This metaphor creates a spooky tone while inspiring the reader's imagination.

LITERARY EXAMPLES OF METAPHOR

A **metaphor** is an implied comparison, i.e., it compares something to something else without using "like", "as", or other comparative words. For example, in "The Tyger" (1794), William Blake writes, "Tyger Tyger, burning bright, / In the forests of the night." Blake compares the tiger to a flame not by saying it is like a fire, but by simply describing it as "burning." Henry Wadsworth Longfellow's poem "O Ship of State" (1850) uses an extended metaphor by referring consistently throughout the entire poem to the state, union, or republic as a seagoing vessel, referring to its keel, mast, sail, rope, anchors, and to its braving waves, rocks, gale, tempest, and "false lights on the shore." Within the extended metaphor, Wordsworth uses a specific metaphor: "the anchors of thy hope!"

TED HUGHES' ANIMAL METAPHORS

Ted Hughes frequently used animal metaphors in his poetry. In "The Thought Fox," a model of concise, structured beauty, Hughes characterizes the poet's creative process with succinct, striking imagery of an idea entering his head like a wild fox. Repeating "loneliness" in the first two stanzas emphasizes the poet's lonely work: "Something else is alive / Beside the clock's loneliness." He treats an idea's arrival as separate from himself. Three stanzas detail in vivid images a fox's approach from the outside winter forest at starless midnight—its nose, "Cold, delicately" touching twigs and leaves; "neat" paw prints in snow; "bold" body; brilliant green eyes; and self-contained, focused progress—"Till, with a sudden sharp hot stink of fox," he metaphorically depicts poetic inspiration as the fox's physical entry into "the dark hole of the head." Hughes ends by summarizing his vision of a poet as an interior, passive idea recipient, with the outside world unchanged: "The window is starless still; the clock ticks, / The page is printed."

Review Video: Metaphors in Writing
Visit mometrix.com/academy and enter code: 133295

Metonymy

Metonymy is naming one thing with words or phrases of a closely related thing. This is similar to metaphor. However, the comparison has a close connection, unlike metaphor. An example of metonymy is to call the news media *the press*. Of course, *the press* is the machine that prints newspapers. Metonymy is a way of naming something without using the same name constantly.

Synecdoche

Synecdoche points to the whole by naming one of the parts. An example of synecdoche would be calling a construction worker a *hard hat*. Like metonymy, synecdoche is an easy way of naming something without having to overuse a name. The device allows writers to highlight pieces of the thing being described. For example, referring to businessmen as *suits* suggests professionalism and unity.

Hyperbole

Hyperbole is excessive exaggeration used for humor or emphasis rather than for literal meaning. For example, in *To Kill a Mockingbird*, Harper Lee wrote, "People moved slowly then. There was no hurry, for there was nowhere to go, nothing to buy and no money to buy it with, nothing to see outside the boundaries of Maycomb County." This was not literally true; Lee exaggerates the scarcity of these things for emphasis. In "Old Times on the Mississippi," Mark Twain wrote, "I... could have hung my hat on my eyes, they stuck out so far." This is not literal, but makes his description vivid and funny. In his poem "As I Walked Out One Evening", W. H. Auden wrote, "I'll love you, dear, I'll love you / Till China and Africa meet, / And the river jumps over the mountain / And the salmon sing in the street." He used things not literally possible to emphasize the duration of his love.

Understatement

Understatement is the opposite of hyperbole. This device discounts or downplays something. Think about someone who climbs Mount Everest. Then, they say that the journey was *a little stroll*. As with other types of figurative language, understatement has a range of uses. The device may show self-defeat or modesty as in the Mount Everest example. However, some may think of understatement as false modesty (i.e., an attempt to bring attention to you or a situation). For example, a woman is praised on her diamond engagement ring. The woman says, *Oh, this little thing?* Her understatement might be heard as stuck-up or unfeeling.

Review Video: Hyperbole and Understatement
Visit mometrix.com/academy and enter code: 308470

Literary Devices

Literary Irony

In literature, irony demonstrates the opposite of what is said or done. The three types of irony are **verbal irony**, **situational irony**, and **dramatic irony**. Verbal irony uses words opposite to the meaning. Sarcasm may use verbal irony. One common example is describing something that is confusing as "clear as mud." For example, in his 1986 movie *Hannah and Her Sisters,* author, director, and actor Woody Allen says to his character's date, "I had a great evening; it was like the Nuremburg Trials." Notice these employ similes. In situational irony, what happens contrasts with what was expected. O. Henry's short story *The Gift of the Magi* uses situational irony: a husband and wife each sacrifice their most prized possession to buy each other a Christmas present. The irony is that she sells her long hair to buy him a watch fob, while he sells his heirloom pocket-watch to buy her the jeweled combs for her hair she had long wanted; in the end, neither of them can use their gifts. In dramatic irony, narrative informs audiences of more than its characters know. For example, in *Romeo and Juliet*, the audience is made aware that Juliet is only asleep, while Romeo believes her to be dead, which then leads to Romeo's death.

Review Video: What is Irony?
Visit mometrix.com/academy and enter code: 374204

IDIOMS

Idioms create comparisons, and often take the form of similes or metaphors. Idioms are always phrases and are understood to have a meaning that is different from its individual words' literal meaning. For example, "break a leg" is a common idiom that is used to wish someone luck or tell them to perform well. Literally, the phrase "break a leg" means to injure a person's leg, but the phrase takes on a different meaning when used as an idiom. Another example is "call it a day," which means to temporarily stop working on a task, or find a stopping point, rather than literally referring to something as "a day." Many idioms are associated with a region or group. For example, an idiom commonly used in the American South is "'til the cows come home." This phrase is often used to indicate that something will take or may last for a very long time, but not that it will literally last until the cows return to where they reside.

ALLUSION

An allusion is an uncited but recognizable reference to something else. Authors use language to make allusions to places, events, artwork, and other books in order to make their own text richer. For example, an author may allude to a very important text in order to make his own text seem more important. Martin Luther King, Jr. started his "I Have a Dream" speech by saying "Five score years ago…" This is a clear allusion to President Abraham Lincoln's "Gettysburg Address" and served to remind people of the significance of the event. An author may allude to a place to ground his text or make a cultural reference to make readers feel included. There are many reasons that authors make allusions.

Review Video: Allusions
Visit mometrix.com/academy and enter code: 294065

COMIC RELIEF

Comic relief is the use of comedy by an author to break up a dramatic or tragic scene and infuse it with a bit of **lightheartedness**. In William Shakespeare's *Hamlet*, two gravediggers digging the grave for Ophelia share a joke while they work. The death and burial of Ophelia are tragic moments that directly follow each other. Shakespeare uses an instance of comedy to break up the tragedy and give his audience a bit of a break from the tragic drama. Authors sometimes use comic relief so that their work will be less depressing; other times they use it to create irony or contrast between the darkness of the situation and the lightness of the joke. Often, authors will use comedy to parallel what is happening in the tragic scenes.

Review Video: Comic Relief
Visit mometrix.com/academy and enter code: 779604

FORESHADOWING

Foreshadowing is a device authors use to give readers **hints** about events that will take place later in a story. Foreshadowing most often takes place through a character's dialogue or actions. Sometimes the character will know what is going to happen and will purposefully allude to future events. For example, consider a protagonist who is about to embark on a journey through the woods. Just before the protagonist begins the trip, another character says, "Be careful, you never know what could be out in those woods!" This alerts the reader that the woods may be dangerous and prompts the reader to expect something to attack the protagonist in the woods. This is an example of foreshadowing through warning. Alternatively, a character may unknowingly foreshadow later events. For example, consider a story where a brother and sister run through their house and knock over a vase and break it. The brother says, "Don't worry, we'll clean it up! Mom will never know!" However, the reader knows that their mother will most likely find out what they have done, so the reader expects the siblings to later get in trouble for running, breaking the vase, and hiding it from their mother.

Symbolism

Symbolism describes an author's use of a **symbol**, an element of the story that **represents** something else. Symbols can impact stories in many ways, including deepening the meaning of a story or its elements, comparing a story to another work, or foreshadowing later events in a story. Symbols can be objects, characters, colors, numbers, or anything else the author establishes as a symbol. Symbols can be clearly established through direct comparison or repetition, but they can also be established subtly or gradually over a large portion of the story. Another form of symbolism is **allusion**, which is when something in a story is used to prompt the reader to think about another work. Many well-known works use **Biblical allusions**, which are allusions to events or details in the Bible that inform a work or an element within it.

Integration of Knowledge and Ideas

Author's Purpose

Author's Purpose

Usually, identifying the author's **purpose** is easier than identifying his or her **position**. In most cases, the author has no interest in hiding his or her purpose. A text that is meant to entertain, for instance, should be written to please the reader. Most narratives, or stories, are written to entertain, though they may also inform or persuade. Informative texts are easy to identify, while the most difficult purpose of a text to identify is persuasion because the author has an interest in making this purpose hard to detect. When a reader discovers that the author is trying to persuade, he or she should be skeptical of the argument. For this reason, persuasive texts often try to establish an entertaining tone and hope to amuse the reader into agreement. On the other hand, an informative tone may be implemented to create an appearance of authority and objectivity.

An author's purpose is evident often in the **organization** of the text (e.g., section headings in bold font points to an informative text). However, you may not have such organization available to you in your exam. Instead, if the author makes his or her main idea clear from the beginning, then the likely purpose of the text is to **inform**. If the author begins by making a claim and provides various arguments to support that claim, then the purpose is probably to **persuade**. If the author tells a story or wants to gain the reader's attention more than to push a particular point or deliver information, then his or her purpose is most likely to **entertain**. As a reader, you must judge authors on how well they accomplish their purpose. In other words, you need to consider the type of passage (e.g., technical, persuasive, etc.) that the author has written and if the author has followed the requirements of the passage type.

Review Video: Understanding the Author's Intent
Visit mometrix.com/academy and enter code: 511819

Informational Texts

An **informational text** is written to educate and enlighten readers. Informational texts are almost always nonfiction and are rarely structured as a story. The intention of an informational text is to deliver information in the most comprehensible way. So, look for the structure of the text to be very clear. In an informational text, the thesis statement is one or two sentences that normally appears at the end of the first paragraph. The author may use some colorful language, but he or she is likely to put more emphasis on clarity and precision. Informational essays do not typically appeal to the emotions. They often contain facts and figures and rarely include the opinion of the author; however, readers should remain aware of the possibility for bias as those facts are presented. Sometimes a persuasive essay can resemble an informative essay, especially if the author maintains an even tone and presents his or her views as if they were established fact.

Review Video: Informational Text
Visit mometrix.com/academy and enter code: 924964

Persuasive Writing

In a persuasive essay, the author is attempting to change the reader's mind or **convince** him or her of something that he or she did not believe previously. There are several identifying characteristics of **persuasive writing**. One is **opinion presented as fact**. When authors attempt to persuade readers, they often present their opinions as if they were fact. Readers must be on guard for statements that sound factual but which cannot be subjected to research, observation, or experiment. Another characteristic of persuasive writing is **emotional language**. An author will often try to play on the emotions of readers by appealing to their sympathy or sense of morality. When an author uses colorful or evocative language with the intent of arousing the reader's passions, then the author may be attempting to persuade. Finally, in many cases, a persuasive text will give an **unfair explanation of opposing positions**, if these positions are mentioned at all.

Entertaining Texts

The success or failure of an author's intent to **entertain** is determined by those who read the author's work. Entertaining texts may be either fiction or nonfiction, and they may describe real or imagined people, places, and events. Entertaining texts are often narratives or poems. A text that is written to entertain is likely to contain **colorful language** that engages the imagination and the emotions. Such writing often features a great deal of figurative language, which typically enlivens the subject matter with images and analogies.

Though an entertaining text is not usually written to persuade or inform, authors may accomplish both of these tasks in their work. An entertaining text may *appeal to the reader's emotions* and cause him or her to think differently about a particular subject. In any case, entertaining texts tend to showcase the personality of the author more than other types of writing.

Descriptive Text

In a sense, almost all writing is descriptive, insofar as an author seeks to describe events, ideas, or people to the reader. Some texts, however, are primarily concerned with **description**. A descriptive text focuses on a particular subject and attempts to depict the subject in a way that will be clear to readers. Descriptive texts contain many adjectives and adverbs (i.e., words that give shades of meaning and create a more detailed mental picture for the reader). A descriptive text fails when it is unclear to the reader. A descriptive text will certainly be informative and may be persuasive and entertaining as well.

Review Video: Descriptive Texts
Visit mometrix.com/academy and enter code: 174903

Expression of Feelings

When an author intends to **express feelings**, he or she may use **expressive and bold language**. An author may write with emotion for any number of reasons. Sometimes, authors will express feelings because they are describing a personal situation of great pain or happiness. In other situations, authors will attempt to persuade the reader and will use emotion to stir up the passions. This kind of expression is easy to identify when the writer uses phrases like *I felt* and *I sense*. However, readers may find that the author will simply describe feelings without introducing them. As a reader, you must know the importance of recognizing when an author is expressing emotion and not to become overwhelmed by sympathy or passion. Readers should maintain some **detachment** so that they can still evaluate the strength of the author's argument or the quality of the writing.

Review Video: Emotional Language in Literature
Visit mometrix.com/academy and enter code: 759390

Expository Passage

An **expository** passage aims to **inform** and enlighten readers. Expository passages are nonfiction and usually center around a simple, easily defined topic. Since the goal of exposition is to teach, such a passage should be as clear as possible. Often, an expository passage contains helpful organizing words, like *first, next, for example,* and *therefore.* These words keep the reader **oriented** in the text. Although expository passages do not need to feature colorful language and artful writing, they are often more effective with these features. For a reader, the challenge of expository passages is to maintain steady attention. Expository passages are not always about subjects that will naturally interest a reader, so the writer is often more concerned with **clarity** and **comprehensibility** than with engaging the reader. By reading actively, you can ensure a good habit of focus when reading an expository passage.

Review Video: Expository Passages
Visit mometrix.com/academy and enter code: 256515

Narrative Passage

A **narrative** passage is a story that can be fiction or nonfiction. However, there are a few elements that a text must have in order to be classified as a narrative. First, the text must have a **plot** (i.e., a series of events). Narratives often proceed in a clear sequence, but this is not a requirement. If the narrative is good, then these events will be interesting to readers. Second, a narrative has **characters**. These characters could be people, animals, or even inanimate objects—so long as they participate in the plot. Third, a narrative passage often contains **figurative language** which is meant to stimulate the imagination of readers by making comparisons and observations. For instance, a *metaphor*, a common piece of figurative language, is a description of one thing in terms of another. *The moon was a frosty snowball* is an example of a metaphor. In the literal sense this is obviously untrue, but the comparison suggests a certain mood for the reader.

Technical Passage

A **technical** passage is written to *describe* a complex object or process. Technical writing is common in medical and technological fields, in which complex ideas of mathematics, science, and engineering need to be explained *simply* and *clearly*. To ease comprehension, a technical passage usually proceeds in a very logical order. Technical passages often have clear headings and subheadings, which are used to keep the reader oriented in the text. Additionally, you will find that these passages divide sections up with numbers or letters. Many technical passages look more like an outline than a piece of prose. The amount of **jargon** or difficult vocabulary will vary in a technical passage depending on the intended audience. As much as possible, technical passages try to avoid language that the reader will have to research in order to understand the message, yet readers will find that jargon cannot always be avoided.

Review Video: Technical Passages
Visit mometrix.com/academy and enter code: 478923

Critical Reading Skills

Opinions, Facts, and Fallacies

Critical thinking skills are mastered through understanding various types of writing and the different purposes of authors can have for writing different passages. Every author writes for a purpose. When you understand their purpose and how they accomplish their goal, you will be able to analyze their writing and determine whether or not you agree with their conclusions.

Readers must always be aware of the difference between fact and opinion. A **fact** can be subjected to analysis and proven to be true. An **opinion**, on the other hand, is the author's personal thoughts or feelings and may not be altered by research or evidence. If the author writes that the distance from New York City to Boston is about two hundred miles, then he or she is stating a fact. If the author writes that New York City is too crowded, then he or she is giving an opinion because there is no objective standard for overpopulation. Opinions are often supported by facts. For instance, an author might use a comparison between the population density of New York City and that of other major American cities as evidence of an overcrowded population. An opinion supported by facts tends to be more convincing. On the other hand, when authors support their opinions with other opinions, readers should employ critical thinking and approach the argument with skepticism.

> **Review Video: Distinguishing Fact and Opinion**
> Visit mometrix.com/academy and enter code: 870899

RELIABLE SOURCES

When you read an argumentative passage, you need to be sure that facts are presented to the reader from **reliable sources**. An opinion is what the author thinks about a given topic. An opinion is not common knowledge or proven by expert sources, instead the information is the personal beliefs and thoughts of the author. To distinguish between fact and opinion, a reader needs to consider the type of source that is presenting information, the information that backs-up a claim, and the author's motivation to have a certain point-of-view on a given topic. For example, if a panel of scientists has conducted multiple studies on the effectiveness of taking a certain vitamin, then the results are more likely to be factual than those of a company that is selling a vitamin and simply claims that taking the vitamin can produce positive effects. The company is motivated to sell their product, and the scientists are using the scientific method to prove a theory. Remember, if you find sentences that contain phrases such as "I think...", then the statement is an opinion.

BIASES

In their attempts to persuade, writers often make mistakes in their thought processes and writing choices. These processes and choices are important to understand so you can make an informed decision about the author's credibility. Every author has a point of view, but authors demonstrate a **bias** when they ignore reasonable counterarguments or distort opposing viewpoints. A bias is evident whenever the author's claims are presented in a way that is unfair or inaccurate. Bias can be intentional or unintentional, but readers should be skeptical of the author's argument in either case. Remember that a biased author may still be correct. However, the author will be correct in spite of, not because of, his or her bias.

A **stereotype** is a bias applied specifically to a group of people or a place. Stereotyping is considered to be particularly abhorrent because it promotes negative, misleading generalizations about people. Readers should be very cautious of authors who use stereotypes in their writing. These faulty assumptions typically reveal the author's ignorance and lack of curiosity.

> **Review Video: Bias and Stereotype**
> Visit mometrix.com/academy and enter code: 644829

Reading Comprehension and Connecting with Texts

Comparing Two Stories

When presented with two different stories, there will be **similarities** and **differences** between the two. A reader needs to make a list, or other graphic organizer, of the points presented in each story. Once the reader has written down the main point and supporting points for each story, the two sets of ideas can be compared. The reader can then present each idea and show how it is the same or different in the other story. This is called **comparing and contrasting ideas**.

The reader can compare ideas by stating, for example: "In Story 1, the author believes that humankind will one day land on Mars, whereas in Story 2, the author believes that Mars is too far away for humans to ever step foot on." Note that the two viewpoints are different in each story that the reader is comparing. A reader may state that: "Both stories discussed the likelihood of humankind landing on Mars." This statement shows how the viewpoint presented in both stories is based on the same topic, rather than how each viewpoint is different. The reader will complete a comparison of two stories with a conclusion.

> **Review Video: How to Compare and Contrast**
> Visit mometrix.com/academy and enter code: 833765

Outlining a Passage

As an aid to drawing conclusions, **outlining** the information contained in the passage should be a familiar skill to readers. An effective outline will reveal the structure of the passage and will lead to solid conclusions. An effective outline will have a title that refers to the basic subject of the text, though the title does not need to restate the main idea. In most outlines, the main idea will be the first major section. Each major idea in the passage will be established as the head of a category. For instance, the most common outline format calls for the main ideas of the passage to be indicated with Roman numerals. In an effective outline of this kind, each of the main ideas will be represented by a Roman numeral and none of the Roman numerals will designate minor details or secondary ideas. Moreover, all supporting ideas and details should be placed in the appropriate place on the outline. An outline does not need to include every detail listed in the text, but it should feature all of those that are central to the argument or message. Each of these details should be listed under the corresponding main idea.

> **Review Video: Outlining as an Aid to Drawing Conclusions**
> Visit mometrix.com/academy and enter code: 584445

Using Graphic Organizers

Ideas from a text can also be organized using **graphic organizers**. A graphic organizer is a way to simplify information and take key points from the text. A graphic organizer such as a timeline may have an event listed for a corresponding date on the timeline, while an outline may have an event listed under a key point that occurs in the text. Each reader needs to create the type of graphic organizer that works the best for him or her in terms of being able to recall information from a story. Examples include a spider-map, which takes a main idea from the story and places it in a bubble with supporting points branching off the main idea. An outline is useful for diagramming the main and supporting points of the entire story, and a Venn diagram compares and contrasts characteristics of two or more ideas.

> **Review Video: Graphic Organizers**
> Visit mometrix.com/academy and enter code: 665513

Making Logical Conclusions about a Passage

A reader should always be drawing conclusions from the text. Sometimes conclusions are **implied** from written information, and other times the information is **stated directly** within the passage. One should always aim to draw conclusions from information stated within a passage, rather than to draw them from mere implications. At times an author may provide some information and then describe a counterargument. Readers should be alert for direct statements that are subsequently rejected or weakened by the author. Furthermore, you should always read through the entire passage before drawing conclusions. Many readers are trained to expect the author's conclusions at either the beginning or the end of the passage, but many texts do not adhere to this format.

Drawing conclusions from information implied within a passage requires confidence on the part of the reader. **Implications** are things that the author does not state directly, but readers can assume based on what the author does say. Consider the following passage: *I stepped outside and opened my umbrella. By the time I got to work, the cuffs of my pants were soaked.* The author never states that it is raining, but this fact is clearly implied. Conclusions based on implication must be well supported by the text. In order to draw a solid conclusion, readers should have **multiple pieces of evidence**. If readers have only one piece, they must be assured that there is no other possible explanation than their conclusion. A good reader will be able to draw many conclusions from information implied by the text, which will be a great help on the exam.

Drawing Conclusions

A common type of inference that a reader has to make is **drawing a conclusion**. The reader makes this conclusion based on the information provided within a text. Certain facts are included to help a reader come to a specific conclusion. For example, a story may open with a man trudging through the snow on a cold winter day, dragging a sled behind him. The reader can logically **infer** from the setting of the story that the man is wearing heavy winter clothes in order to stay warm. Information is implied based on the setting of a story, which is why **setting** is an important element of the text. If the same man in the example was trudging down a beach on a hot summer day, dragging a surf board behind him, the reader would assume that the man is not wearing heavy clothes. The reader makes inferences based on their own experiences and the information presented to them in the story.

Test-taking tip: When asked to identify a conclusion that may be drawn, look for critical "hedge" phrases, such as *likely*, *may*, *can*, and *will often*, among many others. When you are being tested on this knowledge, remember the question that writers insert into these hedge phrases to cover every possibility. Often an answer will be wrong simply because there is no room for exception. Extreme positive or negative answers (such as always or never) are usually not correct. When answering these questions, the reader **should not** use any outside knowledge that is not gathered directly or reasonably inferred from the passage. Correct answers can be derived straight from the passage.

Example

Read the following sentence from *Little Women* by Louisa May Alcott and draw a conclusion based upon the information presented:

> *You know the reason Mother proposed not having any presents this Christmas was because it is going to be a hard winter for everyone; and she thinks we ought not to spend money for pleasure, when our men are suffering so in the army.*

Based on the information in the sentence, the reader can conclude, or **infer**, that the men are away at war while the women are still at home. The pronoun *our* gives a clue to the reader that the character is speaking about men she knows. In addition, the reader can assume that the character is speaking to a brother or sister, since the term "Mother" is used by the character while speaking to another person. The reader can also come to the conclusion that the characters celebrate Christmas, since it is mentioned in the **context** of the sentence. In the sentence, the mother is presented as an unselfish character who is opinionated and thinks about the wellbeing of other people.

Summarizing

A helpful tool is the ability to **summarize** the information that you have read in a paragraph or passage format. This process is similar to creating an effective outline. First, a summary should accurately define the main idea of the passage, though the summary does not need to explain this main idea in exhaustive detail. The summary should continue by laying out the most important supporting details or arguments from the passage. All of the significant supporting details should be included, and none of the details included should be irrelevant or insignificant. Also, the summary should accurately report all of these details. Too often, the desire for brevity in a summary leads to the sacrifice of clarity or accuracy. Summaries are often difficult to read because they omit all of the graceful language, digressions, and asides that distinguish great writing. However, an effective summary should communicate the same overall message as the original text.

Review Video: Summarizing Text
Visit mometrix.com/academy and enter code: 172903

PARAPHRASING

Paraphrasing is another method that the reader can use to aid in comprehension. When paraphrasing, one puts what they have read into their own words by rephrasing what the author has written, or one "translates" all of what the author shared into their own words by including as many details as they can.

EVALUATING A PASSAGE

It is important to understand the logical conclusion of the ideas presented in an informational text. **Identifying a logical conclusion** can help you determine whether you agree with the writer or not. Coming to this conclusion is much like making an inference: the approach requires you to combine the information given by the text with what you already know and make a logical conclusion. If the author intended for the reader to draw a certain conclusion, then you can expect the author's argumentation and detail to be leading in that direction.

One way to approach the task of drawing conclusions is to make brief **notes** of all the points made by the author. When the notes are arranged on paper, they may clarify the logical conclusion. Another way to approach conclusions is to consider whether the reasoning of the author raises any pertinent questions. Sometimes you will be able to draw several conclusions from a passage. On occasion these will be conclusions that were never imagined by the author. Therefore, be aware that these conclusions must be **supported directly by the text**.

EVALUATION OF SUMMARIES

A summary of a literary passage is a condensation in the reader's own words of the passage's main points. Several guidelines can be used in evaluating a summary. The summary should be complete yet concise. It should be accurate, balanced, fair, neutral, and objective, excluding the reader's own opinions or reactions. It should reflect in similar proportion how much each point summarized was covered in the original passage. Summary writers should include tags of attribution, like "Macaulay argues that" to reference the original author whose ideas are represented in the summary. Summary writers should not overuse quotations; they should only quote central concepts or phrases they cannot precisely convey in words other than those of the original author. Another aspect of evaluating a summary is considering whether it can stand alone as a coherent, unified composition. In addition, evaluation of a summary should include whether its writer has cited the original source of the passage they have summarized so that readers can find it.

MAKING CONNECTIONS TO ENHANCE COMPREHENSION

Reading involves thinking. For good comprehension, readers make **text-to-self**, **text-to-text**, and **text-to-world connections**. Making connections helps readers understand text better and predict what might occur next based on what they already know, such as how characters in the story feel or what happened in another text. Text-to-self connections with the reader's life and experiences make literature more personally relevant and meaningful to readers. Readers can make connections before, during, and after reading—including whenever the text reminds them of something similar they have encountered in life or other texts. The genre, setting, characters, plot elements, literary structure and devices, and themes an author uses allow a reader to make connections to other works of literature or to people and events in their own lives. Venn diagrams and other graphic organizers help visualize connections. Readers can also make double-entry notes: key content, ideas, events, words, and quotations on one side, and the connections with these on the other.

READING ARGUMENTATIVE WRITING

AUTHOR'S ARGUMENT IN ARGUMENTATIVE WRITING

In argumentative writing, the argument is a belief, position, or opinion that the author wants to convince readers to believe as well. For the first step, readers should identify the **issue**. Some issues are controversial, meaning people disagree about them. Gun control, foreign policy, and the death penalty are all controversial issues. The next step is to determine the **author's position** on the issue. That position or viewpoint constitutes the author's argument. Readers should then identify the **author's assumptions**: things he or she accepts, believes, or takes for granted without needing proof. Inaccurate or illogical assumptions produce flawed arguments and can mislead readers. Readers should identify what kinds of **supporting evidence** the author offers, such as research results, personal observations or experiences, case studies, facts, examples, expert testimony and opinions, and comparisons. Readers should decide how relevant this support is to the argument.

Review Video: Argumentative Writing
Visit mometrix.com/academy and enter code: 561544

EVALUATING AN AUTHOR'S ARGUMENT

The first three reader steps to **evaluate an author's argument** are to identify the **author's assumptions**, identify the **supporting evidence**, and decide **whether the evidence is relevant**. For example, if an author is not an expert on a particular topic, then that author's personal experience or opinion might not be relevant. The fourth step is to assess the **author's objectivity**. For example, consider whether the author introduces clear, understandable supporting evidence and facts to support the argument. The fifth step is evaluating whether the author's **argument is complete**. When authors give sufficient support for their arguments and also anticipate and respond effectively to opposing arguments or objections to their points, their arguments are complete. However, some authors omit information that could detract from their arguments. If instead they stated this information and refuted it, it would strengthen their arguments. The sixth step in evaluating an author's argumentative writing is to assess whether the **argument is valid**. Providing clear, logical reasoning makes an author's argument valid. Readers should ask themselves whether the author's points follow a sequence that makes sense, and whether each point leads to the next. The seventh step is to determine whether the author's **argument is credible**, meaning that it is convincing and believable. Arguments that are not valid are not credible, so step seven depends on step six. Readers should be mindful of their own biases as they evaluate and should not expect authors to conclusively prove their arguments, but rather to provide effective support and reason.

EVALUATING AN AUTHOR'S METHOD OF APPEAL

To evaluate the effectiveness of an appeal, it is important to consider the author's purpose for writing. Any appeals an author uses in their argument must be relevant to the argument's goal. For example, a writer that argues for the reclassification of Pluto, but primarily uses appeals to emotion, will not have an effective argument. This writer should focus on using appeals to logic and support their argument with provable facts. While most arguments should include appeals to logic, emotion, and credibility, some arguments only call for one or two of these types of appeal. Evidence can support an appeal, but the evidence must be relevant to truly strengthen the appeal's effectiveness. If the writer arguing for Pluto's reclassification uses the reasons for Jupiter's classification as evidence, their argument would be weak. This information may seem relevant because it is related to the classification of planets. However, this classification is highly dependent on the size of the celestial object, and Jupiter is significantly bigger than Pluto. This use of evidence is illogical and does not support the appeal. Even when appropriate evidence and appeals are used, appeals and arguments lose their effectiveness when they create logical fallacies.

Evidence

The term **text evidence** refers to information that supports a main point or minor points and can help lead the reader to a conclusion about the text's credibility. Information used as text evidence is precise, descriptive, and factual. A main point is often followed by supporting details that provide evidence to back up a claim. For example, a passage may include the claim that winter occurs during opposite months in the Northern and Southern hemispheres. Text evidence for this claim may include examples of countries where winter occurs in opposite months. Stating that the tilt of the Earth as it rotates around the sun causes winter to occur at different times in separate hemispheres is another example of text evidence. Text evidence can come from common knowledge, but it is also valuable to include text evidence from credible, relevant outside sources.

Review Video: Textual Evidence
Visit mometrix.com/academy and enter code: 486236

Evidence that supports the thesis and additional arguments needs to be provided. Most arguments must be supported by facts or statistics. A fact is something that is known with certainty, has been verified by several independent individuals, and can be proven to be true. In addition to facts, examples and illustrations can support an argument by adding an emotional component. With this component, you persuade readers in ways that facts and statistics cannot. The emotional component is effective when used alongside objective information that can be confirmed.

Credibility

The text used to support an argument can be the argument's downfall if the text is not credible. A text is **credible**, or believable, when its author is knowledgeable and objective, or unbiased. The author's motivations for writing the text play a critical role in determining the credibility of the text and must be evaluated when assessing that credibility. Reports written about the ozone layer by an environmental scientist and a hairdresser will have a different level of credibility.

Review Video: Author Credibility
Visit mometrix.com/academy and enter code: 827257

Appeal to Emotion

Sometimes, authors will appeal to the reader's emotion in an attempt to persuade or to distract the reader from the weakness of the argument. For instance, the author may try to inspire the pity of the reader by delivering a heart-rending story. An author also might use the bandwagon approach, in which he suggests that his opinion is correct because it is held by the majority. Some authors resort to name-calling, in which insults and harsh words are delivered to the opponent in an attempt to distract. In advertising, a common appeal is the celebrity testimonial, in which a famous person endorses a product. Of course, the fact that a famous person likes something should not really mean anything to the reader. These and other emotional appeals are usually evidence of poor reasoning and a weak argument.

Review Video: Emotional Language in Literature
Visit mometrix.com/academy and enter code: 759390

Counter Arguments

When authors give both sides to the argument, they build trust with their readers. As a reader, you should start with an undecided or neutral position. If an author presents only his or her side to the argument, then they are not exhibiting credibility and are weakening their argument.

Building common ground with readers can be effective for persuading neutral, skeptical, or opposed readers. Sharing values with undecided readers can allow people to switch positions without giving up what they feel is important. People who may oppose a position need to feel that they can change their minds without betraying who they are as a person. This appeal to having an open mind can be a powerful tool in arguing a position without antagonizing other views. Objections can be countered on a point-by-point basis or in a summary paragraph. Be mindful of how an author points out flaws in counter arguments. If they are unfair to the other side of the argument, then you should lose trust with the author.

Chapter Quiz

Ready to see how well you retained what you just read? Scan the QR code to go directly to the chapter quiz interface for this study guide. If you're using a computer, simply visit the bonus page at **mometrix.com/bonus948/act** and click the Chapter Quizzes link.

Science

Transform passive reading into active learning! After immersing yourself in this chapter, put your comprehension to the test by taking a quiz. The insights you gained will stay with you longer this way. Scan the QR code to go directly to the chapter quiz interface for this study guide. If you're using a computer, simply visit the bonus page at **mometrix.com/bonus948/act** and click the Chapter Quizzes link.

Science Overview

The science portion of the ACT is made up of 40 questions in 35 minutes. The test is broken up into various passages, which contain information in written form and in graphs. The primary goal of the science test is to measure your understanding of scientific inquiry, which are represented by the following categories:

- **Interpretation of Data** (40-50%)
- **Scientific Investigation** (20-30%)
- **Evaluation of Models, Inferences, and Experimental Results** (25-35%)

Despite the three scoring categories only mentioning general scientific concepts, to thoroughly understand the passages and information presented, the test-taker will need to be familiar with general concepts related to the following as well:

- **Biology**
- **Chemistry**
- **Earth and Space Science**
- **Physics**

Time Management

The science test may scare you. For even the most accomplished student, many of the terms will be unfamiliar. General test-taking skills will help the most. Make sure you don't run out of time: move quickly and use the easy pacing methods we outline in the test-taking tactics section.

The most important thing you can do is to ignore your fears and jump into the test immediately. Don't be overwhelmed by all of the strange-sounding terms. You have to jump into the test like jumping into a pool; all at once is the easiest way. Once you get past the jargon, you'll find that the science reasoning test is in some ways easier than even the reading test. Unfortunately, most students don't finish this test. This is why managing your time on this test is at least as important as on the math test.

The test lasts 35 minutes, giving 5 minutes per section.

The first thing to do is to read the passage. Use 2 minutes to do this. Really try to understand what's going on, treating all of the scientific terms as you would characters in a novel; just accept their names as they are, and follow the story. Use another 3 minutes to answer as many questions as you can. It's important to answer all of the easy questions.

Overall, the science reasoning is the test that is the hardest to study for and has the lowest test average for all test-takers, even lower than the math. If science is a subject you take because you have to, and not because you want to, your primary goal on science reasoning is damage control; you want to prevent it from dragging down your higher scores when ACT averages your test scores to get the composite.

In addition, the science reasoning test is probably unlike any other science test you've ever taken in high school. It's vital that you work a few practice science reasoning tests before the test day. Familiarity alone will boost your score by 1-2 points.

Scientific Inquiry and Reasoning

Scientific Inquiry

The concept of **scientific inquiry** refers to the idea of how one thinks and asks questions in a logical way to gain trustworthy information. The underlying motivation of science is to try to understand the natural world. Much of human thought is based on assumptions about how things work that may or may not be true. The goal of scientific inquiry is to test those assumptions to gain a greater understanding of the world with good questions and objective tests, and then re-use what was learned to ask better questions. The more we understand about the natural world, the better the questions we can ask, and that is the general idea behind scientific inquiry. The applied practice of scientific inquiry is to ask questions in a systematic method, called the scientific method.

Scientific Knowledge

Scientific knowledge refers to any topic that is studied **empirically**, meaning that it is based on observation of a **phenomenon** in an objective way. The body of **scientific knowledge** is often broken down into several domains including biology, ecology, Earth science, space science, physics, and chemistry. These each have further subdomains and are overlapping in many ways. For instance, ecology is the study of ecosystems, which are made up of biological factors and geological factors, so it contains elements of both biology and Earth science. Each of these domains is subject to the concepts of scientific inquiry, such as the scientific method, scientific facts, hypotheses, and scientific laws.

Important Terminology

- A **phenomenon** is an event or effect that is observed.
- A **scientific fact** is considered an objective and verifiable observation. Usually, a fact can be repeated or demonstrated to others.
- A **scientific theory** is a proposition explaining why or how something happens and is built on scientific facts and laws. Scientific theories can be tested, but are not fully proven. If new evidence is found that disproves the theory, it is no longer considered true.
- A **hypothesis** is an educated guess that is not yet proven. It is used to predict the outcome of an experiment in an attempt to solve a problem or answer a question.
- A **law** is an explanation of events that always leads to the same outcome. It is a fact that an object falls. The law of gravity explains why an object falls. The theory of relativity, although generally accepted, has been neither proven nor disproved.
- A **model** is used to explain something on a smaller scale or in simpler terms to provide an example. It is a representation of an idea that can be used to explain events or applied to new situations to predict outcomes or determine results.

Review Video: Science Process Skills
Visit mometrix.com/academy and enter code: 601624

History of Scientific Knowledge

When one examines the history of **scientific knowledge**, it is clear that it is constantly **evolving**. The body of facts, models, theories, and laws grows and changes over time. In other words, one scientific discovery leads to the next. Some advances in science and technology have important and long-lasting effects on science and society. Some discoveries were so alien to the accepted beliefs of the time that not only were they rejected as wrong, but were also considered outright blasphemy. Today, however, many beliefs once considered incorrect have become an ingrained part of scientific knowledge, and have also been the basis of new advances.

Examples of advances include: Copernicus's heliocentric view of the universe, Newton's laws of motion and planetary orbits, relativity, geologic time scale, plate tectonics, atomic theory, nuclear physics, biological evolution, germ theory, industrial revolution, molecular biology, information and communication, quantum theory, galactic universe, and medical and health technology.

Scientific Inquiry and Scientific Method

Scientists use a number of generally accepted techniques collectively known as the **scientific method**. The scientific method generally involves carrying out the following steps:

- Identifying a problem or posing a question
- Formulating a hypothesis or an educated guess
- Conducting experiments or tests that will provide a basis to solve the problem or answer the question
- Observing the results of the test
- Drawing conclusions

An important part of the scientific method is using acceptable experimental techniques. Objectivity is also important if valid results are to be obtained. Another important part of the scientific method is peer review. It is essential that experiments be performed and data be recorded in such a way that experiments can be reproduced to verify results. Historically, the scientific method has been taught with a more linear approach, but it is important to recognize that the scientific method should be a cyclical or **recursive process**. This means that as hypotheses are tested and more is learned, the questions should continue to change to reflect the changing body of knowledge. One cycle of experimentation is not enough.

Review Video: The Scientific Method
Visit mometrix.com/academy and enter code: 191386

Metric and International System of Units

The **metric system** is the accepted standard of measurement in the scientific community. The **International System of Units (SI)** is a set of measurements (including the metric system) that is almost globally accepted. The United States, Liberia, and Myanmar have not accepted this system. **Standardization** is important because it allows the results of experiments to be compared and reproduced without the need to laboriously convert measurements. The SI is based partially on the **meter-kilogram-second (MKS) system** rather than the **centimeter-gram-second (CGS) system**. The MKS system considers meters, kilograms, and seconds to be the basic units of measurement, while the CGS system considers centimeters, grams, and seconds to be the basic units of measurement. Under the MKS system, the length of an object would be expressed as 1 meter instead of 100 centimeters, which is how it would be described under the CGS system.

Review Video: Metric System Conversions
Visit mometrix.com/academy and enter code: 163709

Basic Units of Measurement

Using the **metric system** is generally accepted as the preferred method for taking measurements. Having a **universal standard** allows individuals to interpret measurements more easily, regardless of where they are located. The basic units of measurement are: the **meter**, which measures length; the **liter**, which measures volume; and the **gram**, which measures mass. The metric system starts with a base unit and increases or decreases in units of 10. The prefix and the base unit combined are used to indicate an amount. For example, deka- is 10 times the base unit. A dekameter is 10 meters; a dekaliter is 10 liters; and a dekagram is 10 grams. The prefix hecto- refers to 100 times the base amount; kilo- is 1,000 times the base amount. The prefixes that indicate a fraction of the base unit are deci-, which is $\frac{1}{10}$ of the base unit; centi-, which is $\frac{1}{100}$ of the base unit; and milli-, which is $\frac{1}{1,000}$ of the base unit.

Common Prefixes

The prefixes for multiples are as follows:

Deka	(da)	**10^1** (deka is the American spelling, but deca is also used)
Hecto	(h)	10^2
Kilo	(k)	10^3
Mega	(M)	10^6
Giga	(G)	10^9
Tera	(T)	10^{12}

The prefixes for subdivisions are as follows:

Deci	(d)	**10^{-1}**
Centi	(c)	10^{-2}
Milli	(m)	10^{-3}
Micro	(μ)	10^{-6}
Nano	(n)	10^{-9}
Pico	(p)	10^{-12}

The rule of thumb is that prefixes greater than 10^3 are capitalized when abbreviating. Abbreviations do not need a period after them. A decimeter (dm) is a tenth of a meter, a deciliter (dL) is a tenth of a liter, and a decigram (dg) is a tenth of a gram. Pluralization is understood. For example, when referring to 5 mL of water, no "s" needs to be added to the abbreviation.

Basic SI Units of Measurement

SI uses **second(s)** to measure time. Fractions of seconds are usually measured in metric terms using prefixes such as millisecond ($\frac{1}{1,000}$ of a second) or nanosecond ($\frac{1}{1,000,000,000}$ of a second). Increments of time larger than a second are measured in **minutes** and **hours**, which are multiples of 60 and 24. An example of this is a swimmer's time in the 800-meter freestyle being described as 7:32.67, meaning 7 minutes, 32 seconds, and 67 one-hundredths of a second. One second is equal to $\frac{1}{60}$ of a minute, $\frac{1}{3,600}$ of an hour, and $\frac{1}{86,400}$ of a day. Other SI base units are the **ampere** (A) (used to measure electric current), the **kelvin** (K) (used to measure thermodynamic temperature), the **candela** (cd) (used to measure luminous intensity), and the **mole** (mol) (used to measure the amount of a substance at a molecular level). **Meter** (m) is used to measure length and **kilogram** (kg) is used to measure mass.

Significant Figures

The mathematical concept of **significant figures** or **significant digits** is often used to determine the accuracy of measurements or the level of confidence one has in a specific measurement. The significant figures of a measurement include all the digits known with certainty plus one estimated or uncertain digit. There are a number of rules for determining which digits are considered "important" or "interesting." They are: all non-zero digits are *significant*, zeros between digits are *significant*, and leading and trailing zeros are *not significant* unless they appear to the right of the non-zero digits in a decimal. For example, in 0.01230 the significant digits are 1230, and this number would be said to be accurate to the hundred-thousandths place. The zero indicates that the amount has actually been measured as 0. Other zeros are considered place holders, and are not important. A decimal point may be placed after zeros to indicate their importance (in 100. for example). **Estimating**, on the other hand, involves approximating a value rather than calculating the exact number. This may be used to quickly determine a value that is close to the actual number when complete accuracy does not matter or is not possible. In science, estimation may be used when it is impossible to measure or calculate an exact amount, or to quickly approximate an answer when true calculations would be time consuming.

Graphs and Charts

Graphs and charts are effective ways to present scientific data such as observations, statistical analyses, and comparisons between dependent variables and independent variables. On a line chart, the **independent variable** (the one that is being manipulated for the experiment) is represented on the horizontal axis (the x-axis). Any **dependent variables** (the ones that may change as the independent variable changes) are represented on the y-axis. An **XY** or **scatter plot** is often used to plot many points. A "best fit" line is drawn, which allows outliers to be identified more easily. Charts and their axes should have titles. The x and y interval units should be evenly spaced and labeled. Other types of charts are **bar charts** and **histograms**, which can be used to compare differences between the data collected for two variables. A **pie chart** can graphically show the relation of parts to a whole.

Review Video: Identifying Variables
Visit mometrix.com/academy and enter code: 627181

Review Video: Data Interpretation of Graphs
Visit mometrix.com/academy and enter code: 200439

Data Presentation

Data collected during a science lab can be organized and **presented** in any number of ways. While **straight narrative** is a suitable method for presenting some lab results, it is not a suitable way to present numbers and quantitative measurements. These types of observations can often be better presented with **tables** and **graphs**. Data that is presented in tables and organized in rows and columns may also be used to make graphs quite easily. Other methods of presenting data include illustrations, photographs, video, and even audio formats. In a **formal report**, tables and figures are labeled and referred to by their labels. For example, a picture of a bubbly solution might be labeled Figure 1, Bubbly Solution. It would be referred to in the text in the following way: "The reaction created bubbles 10 mm in size, as shown in Figure 1, Bubbly Solution." Graphs are also labeled as figures. Tables are labeled in a different way. Examples include: Table 1, Results of Statistical Analysis, or Table 2, Data from Lab 2.

Review Video: Understanding Charts and Tables
Visit mometrix.com/academy and enter code: 882112

Statistical Precision and Errors

Errors that occur during an experiment can be classified into two categories: random errors and systematic errors. **Random errors** can result in collected data that is wildly different from the rest of the data, or they may result in data that is indistinguishable from the rest. Random errors are not consistent across the data set. In large data sets, random errors may contribute to the variability of data, but they will not affect the average. Random errors are sometimes referred to as noise. They may be caused by a student's inability to take the same measurement in exactly the same way or by outside factors that are not considered variables, but influence the data. A **systematic error** will show up consistently across a sample or data set, and may be the result of a flaw in the experimental design. This type of error affects the average, and is also known as bias.

Scientific Notation

Scientific notation is used because values in science can be very large or very small, which makes them unwieldy. A number in **decimal notation** is 93,000,000. In **scientific notation**, it is 9.3×10^7. The first number, 9.3, is the **coefficient**. It is always greater than or equal to 1 and less than 10. This number is followed by a multiplication sign. The base is always 10 in scientific notation. If the number is greater than ten, the exponent is positive. If the number is between zero and one, the exponent is negative. The first digit of the number is followed by a decimal point and then the rest of the number. In this case, the number is 9.3, and the decimal point was moved seven places to the right from the end of the number to get 93,000,000. The number of places moved, seven, is the exponent.

Statistical Terminology

Mean - The average, found by taking the sum of a set of numbers and dividing by the number of numbers in the set.

Median - The middle number in a set of numbers sorted from least to greatest. If the set has an even number of entries, the median is the average of the two in the middle.

Mode - The value that appears most frequently in a data set. There may be more than one mode. If no value appears more than once, there is no mode.

Range - The difference between the highest and lowest numbers in a data set.

Standard deviation - Measures the dispersion of a data set or how far from the mean a single data point is likely to be.

Regression analysis - A method of analyzing sets of data and sets of variables that involves studying how the typical value of the dependent variable changes when any one of the independent variables is varied and the other independent variables remain fixed.

> **Review Video: Mean, Median, and Mode**
> Visit mometrix.com/academy and enter code: 286207
>
> **Review Video: Standard Deviation**
> Visit mometrix.com/academy and enter code: 419469

Physics

Laws of Thermodynamics

The **laws of thermodynamics** are generalized principles dealing with energy and heat.

- The **zeroth law** of thermodynamics states that two objects in thermodynamic equilibrium with a third object are also in equilibrium with each other. Being in thermodynamic equilibrium basically means that different objects are at the same temperature.
- The **first law** deals with conservation of energy. It states that neither mass nor energy can be destroyed; only converted from one form to another.
- The **second law** states that the entropy (the amount of energy in a system that is no longer available for work or the amount of disorder in a system) of an isolated system can only increase. The second law also states that heat is not transferred from a lower-temperature system to a higher-temperature one unless additional work is done.
- The **third law** of thermodynamics states that as temperature approaches absolute zero, entropy approaches a constant minimum. It also states that a system cannot be cooled to absolute zero.

> **Review Video: Laws of Thermodynamics**
> Visit mometrix.com/academy and enter code: 253607

Heat and Temperature

Heat is energy transfer (other than direct work) from one body or system to another due to thermal contact. Everything tends to become less organized and less orderly over time (**entropy**). In all energy transfers, therefore, the overall result is that the energy is spread out uniformly. This transfer of heat energy from hotter to cooler objects is accomplished by conduction, radiation, or convection. **Temperature** is a measurement of an object's stored heat energy. More specifically, temperature is the average kinetic energy of an object's particles. When the temperature of an object increases and its atoms move faster, kinetic energy also increases. Temperature is not energy since it changes and is not conserved. Thermometers are used to measure temperature.

Mass, Weight, Volume, Density, and Specific Gravity

Mass — Mass is a measure of the amount of substance in an object.

Weight — Weight is a measure of the gravitational pull of Earth on an object.

Volume — Volume is a measure of the amount of space occupied. There are many formulas to determine volume. For example, the volume of a cube is the length of one side cubed (a^3) and the volume of a rectangular prism is length times width times height ($l \times w \times h$). The volume of an irregular shape can be determined by how much water it displaces.

Density — Density is a measure of the amount of mass per unit volume. The formula to find density is mass divided by volume ($\mathrm{D} = \mathrm{m/V}$). It is expressed in terms of mass per cubic unit (e.g., grams per cubic centimeter $\frac{g}{cm^3}$).

Specific gravity — This is a measure of the ratio of a substance's density compared to the density of water.

Review Video: Mass, Weight, Volume, Density, and Specific Gravity
Visit mometrix.com/academy and enter code: 920570

Thermal Contact

Thermal contact refers to energy transferred to a body by a means other than work. A system in thermal contact with another can exchange energy with it through the process of heat transfer. Thermal contact does not necessarily involve direct physical contact. **Heat** is energy that can be transferred from one body or system to another without work being done. Everything tends to become less organized and less useful over time (entropy). In all energy transfers, therefore, the overall result is that the heat is spread out so that objects are in thermodynamic equilibrium and the heat can no longer be transferred without additional work.

Models for Flow of Electric Charge

Models that can be used to explain the **flow of electric current, potential, and circuits** include water, gravity, and roller coasters. For example, just as a mass can have a potential for energy based on its location, so can a charge within an electrical field. Just as a force is required to move an object uphill, a force is also required to move a charge from a low to high potential. Another example is water. Water does not flow when it is level. If it is lifted to a point and then placed on a downward path, it will flow. A roller coaster car requires work to be performed to transport it to a point where it has potential energy (the top of a hill). Once there, gravity provides the force for it to flow (move) downward. If either path is broken, the flow or movement stops or is not completed.

Atomic Structures

Magnetic Fields

The motions of subatomic structures (nuclei and electrons) produce a **magnetic field**. It is the direction of the spin and orbit that indicates the direction of the field. The strength of a magnetic field is known as the **magnetic moment**. As electrons spin and orbit a nucleus, they produce a magnetic field. Pairs of electrons that spin and orbit in opposite directions cancel each other out, creating a net magnetic field of zero. Materials that have an unpaired electron are magnetic. Those with a weak attractive force are referred to as paramagnetic materials, while ferromagnetic materials have a strong attractive force. A diamagnetic material has electrons that are paired and, therefore, does not typically have a magnetic moment. There are, however, some diamagnetic materials that have a weak magnetic field.

Electric Charges

The attractive force between the electrons and the nucleus is called the **electric force**. A positive (+) charge or a negative (−) charge creates a field of sorts in the empty space around it, which is known as an **electric field**. The direction of a positive charge is away from the electric field and the direction of a negative charge is towards it. An electron within the force of the field is pulled towards a positive charge because an electron has a negative charge. A particle with a positive charge is pushed away, or repelled, by another positive charge. Like charges repel each other and opposite charges attract. Lines of force show the paths of charges. The **electric force** between two objects is directly proportional to the product of the charge magnitudes and inversely proportional to the square of the distance between the two objects. **Electric charge** is measured with the unit Coulomb (C). It is the amount of charge moved in one second by a steady current of one ampere ($1C = 1A \times 1s$).

> **Review Video: Electric Charge**
> Visit mometrix.com/academy and enter code: 323587

Electric Current Movement Through Circuits

Electric current is the sustained flow of electric charge along a path in a circuit. This differs from a static electric charge, which is a constant non-moving charge rather than a continuous flow. The **rate of flow of electric charge** is expressed using the ampere (amp or A) and can be measured using an ammeter. A current of 1 ampere means that 1 coulomb of charge passes through a given area every second. Electric charges typically only move from areas of high electric potential to areas of low electric potential. To get charges to flow into a high potential area, you must connect it to an area of higher potential by introducing a battery or other voltage source.

Simple Circuits

Movement of electric charge along a path between areas of high electric potential and low electric potential, with a resistor or load device between them, is the definition of a **simple circuit**. It is a closed conducting path between the high and low potential points, such as the positive and negative terminals on a battery. One example of a circuit is the flow from one terminal of a car battery to the other. The electrolyte solution of water and sulfuric acid provides work in chemical form to start the flow. A frequently used classroom example of circuits involves using a D cell (1.5 V) battery, a small light bulb, and a piece of copper wire to create a circuit to light the bulb.

> **Review Video: Resistance of Electric Currents**
> Visit mometrix.com/academy and enter code: 668423

Magnets

A **magnet** is any object or material, such as iron, steel, or magnetite (lodestone), that can affect another substance within its **field of force** that has like characteristics. Magnets can either attract or repel other substances. Magnets have two **poles**: north and south. Like poles repel and opposite poles (pairs of north and south) attract. The magnetic field is a set of invisible lines representing the paths of attraction and repulsion. Magnetism can occur naturally, or ferromagnetic materials can be magnetized. Certain matter that is magnetized can retain its magnetic properties indefinitely and become a permanent magnet. Other matter can lose its magnetic properties. For example, an iron nail can be temporarily magnetized by stroking it repeatedly in the same direction using one pole of another magnet. Once magnetized, it can attract or repel other magnetically inclined materials, such as paper clips. Dropping the nail repeatedly will cause it to lose its charge.

Review Video: Magnets
Visit mometrix.com/academy and enter code: 570803

Magnetic Fields, Current, and Magnetic Domains

A **magnetic field** can be formed not only by a magnetic material, but also by electric current flowing through a wire. When a coiled wire is attached to the two ends of a battery, for example, an electromagnet can be formed by inserting a ferromagnetic material such as an iron bar within the coil. When electric current flows through the wire, the bar becomes a magnet. If there is no current, the magnetism is lost. A **magnetic domain** occurs when the magnetic fields of atoms are grouped and aligned. These groups form what can be thought of as miniature magnets within a material. This is what happens when an object like an iron nail is temporarily magnetized. Prior to magnetization, the organization of atoms and their various polarities are somewhat random with respect to where the north and south poles are pointing. After magnetization, a significant percentage of the poles are lined up in one direction, which is what causes the magnetic force exerted by the material.

Motion and Displacement

Motion is a change in the location of an object and is the result of an unbalanced net force acting on the object. Understanding motion requires an understanding of three basic quantities: displacement, velocity, and acceleration.

When something moves from one place to another, it has undergone **displacement**. Displacement along a straight line is a very simple example of a vector quantity. If an object travels from position $x = -5$ cm to $x = 5$ cm, it has undergone a displacement of 10 cm. If it traverses the same path in the opposite direction, its displacement is -10 cm. A vector that spans the object's displacement in the direction of travel is known as a displacement vector.

Review Video: Displacement in Physics
Visit mometrix.com/academy and enter code: 236197

Gravitational Force

Gravitational force is a universal force that causes every object to exert a force on every other object. The gravitational force between two objects can be described by the formula, $F = Gm_1m_2 / r^2$, where m_1 and m_2 are the masses of two objects, r is the distance between them, and G is the gravitational constant, $G = 6.672 \times 10^{-11}$ N m^2/kg^2. In order for this force to have a noticeable effect, one or both of the objects must be extremely large, so the equation is generally only used in problems involving planetary bodies. For problems involving objects on the earth being affected by earth's gravitational pull, the force of gravity is simply calculated as $F = mg$, where g is 9.81 m/s^2 toward the ground.

Review Video: Newton's Law of Gravitation
Visit mometrix.com/academy and enter code: 709086

Newton's First Two Laws of Motion

Newton's First Law

An object at rest or in motion will remain at rest or in motion unless acted upon by an external force.

This phenomenon is commonly referred to as **inertia**, the tendency of a body to remain in its present state of motion. In order for the body's state of motion to change, it must be acted on by an unbalanced force.

Review Video: Newton's First Law of Motion
Visit mometrix.com/academy and enter code: 590367

Newton's Second Law

An object's acceleration is **directly proportional** to the net force acting on the object and **inversely proportional** to the object's mass.

This law is generally written in equation form $F = ma$, where F is the net force acting on a body, m is the mass of the body, and a is its acceleration. Note that since the mass is always a positive quantity, the acceleration is always in the same direction as the force.

Review Video: Newton's Second Law of Motion
Visit mometrix.com/academy and enter code: 737975

Simple Machines

Simple machines include the inclined plane, lever, wheel and axle, and pulley. These simple machines have no internal source of energy. More complex or compound machines can be formed from them. Simple machines provide a mechanical advantage to make it easier to accomplish a task. The **inclined plane** enables a force less than the object's weight to be used to push an object to a greater height. A **lever** enables a multiplication of force. The wheel and axle allows for movement with less resistance. Single or double **pulleys** allow for easier direction of force. The wedge and screw are forms of the inclined plane. A **wedge** turns a smaller force working over a greater distance into a larger force. The **screw** is similar to an incline that is wrapped around a shaft.

Review Video: Simple Machines
Visit mometrix.com/academy and enter code: 950789

Review Video: Simple Machines - Wheel and Axle
Visit mometrix.com/academy and enter code: 574045

Friction

Friction is a force that arises as a **resistance to motion** where two surfaces are in contact. The maximum magnitude of the frictional force (f) can be calculated as $f = F_c\mu$, where F_c is the contact force between the two objects and μ is a coefficient of friction based on the surfaces' material composition. Two types of friction are static and kinetic. To illustrate these concepts, imagine a book resting on a table. The force of its weight (W) is equal and opposite to the force of the table on the book, or the normal force (N). If we exert a small force (F) on the book, attempting to push it to one side, a frictional force (f) would arise, equal and opposite to our force. At this point, it is a **static frictional force** because the book is not moving. If we increase our force on the book, we will eventually cause it to move. At this point, the frictional force opposing us will be a **kinetic frictional force**. Generally, the kinetic frictional force is lower than static frictional force (because the frictional coefficient for static friction is larger), which means that the amount of force needed to maintain the movement of the book will be less than what was needed to start it moving.

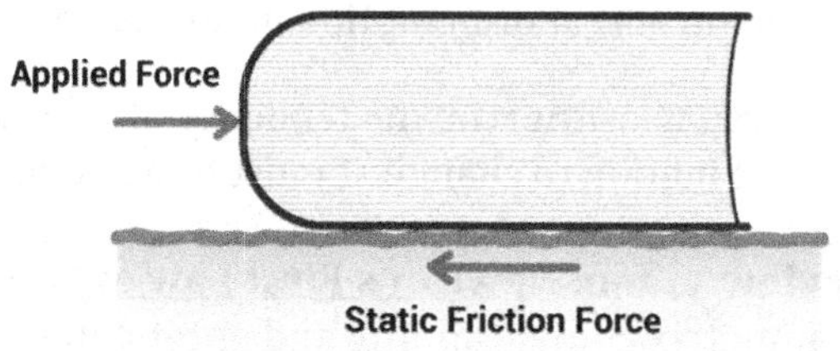

Review Video: Friction
Visit mometrix.com/academy and enter code: 716782

Review Video: Push and Pull Forces
Visit mometrix.com/academy and enter code: 104731

SOUND

Sound is a pressure disturbance that moves through a medium in the form of mechanical waves, which transfer energy from one particle to the next. Sound requires a medium to travel through, such as air, water, or other matter since it is the chain reaction of collisions that transfers energy to adjacent particles, not the actual movement of particles over a great distance. Sound is transferred through the movement of particles, which can be atoms or molecules. Waves of sound energy move outward in all directions from the source. Sound waves consist of compressions (particles are forced together) and rarefactions (particles move farther apart and their density decreases). A wavelength consists of one compression and one rarefaction. Different sounds have different wavelengths. Sound is a form of kinetic energy.

Review Video: Sound
Visit mometrix.com/academy and enter code: 562378

PITCH, LOUDNESS, SOUND INTENSITY, TIMBRE, AND OSCILLATION

Pitch — Pitch is the quality of sound determined by frequency. For example, a musical note can be tuned to a specific frequency. A, for instance, has a frequency of 440 Hz, which is a higher frequency than middle C. Humans can detect frequencies between about 20 Hz to 20,000 Hz.

Loudness — Loudness is a human's perception of sound intensity.

Sound intensity — Sound intensity is measured as the sound power per unit area and can be expressed in decibels.

Timbre — This is a human's perception of the type or quality of sound.

Oscillation — This is a measurement, usually of time, against a basic value, equilibrium, or rest point.

DOPPLER EFFECT

The **Doppler effect** refers to the effect the relative motion of the source of the wave and the location of the observer has on waves. The Doppler effect is easily observable in sound waves. What a person hears when a train approaches or a car honking its horn passes by are examples of the Doppler effect. The pitch of the sound is different not because the *emitted frequency* has changed, but because the *received frequency* has changed. The frequency is higher (as is the pitch) as the train approaches, the same as emitted just as it passes, and lower as the train moves away. This is because the wavelength changes. The Doppler effect can occur when an observer is stationary, and can also occur when two trains approach and pass each other. **Electromagnetic**

waves are also affected in this manner. The motion of the medium can also affect the wave. For waves that do not travel in a medium, such as light waves, it is the difference in velocity that determines the outcome.

Waves

Waves have energy and can transfer energy when they interact with matter. Although waves transfer energy, they do not transport matter. The two basic categories of waves are mechanical and electromagnetic. Mechanical waves are a disturbance of matter that transfers energy from one particle to an adjacent particle. There are many types of mechanical waves, including sound, seismic, and water. **Electromagnetic waves can transmit energy through a vacuum like visible light, microwaves, and radio waves**. A **transverse wave** provides a good illustration of the features of a wave, which include crests, troughs, amplitude, and wavelength.

Electromagnetic Spectrum

The electromagnetic spectrum is defined by frequency (f) and wavelength (λ). Frequency is typically measured in hertz and wavelength is usually measured in meters. Because light travels at a fairly constant speed, frequency is inversely proportional to wavelength, a relationship expressed by the formula $f = c/\lambda$, where c is the speed of light (about 3.0×10^8 m/s). Frequency multiplied by wavelength equals the speed of the wave; for electromagnetic waves, this is the speed of light, with some variance for the medium in which it is traveling. Electromagnetic waves include (from largest to smallest wavelength) radio waves, microwaves, infrared radiation (radiant heat), visible light, ultraviolet radiation, x-rays, and gamma rays. The energy of electromagnetic waves is carried in packets that have a magnitude inversely proportional to the wavelength. Radio waves have a range of wavelengths, from about 10^{-3} to 10^5 meters, while their frequencies range from 10^3 to about 10^{11} Hz.

> **Review Video: Electromagnetic Spectrum**
> Visit mometrix.com/academy and enter code: 771761

Visible Light

Visible light is defined as the portion of the electromagnetic spectrum that stimulates the human retina. It is absorbed and emitted by electrons, atoms, and molecules that move from one energy level to another. Visible light interacts with matter through molecular electron excitation (which occurs in the human retina) and through plasma oscillations (which occur in metals). Visible light is between ultraviolet and infrared light on the spectrum. The wavelengths of visible light cover a range from 380 nm (violet) to 760 nm (red). Different wavelengths correspond to different colors.

> **Review Video: What is Light?**
> Visit mometrix.com/academy and enter code: 900556

Reflection and Refraction

Reflection is the rebounding of a light wave from a surface back toward the medium from where it came. A light wave that hits a reflecting surface at a 90-degree angle retraces its original path back to its source. Striking the surface at any other angle results in reflection of the wave at an angle in the opposite direction. Reflectance is the amount of light a material reflects; metals have high reflectance. The smoother a surface, the higher its reflectance. **Refraction is the change in the direction of a light wave as it passes between transparent mediums with different optical densities**. This results in a change in the wave's velocity. The ratio of the sine of the angle of the incoming ray to the sine of the angle of refraction is equal to the ratio of the speed of light in the original medium to the speed of light in the refracting medium.

$$\frac{\sin\theta_{in}}{\sin\theta_{ref}} = \frac{v_{in}}{v_{ref}}$$

Review Video: Reflection, Transmission, and Absorption of Light
Visit mometrix.com/academy and enter code: 109410

Chemistry

Past Atomic Models and Theories

There have been many revisions to theories regarding the structure of **atoms** and their **particles**. Part of the challenge in developing an understanding of matter is that atoms and their particles are too small to be seen. It is believed that the first conceptualization of the atom was developed by **Democritus** in 400 B.C. Some of the more notable models are the solid sphere or billiard ball model postulated by John Dalton, the plum pudding or raisin bun model by J.J. Thomson, the planetary or nuclear model by Ernest Rutherford, the Bohr or orbit model by Niels Bohr, and the electron cloud or quantum mechanical model by Louis de Broglie and Erwin Schrodinger. Rutherford directed the alpha scattering experiment that discounted the plum pudding model. The shortcoming of the Bohr model was the belief that electrons orbited in fixed rather than changing ecliptic orbits.

Review Video: Atomic Models
Visit mometrix.com/academy and enter code: 434851

Models of Atoms

Atoms are extremely small. A hydrogen atom is about 5×10^{-8} mm in diameter. According to some estimates, five trillion hydrogen atoms could fit on the head of a pin. **Atomic radius** refers to the average distance between the nucleus and the outermost electron. Models of atoms that include the proton, nucleus, and electrons typically show the electrons very close to the nucleus and revolving around it, similar to how the Earth orbits the sun. However, another model relates the Earth as the nucleus and its atmosphere as electrons, which is the basis of the term "**electron cloud**." Another description is that electrons swarm around the nucleus. It should be noted that these atomic models are not to scale. A more accurate representation would be a nucleus with a diameter of about 2 cm in a stadium. The electrons would be in the bleachers. This model is similar to the not-to-scale solar system model. In reference to the periodic table, atomic radius increases as energy levels are added and decreases as more protons are added (because they pull the electrons closer to the nucleus). Essentially, atomic radius increases toward the left and toward the bottom of the periodic table.

Structure of Atoms

All matter consists of **atoms**. Atoms consist of a nucleus and electrons. The **nucleus** consists of protons and neutrons. The properties of these are measurable; they have mass and an electrical charge. The nucleus is positively charged due to the presence of protons. **Electrons** are negatively charged and orbit the nucleus. The nucleus has considerably more mass than the surrounding electrons. Atoms can bond together to make

molecules. Atoms that have an equal number of protons and electrons are electrically neutral. If the number of protons and electrons in an atom is not equal, the atom has a positive or negative charge and is an ion.

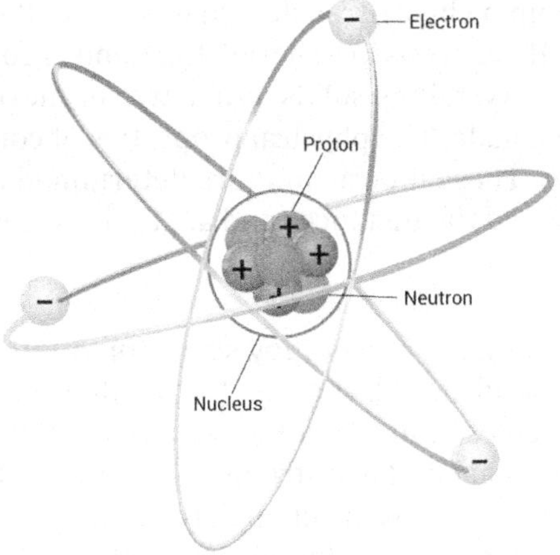

Atomic Number, Neutrons, Nucleon, and Element

- **Atomic number** (proton number) — The atomic number of an element refers to the number of protons in the nucleus of an atom. It is a unique identifier. It can be represented as Z. Atoms with a neutral charge have an atomic number that is equal to the number of electrons.
- **Neutrons** — Neutrons are the uncharged atomic particles contained within the nucleus. The number of neutrons in a nucleus can be represented as "N."
- **Nucleon** — This refers collectively to both neutrons and protons.
- **Element** — An element is matter with one particular type of atom. It can be identified by its atomic number or the number of protons in its nucleus. There are approximately 117 elements currently known, 94 of which occur naturally on Earth. Elements from the periodic table include hydrogen, carbon, iron, helium, mercury, and oxygen.

Molecules

Electrons in an atom can orbit different levels around the nucleus. They can absorb or release energy, which can change the location of their orbit or even allow them to break free from the atom. The outermost layer is the **valence layer**, which contains the valence electrons. The valence layer tends to have or share eight electrons. **Molecules** are formed by a chemical bond between atoms, a bond that occurs at the valence level. Two basic types of bonds are covalent and ionic. A **covalent bond** is formed when atoms share electrons. An **ionic bond** is formed when an atom transfers an electron to another atom. A cation or positive ion is formed when an atom loses one or more electrons. An anion or negative ion is formed when an atom gains one or more electrons. A **hydrogen bond** is a weak bond between a hydrogen atom of one molecule and an electronegative atom (such as nitrogen, oxygen, or fluorine) of another molecule. The **Van der Waals force** is a weak force between molecules. This type of force is much weaker than actual chemical bonds between atoms.

Review Video: Molecules
Visit mometrix.com/academy and enter code: 349910

Review Video: Anion, Cation, and Octet Rule
Visit mometrix.com/academy and enter code: 303525

Review Video: What is an Ionic Bond?
Visit mometrix.com/academy and enter code: 116546

Interaction of Atoms to Form Compounds

Atoms interact by **transferring** or sharing the electrons furthest from the nucleus. Known as the outer or **valence electrons**, they are responsible for the chemical properties of an element. **Bonds** between atoms are created when electrons are paired up by being transferred or shared. If electrons are transferred from one atom to another, the bond is ionic. If electrons are shared, the bond is covalent. Atoms of the same element may bond together to form molecules or crystalline solids. When two or more different types of atoms bind together chemically, a compound is made. The physical properties of compounds reflect the nature of the interactions among their molecules. These interactions are determined by the structure of the molecule, including the atoms they consist of and the distances and angles between them.

Matter

Matter refers to substances that have mass and occupy space (or volume). The traditional definition of matter describes it as having three states: solid, liquid, and gas. These different states are caused by differences in the distances and angles between molecules or atoms, which result in differences in the energy that binds them. **Solid** structures are rigid or nearly rigid and have strong bonds. Molecules or atoms of **liquids** move around and have weak bonds, although they are not weak enough to readily break. Molecules or atoms of **gases** move almost independently of each other, are typically far apart, and do not form bonds. The current definition of matter describes it as having four states. The fourth is **plasma**, which is an ionized gas that has some electrons that are described as free because they are not bound to an atom or molecule.

Review Video: States of Matter
Visit mometrix.com/academy and enter code: 742449

Most Abundant Elements in the Universe and on Earth

Aside from dark energy and dark matter, which are thought to account for all but four percent of the universe, the two most abundant elements in the universe are **hydrogen** (H) and **helium** (He). After hydrogen and helium, the most abundant elements are oxygen, neon, nitrogen, carbon, silicon, and magnesium. The most abundant isotopes in the solar system are hydrogen-1 and helium-4. Measurements of the masses of elements in the Earth's crust indicate that oxygen (O), silicon (Si), and aluminum (Al) are the most abundant on Earth. Hydrogen in its plasma state is the most abundant chemical element in stars in their main sequences but is relatively rare on planet Earth.

Energy Transformations

The following are some examples of energy transformations:

- **Electric to mechanical**: Ceiling fan
- **Chemical to heat**: A familiar example of a chemical to heat energy transformation is the internal combustion engine, which transforms the chemical energy (a type of potential energy) of gas and oxygen into heat. This heat is transformed into propulsive energy, which is kinetic. Lighting a match and burning coal are also examples of chemical to heat energy transformations.
- **Chemical to light**: Phosphorescence and luminescence (which allow objects to glow in the dark) occur because energy is absorbed by a substance (charged) and light is re-emitted comparatively slowly. This process is different from the one involved with glow sticks. They glow due to chemiluminescence, in which an excited state is created by a chemical reaction and transferred to another molecule.
- **Heat to electricity**: Examples include thermoelectric, geothermal, and ocean thermal.
- **Nuclear to heat**: Examples include nuclear reactors and power plants.
- **Mechanical to sound**: Playing a violin or almost any instrument
- **Sound to electric**: Microphone
- **Light to electric**: Solar panels
- **Electric to light**: Light bulbs

Relationship Between Conservation of Matter and Atomic Theory

Atomic theory is concerned with the characteristics and properties of atoms that make up matter. It deals with matter on a *microscopic level* as opposed to a *macroscopic level*. Atomic theory, for instance, discusses the kinetic motion of atoms in order to explain the properties of macroscopic quantities of matter. John Dalton (1766-1844) is credited with making many contributions to the field of atomic theory that are still considered valid. This includes the notion that all matter consists of atoms and that atoms are indestructible. In other words, atoms can be neither created nor destroyed. This is also the theory behind the conservation of matter, which explains why chemical reactions do not result in any detectable gains or losses in matter. This holds true for chemical reactions and smaller-scale processes. When dealing with large amounts of energy, however, atoms can be destroyed by nuclear reactions. This can happen in particle colliders or atom smashers.

> **Review Video: John Dalton**
> Visit mometrix.com/academy and enter code: 565627

Difference Between Atoms and Molecules

Elements from the periodic table such as hydrogen, carbon, iron, helium, mercury, and oxygen are **atoms**. Atoms combine to form molecules. For example, two atoms of hydrogen (H) and one atom of oxygen (O) combine to form one molecule of water (H_2O).

Chemical and Physical Properties

Matter has both physical and chemical properties. **Physical properties** can be seen or observed without changing the identity or composition of matter. For example, the mass, volume, and density of a substance can be determined without permanently changing the sample. Other physical properties include color, boiling point, freezing point, solubility, odor, hardness, electrical conductivity, thermal conductivity, ductility, and malleability. **Chemical properties** cannot be measured without changing the identity or composition of matter. Chemical properties describe how a substance reacts or changes to form a new substance. Examples of chemical properties include flammability, corrosivity, oxidation states, enthalpy of formation, and reactivity with other chemicals.

Chemical and Physical Changes

Physical changes do not produce new substances. The atoms or molecules may be rearranged, but no new substances are formed. Phase changes or changes of state such as melting, freezing, and sublimation are physical changes. For example, physical changes include the melting of ice, the boiling of water, sugar dissolving into water, and the crushing of a piece of chalk into a fine powder. **Chemical changes** involve a chemical reaction and do produce new substances. When iron rusts, iron oxide is formed, indicating a chemical change. Other examples of chemical changes include baking a cake, burning wood, digesting a cracker, and mixing an acid and a base.

Physical and Chemical Properties and Changes

Both physical changes and chemical reactions are everyday occurrences. **Physical changes** do not result in different substances. For example, when water becomes ice it has undergone a physical change, but not a chemical change. It has changed its form, but not its composition. It is still H_2O. **Chemical properties** are concerned with the constituent particles that make up the physicality of a substance. Chemical properties are apparent when **chemical changes** occur. The chemical properties of a substance are influenced by its electron configuration, which is determined in part by the number of protons in the nucleus (the atomic number). Carbon, for example, has 6 protons and 6 electrons. It is an element's outermost valence electrons that mainly determine its chemical properties. Chemical reactions may release or consume energy.

> **Review Video: Chemical and Physical Properties of Matter**
> Visit mometrix.com/academy and enter code: 717349

Elements, Compounds, Solutions, and Mixtures

- **Elements** — These are substances that consist of only one type of atom.
- **Compounds** — These are substances containing two or more elements. Compounds are formed by chemical reactions and frequently have different properties than the original elements. Compounds are decomposed by a chemical reaction rather than separated by a physical one.
- **Solutions** — These are homogeneous mixtures composed of two or more substances that have become one.
- **Mixtures** — Mixtures contain two or more substances that are combined but have not reacted chemically with each other. Mixtures can be separated using physical methods, while compounds cannot.

Heat, Energy, Work, and Thermal Energy

- **Heat** — Heat is the transfer of energy from a body or system as a result of thermal contact. Heat consists of random motion and the vibration of atoms, molecules, and ions. The higher the temperature is, the greater the atomic or molecular motion will be.
- **Energy** — Energy is the capacity to do work.
- **Work** — Work is the quantity of energy transferred by one system to another due to changes in a system that is the result of external forces, or macroscopic variables. Another way to put this is that work is the amount of energy that must be transferred to overcome a force. Lifting an object in the air is an example of work. The opposing force that must be overcome is gravity. Work is measured in joules (J). The rate at which work is performed is known as power.
- **Thermal energy** — Thermal energy is the energy present in a system due to temperature.

Types of Energy

Some discussions of energy consider only two types of energy: **kinetic energy** (the energy of motion) and **potential energy** (which depends on relative position or orientation). There are, however, other types of energy. **Electromagnetic waves**, for example, are a type of energy contained by a field. Another type of potential energy is electrical energy, which is the energy it takes to pull apart positive and negative electrical charges. **Chemical energy** refers to the manner in which atoms form into molecules, and this energy can be released or absorbed when molecules regroup. **Solar energy** comes in the form of visible light and non-visible light, such as infrared and ultraviolet rays. **Sound energy** refers to the energy in sound waves.

Review Video: Potential and Kinetic Energy
Visit mometrix.com/academy and enter code: 491502

Chemical Reactions

Chemical reactions measured in human time can take place quickly or slowly. They can take fractions of a second or billions of years. The rates of chemical reactions are determined by how frequently reacting atoms and molecules interact. Rates are also influenced by the temperature and various properties (such as shape) of the reacting materials. **Catalysts** accelerate chemical reactions, while inhibitors decrease reaction rates. Some types of reactions release energy in the form of heat and light. Some types of reactions involve the transfer of either electrons or hydrogen ions between reacting ions, molecules, or atoms. In other reactions, chemical bonds are broken down by heat or light to form reactive radicals with electrons that will readily form new bonds. Processes such as the formation of ozone and greenhouse gases in the atmosphere and the burning and processing of fossil fuels are controlled by radical reactions.

Review Video: Understanding Chemical Reactions
Visit mometrix.com/academy and enter code: 579876

Review Video: Catalysts
Visit mometrix.com/academy and enter code: 288189

Reading Chemical Equations

Chemical equations describe chemical reactions. The reactants are on the left side before the arrow. The products are on the right side after the arrow. The arrow is the mark that points to the reaction or change. The coefficient is the number before the element. This gives the ratio of reactants to products in terms of moles.

The equation for making water from hydrogen and oxygen is $2H_{2(g)} + O_{2(g)} \rightarrow 2H_2O_{(l)}$. The number 2 before hydrogen and water is the coefficient. This means that there are 2 moles of hydrogen and 2 of water. There is 1 mole of oxygen. This does not need to have the number 1 before the symbol for the element. For additional information, the following subscripts are often included to indicate the state of the substance: (g) stands for gas, (l) stands for liquid, (s) stands for solid, and (aq) stands for aqueous. Aqueous means the substance is dissolved in water. Charges are shown by superscript for individual ions, not for ionic compounds. Polyatomic ions are separated by parentheses. This is done so the kind of ion will not be confused with the number of ions.

Review Video: What is the Process of a Reaction?
Visit mometrix.com/academy and enter code: 808039

Balancing Equations

An **unbalanced equation** is one that does not follow the **law of conservation of mass**, which states that matter can only be changed, not created or destroyed. If an equation is unbalanced, the numbers of atoms indicated by the stoichiometric coefficients on each side of the arrow will not be equal. Start by writing the formulas for each species in the reaction. Count the atoms on each side and determine if the number is equal. Coefficients must be whole numbers. Fractional amounts, such as half a molecule, are not possible. Equations can be balanced by adjusting the coefficients of each part of the equation to the smallest possible whole number coefficient. $H_2 + O_2 \rightarrow H_2O$ is an example of an unbalanced equation. The balanced equation is $2H_2 + O_2 \rightarrow 2H_2O$, which indicates that it takes two moles of hydrogen and one of oxygen to produce two moles of water.

Review Video: How Do You Balance Chemical Equations?
Visit mometrix.com/academy and enter code: 341228

Periodic Table

The **periodic table** groups elements with similar chemical properties together. The grouping of elements is based on **atomic structure**. It shows periodic trends of physical and chemical properties and identifies families of elements with similar properties. It is a common model for organizing and understanding elements. In the periodic table, each element has its own cell that includes varying amounts of information presented in symbol form about the properties of the element. Cells in the table are arranged in **rows** (periods) and **columns** (groups or families). At minimum, a cell includes the symbol for the element and its atomic number. The cell for hydrogen, for example, which appears first in the upper left corner, includes an "H" and a "1" above the letter. Elements are ordered by atomic number, left to right, top to bottom.

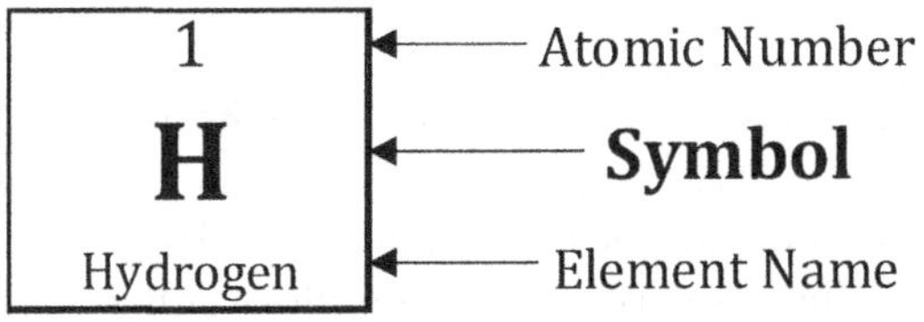

Review Video: Periodic Table
Visit mometrix.com/academy and enter code: 154828

Solutions

A solution is a homogeneous mixture, meaning that it is uniform in composition. Solutions consist of a solute (the substance that is dissolved) and a solvent (the substance that does the dissolving). For example, in sugar water the solvent is the water and the solute is the sugar. The intermolecular attraction between the solvent and the solute is called solvation. **Hydration** refers to solutions in which water is the solvent. Solutions are formed when the forces between the molecules of the solute and the solvent are as strong as the forces holding the solute together. An example is that salt (NaCl) dissolves in water to create a solution. The Na^+ and the Cl^- ions in salt interact with the molecules of water and vice versa to overcome the intramolecular forces of the solute.

Review Video: Solutions
Visit mometrix.com/academy and enter code: 995937

Review Video: Volume Percent of a Solution
Visit mometrix.com/academy and enter code: 400152

Mixtures, Suspensions, Colloids, Emulsions, and Foams

A **mixture** is a combination of two or more substances that are not bonded. **Suspensions** are mixtures of heterogeneous materials. Particles in suspensions are usually larger than those found in true solutions. Dirt mixed vigorously with water is an example of a suspension. The dirt is temporarily suspended in water, but it settles to the bottom of the container once the mixing is ceased. A mixture of large (1 nm to 500 nm) particles is called a **colloidal suspension**. The particles are termed dispersants and the dispersing medium is similar to the solvent in a solution. Sol refers to a liquid or a solid that also has solids dispersed through it, such as milk or gelatin. An aerosol spray is a colloid suspension of gas and the solid or liquid being dispersed. An **emulsion** refers to a liquid or a solid that has small droplets of another liquid dispersed through it. A **foam** is a liquid that has gas dispersed through it.

pH

The **potential of hydrogen** (pH) is a measurement of the concentration of hydrogen ions in a substance in terms of the number of moles of H^+ per liter of solution. All substances fall between 0 and 14 on the pH scale. A lower pH indicates a higher H^+ concentration, while a higher pH indicates a lower H^+ concentration. Pure water has a neutral pH, which is 7. Anything with a pH lower than water (<7) is considered acidic. Anything with a pH higher than water (>7) is a base. Drain cleaner, soap, baking soda, ammonia, egg whites, and sea water are common bases. Urine, stomach acid, citric acid, vinegar, hydrochloric acid, and battery acid are acids. A pH indicator is a substance that acts as a detector of hydrogen or hydronium ions. It is halochromic, meaning it changes color to indicate that hydrogen or hydronium ions have been detected.

Review Video: Overview of pH Levels
Visit mometrix.com/academy and enter code: 187395

Properties of Acids

When they are dissolved in aqueous solutions, some properties of **acids** are that they conduct electricity, change blue litmus paper to red, have a sour taste, react with bases to neutralize them, and react with active metals to free hydrogen. A **weak acid** is one that does not donate all of its protons or disassociate completely. **Strong acids** include hydrochloric, hydriodic, hydrobromic, perchloric, nitric, and sulfuric. They ionize completely. **Superacids** are those that are stronger than 100 percent sulfuric acid. They include fluoroantimonic, magic, and perchloric acids. Acids can be used in pickling, a process used to remove rust and corrosion from metals. They are also used as catalysts in the processing of minerals and the production of salts and fertilizers. Phosphoric acid (H_3PO_4) is added to sodas and other acids are added to foods as preservatives or to add taste.

Review Video: Properties of Acids and Bases
Visit mometrix.com/academy and enter code: 645283

Properties of Bases

When they are dissolved in aqueous solutions, some properties of **bases** are that they conduct electricity, change red litmus paper to blue, feel slippery, and react with acids to neutralize their properties. A **weak base** is one that does not completely ionize in an aqueous solution, and usually has a low pH. **Strong bases** can free protons in very weak acids. Examples of strong bases are hydroxide compounds such as potassium, barium, and lithium hydroxides. Most are in the first and second groups of the periodic table. A **superbase** is extremely strong compared to sodium hydroxide and cannot be kept in an aqueous solution. Superbases are organized into organic, organometallic, and inorganic classes. Bases are used as insoluble catalysts in heterogeneous reactions and as catalysts in hydrogenation.

Properties of Salts

Some properties of **salts** are that they are formed from acid base reactions, are ionic compounds consisting of metallic and nonmetallic ions, dissociate in water, and are comprised of tightly bonded ions. Some common salts are sodium chloride (NaCl), sodium bisulfate ($NaHSO_4$), potassium dichromate ($K_2Cr_2O_7$), and calcium chloride ($CaCl_2$). Calcium chloride is used as a drying agent, and may be used to absorb moisture when freezing mixtures. Potassium nitrate (KNO_3) is used to make fertilizer and in the manufacturing of explosives. Sodium nitrate ($NaNO_3$) is also used in the making of fertilizer. Baking soda [sodium bicarbonate ($NaHCO_3$)] is a salt, as are Epsom salts [magnesium sulfate ($MgSO_4$)]. Salt and water can react to form a base and an acid. This is called a **hydrolysis reaction**.

Unique Properties of Water

The important properties of water (H_2O) are high polarity, hydrogen bonding, cohesiveness, adhesiveness, high specific heat, high latent heat, and high heat of vaporization. Water is vital to life as we know it. The reason is that water is one of the main parts of many living things.

Water is a liquid at room temperature. The high specific heat of water means that it does not easily break its hydrogen bonds. Also, it resists heat and motion. This is why it has a high boiling point and high vaporization point.

Most substances are denser in their solid forms. However, water is different because its solid-state floats in its liquid state. Water is cohesive. This means that it is drawn to itself. It is also adhesive. This means that it draws in other molecules. If water will attach to another substance, the substance is said to be hydrophilic. Because of its cohesive and adhesive properties, water makes a good solvent. Substances with polar ions and molecules easily dissolve in water.

Kinetic Theory of Gases

The **kinetic theory of gases** assumes that gas molecules are small compared to the distances between them and that they are in constant random motion. The attractive and repulsive forces between gas molecules are negligible. Their kinetic energy does not change with time as long as the temperature remains the same. The higher the temperature is, the greater the motion will be. As the temperature of a gas increases, so does the kinetic energy of the molecules. In other words, gas will occupy a greater volume as the temperature is increased and a lesser volume as the temperature is decreased. In addition, the same amount of gas will occupy a greater volume as the temperature increases, but pressure remains constant. At any given temperature, gas molecules have the same average kinetic energy. The **ideal gas law** is derived from the kinetic theory of gases.

Review Video: Ideal Gas vs. Real Gas
Visit mometrix.com/academy and enter code: 619477

Organic Compounds

Two of the main characteristics of organic compounds are that they generally include carbon and are formed by covalent bonds. Carbon can form long chains, double and triple bonds, and rings. While inorganic compounds tend to have high melting points, organic compounds tend to melt at temperatures below 300° C. They also tend to boil, sublimate, and decompose below this temperature. Unlike inorganic compounds, they are not very water-soluble. Organic molecules are organized into functional groups based on their specific atoms, which helps determine how they will react chemically. A few groups are alkanes, nitro, alkenes, sulfides, amines, and carbolic acids. The hydroxyl group (−OH) consists of alcohols. These molecules are polar, which increases their solubility. By some estimates, there are more than 16 million organic compounds.

Review Video: Organic Compounds
Visit mometrix.com/academy and enter code: 264922

Hydrogen Bonds

Hydrogen bonds are weaker than covalent and ionic bonds and refer to the type of attraction in an electronegative atom such as oxygen, fluorine, or nitrogen. Hydrogen bonds can form within a single molecule or between molecules. A water molecule is **polar**, meaning it is partially positively charged on one end (the hydrogen end) and partially negatively charged on the other (the oxygen end). This is because the hydrogen atoms are arranged around the oxygen atom in a close tetrahedron. Hydrogen is **oxidized** (its number of electrons is reduced) when it bonds with oxygen to form water. Hydrogen bonds tend not only to be weak but also short-lived. They also tend to be numerous. Hydrogen bonds give water many of its important properties, including its high specific heat and high heat of vaporization, its solvent qualities, its adhesiveness and cohesiveness, its hydrophobic qualities, and its ability to float in its solid form. Hydrogen bonds are also an important component of proteins, nucleic acids, and DNA.

Inorganic Compounds

The main trait of inorganic compounds is that they generally lack carbon. Inorganic compounds include mineral salts, alloys, non-metallic compounds such as phosphate, and metal complexes. A metal complex has a central atom (or ion) bonded to surrounding ligands (molecules or anions). The ligands sacrifice the donor atoms (in the form of at least one pair of electrons) to the central atom. Many inorganic compounds are ionic, meaning they form ionic bonds rather than share electrons. They may have high melting points because of this. They may also be colorful, but this is not an absolute identifier of an inorganic compound. Salts, which are inorganic compounds, are an example of inorganic bonding of cations and anions. Some examples of salts are magnesium chloride ($MgCl_2$) and sodium oxide (Na_2O). Oxides, carbonates, sulfates, and halides are classes of inorganic compounds. They are typically poor conductors, are very water soluble, and crystallize easily. Minerals and silicates are also inorganic compounds.

Biology

Subfields of Biology

There are a number of subfields of biology:

- **Zoology** – The study of animals
- **Botany** – The study of plants

- **Biophysics** – The application of the laws of physics to the processes of organisms and the application of the facts about living things to human processes and inventions
- **Biochemistry** – The study of the chemistry of living organisms, including diseases and the pharmaceutical drugs used to cure them
- **Cytology** – The study of cells
- **Histology** – The study of the tissues of plants and animals
- **Organology** – The study of tissues organized into organs
- **Physiology** – The study of the way organisms function, including metabolism, the exchange of matter and energy in nutrition, the senses, reproduction and development, and the work of the nervous system and brain
- **Genetics** – The study of heredity as it relates to the transmission of genes
- **Ethology** – The study of animal behavior
- **Ecology** – The study of the relationship of living organisms to their environments

Classification of Life Forms

All living creatures can be classified into one of three domains and then into one of six kingdoms:

- Domain Bacteria
  - **Kingdom Eubacteria**—single celled prokaryotes with little internal complexity, contains peptidoglycan. Members have just one chromosome, reproduce asexually, may have flagella, and are very simple in form.
- Domain Archaea
  - **Kingdom Archaebacteria**—single celled prokaryotes with little internal complexity, does not contain peptidoglycan. Members have just one chromosome, reproduce asexually, may have flagella, and are very simple in form.
- Domain Eukarya
  - **Kingdom Protista**—single celled eukaryotes with greater internal complexity than Bacteria or Archaea. They have a true nucleus surrounded by a membrane that separates it from the cytoplasm. Most are one-celled and have no complex tissues like plants.
  - **Kingdom Fungi**—single celled or multicellular with considerable variation and complexity. Members have no chlorophyll, so they don't make their own food like plants. They reproduce using spores. Fungi are made up of filaments called hyphae that, in larger fungi, can interlace to form a tissue called mycelium.
  - **Kingdom Plantae**—multicellular with great variation and complexity, rigid cell walls. This group consists of organisms that have chlorophyll and make their own food. Plants have differentiated tissues and reproduce either sexually or asexually.
  - **Kingdom Animalia**—multicellular with much variation and complexity, cell membrane. This group consists of organisms that move around and have to feed on existing organic material.

Review Video: Kingdom Animalia
Visit mometrix.com/academy and enter code: 558413

Review Video: Kingdom Fungi
Visit mometrix.com/academy and enter code: 315081

Review Video: Kingdom Plantae
Visit mometrix.com/academy and enter code: 710084

Characteristics of Invertebrates

Invertebrates are animals with no internal skeletons. They can be divided into three groups:

1. **Marine Invertebrates** – Members of this group live in oceans and seas. Marine invertebrates include sponges, corals, jellyfish, snails, clams, octopuses, squids, and crustaceans, none of which live on the surface.
2. **Freshwater Invertebrates** – Members of this group live in lakes and rivers. Freshwater invertebrates include worms on the bottom, microscopic crustaceans, and terrestrial insect larvae that live in the water column, but only where there is no strong current. Some live on the surface of the water.
3. **Terrestrial Invertebrates** – Members of this group live on dry ground. Terrestrial invertebrates include insects, mollusks (snails, slugs), arachnids, and myriapods (centipedes and millipedes). Terrestrial invertebrates breathe through a series of tubes that penetrate into the body (trachea) and deliver oxygen into tissues. Underground terrestrial invertebrates are generally light-colored with atrophied eyes and no cuticle to protect them from desiccation. They include worms that live underground and in caves and rock crevices. This group also includes insects such as ants that create colonies underground.

Characteristics of Vertebrate Groups

The **vertebrates**, animals with an internal skeleton, are divided into four groups:

1. **Fish** – This group is the most primitive, but is also the group from which all other groups evolved. Fish live in water, breathe with gills, are cold-blooded, have fins and scales, and are typically oviparous, which means they lay eggs. Fish typically have either cartilaginous skeletons (such as rays and sharks) or bony skeletons.
2. **Amphibians** – The skin of animals in this group is delicate and permeable, so they need water to keep it moist. Amphibians are oviparous. The young start out in water with gills, but the adults use lungs.
3. **Reptiles and birds** – The skin of animals in this group has very hard, horn-like scales. Birds have exchanged scales for feathers. Reptiles and birds are oviparous, although birds care for their eggs and reptiles do not. Members have a cloaca, an excretory and reproductive cavity that opens to the outside. Reptiles are cold-blooded, but birds are warm-blooded.
4. **Mammals** – Mammals have bodies covered with fur; are warm-blooded; are viviparous, meaning they give birth to live young which are fed with milk from female mammary glands; and are tetrapods (four-legged). Most live on the ground (except whales and dolphins) and a few fly (bats).

Hunters and Prey Animals

The interaction between **predators** and their **prey** is important to controlling the balance of an ecosystem. **Hunters** are **carnivorous** animals at the top of the ecological pyramid that eat other animals. Hunters tend to be territorial, leaving signs to warn others to stay out or risk a fight. Hunters are equipped to capture with claws, curved beaks, spurs, fangs, etc. They try to use a minimum amount of energy for each capture, so they prey upon the more vulnerable (the old, ill, or very young) when given a choice. Predators never kill more than they can eat. Some hunters have great speed, some stalk, and some hunt in groups. **Prey** animals are those that are captured by predators for food. They are usually **herbivores** further down the ecological pyramid. Prey animals have special characteristics to help them flee from predators. They may hide in nests or caves, become totally immobile to escape detection, have protective coloration or camouflage, have warning coloration to indicate being poisonous, or have shells or quills for protection.

Life Processes That All Living Things Have in Common

Living things share many **processes** that are necessary to survival, but the ways these processes and interactions occur are highly diverse. Processes include those related to:

- **Nutrition** – the process of obtaining, ingesting, and digesting foods; excreting unused or excess substances; and extracting energy from the foods to maintain structure.
- **Transport** (circulation) – the process of circulating essential materials such as nutrients, cells, hormones, and gases (oxygen and hydrogen) to the places they are needed by moving them through veins, arteries, and capillaries. Needed materials do not travel alone, but are "piggybacked" on transporting molecules.
- **Respiration** – the process of breathing, which is exchanging gases between the interior and exterior using gills, trachea (insects), or lungs.
- **Regulation** – the process of coordinating life activities through the nervous and endocrine systems.
- **Reproduction and growth** – the process of producing more of one's own kind and growing from birth to adulthood. The more highly evolved an animal is, the longer its growth time is.
- **Locomotion** (in animals) – the process of moving from place to place in the environment by using legs, flight, or body motions.

Organisms That Interfere with Cell Activity

Viruses, bacteria, fungi, and other parasites may infect plants and animals and interfere with normal life functions, create imbalances, or disrupt the operations of cells.

- **Viruses** – These enter the body by inhalation (airborne) or through contact with contaminated food, water, or infected tissues. They affect the body by taking over the cell's protein synthesis mechanism to make more viruses. They kill the host cell and impact tissue and organ operations. Examples of viruses include measles, rabies, pneumonia, and AIDS.
- **Bacteria** – These enter the body through breaks in the skin or contaminated food or water, or by inhalation. They reproduce rapidly and produce toxins that kill healthy host tissues. Examples include diphtheria, bubonic plague, tuberculosis, and syphilis.
- **Fungi** – These feed on healthy tissues of the body by sending rootlike tendrils into the tissues to digest them extracellularly. Examples include athlete's foot and ringworm.
- **Parasites** – These enter the body through the skin, via insect bites, or through contaminated food or water. Examples include tapeworms, malaria, or typhus.

Hydrocarbons and Carbohydrates

Carbon is an element found in all living things. Two types of carbon molecules that are essential to life are hydrocarbons and carbohydrates. **Hydrocarbons**, composed only of hydrogen and carbon, are the simplest organic molecules. The simplest of these is methane, which has one carbon atom and four hydrogen atoms. Methane is produced by the decomposition of animal or vegetable matter, and is part of petroleum and natural gas. **Carbohydrates** are compounds made of hydrogen, carbon, and oxygen. There are three types of these macromolecules (large molecules):

1. **Sugars** are soluble in water and, although they have less energy than fats, provide energy more quickly.
2. **Starches**, insoluble in water, are long chains of glucose that act as reserve substances. Potatoes and cereals are valuable foods because they are rich in starch. Animals retain glucose in their cells as glycogen, a special type of starch.
3. **Cellulose**, composed of glucose chains, makes up the cells and tissues of plants. It is one of the most common organic materials.

Review Video: Basics of Hydrocarbons
Visit mometrix.com/academy and enter code: 824749

Lipids, Proteins, and Nucleic Acids

Besides hydrocarbons and carbohydrates, there are three other types of carbon molecules that are essential to life: lipids, proteins, and nucleic acids. **Lipids** are compounds that are insoluble or only partially soluble in water. There are three main types: fats, which act as an energy reserve for organisms; phospholipids, which are one of the essential components of cell membranes; and steroids such as cholesterol and estrogen, which are very important to metabolism. **Proteins** are complex substances that make up almost half the dry weight of animal bodies. These molecules contain hydrogen, carbon, oxygen, and other elements, chiefly nitrogen and sulfur. Proteins make up muscle fibers and, as enzymes, act as catalysts. **Nucleic acids** are large molecules (polymers) composed of a large number of simpler molecules (nucleotides). Each one has a sugar containing five carbons (pentose), a phosphorous compound (phosphate group), and a nitrogen compound (nitrogenated base). Nucleic acids facilitate perpetuation of the species because they carry genetic information as DNA and RNA.

Cell

The **cell** is the basic organizational unit of all living things. Each component within a cell has a function that helps organisms grow and survive. There are many different types of cells, and they are unique to each type of organism. The one thing that all cells have in common is a **membrane**, which is comparable to a semi-permeable plastic bag. The membrane is composed of phospholipids. There are also some **transport holes**, which are proteins that help certain molecules and ions move in and out of the cell. The cell is filled with a fluid called **cytoplasm** or cytosol. Within the cell are a variety of **organelles**, groups of complex molecules that help a cell survive, each with its own unique membrane that has a different chemical makeup from the cell membrane. The larger the cell, the more organelles it will need to live.

Review Video: Difference Between Plant and Animal Cells
Visit mometrix.com/academy and enter code: 115568

Review Video: Cell Structure
Visit mometrix.com/academy and enter code: 591293

Nucleus and Mitochondria in Eukaryotic Cells

Eukaryotic cells have a nucleus, a big dark spot floating somewhere in the center that acts like the brain of the cell by controlling eating, movement, and reproduction. A **nuclear envelope** surrounds the nucleus and its contents, but allows RNA and proteins to pass through. **Chromatin**, made up of DNA, RNA, and nuclear proteins, is present in the nucleus. The nucleus also contains a nucleolus made of RNA and protein. **Mitochondria** are very small organelles that take in nutrients, break them down, and create energy for the cell through a process called cellular respiration. There might be thousands of mitochondria depending on the cell's purpose. A muscle cell needs more energy for movement than a cell that transmits nerve impulses, for example. Mitochondria have two membranes: a **cover** and the **inner cristae** that folds over many times to increase the surface work area. The fluid inside the mitochondria, the matrix, is filled with water and enzymes that take food molecules and combine them with oxygen so they can be digested.

Review Video: Mitochondria
Visit mometrix.com/academy and enter code: 444287

Chloroplasts of Plant Cells

Chloroplasts, which make plants green, are the food producers of a plant cell. They differ from an animal cell's mitochondria, which break down sugars and nutrients. **Photosynthesis** occurs when the energy from the sun hits a chloroplast and the chlorophyll uses that energy to combine carbon dioxide and water to make sugars and oxygen. The nutrition and oxygen obtained from plants makes them the basis of all life on earth. A chloroplast has two membranes to contain and protect the inner parts. The **stroma** is an area inside the chloroplast where reactions occur and starches are created. A **thylakoid** has chlorophyll molecules on its surface, and a stack of thylakoids is called a granum. The stacks of sacs are connected by **stromal lamellae**, which act like the skeleton of the chloroplast, keeping all the sacs a safe distance from each other and maximizing the efficiency of the organelle.

Passive and Active Transport

Passive transport within a cell does not require additional energy or active work. For example, when there is a large concentration difference between the outside and the inside of a cell, the pressure of the greater concentration, not energy, will move molecules across the lipid bilayer into the cell. Another example of passive transport is osmosis, which is the movement of water across a membrane. Too much water in a cell can cause it to burst, so the cell moves ions in and out to help equalize the amount of water. **Active transport** is when a cell uses energy to move individual molecules across the cell membrane. **Proteins** embedded in the lipid bilayer do most of the transport work. There are hundreds of different types of proteins because they are specific. For instance, a protein that moves glucose will not move calcium. The activity of these proteins can be stopped by inhibitors or poisons, which can destroy or plug up a protein.

Review Video: Passive Transport: Diffusion and Osmosis
Visit mometrix.com/academy and enter code: 642038

Mitotic Cell Replication

Mitosis is the duplication of a cell and all its parts, including the DNA, into two identical daughter cells. There are five phases in the life cycle of a cell:

1. **Prophase** – This is the process of duplicating everything in preparation for division.
2. **Metaphase** – The cell's different pieces align themselves for the split. The DNA lines up along a central axis and the centrioles send out specialized tubules that connect to the centromere. The centromere has two strands of a chromosome (condensed DNA) attached to it.
3. **Anaphase** – Half of the chromosomes go one way and half go another.
4. **Telophase** – When the chromosomes get to the side of the cell, the cell membrane closes in and splits the cell into two pieces. This results in two separate cells, each with half of the original DNA.
5. **Interphase** – This is the normal state of the cell, or the resting stage between divisions. During this stage, the cell duplicates nucleic acids in preparation for the next division.

Review Video: Mitosis
Visit mometrix.com/academy and enter code: 849894

Microbes

Microbes are the smallest, simplest, and most abundant organisms on earth. Their numbers are incalculable, and a microscope is required to see them. There is a huge variety of microbes, including bacteria, fungi, some algae, and protozoa. Microbes can be harmful or helpful.

Microbes can be **heterotrophic** (eat other things) or **autotrophic** (make food for themselves). They can be solitary or colonial, sexual or asexual. Examples include mold, a multi-cellular type of fungus, and yeasts, which are single-celled (but may live in colonies). A **mushroom** is a fungus that lives as a group of strands underground called hyphae that decompose leaves or bark on the ground. When it reproduces, it develops a mushroom whose cap contains spores. **Mold** is a type of zygote fungi that reproduces with a stalk, but releases zygospores. **Good bacteria** can be those that help plants absorb the nitrogen needed for growth or help grazing animals break down the cellulose in plants. Some **bad bacteria** are killed by the penicillin developed from a fungus.

Roots, Stems, and Leaves

Roots are structures designed to pull water and minerals from soil or water. In large plants such as trees, the roots usually go deep into the ground to not only reach the water, but also to support and stabilize the tree.

There are some plant species that have roots above ground, and there are also plants called epiphytes that live in trees with their roots clinging to the branches. Some roots, like carrots and turnips, serve as food. Roots are classified as **primary** and **lateral** (like a trunk and branches). The **apical meristem** is the tip of a root or shoot that helps the plant increase in length. **Root hairs** are fuzzy root extensions that help with the absorption of water and nutrients. The majority of the plant above ground is made up of the stems (trunk and branches) and leaves. **Stems** transport food and water and act as support structures. **Leaves** are the site for photosynthesis, and are connected to the rest of the plant by a vascular system.

Gymnosperms, Cycads, and Conifers

Gymnosperms are plants with vascular systems and seeds but no flowers (flowers are an evolutionary advancement). The function of the seed is to ensure offspring can be produced by the plant by providing a protective coating that lets the plant survive for long periods until it germinates. It also stores food for the new plant to use until it can make its own. Seeds can be spread over a wide area. **Cycads** are sturdy plants with big, waxy fronds that make them look like ferns or palms. They can survive in harsh conditions if there is warm weather. For reproduction, they have big cones located in the center of the plant. The female plant grows a fruit in the middle of the stem. **Conifers** are trees that thrive in northern latitudes and have cones. Examples of conifers are pine, cedar, redwood, and spruce. Conifers are evergreens because they have needles that take full advantage of the sun year-round. They are also very tall and strong because of the chemical substance xylem in their systems.

Angiosperms

Angiosperms are plants that have flowers. This is advantageous because the plant's seeds and pollen can be spread not only by gravity and wind, but also by insects and animals. Flowers are able to attract organisms that can help pollinate the plant and distribute seeds. Some flowering plants also produce fruit. When an animal eats the fruit, the plant seeds within will be spread far and wide in the animal's excrement. There are two kinds of angiosperm seeds: monocotyledons (monocots) and dicotyledons (dicots). A **cotyledon** is the seed leaf or food package for the developing plant. **Monocots** are simple flowering plants such as grasses, corn, palm trees, and lilies. They always have three petals on their flowers, and their leaves are long strands (like a palm frond). A **dicot** has seeds with two cotyledons, or two seed leaves of food. Most everyday flowers are dicots with four or five petals and extremely complex leaves with veins. Examples include roses, sunflowers, cacti, and cherry trees.

Arthropods

Arthropods have a number of unique characteristics:

- They have an **exoskeleton** (outside instead of inside).
- They **molt**. As the arthropod grows, it must shed its old shell and grow a new one.
- They have several **legs**, which are jointed.
- Their advanced **nervous systems** allow for hunting, moving around, finding a mate, and learning new behaviors for adaptation.
- They develop through **metamorphosis**. As arthropods develop, they change body shape. There are two types of metamorphosis:
    - *Complete* – The entire body shape changes. An example is butterflies, which change from worm-like larvae to insects with wings.
    - *Gradual* – The arthropod starts off small with no wings, and then molts and grows wings. Example: Grasshoppers.

Arthropods include spiders, crustaceans, and the enormous insect species (26 orders) called uniramians. Ranging from fleas to mosquitoes, beetles, dragonflies, aphids, bees, flies, and many more, uniramians have exoskeletons made of chitin, compound eyes, complex digestive systems, and usually six legs. This group is extremely diverse. Some can fly, some have toxins or antennae, and some can make wax, silk, or honey.

Reptiles

One group of vertebrates is the **reptile**. This group includes:

- **Crocodilia** – This is a group of reptiles that can grow quite large, and includes alligators and crocodiles. Normally found near the water in warmer climates, Crocodilia might be more closely related to birds than other reptiles.
- **Squamata** – This is the order of reptiles that includes snakes and lizards. Snakes are special because they have no legs and no ears. They feel vibrations, smell with their tongues, have specialized scales, and can unhinge their jaws to swallow prey that is larger than they are. Like snakes, lizards have scales, but they differ in that they have legs, can dig, can climb trees, and can grab things.
- **Chelonia** – This is the order of reptiles that includes turtles and tortoises. It is a special group because its members have shells. Different varieties live in forests, water, and deserts, or anywhere the climate is warm enough. They also live a long time, up to hundreds of years. Turtles are typically found near water and tortoises on land, even dry areas.

Reproduction in Mammals

When classified according to how they reproduce, there are three types of mammals:

1. **Monotremes** are rare mammals that lay eggs. These were the first mammals, and are more closely related to reptiles than other mammals. Examples include the duck-billed platypus and the spiny anteater.
2. **Marsupials** are special mammals. They give birth to live young, but the babies mature in pouches, where they are carried and can feed on milk. Many are found in Australia. The isolation of this island continent prevented placental mammals from taking hold. Examples of marsupials include kangaroos, possums, and koalas.
3. **Placental mammals** give birth from the females' placenta to live young. The young may be able to walk immediately, or they may need to be carried. They are still dependent on parental care for at least a short time. Placental mammals are the dominant form of mammals. Members of this group include cetaceans such as whales and dolphins, which are mammals that evolved but returned to the ocean.

Respiratory System

The **respiratory system** exchanges gases with the environment. Amphibians exchange gases through their moist skin, and fish use gills, but mammals, birds, and reptiles have lungs. The human respiratory system is made up of the nose, mouth, pharynx, trachea, and two lungs. The purpose of the respiratory system is to bring oxygen into the body and expel carbon dioxide. The respiratory system can inhale viruses, bacteria, and dangerous chemicals, so it is vulnerable to toxins and diseases such as pneumonia, which causes the lungs to fill with fluid until they cannot take in enough oxygen to support the body. **Emphysema**, often caused by smoking tobacco, destroys the tissues in the lungs, which cannot be regenerated. The respiratory system interacts with the **digestive system** in that the mouth and pharynx are used to swallow food and drink, as well as to breathe. It interacts with the circulatory system in that it provides fresh oxygen through blood vessels that pass through the lungs. This oxygen is then carried by the circulatory system throughout the body.

Review Video: Respiratory System
Visit mometrix.com/academy and enter code: 783075

Skeletal System

The human body has an **endoskeleton**, meaning it is inside the body. It is made up of bones instead of the hard plate of exoskeletons or fluids in tubes, which comprise the hydrostatic system of the starfish. The purpose of the skeleton is to support the body, provide a framework to which the muscles and organs can connect, and protect the inner organs. The skull protects the all-important brain and the ribs protect the internal organs from impact. The skeletal system interacts with the muscular system to help the body move, and softer cartilage works with the calcified bone to allow smooth movement of the body. The skeletal system also interacts with the circulatory system in that the marrow inside the bones helps produce both white and red blood cells.

Review Video: Skeletal System
Visit mometrix.com/academy and enter code: 256447

Nervous System

The **nervous system** is divided into two parts: the **central nervous system** (brain and spinal cord) and the **peripheral nervous system** (a network of billions of neurons of different types throughout the entire body). The neurons are connected end to end, and transmit electrical impulses to each other. **Efferent neurons** send impulses from the central system to the limbs and organs. **Afferent neurons** receive sensory information and transmit it back to the central system. The nervous system is concerned with **senses and action**. In other words, it senses something and then acts upon it. An example is a predator sensing prey and attacking it. The nervous system also automatically senses activity inside the body and reacts to stimuli. For example, the first bite of a meal sets the whole digestive system into motion. The nervous system **interacts** with every other system in the body because all the tissues and organs need instruction, even when individuals are not aware of any activity occurring. For instance, the endocrine system is constantly working to produce hormones or adrenaline as needed.

Review Video: What is the Function of the Nervous System?
Visit mometrix.com/academy and enter code: 708428

Genetics, Genes, and Chromosomes

Genetics is the science devoted to the study of how characteristics are transmitted from one generation to another. In the 1800s, Gregor Mendel outlined the three laws of heredity that explain how genetics works. Genes are the hereditary units of material that are transmitted from one generation to the next. They are capable of undergoing mutations, can be recombined with other genes, and can determine the nature of an organism, including its color, shape, and size. **Genotype** is the genetic makeup of an individual based on one or more characteristics, while phenotype is the external manifestation of the genotype. For example, genotype determines hair color genes, whereas phenotype is the actual color of the hair observed. **Chromosomes** are the structures inside the nucleus of a cell made up primarily of deoxyribonucleic acid (DNA) and proteins. The chromosomes carry the genes. The numbers vary according to the species, but they are always the same for each species. For example, the human has 46 chromosomes, and the water lily has 112.

Review Video: Chromosomes
Visit mometrix.com/academy and enter code: 132083

Mendel's Contributions to Genetics

Johann Gregor Mendel is known as the father of **genetics**. Mendel was an Austrian monk who performed thousands of experiments involving the breeding of the common pea plant in the garden of his monastery. Mendel kept detailed records including seed color, pod color, seed type, flower color, and plant height for eight years and published his work in 1865. Unfortunately, his work was largely ignored until the early 1900s. Mendel's work showed that genes come in pairs and that dominant and recessive traits are inherited independently of each other. His work established the law of segregation, the law of independent assortment, and the law of dominance.

Darwin's Contributions to the Theory of Evolution

Charles Darwin's theory of evolution is the unifying concept in biology today. From 1831 to 1836, Darwin traveled as a naturalist on a five-year voyage on the *H.M.S. Beagle* around the tip of South America and to the Galápagos Islands. He studied finches, took copious amounts of meticulous notes, and collected thousands of plant and animal specimens. He collected 13 species of finches each with a unique bill for a distinct food source, which led him to believe, due to similarities between the finches, that the finches shared a common ancestor. The similarities and differences of fossils of extinct rodents and modern mammal fossils led him to believe that the mammals had changed over time. Darwin believed that these changes were the result of random genetic changes called mutations. He believed that mutations could be beneficial and eventually result in a different organism over time. In 1859, in his first book, *On the Origin of Species*, Darwin proposed that natural selection was the means by which adaptations would arise over time. He coined the term "natural selection" and said that it is the mechanism of evolution. Because variety exists among individuals of a species, he stated that those individuals must compete for the same limited resources. Some would die, and others would survive. According to Darwin, evolution is a slow, gradual process. In 1871, Darwin published his second book, *Descent of Man, and Selection in Relation to Sex*, in which he discussed the evolution of man.

Contribution to Genetics Made by Alfred Hershey and Martha Chase

Alfred Hershey and Martha Chase did a series of experiments in 1952 known as the **Hershey-Chase experiments**. These experiments showed that deoxyribonucleic acid (DNA), not protein, is the genetic material that transfers information for inheritance. The Hershey-Chase experiments used a bacteriophage, a virus that infects bacteria, to infect the bacteria *Escherichia coli.* The bacteriophage T2 is basically a small piece of DNA enclosed in a protein coating. The DNA contains phosphorus, and the protein coating contains sulfur. In the first set of experiments, the T2 was marked with radioactive phosphorus-32. In the second set of experiments, the T2 was marked with radioactive sulfur-35. For both sets of experiments, after the *E. coli* was infected by the T2, the *E. coli* was isolated using a centrifuge. In the first set of experiments, the radioactive isotope (P-32) was found in the *E. coli*, showing that the genetic information was transferred by the DNA. In the second set of experiments, the radioactive isotope (S-35) was not found in the *E. coli*, showing that the genetic information was not transferred by the protein as was previously thought. Hershey and Chase conducted further experiments allowing the bacteria from the first set of experiments to reproduce, and the offspring was also found to contain the radioactive isotope (P-32) further confirming that the DNA transferred the genetic material.

Ecology

Autotrophs, Producers, Herbivores, Carnivores, Omnivores, and Decomposers

Energy flows in one direction: from the sun, through photosynthetic organisms such as green plants (producers) and algae (autotrophs), and then to herbivores, carnivores, and decomposers. **Autotrophs** are organisms capable of producing their own food. The organic molecules they produce are food for all other organisms (heterotrophs). **Producers** are green plants that manufacture food by photosynthesis. **Herbivores** are animals that eat only plants (deer, rabbits, etc.). Since they are the first animals to receive the energy captured by producers, herbivores are called primary consumers. **Carnivores**, or secondary consumers, are animals that eat the bodies of other animals for food. Predators (wolves, lions, etc.) kill other animals, while scavengers consume animals that are already dead from predation or natural causes (buzzards). **Omnivores** are animals that eat both plants and other animals (humans). **Decomposers** include saprophytic fungi and bacteria that break down the complex structures of the bodies of living things into simpler forms that can be used by other living things. This recycling process releases energy from organic molecules.

ABIOTIC FACTORS AND BIOTIC FACTORS

Abiotic factors are the physical and chemical factors in the environment that are nonliving but upon which the growth and survival of living organisms depends. These factors can determine the types of plants and animals that will establish themselves and thrive in a particular area. Abiotic factors include:

- Light intensity available for photosynthesis
- Temperature range
- Available moisture
- Type of rock substratum
- Type of minerals
- Type of atmospheric gases
- Relative acidity (pH) of the system

Biotic factors are the living components of the environment that affect, directly or indirectly, the ecology of an area, possibly limiting the type and number of resident species. The relationships of predator/prey, producer/consumer, and parasite/host can define a community. Biotic factors include:

- Population levels of each species
- The food requirements of each species
- The interactions between species
- The wastes produced

HOW PLANTS MANUFACTURE FOOD

Plants are the only organisms capable of transforming **inorganic material** from the environment into **organic matter** by using water and solar energy. This transformation is made possible by chloroplasts, flat structures inside plant cells. **Chloroplasts**, located primarily in leaves, contain chlorophyll (the pigment capable of absorbing light and storing it in chemical compounds), DNA, ribosomes, and numerous enzymes. Chloroplasts are surrounded by a membrane. The leaves of plants are the main producers of oxygen, which helps purify the air. The **chlorophyll** in chloroplasts is responsible for the light, or luminous, phase of photosynthesis. The energy it absorbs breaks down water absorbed through the roots into hydrogen and oxygen to form ATP molecules that store energy. In the dark phase, when the plant has no light, the energy molecules are used to attach carbon dioxide to water and form glucose, a sugar.

PRODUCERS, CONSUMERS, AND DECOMPOSERS

The **food chain**, or food web, is a series of events that happens when one organism consumes another to survive. Every organism is involved in dozens of connections with others, so what happens to one affects the environment of the others. In the food chain, there are three main categories:

- **Producers** – Plants and vegetables are at the beginning of the food chain because they take energy from the sun and make food for themselves through photosynthesis. They are food sources for other organisms.
- **Consumers** – There are three levels of consumers: the organisms that eat plants (primary consumers, or herbivores); the organisms that eat the primary consumers (secondary consumers, or carnivores); and, in some ecosystems, the organisms that eat both plants and animals (tertiary consumers, or omnivores).
- **Decomposers** – These are the organisms that eat dead things or waste matter and return the nutrients to the soil, thus returning essential molecules to the producers and completing the cycle.

Review Video: Food Webs
Visit mometrix.com/academy and enter code: 853254

System of Classification for Living Organisms

The main characteristic by which living organisms are classified is the degree to which they are **related**, not the degree to which they resemble each other. The science of classification is called **taxonomy**. This classification is challenging since the division lines between groups is not always clear. Some animals have characteristics of two separate groups. The current system of taxonomy involves placing an organism into a **domain** (Bacteria, Archaea, and Eukarya), and then into a **kingdom** (Eubacteria, Archaeabacteria, Protista, Fungi, Plantae, and Animalia). The kingdoms are divided into phyla, then classes, then orders, then families, and finally genuses and species. For example, the family cat is in the domain of eukaryotes, the kingdom of animals, the phylum of chordates, the class of mammals, the order of carnivores, the family of felidae, and the genus of felis. All species of living beings can be identified with Latin scientific names that are assigned by the worldwide binomial system. The genus name comes first, and is followed by the name of the species. The family cat is *felis domesticus*.

Review Video: Biological Classification Systems
Visit mometrix.com/academy and enter code: 736052

Properties That Contribute to Earth's Life-Sustaining System

Life on earth is dependent on:

- All three states of **water** – gas (water vapor), liquid, and solid (ice)
- A variety of forms of **carbon**, the basis of life (carbon-based units)
- In the atmosphere, carbon dioxide, in the forms of methane and black carbon soot, produces the **greenhouse effect** that provides a habitable atmosphere.
- The earth's **atmosphere and electromagnetic field**, which shield the surface from harmful radiation and allow useful radiation to go through.
- The **earth's relationship to the sun and the moon**, which creates the four seasons and the cycles of plant and animal life.
- The combination of **water, carbon, and nutrients** that provides sustenance for life and regulates the climate system in a habitable temperature range with non-toxic air.

Geology

Earth System Science

The complex and interconnected dynamics of the continents, atmosphere, oceans, ice, and life forms are the subject of Earth system science. These interconnected dynamics require an interdisciplinary approach that includes chemistry, physics, biology, mathematics, and applied sciences in order to study the Earth as an integrated system and determine (while considering human impact and interaction) the past, present, and future states of the Earth. Scientific inquiry in this field includes exploration of:

- Extreme weather events as they pertain to a changing climate
- Earthquakes and volcanic eruptions as they pertain to tectonic shifts
- Losses in biodiversity in relation to the changes in the Earth's ecosystems
- Causes and effects in the environment
- The Sun's solar variability in relation to the Earth's climate
- The atmosphere's increasing concentrations of carbon dioxide and aerosols
- Trends in the Earth's systems in terms of changes and their consequences

TRADITIONAL EARTH SCIENCE DISCIPLINES

Modern science is approaching the study of the Earth in an integrated fashion that sees the Earth as an interconnected system that is impacted by humankind and, therefore, must include social dimensions. Traditionally, though, the following were the Earth science disciplines:

- **Geology** – This is the study of the origin and structure of the Earth and of the changes it has undergone and is in the process of undergoing. Geologists work from the crust inward.
- **Meteorology** – This is the study of the atmosphere, including atmospheric pressure, temperature, clouds, winds, precipitation, etc. It is also concerned with describing and explaining weather.
- **Oceanography** – This is the study of the oceans, which includes studying their extent and depth, the physics and chemistry of ocean waters, and the exploitation of their resources.
- **Ecology** – This is the study of living organisms in relation to their environment and to other living things. It is the study of the interrelations between the different components of the ecosystem.

GEOLOGICAL ERAS

Geologists divide the history of the Earth into units of time called eons, which are divided into **eras**, then into **periods**, then into **epochs** and finally into **ages**. Dates are approximate of course, and there may be variations of a few million years. (Million years ago is abbreviated as Ma.) Some of the most commonly known time periods are:

- **Hadean Eon** – About 4.5 to 3.8 billion years ago
- **Archaean Eon** – 3.8 to 2.5 billion years ago
- **Proterozoic Eon** – 2.5 billion to 542 Ma
- **Phanerozoic Eon** – 542 Ma to the present
  - **Paleozoic Era** – 542 Ma to 251 Ma
    - **Cambrian Period** – 542 to 488 Ma
    - **Ordovician Period** – 488 to 443 Ma
    - **Silurian Period** – 443 to 416 Ma
    - **Devonian Period** – 416 to 359 Ma
    - **Carboniferous Period** – 359 to 290 Ma
    - **Permian Period** – 290 to 252 Ma
  - **Mesozoic Era** – 252 to 65 Ma
    - **Triassic Period** – 252 to 200 Ma
    - **Jurassic Period** – 200 to 150 Ma
    - **Cretaceous Period** – 150 to 65 Ma
  - **Cenozoic Era** – 65 Ma to the present
    - **Paleogene Period** – 65 to 28 Ma
    - **Neogene Period** – 28 to 2 Ma
    - **Quaternary Period** – about 2 Ma to the present

DEVELOPMENT OF LIFE ON EARTH ACCORDING TO TIME PERIODS

The evolution of life on Earth is believed to have occurred as follows:

- Igneous rocks formed. (Hadean Eon)
- The continents formed. (Archaean Eon)
- The first multi-cellular creatures such as hydras, jellyfish, and sponges appeared about 600 Ma.
- Flatworms, roundworms, and segmented worms appeared about 550 Ma.
- Moss, arthropods, octopus, and eels appeared. (Cambrian Period)
- Mushrooms, fungi, and other primitive plants appeared; sea animals began to use calcium to build bones and shells. (Ordovician Period)

- Fish with jaws appeared. (Silurian Period)
- Fish developed lungs and legs (frogs) and went on land; ferns appeared. (Devonian period)
- Reptiles developed the ability to lay eggs on land and pine trees appeared. (Carboniferous Period)
- Dinosaurs dominated the land during the Triassic and Jurassic Periods.
- Flying insects, birds, and the first flowering plants appeared; dinosaurs died out. (Cretaceous Period)
- Mammals evolved and dominated; grasses became widespread. (50 Ma)
- Hominids appeared more than 2 Ma.

Hydrosphere and Hydrologic Cycle

The **hydrosphere** is anything on Earth that is related to water, whether it is in the air, on land, or in a plant or animal system. A water molecule consists of only two atoms of hydrogen and one of oxygen, yet it is what makes life possible. Unlike any other planets that have been discovered, Earth is able to sustain water in a liquid state most of the time. Water vapor and ice are of no use to living organisms. The **hydrologic cycle** is the journey water takes as it proceeds through different forms. Liquid surface water evaporates to form the gaseous state of a cloud, and then becomes liquid again in the form of rain. This process takes about 10 days. This cycle is for surface water only: rivers, lakes, groundwater, ocean surface, etc. Water in the deep ocean and in the heart of glaciers is typically sequestered from the cycle for many thousands of years.

Review Video: Hydrologic Cycle
Visit mometrix.com/academy and enter code: 426578

Aquifers

An **aquifer** is an underground water reservoir formed from groundwater that has infiltrated from the surface by passing through the soil and permeable rock layers to whereever the rock layer is impermeable. The section of permeable layers with water present is called the zone of saturation, and the area above that (with no water) is the zone of aeration. There are two types of aquifers. In one, the water is under pressure (**confined**) as the supply builds up between layers of impermeable rocks and has to move back towards the surface, resulting in a spring or artesian well. The second type of aquifer is called "**unconfined**" because it has room to expand and contract, and the water has to be pumped out. The highest level of the aquifer is called the water table. If water is pumped out of the aquifer such that the water table dips in a specific area, that area is called a cone of depression.

Biosphere

Biosphere is the term used by physical geographers to describe the living world of trees, bugs, and animals. It refers to any place where life exists on Earth, and is the intersection of the hydrosphere, the atmosphere, the land, and the energy that comes from space. The biosphere includes the upper areas of the atmosphere where birds and insects can travel, areas deep inside caves, and hydrothermal vents at the bottom of the ocean.

Factors that affect the biosphere include:

- The **distance and tilt** between the Earth and the Sun – This produces temperatures that are conducive to life and causes the seasons.
- **Climate, daily weather, and erosion** – These change the land and the organisms on and in it.
- Earthquakes, tornadoes, volcanoes, tsunamis, and other **natural phenomena** – These all change the land.
- **Chemical erosion** – This changes the composition of rocks and organic materials.
- **Biological erosion** – This is bacteria and single-celled organisms breaking down organic and inorganic materials.

Ecological System and Biome

An **ecological system**, or ecosystem, is the community of all the living organisms in a specific area interacting with non-living factors such as temperature, sunlight, atmospheric pressure, weather patterns, wind, types of nutrients, etc. An ecosystem's development depends on the energy that passes in and out of it. The boundaries of an ecosystem depend on the use of the term, whether it refers to an ecosystem under a rock or in a valley, pond, or ocean.

A **biome** is a general ecosystem type defined by the plants and animals that live there and the local climate patterns. Examples include tropical rainforests or savannas, deserts, grasslands, deciduous forests, tundra, woodlands, and ice caps. There can be more than one type of biome within a larger climate zone. The transition area between two biomes is an ecotone, which may have characteristics of both biomes.

Erosion

Erosion is the process that breaks down matter, whether it is a rock that is broken into pebbles or mountains that are blown by wind and rained on until they become hills. . The erosion of land by weather or breaking waves is called **denudation**. **Mass wasting** is the movement of masses of dirt and rock from one place to another. This can occur in two ways: **mechanical** (such as breaking a rock with a hammer) or **chemical** (such as pouring acid on a rock to dissolve it). If the material changes color, it indicates that a break down was chemical in nature. Whatever is broken down must go somewhere, so erosion eventually builds something up. For example, an eroded mountain ends up in a river that carries the sediment towards the ocean, where it builds up and creates a wetland or delta at the mouth of the river.

Climates

Scientists have determined the following different types of **climates**:

- Polar (ice caps)
- Polar (tundra)
- Subtropical (dry summer)
- Subtropical (dry winter)
- Subtropical (humid)
- Subtropical (marine west coast)
- Subtropical (Mediterranean)
- Subtropical (wet)
- Tropical (monsoon)
- Tropical (savannah/grasslands)
- Tropical (wet)

Several factors make up and affect climates. These include:

- Temperature
- Atmospheric pressure
- The number of clouds and the amount of dust or smog
- Humidity
- Winds

The moistest and warmest of all the climates is that of the tropical rainforest. It has daily convection thunderstorms caused by the surface daytime heat and the high humidity, which combine to form thunderclouds.

Review Video: Climates
Visit mometrix.com/academy and enter code: 991320

LAYERS OF THE EARTH

The Earth has several distinct layers, each with its own properties:

- **Crust** – This is the outermost layer of the Earth that is comprised of the continents and the ocean basins. It has a variable thickness (35-70 km in the continents and 5-10 km in the ocean basins) and is composed mostly of alumino-silicates.
- **Mantle** – This is about 2900 km thick, and is made up mostly of ferro-magnesium silicates. It is divided into an upper and lower mantle. Most of the internal heat of the Earth is located in the mantle. Large convective cells circulate heat, and may cause plate tectonic movement.
- **Core** – This is separated into the liquid outer core and the solid inner core. The outer core is 2300 km thick (composed mostly of nickel-iron alloy), and the inner core (almost entirely iron) is 12 km thick. The Earth's magnetic field is thought to be controlled by the liquid outer core.

COMPOSITION OF EARTH'S ATMOSPHERE

The Earth's atmosphere is 79% nitrogen, 20% oxygen, and 1% other gases. The oxygen was originally produced almost entirely by algae-type plants. The atmosphere has four layers:

- **Troposphere** – This is the layer closest to the Earth where all weather takes place. It is the region that contains rising and falling packets of air. Air pressure at sea level is 0.1 atmospheres, but the top of the troposphere is about 10% of that amount.
- **Stratosphere** – In this layer, air flow is mainly horizontal. The upper portion has a thin layer of concentrated ozone (a reactive form of oxygen) that is largely responsible for absorbing the Sun's ultraviolet rays.
- **Mesosphere** – This is the coldest layer. Temperatures drop to -100°C at the top.
- **Thermosphere** – This is divided into the lower ionosphere and the higher exosphere. This layer is very thin and has many ionized atoms with a net electrical charge. The aurora and Van Allen Belts are here. This layer also absorbs the most energetic photons from the Sun and reflects radio waves, enabling long distance radio communication.

Review Video: Earth's Atmosphere
Visit mometrix.com/academy and enter code: 417614

PALEONTOLOGY

Paleontology is the study of prehistoric plant and animal life through the analysis of **fossil remains**. These fossils reveal the ecologies of the past and the path of evolution for both extinct and living organisms. A historical science, paleontology seeks information about the identity, origin, environment, and evolution of past organisms and what they can reveal about the past of the Earth as a whole. Paleontologists seek to explain causes rather than conduct experiments to observe effects. It is related to the fields of biology, geology, and archaeology, and is divided into several sub-disciplines concerned with the types of fossils studied, the process of fossilization, and the ecology and climate of the past. Paleontologists also help identify the composition of the Earth's rock layers by the fossils that are found, thus identifying potential sites for oil, mineral, and water extraction.

DETERMINING THE ORDER IN WHICH GEOLOGIC EVENTS OCCURRED USING THE ROCK RECORD

The **Law of Superposition** logically assumes that the bottom layer of a series of sedimentary layers is the oldest, unless it has been overturned or older rock has been pushed over it. In addition, igneous intrusions can cut through or flow above already present rocks (e.g., lava flows). This is a further indication that the lower rock layers are older. Another guideline for the rock record is that **rock layers** are older than the folds and faults in them because the rocks must exist before they can be folded or faulted. If a rock contains **atomic nuclei**, reference tables of the half-lives of commonly used radio isotopes can be used to match the decay rate of known substances to the nuclei in a rock, and thereby determine its age. Ages of rocks can also be determined from **contact metamorphism**, the re-crystallization of pre-existing rocks due to changes in physical and chemical conditions, such as heat, pressure, and chemically active fluids that might be present in lava or polluted waters.

Matching Rocks and Geologic Events in One Place with Those of Another

Geologists physically follow rock layers from one location to another by a process called "walking the outcrop." Geologists walk along the outcropping to see where it goes and what the differences and similarities of the neighboring locations they cross are. Similar rock **types** or **patterns** of rock layers that are similar in terms of thickness, color, composition, and fossil remains tell geologists that two locations have a similar geologic history. Fossils are found all over the Earth, but are from a relatively **small time period** in Earth's history. Therefore, fossil evidence helps date a rock layer, regardless of where it occurs. **Volcanic ash** is a good time indicator since ash is deposited quickly over a widespread area. Matching the date of an eruption to the ash allows for a precise identification of time. Similarly, the **meteor impact** at the intersection of the Cretaceous and Tertiary Periods left a time marker. Wherever the meteor's iridium content is found, geologists are able to date rock layers.

Sequencing the Earth's Geologic History from the Fossil and Rock Record

Reference tables are used to match specimens and time periods. For example, the fossil record has been divided into time units of the Earth's history. Rocks can therefore be dated by the fossils found with them. There are also reference tables for dating plate motions and mountain building events in geologic history. Since humans have been around for a relatively short period of time, **fossilized human remains** help to affix a date to a location. Some areas have missing **geologic layers** because of erosion or other factors, but reference tables specific to a region will list what is complete or missing. The theory of **uniformitarianism** assumes that geologic processes have been the same throughout history. Therefore, the way erosion or volcanic eruptions happen today is the same as the way these events happened millions of years ago because there is no reason for them to have changed. Therefore, knowledge about current events can be applied to the past to make judgments about events in the rock record.

Revealing Changes in Earth's History by the Fossil and Rock Records

Fossils can show how animal and plant life have changed or remained the same over time. For example, fossils have provided evidence of the existence of dinosaurs even though they no longer roam the Earth, and have also been used to prove that certain insects have been around for hundreds of millions of years. Fossils have been used to identify four basic eras: **Proterozoic**, the age of primitive life; **Paleozoic**, the age of fishes; **Mesozoic**, the age of dinosaurs; and **Cenozoic**, the age of mammals. Most ancient forms of life have disappeared, and there are reference tables that list when this occurred. Fossil records also show the evolution of certain life forms, such as the horse from the eohippus. However, the majority of changes do not involve evolution from simple to complex forms, but rather an increase in the variety of forms.

Mountains

A **mountain** is a portion of the Earth that has been raised above its surroundings by volcanic action or tectonic plate movement. Mountains can be made of any type of rock and most lie along active plate boundaries. There are two major mountain systems. The **Circum-Pacific** encircles the entire Pacific Ocean, from New Guinea up across Japan and the Aleutians and down to southern South America. The **Alpine-Himalaya** stretches from northern Africa across the Alps and to the Himalayas and Indonesia. **Orogeny** is the term for the process of natural mountain formation. Therefore, physical mountains are orogens. **Folded mountains** are created through the folding of rock layers when two crustal plates come together. The Alps and Himalayas are folded mountains. The latter was formed by the collision of India with Asia. **Fault-block mountains** are created from the tension forces of plate movements. These produce faults that vertically displace one section to form a mountain. **Dome mountains** are created from magma pushing up through the Earth's crust.

Volcanoes and Volcanic Mountains

Volcanoes are classified according to their activity level. An **active** volcano is in the process of erupting or building to an eruption; a dormant volcano has erupted before and may erupt again someday, but is not currently active; and an **extinct** volcano has died out volcanically and will not erupt ever again. Active volcanoes endanger plant and animal life, but lava and ash add enriching minerals to the soil. There are three types of volcanic mountains:

- **Shield volcanoes** are the largest volcanic mountains because of a repeated, viscous lava flow from small eruptions over a long period of time that cause the mountain to grow.
- **Cinder cone volcanoes**, or linear volcanoes, are small in size, but have massive explosions through linear shafts that spread cinders and ash around the vent. This results in a cone-shaped hill.
- **Composite volcanoes** get their name from the mix of lava and ash layers that build the mountain.

Subdivisions of Rock

The three major subdivisions of rock are:

- **Igneous** (magmatites) – This type is formed from the cooling of liquid magma. In the process, minerals crystallize and amalgamate. If solidification occurs deep in the Earth (plutonic rock), the cooling process is slow. This allows for the formation of large crystals, giving rock a coarse-grained texture (granite). Quickly cooled magma has a glassy texture (obsidian).
- **Metamorphic** – Under conditions of high temperature and pressure within the Earth's crust, rock material melts and changes structure, transitioning or metamorphosing into a new type of rock with different minerals. If the minerals appear in bands, the rock is foliated. Examples include marble (unfoliated) and slate (foliated).
- **Sedimentary** – This is the most common type of rock on Earth. It is formed by sedimentation, compaction, and then cementation of many small particles of mineral, animal, or plant material. There are three types of sedimentary rocks: clastic, clay, and sand that came from disintegrated rocks; chemical (rock salt and gypsum), formed by evaporation of aqueous solutions; and biogenic (coal), formed from animal or plant remnants.

> **Review Video: Igneous, Sedimentary, and Metamorphic Rocks**
> Visit mometrix.com/academy and enter code: 689294

Glaciers

Glaciers start high in the mountains, where snow and ice accumulate inside a cirque (a small semicircular depression). The snow becomes firmly packed into masses of coarse-grained ice that are slowly pulled down a slope by gravity. Glaciers grow with large amounts of snowfall and retreat (diminish) if warm weather melts more ice than can be replaced. Glaciers once covered large areas of both the northern and southern hemispheres with mile-thick ice that carved out valleys, fjords, and other land formations. They also moved plants, animals, and rocks from one area to another. There were two types of glaciers: **valley**, which produced U-shaped erosion and sharp-peaked mountains; and **continental**, which moved over and rounded mountain tops and ridges. These glaciers existed during the ice ages, the last of which occurred from 2.5 million years ago to 12,000 years ago.

Earth Science and Weather

Layers Above the Surface of Earth

The **ozone layer**, although contained within the stratosphere, is determined by ozone (O_3) concentrations. It absorbs the majority of ultraviolet light from the Sun. The ionosphere is part of both the exosphere and the thermosphere. It is characterized by the fact that it is a plasma, a partially ionized gas in which free electrons and positive ions are attracted to each other, but are too energetic to remain fixed as a molecule. It starts at about 50 km above Earth's surface and goes to 1,000 km. It affects radio wave transmission and auroras. The ionosphere pushes against the inner edge of the Earth's magnetosphere, which is the highly magnetized, non-spherical region around the Earth. The homosphere encompasses the troposphere, stratosphere, and mesosphere. Gases in the homosphere are considered well mixed. In the heterosphere, the distance that particles can move without colliding is large. As a result, gases are stratified according to their molecular weights. Heavier gases such as oxygen and nitrogen occur near the bottom of the heterosphere, while hydrogen, the lightest element, is found at the top.

Review Video: Earth's Atmosphere
Visit mometrix.com/academy and enter code: 417614

Tropospheric Circulation

Most weather takes place in the **troposphere**. Air circulates in the atmosphere by convection and in various types of "cells." Air near the equator is warmed by the Sun and rises. Cool air rushes under it, and the higher, warmer air flows toward Earth's poles. At the poles, it cools and descends to the surface. It is now under the hot air, and flows back to the equator. Air currents coupled with ocean currents move heat around the planet, creating winds, weather, and climate. Winds can change direction with the seasons. For example, in Southeast Asia and India, summer monsoons are caused by air being heated by the Sun. This air rises, draws moisture from the ocean, and causes daily rains. In winter, the air cools, sinks, pushes the moist air away, and creates dry weather.

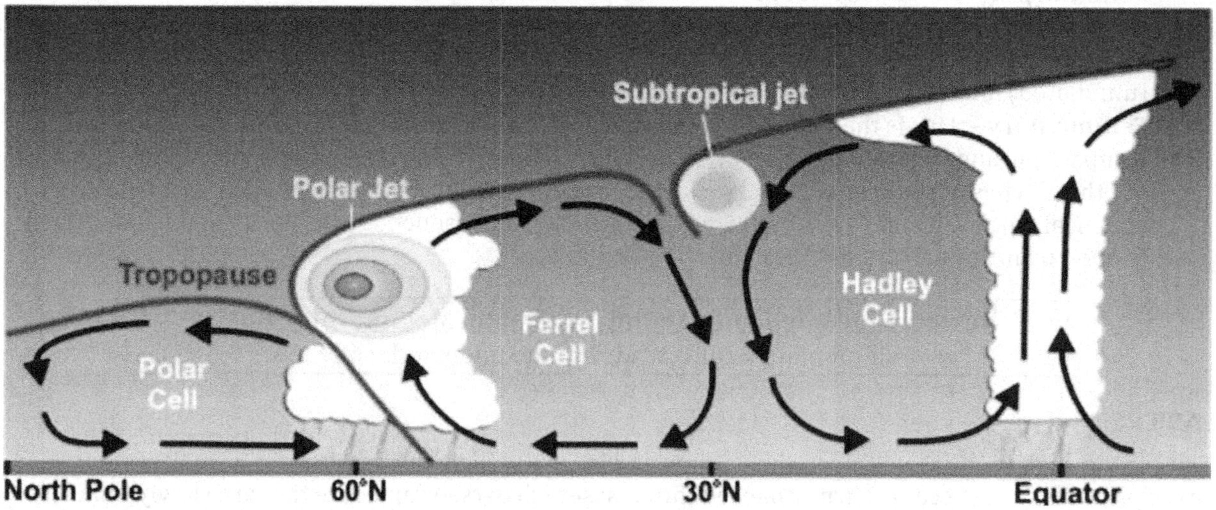

Common Weather Phenomena and Equipment to Measure Them

Common **atmospheric conditions** that are frequently measured are temperature, precipitation, wind, and humidity. These weather conditions are often measured at permanently fixed **weather stations** so weather data can be collected and compared over time and by region. Measurements may also be taken by ships, buoys, and underwater instruments. Measurements may also be taken under special circumstances. Common instruments used and measurements taken include:

- A **thermometer** for measuring temperature
- A **barometer** for measuring barometric/air pressure
- A **hygrometer** for measuring humidity
- An **anemometer** for measuring wind speed
- A **weather vane** for measuring wind direction
- A **rain gauge** for measuring precipitation

Weather, Climate, and Meteorology

Meteorology is the study of the atmosphere, particularly as it pertains to forecasting the weather and understanding its processes. **Weather** is the condition of the atmosphere at any given moment. Most weather occurs in the troposphere and includes changing events such as clouds, storms, and temperature, as well as more extreme events such as tornadoes, hurricanes, and blizzards. **Climate** refers to the average weather for a particular area over time, typically at least 30 years. Latitude is an indicator of climate. Changes in climate occur over long time periods.

Winds and Global Wind Belts

Winds are the result of air moving by convection. Masses of warm air rise, and cold air sweeps into their place. The warm air also moves, cools, and sinks. The term "prevailing wind" refers to the wind that usually blows in an area in a single direction. **Dominant winds** are the winds with the highest speeds. Belts or bands that run latitudinally and blow in a specific direction are associated with **convection cells. Hadley cells** are formed directly north and south of the equator. The **Farrell cell*s*** occur at about 30° to 60°. The jet stream runs between the Farrell cells and the polar cells. At the higher and lower latitudes, the direction is easterly. At mid latitudes, the direction is westerly. From the North Pole to the south, the surface winds are Polar High Easterlies, Subpolar Low Westerlies, Subtropical High or Horse Latitudes, North-East Trade winds, Equatorial Low or Doldrums, South-East Trades, Subtropical High or Horse Latitudes, Subpolar Low Easterlies, and Polar High.

Review Video: Where Does Wind Come From?
Visit mometrix.com/academy and enter code: 451712

Relative Humidity, Absolute Humidity, and Dew Point Temperature

Humidity refers to water vapor contained in the air. The amount of moisture contained in air depends upon its temperature. The higher the air temperature, the more moisture it can hold. These higher levels of moisture are associated with higher humidity. **Absolute humidity** refers to the total amount of moisture air is capable of holding at a certain temperature. **Relative humidity** is the ratio of water vapor in the air compared to the amount the air is capable of holding at its current temperature. As temperature decreases, absolute humidity stays the same and relative humidity increases. A hygrometer is a device used to measure humidity. The **dew point** is the temperature at which water vapor condenses into water at a particular humidity.

Precipitation

After clouds reach the dew point, **precipitation** occurs. Precipitation can take the form of a liquid or a solid. It is known by many names, including rain, snow, ice, dew, and frost. **Liquid** forms of precipitation include rain and drizzle. Rain or drizzle that freezes on contact is known as freezing rain or freezing drizzle. **Solid or frozen** forms of precipitation include snow, ice needles or diamond dust, sleet or ice pellets, hail, and graupel or snow pellets. Virga is a form of precipitation that evaporates before reaching the ground. It usually looks like sheets or shafts falling from a cloud. The amount of rainfall is measured with a rain gauge. Intensity can be measured according to how fast precipitation is falling or by how severely it limits visibility. Precipitation plays a major role in the water cycle since it is responsible for depositing much of the Earth's fresh water.

Clouds

Clouds form when air cools and warm air is forced to give up some of its water vapor because it can no longer hold it. This vapor condenses and forms tiny droplets of water or ice crystals called clouds. Particles, or aerosols, are needed for water vapor to form water droplets. These are called **condensation nuclei**. Clouds are created by surface heating, mountains and terrain, rising air masses, and weather fronts. Clouds precipitate, returning the water they contain to Earth. Clouds can also create atmospheric optics. They can scatter light, creating colorful phenomena such as rainbows, colorful sunsets, and the green flash phenomenon.

Review Video: Types of Clouds
Visit mometrix.com/academy and enter code: 803166

High, Middle, and Low Cloud Types

Most clouds can be classified according to the altitude of their base above Earth's surface. **High clouds** occur at altitudes between 5,000 and 13,000 meters. **Middle clouds** occur at altitudes between 2,000 and 7,000 meters. **Low clouds** occur from the Earth's surface to altitudes of 2,000 meters. Types of high clouds include cirrus (Ci), thin wispy mare's tails that consist of ice; cirrocumulus (Cc), small, pillow-like puffs that often appear in rows; and cirrostratus (Cs), thin, sheet-like clouds that often cover the entire sky. Types of middle clouds include altocumulus (Ac), gray-white clouds that consist of liquid water; and altostratus (As), grayish or blue-gray clouds that span the sky. Types of low clouds include stratus (St), gray and fog-like clouds consisting of water droplets that take up the whole sky; stratocumulus (Sc), low-lying, lumpy gray clouds; and nimbostratus (Ns), dark gray clouds with uneven bases that indicate rain or snow. Two types of clouds, cumulus (Cu) and cumulonimbus (Cb), are capable of great vertical growth. They can start at a wide range of altitudes, from the Earth's surface to altitudes of 13,000 meters.

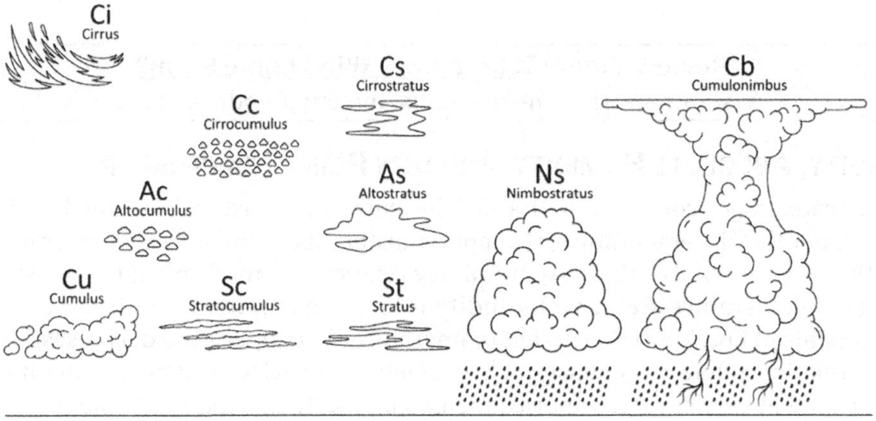

Air Masses

Air masses are large volumes of air in the troposphere of the Earth. They are categorized by their temperature and by the amount of water vapor they contain:

- **Arctic** and **Antarctic** air masses are cold
- **Polar** air masses are cool
- **Tropical** and **equatorial** air masses are hot
- **Maritime** and **monsoon** air masses are moist and unstable
- **Continental** and **superior** air masses are dry

Weather Fronts and Weather Maps

A **weather front** is the area between two differing masses of air that affects weather. Movement of a front is influenced by the jet stream and other high winds as well as the type of front; cold fronts move up to twice as fast as warm ones. It is in the turbulent frontal area that weather events take place, both commonplace and dramatic. This area also creates temperature changes. Weather phenomena include rain, thunderstorms, high winds, tornadoes, cloudiness, clear skies, and hurricanes. Different fronts can be plotted on weather maps using a set of designated symbols. Surface weather maps can also include symbols representing clouds, rain, temperature, air pressure, and fair weather.

Space Science

Astronomy

Astronomy is the scientific study of celestial objects and their positions, movements, and structures. *Celestial* does not refer to the Earth by itself, but does include its movement through space. Other celestial objects include the Sun, the Moon, planets, satellites, asteroids, meteors, comets, stars, galaxies, the universe, and other space phenomena. The term astronomy has its roots in the Greek words *astro* and *nomos*, which means "laws of the stars."

> **Review Video: Astronomy**
> Visit mometrix.com/academy and enter code: 640556

Universe

Origin

The **universe** can be said to consist of everything and nothing. The universe contains all of space, matter, energy, and time. There are likely still phenomena that have yet to be discovered. The universe can also be thought of as nothing, since a vast portion of the known universe is empty space. It is believed that the universe is expanding. The **Big Bang** is a core part of a theory developed to explain the origin of the universe. It is widely accepted among astronomers, though there are other theories regarding the origin of the universe, such as the **Steady-State theory** and the **Creationist theory**. According to the Big Bang model, all the matter in the universe was once in one place. This matter underwent a huge explosion that spread it into space. Galaxies formed from, this material and the universe is still expanding.

Structure

What can be seen of the universe is believed to be at least 93 billion light years across. To put this into perspective, the Milky Way galaxy is about 100,000 light years across. Our view of matter in the universe is that it forms into clumps which become stars, galaxies, clusters of galaxies, superclusters, and the Great Wall of galaxies. **Galaxies** consist of stars, some with planetary systems. Some estimates state that the universe is about 13 billion years old. It is not considered dense and is believed to consist of 73% dark energy, 23% cold dark matter, and 4% regular matter. Cosmology is the study of the universe. Interstellar medium (ISM) is the gas and dust in the interstellar space between a galaxy's stars.

> **Review Video: Dark Matter**
> Visit mometrix.com/academy and enter code: 251909

Galaxies

Galaxies consist of stars, stellar remnants, and dark matter. **Dwarf galaxies** contain as few as 10 million stars, while giant galaxies contain as many as 1 trillion stars. Galaxies are gravitationally bound, meaning that stars, star systems, other gases, and dust orbit the galaxy's center. The Earth exists in the **Milky Way galaxy** and the nearest galaxy to ours is the **Andromeda galaxy**. Galaxies can be classified by their visual shape into elliptical, spiral, irregular, and starburst galaxies. It is estimated that there are more than 100 billion galaxies in the universe ranging from 1,000 to 100,000 parsecs in diameter. Galaxies can be megaparsecs apart. Intergalactic space consists of a gas with an average density of less than one atom per cubic meter. Galaxies are organized into clusters which form superclusters. Dark matter may account for up to 90% of the mass of galaxies. Dark matter is still not well understood.

Planets

In order of their distance from the Sun (closest to furthest away), the **planets** are: Mercury, Venus, Earth, Mars, Jupiter, Saturn, Uranus, and Neptune (Pluto is now considered to be a dwarf planet). All the planets revolve around the Sun, which is an average-sized star in the spiral Milky Way galaxy. They revolve in the same direction in nearly circular orbits. If the planets were viewed by looking down from the Sun, they would rotate in a counter-clockwise direction. All the planets are in, or near, the same plane, called the ecliptic, and their axis of rotation is nearly perpendicular to the ecliptic. The only exception is Uranus, which is tipped on its side.

Terrestrial Planets, Jovian Planets, and Mass of Planets

The **Terrestrial Planets** are: Mercury, Venus, Earth, and Mars. These are the four planets closest to the Sun. They are called terrestrial because they all have a compact, rocky surface similar to the Earth's. Venus, Earth, and Mars have significant atmospheres, but Mercury has almost no atmosphere.

The **Jovian Planets** are: Jupiter (the largest planet), Saturn, Uranus, and Neptune. They are called Jovian (Jupiter-like) because of their huge sizes in relation to that of the Earth, and because they all have a gaseous nature like Jupiter. Although gas giants, some or all of the Jovian Planets may have small, solid cores.

The Sun represents 99.85% of all the matter in our solar system. Combined, the planets make up only 0.135% of the mass of the solar system, with Jupiter having twice the mass of all the other planets combined. The remaining 0.015% of the mass comes from comets, planetary satellites, asteroids, meteoroids, and interplanetary medium.

Review Video: Terrestrial Planets
Visit mometrix.com/academy and enter code: 100346

Definition of Planet

On August 24, 2006, the International Astronomical Union redefined the criteria a body must meet to be classified as a planet, stating that the following conditions must be met:

- "A planet orbits around a star and is neither a star nor a moon."
- "Its shape is spherical due to its gravity."
- "It has 'cleared' the space of its orbit."

A **dwarf planet** such as Pluto does not meet the third condition. Small solar system bodies such as asteroids and comets meet only the first condition.

Solar System

The **solar system** developed about 4.6 billion years ago out of an enormous cloud of dust and gas circling around the Sun. Four rocky planets orbit relatively close to the Sun. Their inside orbits are separated from the outside orbits of the four, larger gaseous planets by an asteroid belt. Pluto, some comets, and several small objects circle in the Kuiper belt outside Neptune's orbit. The Oort cloud, composed of icy space objects, encloses the planetary system like a shell.

Review Video: The Solar System
Visit mometrix.com/academy and enter code: 273231

Earth's Moon

The Moon is the closest celestial body to Earth. Its proximity has allowed it to be studied since the invention of the telescope. As a result, its landforms have been named after astronomers, philosophers, and other scholars. Its surface has many craters created by asteroids since it has no protective atmosphere. These dark lowlands looked like seas to early astronomers, so many have been given names like the Sea of Tranquility, even though there is virtually no water on the Moon except possibly in its polar regions. These impact craters and depressions actually contain solidified lava flows. The bright highlands were thought to be continents, and were named terrae. The rocks of the Moon have been pounded by asteroids so often that there is a layer of rubble and dust called the regolith. Also, because there is no protective atmosphere, temperatures on the Moon vary widely, from 265°F to -255°F.

EARTH'S SUN AND OTHER STARS

A **star** begins as a cloud of hydrogen and some heavier elements drawn together by their own mass. As the matter coalesces due to its own gravity, it begins to rotate. Once there is sufficient mass, the core heats up to several million degrees Fahrenheit, which causes the hydrogen atoms to lose their shells and their nuclei to fuse. This releases enormous amounts of energy, generates an outward pressure that is balanced by the pull of gravity, and enables the star to become stable. At this point the star is in a stage called the **main sequence**. This is the stage our Sun is in, and it will remain in this stage until its supply of hydrogen fuel runs out. Stars are not always alone like our Sun, and may exist in pairs or groups. The hottest stars shine blue-white; medium-hot stars like our Sun glow yellow; and cooler stars appear orange. The Sun is an **average star** in terms of mass, light production, and size. All stars, including our Sun, have a **core** where fusion happens; a **photosphere** (surface) that produces sunspots (cool, dark areas); a red **chromosphere** that emits solar (bright) flares and shooting gases; and a **corona**, the transparent area only seen during an eclipse.

Review Video: The Sun
Visit mometrix.com/academy and enter code: 699233

COMETS, ASTEROIDS, AND METEOROIDS

Comets are celestial bodies composed of dust, rock, frozen gases, and ice. Invisible until they near the Sun, comets emit volatile components in jets of gas and dust when exposed to the Sun's heat. The **coma** is the comet's fog-like envelope that glows as it reflects sunlight and releases radiation. **Solar winds** blow a comet away from the Sun and give it a tail of dust or electrically charged molecules. Each orbit of a comet causes it to lose matter until it breaks up or vaporizes into the Sun.

Asteroids are irregularly-shaped boulders, usually less than 60 miles in diameter, that orbit the Sun. Most are made of graphite; about 25% are silicates, or iron and nickel. Collisions or gravitational forces can cause them to fly off and possibly hit a planet.

Meteoroids are fragments of asteroids of various sizes. If they come through Earth's atmosphere, they are called meteors or shooting stars. If they land on Earth, they are called meteorites, and create craters on impact (the Barringer Crater in Arizona).

Chapter Quiz

Ready to see how well you retained what you just read? Scan the QR code to go directly to the chapter quiz interface for this study guide. If you're using a computer, simply visit the bonus page at **mometrix.com/bonus948/act** and click the Chapter Quizzes link.

Writing

Transform passive reading into active learning! After immersing yourself in this chapter, put your comprehension to the test by taking a quiz. The insights you gained will stay with you longer this way. Scan the QR code to go directly to the chapter quiz interface for this study guide. If you're using a computer, simply visit the bonus page at **mometrix.com/bonus948/act** and click the Chapter Quizzes link.

Writing Overview

The ACT writing section is an optional, 40-minute essay test. The prompt presents a common problem and gives several perspectives on that issue. In the response, the test-taker must address the issue by presenting his or her own perspective and relate it to the other perspectives. The scoring rubric consists of a rounded average score from 2-12 based on the following four categories:

- **Ideas and Analysis** – Writers must provide relevant and helpful information in addressing the given prompt.
- **Development and Support** – Writers must use good logic and strong arguments in supporting their own viewpoint.
- **Organization** – Writers must use a good organizational scheme that supports clarity and purposefully connects ideas.
- **Language Use and Conventions** – Writers must present strong grammar, syntax, word usage, and mechanics.

Preparing for an Essay Question

Brainstorm

Spend the first three to five minutes brainstorming for ideas. Write down any ideas that you might have on the topic. The purpose is to pull any helpful information from the depths of your memory. In this stage, anything goes down in a margin for notes regardless of how good or bad the idea may seem at first glance.

Strength Through Different Viewpoints

The best papers will contain several examples and mature reasoning. As you brainstorm, you should consider different perspectives. There are more than two sides to every topic. In an argument, there are countless perspectives that can be considered. On any topic, different groups are impacted and many reach the same conclusion or position. Yet, they reach the same conclusion through different paths. Before writing your essay, try to *see* the topic through as many different *eyes* as you can.

In addition, you don't have to use information on how the topic impacts others. You can draw from your own experience as you wish. If you prefer to use a personal narrative, then explain the experience and your emotions from that moment. Anything that you've seen in your community can be expanded upon to round out your position on the topic.

Once you have finished with your creative flow, you need to stop and review what you brainstormed. *Which idea allowed you to come up with the most supporting information?* Be sure to pick an angle that will allow you to have a thorough coverage of the prompt.

Every garden of ideas has weeds. The ideas that you brainstormed are going to be random pieces of information of different values. Go through the pieces carefully and pick out the ones that are the best. The best ideas are strong points that will be easy to write a paragraph in response.

Now, you have your main ideas that you will focus on. So, align them in a sequence that will flow in a smooth, sensible path from point to point. With this approach, readers will go smoothly from one idea to the next in a reasonable order. Readers want an essay that has a sense of continuity (i.e., Point 1 to Point 2 to Point 3 and so on).

START YOUR ENGINES

Now, you have a logical flow of the main ideas for the start of your essay. Begin by expanding on the first point, then move to your second point. Pace yourself. Don't spend too much time on any one of the ideas that you are expanding on. You want to have time for all of them. Make sure that you watch your time. If you have twenty minutes left to write out your ideas and you have four ideas, then you can only use five minutes per idea. Writing so much information in so little time can be an intimidating task. Yet, when you pace yourself, you can get through all of your points. If you find that you are falling behind, then you can remove one of your weaker arguments. This will allow you to give enough support to your remaining paragraphs.

Once you finish expanding on an idea, go back to your brainstorming session where you wrote out your ideas. You can scratch through the ideas as you write about them. This will let you see what you need to write about next and what you have left to cover.

Your introductory paragraph should have several easily identifiable features.

- First, the paragraph should have a quick description or paraphrasing of the topic. Use your own words to briefly explain what the topic is about.
- Second, you should list your writing points. What are the main ideas that you came up with earlier? If someone was to read only your introduction, they should be able to get a good summary of the entire paper.
- Third, you should explain your opinion of the topic and give an explanation for why you feel that way. What is your decision or conclusion on the topic?

Each of your following paragraphs should develop one of the points listed in the main paragraph. Use your personal experience and knowledge to support each of your points. Examples should back up everything.

Once you have finished expanding on each of your main points, you need to conclude your essay. Summarize what you have written in a conclusion paragraph. Explain once more your argument on the prompt and review why you feel that way in a few sentences. At this stage, you have already backed up your statements. So, there is no need to do that again. You just need to refresh your readers on the main points that you made in your essay.

DON'T PANIC

Whatever you do during essay, do not panic. When you panic, you will put fewer words on the page and your ideas will be weak. Therefore, panicking is not helpful. If your mind goes blank when you see the prompt, then you need to take a deep breath. Force yourself to go through the steps listed above: brainstorm and put anything on scratch paper that comes to mind.

Also, don't get clock fever. You may be overwhelmed when you're looking at a page that is mostly blank. Your mind is full of random thoughts and feeling confused, and the clock is ticking down faster. You have already brainstormed for ideas. Therefore, you don't have to keep coming up with ideas. If you're running out of time and you have a lot of ideas that you haven't written down, then don't be afraid to make some cuts. Start picking the best ideas that you have left and expand on them. Don't feel like you have to write on all of your ideas.

A short paper that is well written and well organized is better than a long paper that is poorly written and poorly organized. Don't keep writing about a subject just to add sentences and avoid repeating a statement or idea that you have explained already. The goal is 1 to 2 pages of quality writing. That is your target, but you should not mess up your paper by trying to get there. You want to have a natural end to your work without having to cut something short. If your essay is a little long, then that isn't a problem as long as your ideas are clear and flow well from paragraph to paragraph. Remember to expand on the ideas that you identified in the brainstorming session.

Leave time at the end (at least three minutes) to go back and check over your work. Reread and make sure that everything you've written makes sense and flows well. Clean up any spelling or grammar mistakes. Also, go ahead and erase any brainstorming ideas that you weren't able to include. Then, clean up any extra information that you might have written that doesn't fit into your paper.

As you proofread, make sure that there aren't any fragments or run-ons. Check for sentences that are too short or too long. If the sentence is too short, then look to see if you have a specific subject and an active verb. If it is too long, then break up the long sentence into two sentences. Watch out for any "big words" that you may have used. Be sure that you are using difficult words correctly. Don't misunderstand; you should try to increase your vocabulary and use difficult words in your essay. However, your focus should be on developing and expressing ideas in a clear and precise way.

THE SHORT OVERVIEW

Depending on your preferences and personality, the essay may be your hardest or your easiest section. You are required to go through the entire process of writing a paper in a limited amount of time which is very challenging.

Stay focused on each of the steps for brainstorming. Go through the process of creative flow first. You can start by generating ideas about the prompt. Next, organize those ideas into a smooth flow. Then, pick out the ideas that are the best from your list.

Create a recognizable essay structure in your paper. Start with an introduction that explains what you have decided to argue. Then, choose your main points. Use the body paragraphs to touch on those main points and have a conclusion that wraps up the topic.

Save a few moments to go back and review what you have written. Clean up any minor mistakes that you might have made and make those last few critical touches that can make a huge difference. Finally, be proud and confident of what you have written!

Chapter Quiz

Ready to see how well you retained what you just read? Scan the QR code to go directly to the chapter quiz interface for this study guide. If you're using a computer, simply visit the bonus page at **mometrix.com/bonus948/act** and click the Chapter Quizzes link.

Practice Test #1

Want to take this practice test in an online interactive format?
Check out the bonus page, which includes interactive practice questions and much more: **<u>mometrix.com/bonus948/act</u>**

SCAN HERE

English

Refer to the following for questions 1 - 15:

United States Coast Guard

The United States Coast Guard <u>was founded in 1790</u> as the branch of military service responsible for safeguarding the country's sea-related interests. <u>It was originally created</u> to protect the US <u>from smugglers, and to enforce</u> tariff and trade laws. While this may seem like a job for the Navy, the Navy's purpose is very different from that of the Coast Guard. The Navy's job is <u>to engage in combat, defend the seas</u> from threats <u>to the US and its interests</u> worldwide. <u>The United States Coast Guard is actually a part of the Department of Homeland Security and is considered a federal law enforcement agency</u>. <u>The mission of the department is to protect the US coastlines and American waters through enforcing US and international laws.</u>

In addition to enforcing maritime <u>law, we need to recognize that the United States Coast Guard also serves</u> as a guardian of the environment. One of the Coast Guard's main missions is the Marine Environmental Protection mission. The <u>responsibilities of this mission included stopping</u> waste and pollutants from entering the ocean and helping to prevent and clean oil spills. <u>This is a real important</u> job for the Coast Guard because there would not be much of a coastline to protect if the seas were too polluted to entertain or to sustain life.

<u>Performing in a single day</u>, the United States Coast Guard personnel save 12 lives, respond to 64 search and rescue cases, keep 842 pounds of cocaine off the streets, service 116 buoys and fix 24 discrepancies, screen 720 commercial vessels and 183,000 crew and passengers, issue 173 credentials to merchant mariners, investigate 13 marine accidents, inspect 68 containers and 29 vessels for compliance with air emissions standards, perform 28 safety and environmental examinations of foreign vessels, board 13 fishing boats to ensure compliance with fisheries laws, and <u>explore and investigate 10 pollution incidents</u>.

1. The United States Coast Guard <u>was founded in 1790</u> as the branch of military service responsible for safeguarding the country's sea-related interests.

A. NO CHANGE
B. was founded in 1790,
C. were founded in 1790
D. will have been founded in 1790

2. The author wants to add the following statement:

While this branch of military service has seen several changes in its tasks, the mission of the branch has not changed since its founding.

Should the author make this addition between the first and second sentences in the passage?

F. Yes, this sentence offers a smooth transition to the following sentence and informs readers of what they can expect for the remainder of the passage.
G. No, this sentence is vague and distracting for readers.
H. Yes, the purpose of the passage is to address the many responsibilities of the US Coast Guard.
J. No, the dependent phrase of this sentence is already addressed in the next sentence, and the independent clause is addressed in the following paragraphs.

3. <u>It was originally created</u> to protect the US from smugglers, and to enforce tariff and trade laws.

A. NO CHANGE
B. It was originally established
C. The branch was originally created
D. Originally, it was created

4. It was originally created to protect the US <u>from smugglers, and to enforce</u> tariff and trade laws.

F. NO CHANGE
G. from smugglers, and enforce
H. from smugglers, and to promote
J. from smugglers and to enforce

5. The Navy's job is <u>to engage in combat, defend the seas</u> from threats to the US and its interests worldwide.

A. NO CHANGE
B. to engage in combats and defend the seas
C. to engage in combat, and defend the seas
D. to engage in combat and defend the seas

6. How can this sentence be revised for conciseness?

The United States Coast Guard is actually a part of the Department of Homeland Security and is considered a federal law enforcement agency.

F. NO CHANGE
G. As part of the Department of Homeland Security, the United States Coast Guard is considered a federal law enforcement agency.
H. As part of the Department of Homeland Security, we know the United States Coast Guard to be a federal law enforcement agency.
J. The Department of Homeland Security considers the United States Coast Guard to be actually a part of a federal law enforcement agency.

7. In addition to enforcing maritime <u>law, we need to recognize that the United States Coast Guard also serves</u> as a guardian of the environment.

A. NO CHANGE
B. law, also serving the United States Coast Guard
C. law we need to recognize that the United States Coast Guard serves
D. law, the United States Coast Guard also serves

8. <u>This is a real important</u> job for the Coast Guard because there would not be much of a coastline to protect if the seas were too polluted to entertain or to sustain life.

F. NO CHANGE
G. Truly, this is not an important
H. This is a truly, valuable
J. This is a critical

9. Performing in a single day, the United States Coast Guard personnel save 12 lives, respond to 64 search and rescue cases, keep 842 pounds of cocaine off the streets, service 116 buoys and fix 24 discrepancies, screen 720 commercial vessels and 183,000 crew and passengers, issue 173 credentials to merchant mariners, investigate 13 marine accidents, inspect 68 containers and 29 vessels for compliance with air emissions standards, perform 28 safety and environmental examinations of foreign vessels, board 13 fishing boats to ensure compliance with fisheries laws, and <u>explore and investigate 10 pollution incidents</u>.

A. NO CHANGE
B. investigate 10 pollution incidents
C. explore, and investigate 10 pollution incidents
D. explore to investigate 10 pollution incidents

10. At the end of the passage, the author wants to add the following statement:

If we do our part to maintain clean coastlines, this will allow the Coast Guard to focus more on performing routine inspections or search and rescue missions.

Should the author make the addition here?

F. Yes, this comes as helpful information to readers who are not familiar with the responsibilities of the Coast Guard.
G. No, this sentence would distract from the author's original purpose of the passage, which is to inform, not persuade.
H. Yes, this encourages readers to be responsible citizens, assisting the Coast Guard in a task that is too large for them to complete on their own.
J. No, this sentence suggests that readers are responsible for cleaning coastlines.

11. If the writer's main goal were to explain the requirements for becoming a member of the United States Coast Guard, then would this passage achieve that goal?

A. Yes, the author lists the daily objectives of Coast Guard members and describes how a member is "a guardian of the environment."
B. No, the author provides only a partial list of the things that Coast Guard members are expected to accomplish each day.
C. Yes, the author notes the difference between the US Navy and the Coast Guard in the first paragraph.
D. No, the author gives clarity on some of the differences between the US Navy and the Coast Guard but mentions none of the necessary steps to becoming a member of the US Coast Guard.

12. Which of the following would be the best conclusion for this essay?

F. There is much more that we can learn about the Coast Guard. To list all of the great things about this organization would take all day. The opportunities available to members of the Coast Guard are endless, and we should all consider becoming a "Coastie."

G. Being a "Coastie" would be the fulfillment of many people's dreams. To have a career of adventure and honor, and to make a difference in the lives of fellow countrymen daily, are high aspirations. Few jobs are more fulfilling or more necessary.

H. The Coast Guard is a very diverse branch of the US military. Though some may not believe it is as important as the Navy, the Army, the Marines, or the Air Force, it's plain to see that the Coast Guard plays a vital role in ensuring our nation's security and prosperity.

J. The Coast Guard provides little support toward defending our nation from threats, as its members are always so close to home. They do an excellent job of patrolling the coastline, but the threats that the Coast Guard faces are insignificant when compared to those faced by the Army, the Navy, the Marines, or the Air Force.

13. The Navy's job is to engage in combat, defend the seas from threats <u>to the US, and its interests</u> worldwide.

A. NO CHANGE
B. to the US, and it's interests
C. to the US and its interests
D. to the US with its interests worldwide

14. The <u>responsibilities of this mission included stopping</u> waste and pollutants from entering the ocean, helping to prevent and clean oil spills, and protecting existing ecosystems from invasive marine species.

F. NO CHANGE
G. responsibilities of this mission will include stopping
H. responsibilities of this mission include stopping
J. responsibilities of this mission might include stopping

15. What is the best revision to this sentence?

The mission of the department is to protect the US coastlines and American waters through enforcing US and international laws.

A. NO CHANGE
B. The mission of the department, is to protect the US coastlines, and American waters through enforcing US and international laws.
C. The mission of the department is to protect the US coastlines and American waters, through enforcing US and international laws
D. The mission of the department is to protect the coastlines, and American waters, through enforcing US and international laws.

Refer to the following for questions 16 - 30:

New Zealand Inhabitants

(1) The islands of New Zealand are among the most remote of all the Pacific islands. (2) New Zealand is an archipelago, with two large islands, and a number of smaller ones. (3) Its climate is far cooler than the rest of Polynesia. (4) Nevertheless, according to Maori legends, it was colonized in the early fifteenth century by a wave of Polynesian voyagers who traveled southward in their canoes and settled on North Island. (5) At this

time, New Zealand will already be known to the Polynesians, who had probably first landed there some 400 years earlier.

(6) The Polynesian southward migration was limited by the availability of food. (7) Traditional Polynesian tropical crops such as taro and yams will grow on North Island, but the climate of the South Island is too cold for them. (8) The first settlers were forced to rely on hunting and gathering, and, of course, fishing. (9) Especially on the South Island, most settlements remained close to the sea. (10) At the time of the Polynesian incursion, enormous flocks of moa birds had their rookeries on the island shores. (11) These flightless birds were easy prey for the settlers, and within a few centuries had been hunted to extinction. (12) Fish, shellfish and the roots of the fern were other important sources of food, but even these began to diminish in quantity as the human population increased. (13) The Maori had few other sources of meat: dogs, smaller birds, and rats. (14) Archaeological evidence shows that human flesh was also eaten, and that tribal warfare increased markedly after the moa disappeared.

(15) By far the most important farmed crop in prehistoric New Zealand was the sweet potato. (16) This tuber is hearty enough to grow throughout the islands, and could be stored to provide food during the winter months, when other food-gathering activities were difficult. (17) The availability of the sweet potato made possible a significant increase in the human population. (18) Thus, Maori tribes were often located near the most fertile farmlands in encampments called pa, which were fortified with earthen embankments.

16. What is the best revision for the underlined portion?

(1) The islands of New Zealand are among the most remote of all the Pacific islands.

F. NO CHANGE
G. The island of New Zealand is among the most remote
H. The islands of New Zealand are between the most remote
J. The islands of New Zealand are among the more remote

17. The author wants to add the following statement after sentence 1:

New Zealand is one of the most popular tourist destinations in the southern hemisphere.

Should the author make this addition between the first and second sentences in the passage?

A. Yes, because this is an important detail for introducing the reader to the islands of New Zealand.
B. No, because this detail would be more appropriately placed in the third paragraph.
C. Yes, because the description of the islands' geography in this paragraph helps to explain the reason for New Zealand's popularity.
D. No, because this detail is not at all relevant to the author's purpose in this passage.

18. What is the best revision for the underlined portion?

(2) New Zealand is an archipelago, with two large islands, and a number of smaller ones.

F. NO CHANGE
G. islands and the amount of smaller
H. islands and a number of smaller
J. islands and an amount of smaller

19. How can the following sentence be revised for precision and conciseness?

(4) Nevertheless, according to Maori legends, it was colonized in the early fifteenth century by a wave of Polynesian voyagers who traveled southward in their canoes and settled on North Island.

A. NO CHANGE
B. According to Maori legends, New Zealand was colonized in the early fifteenth century by Polynesian voyagers who traveled in their canoes to settle on North Island.
C. Nevertheless, it was colonized according to Maori legends, by a wave of Polynesian voyagers who traveled southward in their canoes and settled on North Island.
D. Those who traveled southward in their canoes settled on North Island because it was colonized in the early fifteenth century by a wave of Polynesian voyagers according to Maori legends.

20. What is the best revision for the following sentence?

(5) At this time, New Zealand has been known already to the Polynesians, who had probably first landed there some 400 years earlier.

F. NO CHANGE
G. New Zealand will have been known already to the Polynesians who had probably first landed there some 400 years earlier.
H. The Polynesians, who had probably first landed there some 400 years earlier, at this time have known New Zealand.
J. At this time, the Polynesians knew their surroundings in New Zealand since they had probably first landed some 400 years earlier.

21. What is the best revision for the underlined portion?

(6) The Polynesian <u>southward migration was limited by</u> the availability of food.

A. NO CHANGE
B. Southward migration is limited by
C. southward migration had been limited by
D. Southward migration has been limited by

22. The author wants to add the following statement:

Coconuts, a staple in many tropical cultures, will not grow on either island.

Should the author make this addition after sentence 8?

F. Yes. This information is evidence that will help readers understand the predicament of Polynesian people.
G. No. This statement is not relevant to the discussion.
H. Yes. This statement transitions well from the previous sentence to the next on the struggle to find and maintain food for Polynesians.
J. No. This statement does not include an explanation of the purpose of coconuts to the Polynesian people.

23. What is the best revision for the underlined portion?

(8) <u>The first settlers were forced</u> to rely on hunting, gathering, and fishing.

A. NO CHANGE
B. The first settlers forced themselves
C. The first settlers will have been forced
D. This harsh environment forced the first settlers

24. Which choice most effectively transitions between sentences 8 and 9?

The first settlers were forced to rely on hunting, gathering, and fishing. Especially on the South Island, most settlements remained close to the sea.

F. fishing, but especially on South Island
G. fishing; however, on South Island
H. fishing: especially on South Island
J. fishing; therefore, on South Island

25. What is the best revision for the underlined portion?

(12) Fish, shellfish and the roots of the fern, were other important sources of food, but even these began to diminish in quantity as the human population increased.

A. NO CHANGE
B. Fish, shellfish, and the roots of the fern
C. Fish, Shellfish, and the roots of the fern
D. Fish, shellfish and the root of the fern,

26. What is the best revision for the underlined portion?

(13) The Maori had few other choices of meat among: dogs, smaller birds, and rats.

F. NO CHANGE
G. of meat among: dogs, smaller birds and rats
H. with: dogs, smaller birds, and rats
J. of meat: dogs, smaller birds, and rats

27. What is the best revision for the underlined portion?

(14) Archaeological evidence shows that human flesh was also eaten, and that tribal warfare increased after the markedly disappearance of the moa.

A. NO CHANGE
B. increased markedly after the moa disappeared.
C. increased after they disappeared.
D. increased markedly after their disappearance.

28. What is the most appropriate location for sentence 17?

The availability of the sweet potato made possible a significant increase in the human population.

F. In its current location
G. At the end of the second paragraph
H. At the beginning of the final paragraph
J. In the middle of the final paragraph

29. What is the best revision for the underlined portion?

(17) The availability of the sweet potato made possible a significant increase in the human population.

A. NO CHANGE
B. increase in the human population.
C. significant increase in the Maori population.
D. significant increase in the population.

30. The author is reconsidering sentence (18):

Thus, Maori tribes were often located near the most fertile farmlands in encampments called pa, which were fortified with earthen embankments.

Should the author keep the addition at the end of this passage?

F. Yes, this information is evidence that supports the topic of the third paragraph.
G. No, this sentence is unnecessary and does not support the topic of the third paragraph.
H. Yes, this sentence is further proof that the Maori tribe was the most advanced of New Zealand inhabitants.
J. No. While this information supports the topic, the author should reconsider the placement of the sentence in this passage.

Refer to the following for questions 31 - 45:

Early Twentieth Century Flight

After Orville and Wilbur Wright will have flown their first airplane in 1903, the age of flying slowly began. Many new pilots learned how to fly in World War I, that the United States joined in 1917. During the war, the American public loved hearing stories about the daring pilots and their air fights. But after the war ended, many Americans thought that men and women belonged on the ground and not in the air. [**A**]

In the years after the war and through the Roaring Twenties, America's pilots found themselves without jobs. Some of them gave up flying altogether. [**B**] Pilot Eddie Rickenbacker, who used to be called America's Ace of Aces, became a car salesman. But other pilots found new and creative things to do with their airplanes. The airplane was used by pilot Casey Jones to help get news across the country. When a big news story broke, Jones flew photos to newspapers in different cities. A pilot, Roscoe Turner, traveled around the country with a lion cub in his plane. The cub was the mascot of an oil company, and Turner convinced the company that flying the cub around would be a good advertisement. The Humane Society was not pleased with this idea, and they convinced Turner to make sure the lion cub always wore a parachute. [**C**] Other pilots took people for short airplane rides, often charging five dollars for a five-minute ride (by comparison, you could buy a loaf of bread for about ten cents in 1920). These pilots, called barnstormers, often used dangerous tricks to win customers: two barnstormers once stood on a plane's wings and played tennis while the plane flew at 70 miles per hour! Many barnstormers advertised their shows as a "flying circus."

During the 1920s, the US Post Office developed airmail. [**D**] The Airmail Act of 1925 was passed to make airmail routes more efficient. The first commercial airmail flight takes place on February 15th, 1926. Before airmail the post traveled on trains and can take weeks to reach a destination. Flying for the post office was dangerous work. Early pilots didn't have sophisticated instruments and safety equipment on their planes. Many of them had to bale out and use their parachutes when their planes iced up in the cold air or had other trouble.

31. After Orville and Wilbur Wright will have flown their first airplane in 1903, the age of flying slowly began.

A. NO CHANGE
B. Wilbur Wright have flown their
C. Wilbur Wright flew their
D. Wilbur Wright will have flew their

32. Many new pilots learned how to fly in World War I, that the United States joined in 1917.

F. NO CHANGE
G. trained for flight in World War I, that
H. studied flying during World War I which
J. learned how to fly during World War I, which

33. What is the best way to combine these two sentences?

In the years after the war and through the Roaring Twenties, America's pilots found themselves without jobs.
Some of them gave up flying altogether.

A. Some of America's pilots in the years after the war and through the Roaring Twenties found themselves without jobs because they gave up flying altogether.
B. In the years after the war and through the Roaring Twenties, America's pilots found themselves without jobs; thus, some of them gave up flying altogether.
C. Some of America's pilots gave up flying altogether in the years after the war and through the Roaring Twenties, and they found themselves without jobs.
D. In the years after the war and through the Roaring Twenties, America's pilots found themselves without jobs because some of them gave up flying altogether.

34. But other pilots found new and creative things to do with their airplanes.

F. NO CHANGE
G. pilots found creative things
H. pilots attempted new and creative things
J. pilots found new, creative tricks

35. When a big news story broke, Jones flew photos to newspapers in different cities.

A. NO CHANGE
B. When a big, news story broke, Jones
C. When an important story broke, Jones
D. When a big news story arrived, Jones

36. The Humane Society was not pleased with this idea, and they convinced Turner to make sure the lion cub always wore a parachute.

F. NO CHANGE
G. with this idea: they convinced Turner
H. with this idea; Turner was convinced
J. with this idea; and they convinced Turner

37. What is the best revision to this sentence?

Other pilots took people for short airplane rides, often charging five dollars for a five-minute ride (by comparison, you could buy a loaf of bread for about ten cents in 1920).

A. NO CHANGE
B. In the same time period that one could buy a loaf of bread for about ten cents, pilots took people for short airplane rides, often charging five dollars for a five-minute ride.
C. Pilots took people for short airplane rides by charging five dollars for a five-minute ride, or you could buy a loaf of bread for about ten cents in 1920.
D. Often charging five dollars for a five-minute ride, pilots took people for short airplane rides; however, you could buy a loaf of bread for about ten cents in 1920 by comparison.

38. These pilots, called barnstormers, often used dangerous tricks to win <u>customers: two barnstormers once stood</u> on a plane's wings and played tennis while the plane flew at 70 miles per hour!

F. NO CHANGE
G. customers, two barnstormers once stood
H. customers: two barnstormers were once standing
J. customers: two barnstormers stood

39. The author wants to add the following statement:

The most famous pilot of the 1920s, Charles A. Lindbergh, participated in an air race to fly across the Atlantic Ocean in May 1927.

Where is the best place for this sentence to be added in the passage?

A. Point A in Paragraph 1
B. Point B in Paragraph 2
C. Point C in Paragraph 2
D. Point D in Paragraph 3

40. If the author wanted to argue that the purpose of the passage was to explain the reasons for men and women needing to remain on the ground after the war, would the author be able to maintain this claim?

F. Yes, the first paragraph reviews the contribution that pilots made during WWI.
G. No, the passage does not focus enough on the practical aspects of the airplane compared to entertainment.
H. Yes, the author gives context to the privileges of flight and the early achievements of flight.
J. No, the author does not provide reasons for why the American public thought that the pilots should remain on the ground instead of pursuing more opportunities with flight.

41. Many <u>barnstormers advertised</u> their shows as a "flying circus."

A. NO CHANGE
B. barnstormer's advertised
C. barnstormers' advertised
D. barnstormer advertised

42. Many of them <u>had to bale out</u> and use their parachutes when their planes iced up in the cold air or had other trouble.

F. NO CHANGE
G. had to bail out
H. had to baile out
J. had to bell out

43. The first commercial airmail <u>flight takes place on</u> February 15th, 1926.

A. NO CHANGE
B. flight will take place on
C. flight was to take place on
D. flight took place on

44. The Airmail Act of 1925 <u>was passed to make</u> airmail routes more efficient.

F. NO CHANGE
G. will pass to make
H. can pass to make
J. were passed to make

45. <u>Before airmail the post</u> traveled on trains and can take weeks to reach a destination.

A. NO CHANGE
B. Before airmail: the post
C. Before airmail, the post
D. Before airmail; the post

Refer to the following for questions 46 - 60:

Buddhism, Western Society, and the Self

<u>In Western society, the American individual self</u> is generally prioritized over the collective self. This is evidenced in such things as the privatization of medicine and conceptions of ownership. In recent decades, however, there has been an increased tension <u>beside Western societies</u> with institutions and ideologies that prioritize the individual and those that prioritize the collective. This is evidenced in the struggles <u>that Western Buddhists faced.</u>

Central to Buddhist belief is the idea of "egolessness." While this term may seem to imply the absence of the individual ego or selfhood, this is <u>not the case; consequently, "egolessness" is a prioritization of the relationships</u> between and among people over selfish concerns. "Egolessness" may also be thought of as an antonym of "ego-toxicity," that condition where an individual <u>places his or her concerns before any other person or group's concerns.</u> <u>In Western societies, ego-toxicity is the reigning condition</u>. Buddhists who live in such societies often find themselves caught between their ideology of egolessness and environmental ego-toxicity.

While a Western perspective might find it difficult to <u>understand how a Buddhist can keep egolessness;</u> in Western society, Buddhists are able to maintain such a perspective as a natural consequent of their beliefs. The Western perspective expects moral actions to be quid pro quo; to put it another way, a Westerner assumes that if he or she does something considered "good," then <u>he or she was rewarded</u>. Buddhists, on the other hand, believe that good should be done out of compassion for all <u>beings, and to do good is to do good for all beings, including</u> the self. Approaching society and social action in an egoless manner is becoming more prevalent in secular institutions and movements, <u>as can be seen in the healthcare field</u>. The struggle between the ego and the collective <u>continues; however.</u>

Buddhist practitioners <u>show through they're actions that</u> it is possible to do good in the world without giving up one's personhood. <u>When ego-toxicity is abandoned, it is possible to care for one's self in the rest of the world through compassionate, egoless behavior</u>.

46. <u>In Western society, the American individual self</u> is generally prioritized over the collective self.

F. NO CHANGE
G. In Western society, the self
H. In western society, the American self
J. In Western society, the individual self

47. In recent decades, however, there has been an increased tension <u>beside Western societies</u> with institutions and ideologies that prioritize the individual and those that prioritize the collective.

A. NO CHANGE
B. among Western societies
C. between Western societies
D. underneath western societies

48. What is the author's purpose in the first paragraph?

F. To criticize Buddhist notions of the self.
G. To criticize contemporary Western notions of the self.
H. To introduce the tension between individuality and collectivity in Western society.
J. To introduce the idea of "egolessness."

49. While this term may seem to imply the absence of the individual ego or selfhood, this is <u>not the case; consequently, "egolessness" is a prioritization</u> of the relationships between and among people over selfish concerns.

A. NO CHANGE
B. not the case; rather, "egolessness" is a prioritization
C. not the case; therefore, "egolessness" is a prioritization
D. not the case; accordingly, "egolessness" is a priority

50. "Egolessness" may also be thought of as an antonym of "ego-toxicity," that condition where an individual <u>places his or her concerns before any other person or group's concerns</u>.

F. NO CHANGE
G. places his or her concerns before any other person's concerns.
H. places his or her concerns before any other person's or group's concerns.
J. places his or her concerns before any other person or group concern.

51. Which of the following best describes the purpose of the second paragraph?

A. It introduces the distinction between egolessness and ego-toxicity.
B. It makes light of the conflicts that Buddhists in Western societies experience.
C. It praises egolessness as the only moral way of living.
D. It harshly denounces ego-toxicity.

52. While a Western perspective might find it difficult to <u>understand how a Buddhist can keep egolessness;</u> in Western society, Buddhists are able to maintain such a perspective as a natural consequent of their beliefs.

F. NO CHANGE
G. understand how a Buddhist could maintain egolessness,
H. understand how a Buddhist could stay egolessness
J. believe what a Buddhist could maintain egolessness

53. The Western perspective expects moral actions to be quid pro quo; to put it another way, a Westerner assumes that if he or she does something considered "good," then <u>he or she was rewarded</u>.

A. NO CHANGE
B. then he or she will be rewarded.
C. then he or she should be rewarded.
D. then he or she were to be rewarded.

54. Buddhists, on the other hand, believe that good should be done out of compassion for all <u>beings, and to do good is to do good for all beings, including</u> the self.

F. NO CHANGE
G. beings, and to do good is good for all beings, including
H. beings and to do good is to do good for all beings including
J. beings, and this is done for all beings including

55. <u>When ego-toxicity is abandoned, it is possible to care for one's self in the rest of the world through compassionate, egoless behavior</u>.

A. NO CHANGE
B. When ego-toxicity can be abandoned it is possible for one's self to care for the rest of the world through compassionate, egoless behavior.
C. When ego-toxicity is abandoned it could be possible to care for one's self and the rest of the world through compassionate, egoless behavior.
D. When ego-toxicity is abandoned, it is possible to care for one's self and the rest of the world through compassionate, egoless behavior.

56. In this passage, which sentence in the first paragraph states a main idea that is developed in subsequent paragraphs?

F. The second sentence
G. The fourth sentence
H. The third sentence
J. The first sentence

57. Which of these accurately describes a pattern in the first and/or last sentences of all the paragraphs in this passage?

A. The last sentence of each paragraph identifies half a main conflict; the final sentence in the passage completes it.
B. The first sentence of each paragraph identifies a main conflict, with the final sentence in the passage reiterating.
C. The first sentence of each paragraph identifies a main conflict, with the final sentence in the passage resolving it.
D. The last sentence in all but the final paragraph identifies a main conflict, with the final sentence in the passage resolving it.

58. The struggle between the ego and the collective <u>continues; however.</u>

F. NO CHANGE
G. continues, however
H. continues: however
J. continues however

59. Buddhist practitioners <u>show through they're actions that</u> it is possible to do good in the world without giving up one's personhood.

A. NO CHANGE
B. show through their actions that
C. show thru their actions that
D. show threw they're actions that

60. This is evidenced in the struggles <u>that Western Buddhists faced.</u>

F. NO CHANGE
G. that Western Buddhists faces
H. that Western Buddhists did face
J. that Western Buddhists face

Refer to the following for questions 61 - 75:

The Beginnings of Basketball

One of the most popular and exciting sports of our time, is basketball. Behind this fast-paced sport, however, is a rich history. There have been many changes made to the game over the years, but the essence remains the same. [**A**] From its humble beginnings in 1891, basketball has grown to have worldwide appeal.

[**B**] In 1891, Dr. James Naismith, a teacher and Presbyterian minister, needed an indoor game to keep college students busy during long winter days in Springfield, Massachusetts at the Springfield YMCA Training School. This need prompted the creation of basketball, which was originally played by tossing a soccer ball into an empty peach basket nailed to the gym wall. Additionally, there was two teams but only one basket in the original game.

Because of the simplicity of basketball, the game spread across the nation within 30 years of its invention in Massachusetts. [**C**] As more teams formed, the need for a league became apparent. The smaller National Basketball League (NBL) formed soon after. On June 6, 1946 the Basketball Association of America (BAA) was formed. In 1948, the BAA merged with the NBL, and the National Basketball Association (NBA) was born. The NBA played its first full season in 1948–49 and is still going strong today.

Though much has changed in our world since 1891, the popularity of the sport of basketball has remained strong. [**D**] From it's humble start in a YMCA gym to the multi-million-dollar empire it is today, the simple fun of the sport has endured. Although many changes have been made over the years, the essence of basketball has remained constant. Its rich history and simplicity ensure that basketball will always be a popular sport around the world.

61. One of the most popular and exciting sports of our time, is basketball.

A. NO CHANGE
B. of our time is basketball.
C. among our time, is basketball.
D. of our day and age, is basketball.

62. What is the BEST way to revise and combine these two sentences?

Behind this fast-paced sport, however, is a rich history.
There have been many changes made to the game over the years, but the essence remains the same.

F. Behind this fast-paced sport is a rich history; however, there have been many changes made to the game over the years.
G. Over the years the essence remains the same for this fast-paced sport with its rich history.
H. Behind this fast-paced sport is a rich history, but the essence remains the same.
J. Though there have been many changes made to the game over the years, the essence remains the same for this fast-paced sport with its rich history.

63. From its humble beginnings in 1891, <u>basketball has grown to have worldwide appeal</u>.

A. NO CHANGE
B. basketball has grown to have world-wide appeal.
C. basketball grew to have worldwide appeal.
D. basketball has grown due to its worldwide appeal.

64. In 1891, Dr. James Naismith, a teacher and <u>Presbyterian minister, needed</u> an indoor game to keep college students busy during long winter days in Springfield, Massachusetts at the Springfield YMCA Training School.

F. NO CHANGE
G. Presbyterian Minister needed
H. presbyterian minister, needed
J. a Presbyterian Minister, founded

65. In 1891, Dr. James Naismith, a teacher and Presbyterian minister, needed an indoor game to keep college students busy during long winter days in Springfield, <u>Massachusetts at the Springfield YMCA Training School</u>.

A. NO CHANGE
B. Massachusetts, at the Springfield YMCA training school
C. Massachusetts, at the Springfield YMCA Training School
D. Massachusetts at the Springfield YMCA training school

66. Additionally, <u>there was two teams</u> but only one basket in the original game.

F. NO CHANGE
G. there were two teams; but only one
H. there was two teams, but only one
J. there were two teams but only one

67. Because of the simplicity of <u>basketball, the game spread</u> across the nation within 30 years of its invention in Massachusetts.

A. NO CHANGE
B. basketball, the sport had spread
C. basketball the game spread
D. basketball, the game had spread

68. Where should this sentence be located to achieve the best organization and clarity for the paragraph?

<u>The smaller National Basketball League (NBL) formed soon after</u>.

F. It should remain where it is.
G. It should be moved one sentence earlier.
H. It should be moved one sentence later.
J. It should be moved to the end of the paragraph.

69. On <u>June 6, 1946 the Basketball Association of America (BAA)</u> was formed.

A. NO CHANGE
B. June 6, 1946, the Basketball Association of America (BAA)
C. June 6, 1946 the basketball association of America (BAA)
D. June 6, 1946; the Basketball Association of America (BAA)

70. Though much has changed in our world since 1891, the <u>popularity of the sport of basketball has remained strong</u>.

F. NO CHANGE
G. popularity of basketball has remained strong.
H. popularity of the sport of basketball has been constant.
J. attention of the sport of basketball has been constant.

71. From <u>it's humble start in a YMCA gym to the multi-million-dollar empire</u> it is today, the simple fun of the sport has endured.

A. NO CHANGE
B. it's humble start in a YMCA gymnasium to the multi-million-dollar
C. it's humble start in a YMCA gym to the multi-million dollar
D. its humble start in a YMCA gym to the multi-million-dollar

72. From it's humble start in a YMCA gym to the multi-million-dollar empire it is <u>today, the simple fun of the sport has endured</u>.

F. NO CHANGE
G. today, the fun of the sport has
H. today: the simple fun of the sport has
J. today, the simple fun of the sport had

73. The author wants to add the following statement to the passage:

One thing that sets the history of basketball apart from other major sports is the fact that it was created with the intent of playing indoors.

Where should this sentence be added?

A. Point A in Paragraph 1
B. Point B in Paragraph 2
C. Point C in Paragraph 3
D. Point D in Paragraph 4

74. The style, mode, or type of text in this passage is best characterized as which of these?

F. Description
G. Persuasion
H. Exposition
J. Narration

75. If the author wanted to argue that the purpose of the passage was to explain the influence of the YMCA on sports, would the author be able to maintain this claim?

A. Yes, the author demonstrated that James Naismith invented a sport.
B. No, the thirty years after its invention were more influential than the YMCA.
C. Yes, some of the most respected athletes in America were members at a YMCA.
D. No, the author would need to show how the YMCA influenced more than just basketball.

Mathematics

1. Elijah spent \$30 for a state fair ticket and \$3.50 per ride. Which of the following equations can be used to find the total amount Elijah spent (y) if he rode x rides?

A. $y = 30x + 3.50$
B. $y = 33.50x$
C. $y = 3.50x + 30$
D. $y = 3.50x + 33.50$
E. $y = -3.50x + 33.50$

2. If $g(x) = 3x + x + 5$, evaluate $g(2)$.

F. $g(2) = 8$
G. $g(2) = 9$
H. $g(2) = 13$
J. $g(2) = 17$
K. $g(2) = 19$

3. Given the equation, $ax + b = c$, what is the value of x?

A. $\frac{c+b}{a}$
B. $\frac{ca}{b}$
C. $c - ba$
D. $\frac{c-b}{a}$
E. $c + ba$

4. Put the following numbers in order from the least to greatest $2^3, 4^2, 6^0, 9, 10^1$.

F. $2^3, 4^2, 6^0, 9, 10^1$
G. $6^0, 9, 10^1, 2^3, 4^2$
H. $10^1, 2^3, 6^0, 9, 4^2$
J. $6^0, 2^3, 9, 10^1, 4^2$
K. $2^3, 9, 10^1, 4^2, 6^0$

5. Given the partial table of values for $f(x)$ and $g(x)$, find $f(g(3))$. Assume that $f(x)$ and $g(x)$ are the simplest polynomials that fit the data.

x	$f(x)$	$g(x)$
-2	-16	-11
-1	-2	-8
0	0	-5
1	2	-2
2	16	1

A. 169
B. 128
C. 72
D. 16
E. 4

6. What is the approximate area of the shaded region between the circle and the square in the figure shown below? Use 3.14 for π.

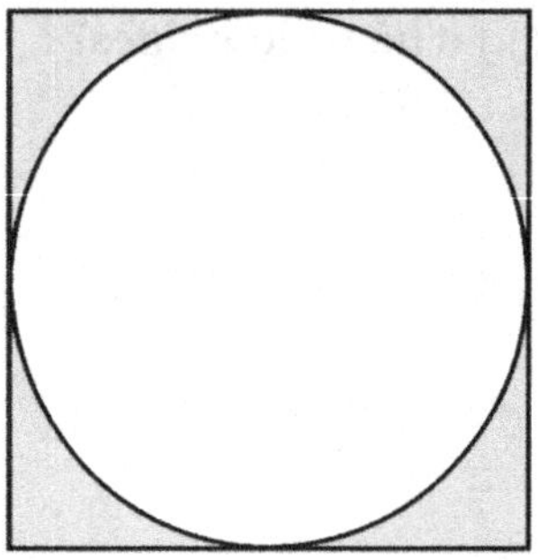

F. $177\ \text{cm}^2$
G. $181\ \text{cm}^2$
H. $187\ \text{cm}^2$
J. $190\ \text{cm}^2$
K. $193\ \text{cm}^2$

7. Which of the following expressions is equivalent to $(x-3)^2$?

A. $x^2 - 3x + 9$
B. $x^2 - 6x - 9$
C. $x^2 - 6x + 9$
D. $x^2 + 3x - 9$
E. $x^2 + 3x + 9$

8. Tim is paid $5.00 an hour to babysit his neighbor's child. The neighbor says she will give Tim a 20% bonus for today's babysitting if he takes care of their puppy too. Tim works for four hours. How much is he paid for his work today if he takes care of the puppy along with the child?

F. $20.00
G. $20.40
H. $22.00
J. $24.00
K. $24.50

9. The possible combinations of candy bars and packages of suckers that Amanda may purchase are represented by the graph shown below.

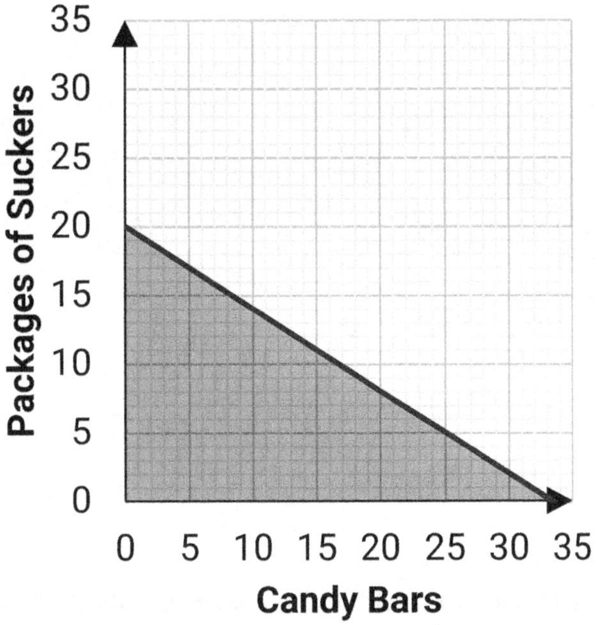

Which of the following inequalities represents the possible combinations of candy bars and packages of suckers that she may purchase?

A. $y \le -\frac{1}{2}x + \frac{40}{3}$
B. $y \le -\frac{2}{5}x + 20$
C. $y \le -\frac{3}{5}x + 20$
D. $y \le -\frac{5}{3}x + \frac{80}{3}$
E. $y \le -\frac{2}{3}x + \frac{80}{3}$

10. If $A = \begin{bmatrix} 1 & -3 \\ -4 & 2 \end{bmatrix}$ and $B = \begin{bmatrix} 1 & -3 \\ -4 & -2 \end{bmatrix}$, then what is $A - B$?

F. $\begin{bmatrix} 2 & -6 \\ -8 & 0 \end{bmatrix}$
G. $\begin{bmatrix} 0 & 0 \\ 0 & 0 \end{bmatrix}$
H. $\begin{bmatrix} 0 & 0 \\ 0 & 4 \end{bmatrix}$
J. $\begin{bmatrix} 0 & 3 \\ 4 & 2 \end{bmatrix}$
K. $\begin{bmatrix} 0 & -6 \\ -8 & 4 \end{bmatrix}$

11. A scaled drawing for a new building has walls measuring 4 inches in height. The key indicates that each inch on the drawing represents 2 feet in real life. Based on the scaled drawing, how tall will the actual walls measure?

A. 8 feet
B. 4 feet
C. 12 feet
D. 21 feet
E. 32 feet

12. Solve: $\begin{bmatrix} 4 & 2 \\ 7 & 12 \end{bmatrix} + \begin{bmatrix} -1 & 15 \\ 3 & -5 \end{bmatrix}$

F. $\begin{bmatrix} 3 & 17 \\ 10 & 7 \end{bmatrix}$
G. $\begin{bmatrix} 3 & 1 \\ 10 & 15 \end{bmatrix}$
H. $\begin{bmatrix} 19 & 17 \\ 2 & 7 \end{bmatrix}$
J. $\begin{bmatrix} 19 & 1 \\ 2 & 15 \end{bmatrix}$
K. $\begin{bmatrix} 3 & 17 \\ 2 & 15 \end{bmatrix}$

13. In the figure below, circle O is a unit circle, and the measure of $\angle AOB$ is $\frac{\pi}{3}$ (radians).

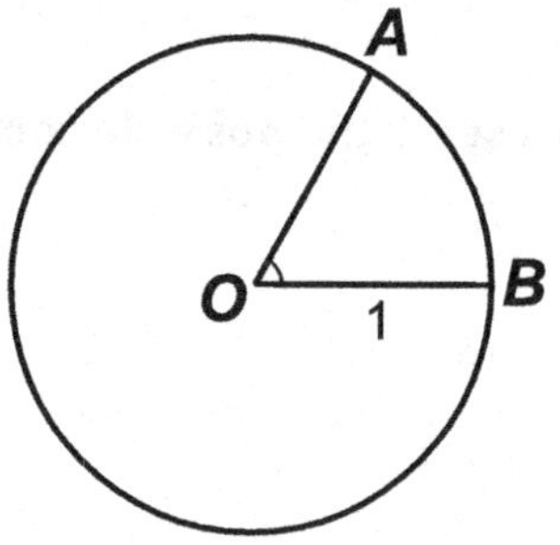

What is the length of $\widehat{AB}$?

A. $\frac{\pi}{6}$
B. $\frac{\pi}{3}$
C. $\frac{2\pi}{3}$
D. π
E. 2π

14. A pump fills a cylindrical tank with water at a constant rate. The function $L(g) = 0.3g$ represents the water level of the tank (in feet) after g gallons are pumped into the tank. The function $w(t) = 1.2t$ represents the number of gallons that can be pumped into the tank in t minutes. Write a function $L(t)$ for the water level of the tank after t minutes.

F. $L(t) = 0.25t$
G. $L(t) = 0.36t$
H. $L(t) = 0.9t$
J. $L(t) = 3.6t$
K. $L(t) = 4t$

15. Evaluate the quotient and express in standard form: $\frac{15-5i}{4-2i}$.

A. $\frac{25+5i}{6}$
B. $\frac{7+5i}{2}$
C. $\frac{5+i}{2}$
D. $\frac{7+i}{2}$
E. $\frac{7+5i}{6}$

16. There are 100 bacteria in a Petri dish. The number of bacteria doubles every day, so that on the first day, there are 100 bacteria; on the second, there are 200; on the third, there are 400; and so on. Write a formula for the number of bacteria on the nth day.

F. $b(n) = 100 \times 2^{n-1}$
G. $b(n) = 100n$
H. $b(n) = 100n^2$
J. $b(n) = 200(n-1)$
K. $b(n) = 200n^2$

17. On Day 1, a driver averages 60 miles per hour for 15 hours of a 2,000-mile car trip. If he maintains this average speed and duration on Day 2, how far will he be from his destination at the end of the day?

A. 200 miles
B. 400 miles
C. 500 miles
D. 700 miles
E. 900 miles

18. In the figure below, ΔJKL is dilated to the image $\Delta J'K'L'$.

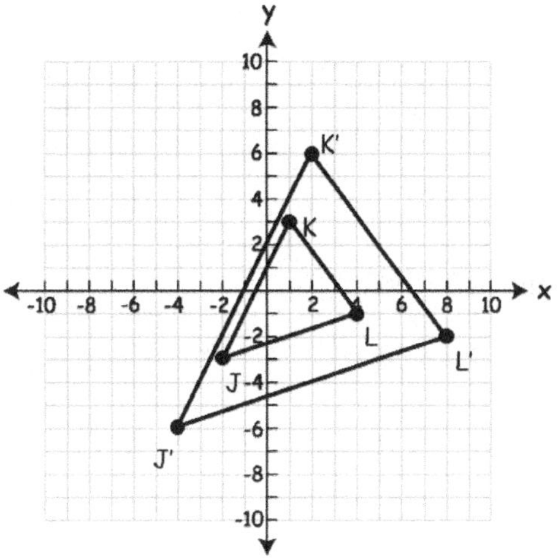

What is the scale factor of the dilation?

F. $\frac{1}{3}$
G. $\frac{1}{2}$
H. 2
J. 3
K. $\frac{1}{4}$

19. Mike is at a Pay-By-The-Ounce salad bar. He places a quarter-pound of blueberries, a half-pound of strawberries, a half-pound of yogurt, and a quarter-pound of walnuts into his bowl. A sign says that the salad bar costs fifteen cents an ounce. How much will Mike's salad cost?

A. $1.80
B. $2.75
C. $3.00
D. $3.60
E. $4.10

20. A hotel's Internet service costs guests $3.00 for the first hour of use and $0.15 for each five minutes over that. A woman uses the service for 3 hours and 10 minutes. What will her Internet charge be?

F. $3.90
G. $5.60
H. $6.90
J. $7.20
K. $9.30

21. Abe averages 3 miles per hour running and Beatriz averages 4 miles per hour running. How much further can Beatriz go in half an hour than Abe can?

A. 2 miles
B. 1 mile
C. $\frac{1}{2}$ mile
D. $\frac{1}{4}$ mile
E. $\frac{1}{8}$ mile

22. A woman wants to park her 15-foot-long car in a garage that is 19 feet long. How far from the front of the garage will the front of her car need to be so that the car is centered on the floor of the garage?

F. 2 feet
G. $2\frac{1}{2}$ feet
H. 3 feet
J. $3\frac{1}{2}$ feet
K. 4 feet

23. Approximately what percentage of 81 is 36?

A. 34%
B. 44%
C. 54%
D. 64%
E. 74%

24. $\overline{AB}$ is tangent to circle O. Find the length of $\overline{OB}$.

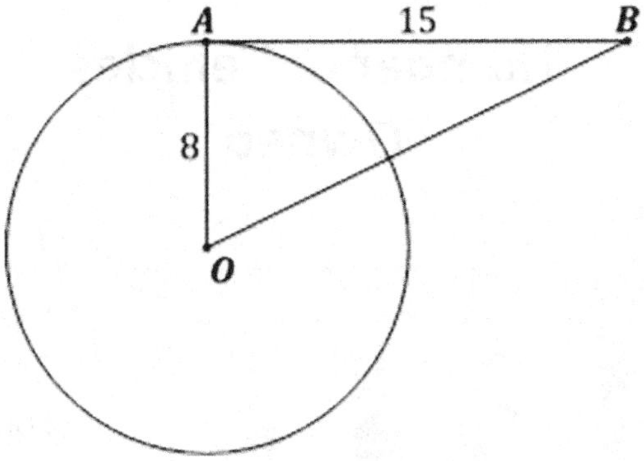

F. 13
G. 16
H. 17
J. 23
K. 64

25. Natasha designs a square pyramidal tent for her children. Each of the sides of the square base measures x ft, and the tent's height is h feet. If Natasha were to increase by 1 ft the length of each side of the base, how much more interior space would the tent have?

A. $\frac{h(x^2+2x+1)}{3}$ ft^3
B. $\frac{h(2x+1)}{3}$ ft^3
C. $\frac{x^2h+3}{3}$ ft^3
D. $\frac{x^2h}{3}$ ft^3
E. 1 ft^3

26. The table below displays the value of the linear function $g(x)$ for different values of x.

x	−2	−1	0	1	2
$g(x)$	10	7	4	1	-2

Write an explicit formula for $g(x)$.

F. $g(x) = -4x + 3$
G. $g(x) = -4x + 4$
H. $g(x) = -3x + 3$
J. $g(x) = -3x + 4$
K. $g(x) = -2x + 4$

27. Andre is traveling at a speed of 65 miles per hour. At this rate, how long will it take Andre to travel 195 miles?

A. 2.17 hours
B. 3 hours
C. 3.25 hours
D. 4.5 hours
E. 585 minutes

28. Given the double bar graph shown below, which of the following statements is true?

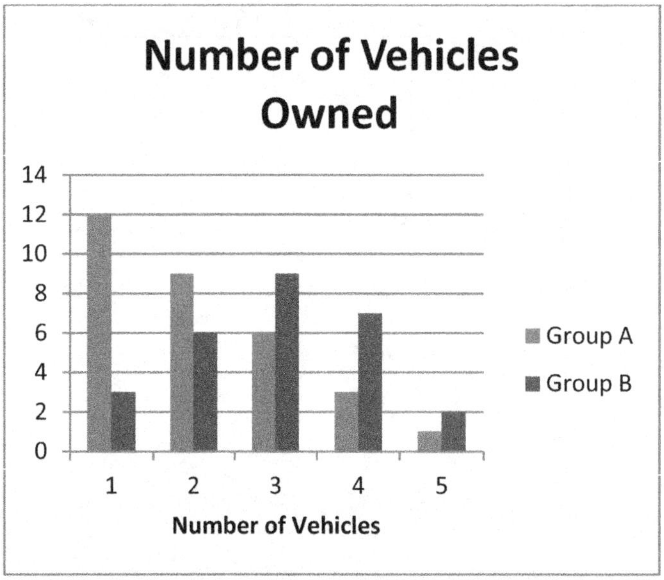

F. Group A is negatively skewed, while Group B is approximately normal.
G. Group A is positively skewed, while Group B is approximately normal.
H. Group A is positively skewed, while Group B is neutral.
J. Group A is approximately normal, while Group B is negatively skewed.
K. Group A is approximately normal, while Group B is positively skewed.

29. A $1,000 lottery winner had 35% deducted for taxes. How much was the winning check?

A. $300
B. $350
C. $650
D. $700
E. $965

30. Edward draws a card from a standard deck of cards, does not replace it, and then draws another card. What is the probability that he draws a heart and then a spade?

F. $\frac{1}{16}$
G. $\frac{1}{2}$
H. $\frac{1}{17}$
J. $\frac{13}{204}$
K. $\frac{1}{3}$

Refer to the following for questions 31 - 32:

The 180 campers in Group A got to choose which kind of sandwich they wanted on the picnic. The results of the choice are given in the table below.

Sandwich	# of Campers
PB & J	60
Turkey	45
Egg salad	15
Veggie	60

31. Which expression correctly provides the ratio of campers who chose veggie sandwiches to those who chose turkey?

A. 1 : 3
B. 1 : 4
C. 2 : 3
D. 3 : 2
E. 4 : 3

32. Approximately what percentage of the campers chose either turkey or egg salad?

F. 66%
G. 45%
H. 33%
J. 15%
K. 7%

33. A new ramp is being installed at the entrance to a building.

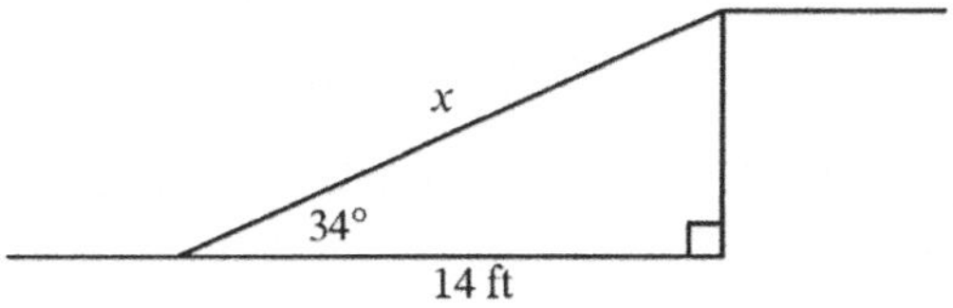

Based on the figure above, what is the length of the ramp, shown by x?

A. $14\cos 34°$ ft
B. $\frac{14}{\cos 34°}$ ft
C. $\frac{14}{\tan 34°}$ ft
D. $\frac{14}{\sin 34°}$ ft
E. $14\sin 34°$ ft

34. Sara and her sister Kate are standing next to one another on the beach. Kate casts a shadow that is 32 inches long. Sara's shadow is 16 inches longer than her sister's. If Kate is 40 inches tall, how tall is Sara?

F. 48 inches
G. 52 inches
H. 60 inches
J. 72 inches
K. Not enough information is given

35. Sophie is painting a wall in her living room red. She can cover 36 square feet with one gallon of paint. If the wall is 8 feet high and 15 feet long, how many gallons will she need to purchase if she can only purchase whole gallons of paint?

A. 2 gallons
B. 3 gallons
C. 4 gallons
D. 5 gallons
E. 6 gallons

36. If Fahrenheit, (°F) and Celsius, (°C) are related by the formula °F $= \left(\frac{9}{5}\right)$°C $+ 32$, what is the temperature in Fahrenheit of a location with an average temperature of 20 °C?

F. 58°
G. 63°
H. 68°
J. 73°
K. 78°

37. Hector's car holds 12 gallons of gasoline. He filled his tank for $22.44. Assuming Hector's tank was completely empty when he filled up, how much money did Hector pay per gallon of gasoline?

A. $1.87
B. $2.05
C. $2.22
D. $18.70
E. $269.28

38. A dress is marked down by 20% and placed on a clearance rack, on which is posted a sign reading, "Take an extra 25% off already reduced merchandise." What fraction of the original price is the final sale price of the dress?

F. $\frac{1}{4}$
G. $\frac{2}{5}$
H. $\frac{3}{5}$
J. $\frac{9}{20}$
K. $\frac{11}{20}$

39. The graph of the parent function $y = x^2$ is shifted 5 units to the left and 4 units down. Which of the following equations represents the transformed function?

A. $y = (x - 5)^2 - 4$
B. $y = (x + 5)^2 - 4$
C. $y = (x - 5)^2 + 4$
D. $y = (x + 5)^2 + 4$
E. $y = (x + 4)^2 + 5$

40. Of the twenty students in the classroom, half are boys and half are girls. If all students handed in their homework, what is the probability that the top homework sheet belongs to a girl?

F. 20%
G. 25%
H. 30%
J. 40%
K. 50%

41. The sides of quadrilateral *PQRS* are tangent to the circle. What is the perimeter of quadrilateral *PQRS*?

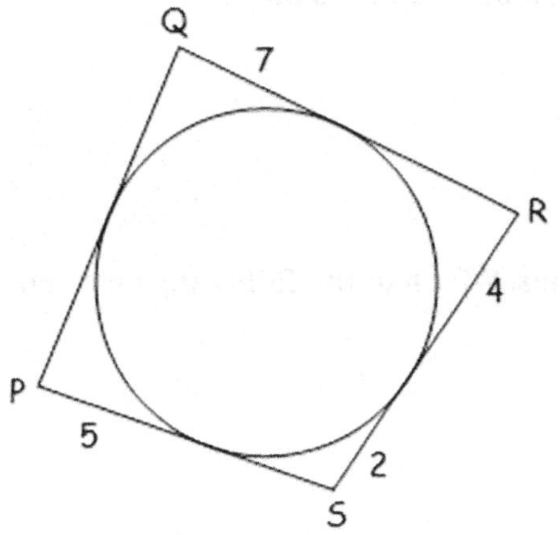

A. 36
B. 30
C. 24
D. 20
E. 18

42. A librarian makes time-and-a-half for each hour that he works over 40 hours per week. The linear function $s(h) = 27h + 720$ represents his weekly salary (in dollars) if he works *h* hours more than 40 hours that week. For example, his weekly salary is $s(10) = 990$ dollars if he works 50 hours in one week (because 50 hours means 10 hours of overtime). What is his hourly salary after he has already worked the initial 40 hours in one week?

F. $7.20 per hour
G. $18.00 per hour
H. $27.00 per hour
J. $48.00 per hour
K. $72.00 per hour

43. Three rectangular gardens, each with an area of 36 square feet, are created on a tract of land. Garden A measures 4 feet by 9 feet; Garden B measures 12 feet by 3 feet; Garden C measures 18 feet by 2 feet. Which garden will require the most fencing to surround it?

A. Garden A
B. Garden B
C. Garden C
D. All gardens will require the same amount of fencing
E. It cannot be determined from the information provided

44. John puts his money into a bank account that pays monthly interest. His monthly balance (in dollars) after *t* months is given by the exponential function $b(t) = 315(1.05)^t$. How much money did John initially put into the account?

F. $5
G. $105
H. $300
J. $315
K. $350

45. On Peter's homework assignment of a state map, $\frac{1}{2}$ inch represents 12 miles. If a distance is 84 miles, how many inches long will it be on Peter's map?

A. 3
B. 3.5
C. 5
D. 5.5
E. 6

46. Portia tosses a coin 1,000 times. Which of the following best represents the number of times she can expect to get tails?

F. 350
G. 400
H. 450
J. 500
K. 1,000

47. Dale made service calls at a rate of $45/hour last year. He is raising his rates 7% this year. What would a $135.00 bill from the last year cost this year with the increase in rates?

A. $138.00
B. $138.15
C. $142.00
D. $144.45
E. $150.00

48. On a road map, $\frac{1}{4}$ inch represents 8 miles of actual road distance. The towns of Dinuba and Clovis are measured to be $2\frac{1}{8}$ inches apart on the map. What is the actual distance, in miles, between the two towns?

F. 32
G. 40
H. 60
J. 64
K. 68

49. Brenda buys a pair of shoes for $62.00. The next day she sees that the shoes are on sale for 25% off. How much money would Brenda have saved if she had waited a day?

A. $9.92
B. $15.50
C. $25.00
D. $46.50
E. $52.08

50. The ratio of boys to girls in a math class is 3 to 4. If there are 12 boys in the class, how many total students are in the class?

F. 7 students
G. 16 students
H. 19 students
J. 28 students
K. 34 students

51. The table below shows the average amount of rainfall Houston receives during the summer and autumn months.

Month	Rainfall (inches)
June	5.35
July	3.18
August	3.83
September	4.33
October	4.5
November	4.19

What percentage of rainfall in this timeframe occurs during October?

A. 13.5%
B. 15.1%
C. 16.9%
D. 17.7%
E. 18.38%

52. Find the area of the rectangle.

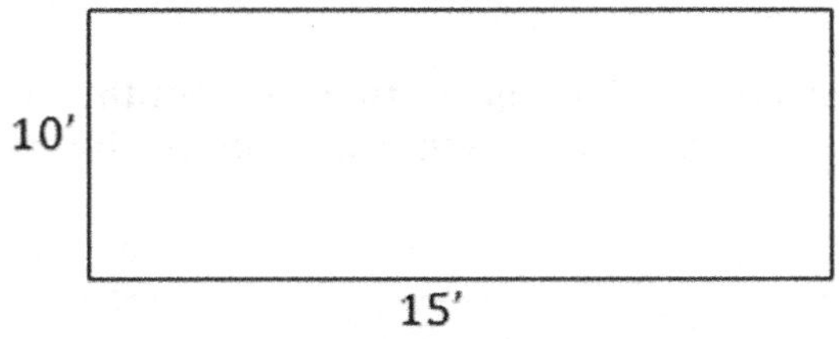

F. 50 ft^2
G. 75 ft^2
H. 100 ft^2
J. 125 ft^2
K. 150 ft^2

53. James won a cash raffle prize. He paid taxes of 30% on the prize and had $14,000 remaining. How much was the original prize?

A. $42,000
B. $40,000
C. $30,000
D. $20,000
E. $18,000

54. Which of these statements is true for functions $f(x)$, $g(x)$, and $h(x)$?

$$f(x) = 2x - 2$$
$$g(x) = 2x^2 - 2$$
$$h(x) = 2x^3 - 2$$

F. The degree of each polynomial function is 2.
G. The leading coefficient of each function is –2.
H. Each function has exactly one real zero at $x = 1$.
J. All three functions are trinomials.
K. None of these is true for functions $f(x)$, $g(x)$, and $h(x)$.

55. What is the expression $-2i \times 7i$ is equal to?

A. -14
B. 14
C. $14i$
D. $-14i$
E. $-9i$

56. Given the table below, which of the following best represents the probability that a student is enrolled at TAMU or prefers lattes?

	Latte	Cappuccino	Frappuccino	Total
TAMU	350	225	175	750
NMSU	325	300	275	900
Total	675	525	450	1,650

F. 55%
G. 60%
H. 65%
J. 70%
K. 75%

57. Molly borrows $12,000 from a friend. She agrees to make monthly payments to repay the loan in two years along with an additional 10% of the original amount for interest. What are her monthly payments?

A. $465
B. $550
C. $650
D. $700
E. $1,010

58. The volume of a rectangular box is found by multiplying its length, width, and height. If the dimensions of a box are $\sqrt{3}$, $2\sqrt{5}$, and 4, what is its volume?

F. $2\sqrt{60}$
G. $2\sqrt{15}$
H. $4\sqrt{15}$
J. $8\sqrt{15}$
K. $24\sqrt{5}$

59. Given the equation $\frac{2}{x-8} = \frac{3}{x}$, what is the value of x?

A. 16
B. 20
C. 24
D. 28
E. 32

60. Which of the following is true about the relationship between the two triangles shown below?

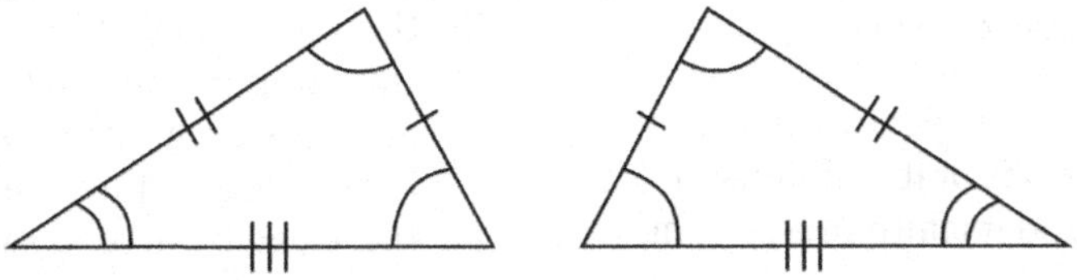

F. The triangles are similar.
G. The triangles are congruent.
H. The triangles are equilateral.
J. The triangles are both congruent and equilateral.
K. The triangles are both similar and congruent.

Reading

Refer to the following for questions 1 - 10:

This passage is adapted from President Franklin D. Roosevelt's *State of the Union Address* in January of 1941.

Many subjects connected with our social economy call for immediate improvement. As examples:

We should bring more citizens under the coverage of old-age pensions and unemployment insurance. We should widen the opportunities for adequate medical care. We should plan a better system by which persons deserving or needing gainful employment may obtain it.

I have called for personal sacrifice. And I am assured of the willingness of almost all Americans to respond to that call. A part of the sacrifice means the payment of more money in taxes. In my Budget Message I will recommend that a greater portion of this great defense program be paid for from taxation than we are paying for today. No person should try, or be allowed, to get rich out of the program; and the principle of tax payments in accordance with ability to pay should be constantly before our eyes to guide our legislation. If the Congress maintains these principles, the voters, putting patriotism ahead of pocketbooks, will give you their applause.

In the future days, which we seek to make secure, we look forward to a world founded upon four essential human freedoms. The first is freedom of speech and expression—everywhere in the world. The second is freedom of every person to worship God in his own way—everywhere in the world. The third is freedom from want—which, translated into world terms, means economic understandings which will secure to every nation a healthy peacetime life for its inhabitants—everywhere in the world. The fourth is freedom from fear—which, translated into world terms, means a world-wide reduction of armaments to such a point and in such a thorough fashion that no nation will be in a position to commit an act of physical aggression against any neighbor—anywhere in the world.

That is no vision of a distant millennium. It is a definite basis for a kind of world attainable in our own time and generation. That kind of world is the very antithesis of the so-called new order of tyranny which the dictators seek to create with the crash of a bomb. To that new order we oppose the greater conception—the moral order. A good society is able to face schemes of world domination and foreign revolutions alike without fear.

Since the beginning of our American history, we have been engaged in change—in a perpetual peaceful revolution—a revolution which goes on steadily, quietly adjusting itself to changing conditions—without the concentration camp or the quick-lime in the ditch. The world order which we seek is the cooperation of free countries, working together in a friendly, civilized society.

This nation has placed its destiny in the hands and heads and hearts of its millions of free men and women; and its faith in freedom under the guidance of God. Freedom means the supremacy of human rights everywhere. Our support goes to those who struggle to gain those rights and keep them. Our strength is our unity of purpose. To that high concept there can be no end save victory.

1. Which statement best supports the idea that FDR believed America is constantly evolving toward a better situation?

A. Since the beginning of our American history, we have been engaged in change—in a perpetual peaceful revolution—a revolution which goes on steadily, quietly adjusting itself to changing conditions—without the concentration camp or the quick-lime in the ditch.
B. This nation has placed its destiny in the hands and heads and hearts of its millions of free men and women; and its faith in freedom under the guidance of God.
C. To that new order we oppose the greater conception—the moral order. A good society is able to face schemes of world domination and foreign revolutions alike without fear.
D. The fourth is freedom from fear—which, translated into world terms, means a world-wide reduction of armaments to such a point and in such a thorough fashion that no nation will be in a position to commit an act of physical aggression against any neighbor—anywhere in the world.

2. In this text, FDR claims that raising taxes will result in a patriotic populace that will happily support the government. What might be one argument against this idea?

F. Americans are uninterested in pursuing freedom of any kind, and the four freedoms listed here are not considered important.
G. The average citizen already feels overburdened by taxes and feels the money is not being well-spent by the government.
H. Individuals will easily assent to the idea of a greater tax burden since it will naturally lead to a more prosperous state.
J. Patriots of all kinds are part of the natural makeup of America, and some will feel that the support of government is something that should be contemplated and debated.

3. What is a major theme that Roosevelt articulates in his speech?

A. It is important for all people to have access to the benefits of an old-age system that supports citizens when they can no longer work.
B. Patriotic people will feel the need to pay more taxes to the government in order to obtain certain benefits they would not be able to afford.
C. People who want to work should be able to find work without bias and without undue hardship.
D. There are four basic freedoms that are vital to the health of people: speech, worship, freedom from want, and freedom from fear.

4. The last sentence in this passage is, "To that high concept there can be no end save victory" (lines 73-74). In the context of the preceding text, which of the following is the most precise meaning of the word "end"?

F. Death
G. Purpose
H. Outcome
J. Conclusion

5. FDR spoke of "the so-called new order of tyranny which the dictators seek to create with the crash of a bomb" (lines 50–52). In the context of this passage, which is the most accurate meaning of the word "order"?

A. A command given by a military leader
B. An authoritative decision or direction
C. An arrangement of items in sequence
D. A system of societal and world politics

6. When FDR spoke of "personal sacrifice" (line 11), which of these did he explicitly give as an example of it?

F. Higher taxation
G. Military service
H. Arms reduction
J. Four freedoms

7. According to lines 57–65, what does Roosevelt's view of American "change" involve?

A. Ending wars and the atrocities they cause so that all humanity can enjoy the freedom they deserve
B. Reform of social and financial systems so that all Americans are taken care of in the current generation's lifetime
C. Establishing treaties with all other free countries for a peaceful global network
D. Gradual movement toward goals, adjusting as needed when conditions change

8. FDR identified aspects of the social economy needing to be improved immediately. As evidence of this need, which example did he NOT cite in this passage?

F. Expanding retirement benefits
G. Expanding healthcare benefits
H. Expanding draft by the military
J. Expanding labor opportunities

9. As represented in this passage, the power and tone of FDR's speech are enhanced by which of the following?

A. Short, simple sentences
B. Long, complex sentences
C. Long, compound sentences
D. Answer choices B, C, and complex-compound sentences

10. What can readers infer from lines 27–45 of President Roosevelt's message?

F. The President attempted to name every right in the First Amendment but failed.
G. Roosevelt is more concerned about the people of other nations than American citizens.
H. The President is uncertain on whether he can deliver on such a large promise.
J. President Roosevelt is deeply concerned with individual rights and liberties.

Refer to the following for questions 11 - 20:

The following passage is adapted from Albert Einstein's paper on *Relativity: The Special and General Theory* (1916, revised 1924).

In order to attain the greatest possible clearness, let us return to our example of the railway carriage supposed to be travelling uniformly. We call its motion a uniform translation ("uniform" because it is of constant velocity and direction, "translation" because although the carriage changes its position relative to the embankment yet it does not rotate in so doing). Let us imagine a raven flying through the air in such a manner that its motion, as observed from the embankment, is uniform and in a straight line. If we were to observe the flying raven from the moving railway carriage, we should find that the motion of the raven would be one of different velocity and direction, but that it would still be uniform and in a straight line. Expressed in an abstract manner we may say: If a mass m is moving uniformly in a straight line with respect to a co-ordinate system K, then it will also be moving uniformly and in a straight line relative to a second co-ordinate system K1 provided that the latter is executing a uniform translatory motion with respect to K. In accordance with the discussion contained in the preceding section, it follows that:

If K is a Galilean co-ordinate system, then every other co-ordinate system K' is a Galilean one, when, in relation to K, it is in a condition of uniform motion of translation. Relative to K1 the mechanical laws of Galilei-Newton hold good exactly as they do with respect to K.

We advance a step farther in our generalization when we express the tenet thus: If, relative to K, K1 is a uniformly moving co-ordinate system devoid of rotation, then natural phenomena run their course with respect to K1 according to exactly the same general laws as with respect to K. This statement is called the principle of relativity (in the restricted sense).

As long as one was convinced that all-natural phenomena were capable of representation with the help of classical mechanics, there was no need to doubt the validity of this principle of relativity...

Nevertheless, there are two general facts which at the outset speak very much in favor of the validity of the principle of relativity. Even though classical mechanics does not supply us with a sufficiently broad basis for the theoretical presentation of all physical phenomena, still we must grant it a considerable measure of "truth," since it supplies us with the actual motions of the heavenly bodies with a delicacy of detail little short of wonderful. The principle of relativity must therefore apply with great accuracy in the domain of mechanics. But that a principle of such broad generality should hold with such exactness in one domain of phenomena, and yet should be invalid for another, is a priori not very probable.

We now proceed to the second argument, to which, moreover, we shall return later. If the principle of relativity (in the restricted sense) does not hold, then the Galilean co-ordinate systems K, K1, K2, etc., which are moving uniformly relative to each other, will not be equivalent for the description of natural phenomena. In this case we should be constrained to believe that natural laws are capable of being formulated in a particularly simple manner, and of course only on condition that, from amongst all possible Galilean co-ordinate systems, we should have chosen one (K[0]) of a particular state of motion as our body of reference. We should then be justified (because of its merits for the description of natural phenomena) in calling this system "absolutely at rest," and all other Galilean systems K "in motion." If, for instance, our embankment were the system K[0] then our railway carriage would be a system K, relative to which less simple laws would hold than with respect to K[0]. This diminished simplicity would be due to the fact that the carriage K would be in motion (i.e. “really”) with respect to K[0]. In the general laws of nature which have been formulated with reference to K, the magnitude and direction of the velocity of the carriage would necessarily play a part. We should expect, for instance, that the note emitted by an organ pipe placed with its axis parallel to the direction of travel would be different from that emitted if the axis of the pipe were placed perpendicular to this direction.

Now in virtue of its motion in an orbit round the sun, our earth is comparable with a railway carriage travelling with a velocity of about 30 kilometers per second. If the principle of relativity were not valid, we should therefore expect that the direction of motion of the Earth at any moment would enter into the laws of nature, and also that physical systems in their behavior would be dependent on the orientation in space with respect to the Earth. For owing to the alteration in direction of the velocity of revolution of the Earth in the course of a year, the Earth cannot be at rest relative to the hypothetical system K[0] throughout the whole year. However, the most careful observations have never revealed such anisotropic properties in terrestrial physical space, i.e. a physical non-equivalence of different directions. This is a very powerful argument in favor of the principle of relativity.

11. Which of the following choices best supports the claim of Einstein's theory of special relativity as accurate?

A. The movement of the Earth around the sun
B. Galilean co-ordinate systems and their application in classical mechanics
C. The idea of chance in quantum mechanics
D. The two different parts of relativity

12. What might be one question to ask to begin an argument against Einstein's theory of relativity?

F. If relativity holds true, what does that say about the classical rules of motion?
G. If relativity is valid, then why can it not explain all parts of the natural world, including the rules of quantum mechanics?
H. If the natural laws concerning quantum mechanics are true, then shouldn't the classical rules of motion be suspect?
J. If the natural laws formulated with reference to K are measurable, then wouldn't the magnitude and direction of the velocity of the carriage be important?

13. Which of the following choices provides the best meaning for the "truth"?

Even though classical mechanics does not supply us with a sufficiently broad basis for the theoretical presentation of all physical phenomena, still we must grant it a considerable measure of "truth," since it supplies us with the actual motions of the heavenly bodies with a delicacy of detail little short of wonderful.

A. Correctness regarding the abstract meaning of classical mechanics
B. Honesty regarding the movement of objects according to the rules of relativity
C. Validity regarding an understanding of the classical rules of motion
D. Exactness regarding the movement of small bodies on a coordinate plane

14. In lines 58–59, Einstein writes that classical mechanics describes astronomical movements with "a delicacy of detail little short of wonderful." In this context, what is the best synonym for the meaning of "delicacy"?

F. A fragility
G. A sensitivity
H. A rare delight
J. A soft texture

15. If a reader did not know the meaning of the phrase *a priori*, she could ascertain it from the sentence: "But that a principle of such broad generality should hold with such exactness in one domain of phenomena, and yet should be invalid for another, is *a priori* not very probable" (lines 61–65). Based on this context, to which of these is its meaning closest?

A. Existing in the first place
B. Having the highest priority
C. Something happening after the fact
D. Independently true

16. Einstein describes the detail with which classical mechanics describes celestial motions as "little short of wonderful" (lines 58–59). Rhetorically, this is most an example of which of these?

F. Understatement
G. Overstatement
H. Amplification
J. Metabasis

17. Within this passage, which of the following conclusions proposed by Einstein is predicated upon the condition that the principle of relativity is valid?

A. "then the Galilean co-ordinate systems K, K1, K2, etc., which are moving uniformly relative to each other, will not be equivalent for the description of natural phenomena" (lines 69–73)
B. "natural laws are capable of being formulated in a particularly simple manner, and...only on condition that...we...have chosen one...of a particular state of motion as our body of reference" (lines 74–80)
C. "If, relative to K, K1 is a uniformly moving co-ordinate system devoid of rotation...then natural phenomena run their course with respect to K1 according to exactly the same general laws as with respect to K" (lines 37–41)
D. "we should therefore expect that the direction of motion of the Earth at any moment would enter into the laws of nature, and also that physical systems in their behavior would be dependent on the orientation in space with respect to the Earth" (lines 106–112)

18. What might Einstein mean when he writes that "we must grant it a considerable measure of 'truth,'" in paragraph five?

F. Correctness regarding the abstract meaning of classical mechanics
G. Honesty regarding the movement of objects according to the rules of relativity
H. Validity regarding an understanding of the classical rules of motion
J. Exactness regarding the movement of small bodies on a coordinate plane

19. Which of the following most accurately represents Einstein's use of claims and counterclaims in this passage?

A. From one paragraph to the next, statements of claims and statements of counterclaims are presented alternately; the last two sentences summarize how these contrast.
B. The first three paragraphs present a series of counterclaims; the following four present arguments that logically refute those counterclaims and then support his claims.
C. The first five paragraphs mainly explain his claims; the last two state counterclaims, explaining results to expect if they were true; the last two sentences reassert his claims.
D. Every paragraph begins by presenting a claim, then a counterclaim, then refutation of the counterclaim; and ends with repeating the original claim for emphasis.

20. Among the following, which sentence introduces evidence supporting Einstein's assertions?

F. "This is a very powerful argument in favor of the principle of relativity" (lines 121–123)
G. "We now proceed to the second argument, to which, moreover, we shall return later" (lines 66–67)
H. "Nevertheless, there are two general facts...in favor of the validity of the principle of relativity" (lines 49–51)
J. "In order to attain the greatest possible clearness, let us return to our example of the railway carriage" (lines 1–3)

Refer to the following for questions 21 - 30:

Passage A

Black History Month is unnecessary. In a place and time in which we overwhelmingly elected an African American president, we can and should move to a post-racial approach to education. As Detroit Free Press columnist Rochelle Riley wrote in a February 1 column calling for an end to Black History Month, "I propose that, for the first time in American history, this country has reached a point where we can stop celebrating separately, stop learning separately, stop being American separately."

In addition to being unnecessary, the idea that African American history should be focused on in a given month suggests that it belongs in that month alone. It is important to instead incorporate African American history into what is taught every day as American history. It needs to be recreated as part of mainstream thought and not as an optional, often irrelevant, side note. We should focus efforts on pushing schools to diversify and broaden their curricula.

There are a number of other reasons to abolish it: first, it has become a shallow commercial ritual that does not even succeed in its (limited and misguided) goal of focusing for one month on a sophisticated, intelligent appraisal of the contributions and experiences of African Americans throughout history. Second, there is a paternalistic flavor to the mandated bestowing of a month in which to study African American history that is overcome if we instead assert the need for a comprehensive curriculum. Third, the idea of Black History Month suggests that the knowledge imparted in that month is for African Americans only, rather than for all people.

Passage B

Black History Month is still an important observance. Despite the election of our first African American president being a huge achievement, education about African American history is still unmet to a substantial degree. Black History Month is a powerful tool in working towards meeting that need. There is no reason to give up that tool now, and it can easily coexist with an effort to develop a more comprehensive and inclusive yearly curriculum.

Having a month set aside for the study of African American history doesn't limit its study and celebration to that month; it merely focuses complete attention on it for that month. There is absolutely no contradiction between having a set-aside month and having it be present in the curriculum the rest of the year.

Equally important is that the debate *itself* about the usefulness of Black History Month can, and should, remind parents that they can't necessarily count on schools to teach African American history as thoroughly as many parents would want.

Although Black History Month has, to an extent, become a shallow ritual, it doesn't have to be. Good teachers and good materials could make the February curriculum deeply informative, thought-provoking, and inspiring. The range of material that can be covered is rich, varied, and full of limitless possibilities.

Finally, it is worthwhile to remind ourselves and our children of the key events that happened during the month of February. In 1926, Woodson organized the first Black History Week to honor the birthdays of essential civil rights activists Abraham Lincoln and Frederick Douglass. W. E. B. DuBois was born on February 23, 1868. The 15th Amendment, which granted African Americans the right to vote, was ratified on February 3, 1870. The first black US senator, Hiram R. Revels, took his oath of office on February 25, 1870. The National Association for the Advancement of Colored People (NAACP) was founded on February 12, 1909. Malcolm X was shot on February 21, 1965.

21. The author's primary purpose in Passage A is to:

A. argue that Black History Month should not be so commercial.
B. argue that Black History Month should be abolished.
C. argue that Black History Month should be maintained.
D. suggest that African American history should be taught in two months rather than just one.

22. It can be inferred that the term "post-racial" in the second sentence of Passage A refers to an approach that:

F. treats race as the most important factor in determining an individual's experience.
G. treats race as one factor, but not the most important, in determining an individual's experience.
H. considers race after considering all other elements of a person's identity.
J. is not based on or organized around concepts of race.

23. Which of the following does the author of Passage A not give as a reason for abolishing Black History Month?

A. It has become a shallow ritual.
B. There is a paternalistic feel to being granted one month of focus.
C. It suggests that the month's education is only for African Americans.
D. No one learns anything during the month.

24. Which event happened first?

F. The ratifying of the 15th Amendment
G. The birth of W.E.B. DuBois
H. The establishment of Black History Month
J. The founding of the NAACP

25. Why does the author of Passage B believe that the debate itself about Black History Month can be useful?

A. The people on opposing sides can come to an intelligent resolution about whether to keep it.
B. African American history is discussed in the media when the debate is ongoing.
C. The debate is a reminder to parents that they can't count on schools to teach their children about African American history.
D. Black History Month doesn't have to be a shallow ritual.

26. What does the author of Passage B say about the range of material that can be taught during Black History Month?

F. It is rich and varied.
G. It is important.
H. It is an unmet need.
J. It is comprehensive.

27. The author of Passage A argues that celebrating Black History Month suggests that the study of African American history can and should be limited to one month of the year. What is the author of Passage B's response?

A. Black History Month is still an important observance.
B. Black History Month is a powerful tool in meeting the need for education about African American history.
C. Having a month set aside for the study of African American history does not limit its study and celebration to that month.
D. Black History Month does not have to be a shallow ritual.

28. From both passages, readers can infer that the authors:

F. voted for Barack Obama to become president.
G. are well connected to the media.
H. think that February is not the best time for Black History Month.
J. are concerned with the current education system.

29. Which of the following statements is true?

A. The author of Passage A thinks that it is important for students to learn about the achievements and experience of African Americans, while the author of Passage B does not think this is important.
B. The author of Passage B thinks that it is important for students to learn about the achievements and experience of African Americans, while the author of Passage A does not think this is important.
C. Neither author thinks that it is important for students to learn about the achievements and experience of African Americans.
D. Both authors think that it is important for students to learn about the achievements and experience of African Americans.

30. Which individuals are described in either Passage A or Passage B as "essential civil rights activists?"

F. Abraham Lincoln and Malcolm X
G. Abraham Lincoln and W.E.B. DuBois
H. Malcolm X and W.E.B. DuBois
J. Abraham Lincoln and Frederick Douglass

Refer to the following for questions 31 - 40:

<u>Ernst Lubitsch</u>

The comedy of manners was a style of film popular in the 1930s. These movies expressed the frustrations of the depression-era poor by mocking the swells of the upper classes, and contrasting their gilded lives to the daily grind of the downtrodden masses. One of the greatest directors of this type of film was Ernst Lubitsch, a German filmmaker who eventually came to Hollywood to make some of his greatest films.

Lubitsch's film career began in the silent era. Born in Berlin, in 1892, he worked at first as an actor, subsequently debuting as a director with the film *Passion* in 1912. He made more than 40 films in Germany, but the advent of sound brought him to Hollywood, where the new technology was most readily available. After the producer Albert Zukor invited him to come to the US in 1923, he pursued his career in the capital of film until the late 1940s. His signature style – a focus on seemingly insignificant details that imbued them with symbolism in the context of the film – was just as effective in the "talkies" as it had been in silent films. One of his greatest comedies, *Trouble in Paradise*, starred Herbert Marshall and Miriam Hopkins and was shot in 1932. A stinging social comedy that skewers the illusions of the upper classes, it would not have been well received in his native Germany of the time.

Trouble in Paradise tells the story of a charming, elegant thief. Marshall plays Gaston Monescu, a man whose charm and elegant manners allow him to work his way into the bosom of high society. In the hotels and clubs of the rich, he manages to gain the trust of wealthy individuals until he swindles them. Monescu courts the rich perfume heiress, Mariette, and we are never certain of how sincere his affection for her may be. But he is also in love with his accomplice, Lily, a clever thief in her own right. His eventual decision to leave Mariette for her can be seen as an affirmation of the unity of the working class in this very class-conscious film.

The opening scenes of the film provide a classic example of Lubitsch's wry symbolism. The opening shot is of a garbage can, which is duly picked up by a garbage man and dumped onto what seems to be a truck. But, as the camera pans back, we realize that the truck is, in fact, a gondola, and that the scene takes place in Venice. As the gondolier-garbage man breaks into a romantic song, the camera contrasts the elegant city, its palaces and beautiful canals, with the mundane reality of garbage and necessary, low-wage work.

The film continues to contrast the elegant surfaces of society with the corruption that lies beneath. A classic scene is the first meeting between Monescu and Lily, two thieves with polished manners. In an elegant hotel room, the two engage in a genteel banter filled with seductive double-entendres and urbane banalities. But they are not the Baron and Countess they profess to be, as their behavior soon makes clear. As the supper progresses, they manage to steal one another's wallets, jewelry, and watches. Finally, they reveal the thefts to one another and sort out their belongings, but Monescu has been won over by Lily's cleverness, for he admires her resourcefulness far more than the undeserved wealth of the upper classes.

Lubitsch went on to make many more films during the 1930s, comedies of manners and musical comedies as well. Among his greatest Hollywood films are *Design for Living* (1933), *The Merry Widow* (1934), *Ninotchka* (1939), and *Heaven Can Wait* (1943). One of the wittiest directors of all time, he made films in English, German, and French, always exhibiting the sharpest eye for detail. His films challenged the intellect of his viewers, and they never disappointed. The juxtaposition of seemingly contradictory elements was always central to his style, as he exposed the falsehoods he found in his world.

31. Which of the following terms would not be a good description of Lubitsch's film style, as it is described in the text?

A. Sophisticated
B. Erudite
C. Chic
D. Boisterous

32. One of the tools that Lubitsch used to mock the upper classes, as shown in the text, was

F. Lighting
G. Talking pictures
H. Juxtaposition of contradictory elements
J. Urbane banalities

33. Lubitsch's signature style can be described as

A. Double-entendres and urbane banalities
B. Using apparently insignificant details as symbols
C. Charm and elegant manners
D. Corruption underlying high society

34. Lubitsch first came to the US in 1923 because

F. His films were not well received in Germany.
G. He was fleeing the Nazi regime.
H. He was invited by a producer.
J. He could not make films with sound in Germany.

35. The text tells us that Lubitsch's first film, *Passion* was

A. An early "talkie."
B. A comedy of manners.
C. A film starring Miriam Hopkins.
D. None of the above.

36. Without considering gender, which two characters have the most in common?

F. Monescu and Lily
G. Monescu and Mariette
H. Lily and Mariette
J. Monescu and Lubitsch

37. The scene with the garbage gondola at the opening of the film shows that

A. The rich need supporting services.
B. Venice is kept clean by gondoliers.
C. Elegance may be only a veneer.
D. Gondoliers sing romantic ballads.

38. Monescu most admires

F. Lily's wealth
G. Lily's cleverness
H. Mariette's money
J. Venetian gondolas

39. In the film, Lily pretends to be

A. A perfume heiress
B. A countess
C. A wealthy dowager
D. Monescu's partner

40. In addition to the films he made in Hollywood and Germany, the text suggests that Lubitsch made movies in

F. England
G. France
H. Spain
J. Lisbon

Science

Refer to the following for questions 1 - 6:

Although only ninety-four elements occur naturally on Earth, many more have been produced artificially in laboratories. All of these elements are heavier than the natural elements, and many are generally extremely short-lived, lasting only a tiny fraction of a second before decaying into other elements. Still, their presence can be reliably detected, and different labs race to produce new elements first to win naming rights. The latest four elements to be given official names are nihonium, moscovium, tennessine, and oganesson, elements 113, 115, 117, and 118, respectively. There may be a limit to the number of elements that can be discovered, however. Two scientists express their views on the matter.

Scientist 1

Atoms exist because the strong nuclear force causes protons to be attracted to each other, overcoming their electrical repulsion—although not indefinitely for radioactive isotopes. However, the strong nuclear force operates over only short distances. If an atomic nucleus becomes too large, the distance between protons will become too great for the strong nuclear force to hold it together even for a brief period of time. Calculation shows that the threshold occurs at about 173 protons. Therefore, there can never be an element with an atomic number greater than this. There still may remain some fifty-odd elements to be discovered but certainly not much more than sixty at the most.

Scientist 2

Because of the short lifetime of most heavy elements and the difficulty of creating them in the lab, it's not easy to study their properties. It's likely that as the atomic number increases, the configuration of the nucleus changes, possibly in ways that lead to atoms more stable than one might expect—there are sound reasons to expect "islands of stability," perhaps centered around elements 126 and 164, in which certain heavy elements are unusually stable relative to the atoms around them. In any case, we know too little about the arrangement of heavy atoms to confidently name a limit to their size, and I don't think there's any good reason to doubt that the periodic table can be extended indefinitely.

1. What is the main point of disagreement between the two scientists?

A. Scientist 1 thinks there is a limited number of elements; scientist 2 does not.
B. Scientist 2 thinks there is a limited number of elements; scientist 1 does not.
C. Scientist 1 thinks there are stable elements that have not yet been discovered; scientist 2 does not.
D. Scientist 2 thinks there are stable elements that have not yet been discovered; scientist 1 does not.

2. Which statement would both scientists likely agree on?

F. The higher the atomic number of an element, the less stable it is.
G. There are still new elements remaining to be discovered.
H. The procedure for naming elements needs to be changed.
J. No elements of atomic number greater than 94 could possibly exist anywhere in nature.

3. What hypothetical piece of evidence would support Scientist 2's view and contradict Scientist 1's?

A. The discovery of element 200
B. The discovery that element 126 is stable
C. The discovery that element 126 is highly unstable
D. The discovery of three elements with atomic numbers between 150 and 160

4. Which statement would be MOST consistent with both scientists' views?

F. Labs investigating heavy elements need better safety precautions.
G. Heavy elements that do not occur in nature can be created in the lab.
H. Elements above number 126 are too short-lived to ever be detectable in a laboratory setting.
J. The arrangement of the particles in an atom changes in predictable ways as the atomic number increases.

5. According to Scientist 1, what force would prevent the formation of elements of atomic number above 173?

A. The strong nuclear force
B. The weak nuclear force
C. Electromagnetism
D. Gravity

6. If the "islands of stability" that Scientist 2 mentions exist where Scientist 2 says they might, which element is likely to be the LEAST stable?

F. Element 8
G. Element 126
H. Element 145
J. Element 164

Refer to the following for questions 7 - 11:

Genetic profiling refers to the analysis of an individual's DNA, either for the purpose of identifying specific genes that might imply a risk of inherited conditions or to compare two DNA samples to see how well they match.

One method of genetic profiling involves first heating the DNA sample to separate the strands. Then small bits of DNA called primers are added that bind to the selected regions of interest, called "markers," and then these regions are duplicated with an enzyme called a DNA polymerase. Finally, the replicated DNA samples are subjected to a process called gel electrophoresis: an electric current is used to move the DNA fragments through a gel, and the distance they move depends on the size of the fragment. Finally, the DNA fragments are dyed to form visible bands. If the bands in two DNA samples match, they likely came from the same person. Genetic profiling can also be used to determine paternity—because a person's genes come from his or her parents, each band in the DNA profile must match a band from either the person's mother or father. (There may be exceptions due to mutated genes, but they are rare enough not to play a major role.) Identifying siblings is more difficult because a child may get genes from either parent, and the number of markers shared by two siblings is unpredictable. (In principle, we would expect siblings to share about half their markers on average, but unless a large number of markers are used there's too much variability for this to be reliable.)

Consider the following DNA profiles. Profile 2 represents the DNA profile of the mother of the individual in DNA profile 1.

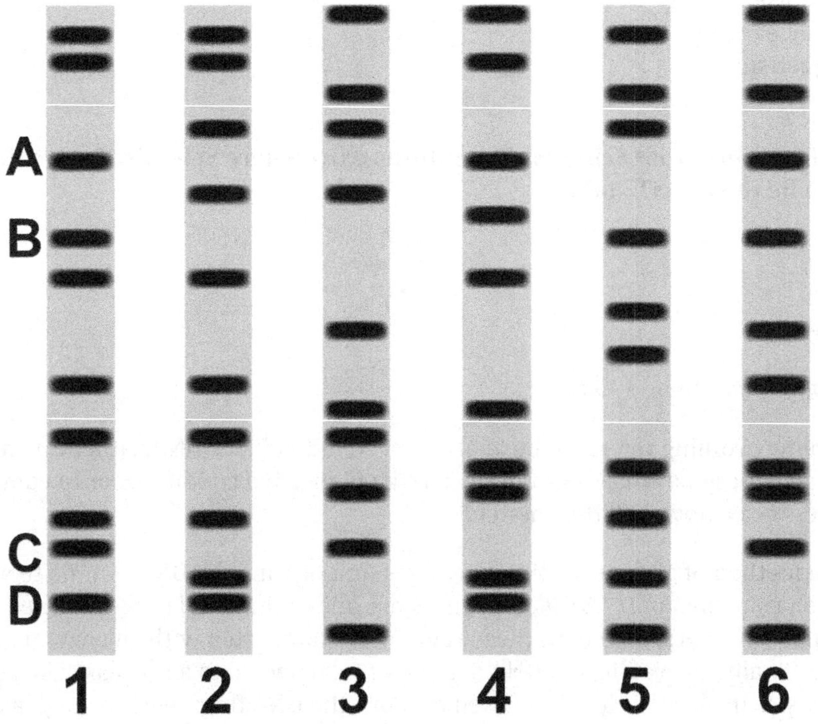

7. Which of the labeled bands in Profile 1 matches a band in Profile 2?

A. Band A
B. Band B
C. Band C
D. Band D

8. How many bands in Profiles 1 and 2 match?

F. 5
G. 6
H. 7
J. 8

9. Which profile likely represents the father of the individual in DNA profile 1?

A. Profile 3
B. Profile 4
C. Profile 5
D. Profile 6

10. Which profile could belong to a child of the individuals in Profiles 3 and 4?

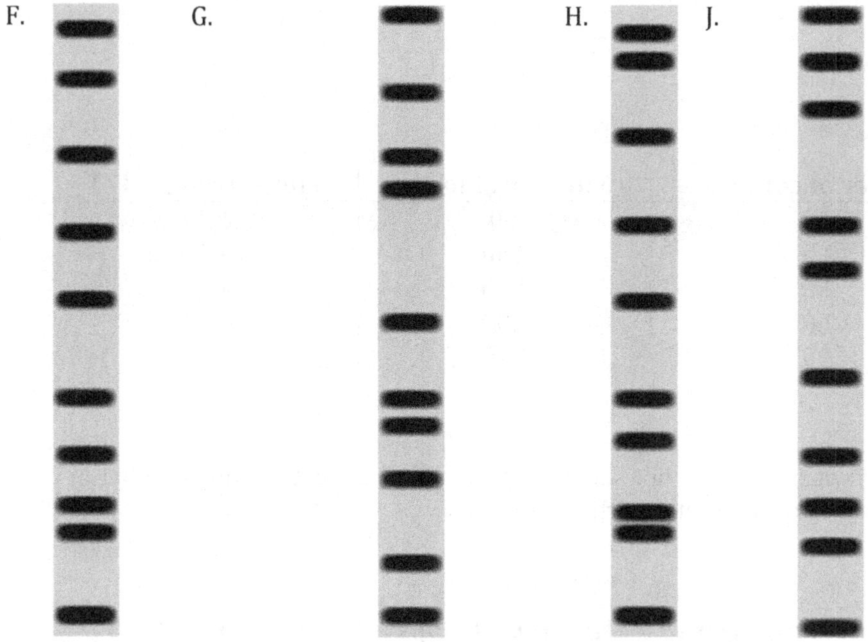

11. Is it possible that Profiles 5 and 6 belong to siblings?

A. Yes; they share more than half their markers.
B. Yes; the number of markers siblings share is unpredictable.
C. No; the two profiles share too few markers to be siblings.
D. No; the two profiles share too many markers to be siblings.

Refer to the following for questions 12 - 17:

A simple electromagnet can be produced by wrapping a coil of insulated wire around an iron rod and connecting both ends of the rod to a battery or another voltage source. This works because moving electrical charges, such as those in an electric current, produce a magnetic field. Although the magnetic field around a single current-carrying wire may be weak, the field due to each turn of the coil will build and accumulate. Wrapping the coil around a core made of some magnetic material can further increase the magnetic field produced.

A student wants to test the effect of different factors on the strength of an electromagnet. The student first constructs a number of electromagnets by wrapping insulated copper wire around cylindrical iron cores. The same voltage and identical iron cores are used for each trial but the number of loops in the coil varies. The student then uses a magnetometer to measure the strength of the magnetic field in teslas produced by each electromagnet at a constant distance of 5 cm axially from the end of the coil. (The tesla is the standard SI unit for magnetic field strength.)

Study 1

Table 1

Trial	Diameter of core (cm)	Number of loops	Field strength (T)
1	2.0	50	1.11
2	2.0	100	1.24
3	2.0	150	1.29
4	2.0	200	1.21
5	2.0	250	1.33

Study 2

The student then constructs another set of electromagnets using the same number of loops for each set but varying the diameter of the metal core.

Table 2

Trial	Diameter of core (cm)	Number of loops	Field strength (T)
6	1.0	100	0.57
7	2.0	100	1.24
8	3.0	100	1.86
9	4.0	100	2.40

12. In which trial did the student use the most loops in the coil?

F. Trial 1
G. Trial 3
H. Trial 5
J. Trial 9

13. After performing the experiment, the student realizes a mistake was made recording the measurement in one of the trials, creating an outlier in the data that should be thrown out. Which trial is likely to have been the one with the mistake?

A. Trial 2
B. Trial 4
C. Trial 6
D. Trial 8

14. Overall, according to the student's data, which action is MOST likely to result in an increase in the magnetic field strength?

F. Increasing the diameter of the core and the number of loops
G. Decreasing the diameter of the core and the number of loops
H. Increasing the diameter of the core and decreasing the number of loops
J. Decreasing the diameter of the core and increasing the number of loops

15. The Earth itself has a magnetic field, which the magnetometer will also detect. What is one way the student can prevent this field from affecting the measurements?

A. Perform the experiment indoors in a closed room.
B. Align the electromagnet perpendicular to the Earth's magnetic field.
C. Perform the experiment quickly before the Earth's magnetic field has a chance to affect it.
D. Measure the magnetic field when the electromagnet is not present, and subtract the value from the readings when it is.

16. Based on theoretical considerations, the student expected the magnetic field to be proportional to the number of coils and is puzzled that this is not the case. Considering the matter further, the student hypothesizes that the discrepancy is because the electromagnets with more coils use longer wires, which have more resistance, reducing the current through the wires. To test this, instead of applying a constant voltage, the student attaches an ammeter to the circuit to measure the current and adjusts the voltage so that the same current runs through the electromagnet each trial, obtaining the following data:

Table 3

Trial	Diameter of core (cm)	Number of loops	Field strength (T)
10	2.0	50	1.16
11	2.0	100	2.32
12	2.0	150	3.48
13	2.0	200	4.64

Do these data support the student's hypothesis that the resistance of the wire affected the results?

F. Yes; these data are consistent with the student's hypothesis.
G. No; these data show that the resistance of the wire did not affect the results.
H. No; these data show that the resistance of the wire had the opposite effect from what the student hypothesized.
J. These data have no bearing on the student's hypothesis.

17. Suppose the student wanted to eliminate the confounding effect that the length of the wire affects the current but didn't have an ammeter or a variable voltage source. How else might the student control for this factor?

A. Make sure that the number of coils is always a prime number.
B. Use wires made out of different metals for the different numbers of coils.
C. Use wires of the same length for each trial even if that means the electromagnets with fewer coils leave a lot of extra wire between the electromagnet and the voltage source.
D. Add an extra length of wire directly connecting the two ends of the electromagnet, creating a short circuit that will have a consistent length regardless of the number of coils.

Refer to the following for questions 18 - 22:

A scientist wishes to test the effectiveness of an antibiotic. To do this, she takes nine Petri dishes filled with agar, a nutrient substrate on which bacteria grow readily, and labels them with the numbers 1 through 9. She then introduces bacterial cultures into each Petri dish, taking care to spread them evenly along the surfaces.

In dishes 1 through 3, the scientist then places a drop of solution of the antibiotic to be tested at a concentration of 2 parts per thousand. (The rest of the solution is water.) She does the same to dishes 4 through 6 but with a solution at a concentration of one part per thousand. In dishes 7 through 9, the scientist places a drop of a control liquid. The scientist covers the Petri dishes, leaves them in a cool location for five days, and then examines the results. The diagrams below show the growth of bacteria in each dish after five days; the gray areas show where on the Petri dish bacterial cultures have grown, whereas the white areas show parts of the agar that are clear of bacteria.

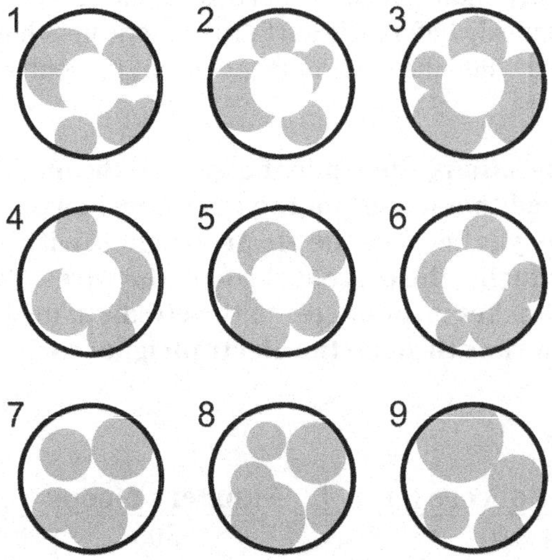

18. The passage says that dishes 7 through 9 are treated with a "control liquid." What would be the best choice as a control liquid?

F. A solution of the antibiotic at an intermediate concentration of 1.5 parts per thousand
G. A solution of the antibiotic at a lower concentration of 0.5 parts per thousand
H. A solution of a different antibiotic
J. Pure distilled water

19. The scientist discovers that her assistant inadvertently switched the labels on two of the Petri dishes. Although at first upset, she soon realizes that this mistake did not affect her results. Which choice could have been the numbers of the two dishes that were switched?

A. 3 and 9
B. 4 and 6
C. 5 and 7
D. 6 and 7

20. What is the best conclusion that can be drawn from the given data?

F. The antibiotic has no effect on bacterial growth.
G. The antibiotic has an effect on bacterial growth that increases with its concentration.
H. The antibiotic impedes bacterial growth, but increasing the concentration above one part per thousand does not increase the effect.
J. The antibiotic is only effective at concentrations greater than one part per thousand.

21. To see how the effectiveness of the antibiotic changes over time, the scientist leaves the Petri dishes for an additional 3 days. Which diagrams is MOST likely to show how dish 8 looks after this time?

A. 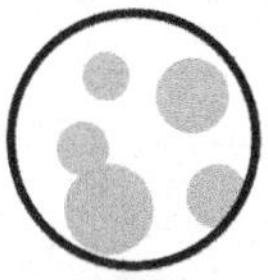

B. 

C. 

D. 

22. Another scientist decides to replicate the first scientist's work, but at a higher temperature, to see if the antibiotic's effectiveness changes at different temperatures. Unlike the first scientist, however, the second scientist neglects to use a control group. The second scientist finds that at this higher temperature, all the Petri dishes treated with the antibiotic are completely free of bacteria and concludes that the antibiotic is more effective at this higher temperature. Given the lack of a control group, what is another possible interpretation of the second scientist's data?

F. The antibiotic is ineffective at the higher temperature.
G. The antibiotic requires a higher concentration to work at the higher temperature.
H. The bacteria are unable to grow in agar.
J. The bacteria are unable to grow at the higher temperature.

Refer to the following for questions 23 - 28:

Carbon dating is the most famous type of radiometric dating, a process in which the amount of some radioactive isotope that remains in a sample is used to estimate the age of the sample. Carbon dating relies on the carbon isotope carbon-14, or ^{14}C, which decays into the stable nitrogen isotope ^{14}N. In the atmosphere, the amount of ^{14}C is continually being replenished by cosmic rays interacting with atmospheric gases. Living creatures take in carbon from the environment, so the proportion of carbon in their tissues that is the isotope ^{14}C is roughly the same as in the environment. Once they die, however, they cease to take in more carbon from their environment, so the ^{14}C in their bodies decays and is not replenished. This means that from the proportion of ^{14}C in an object made from once-living tissue—such as bone or wood—we can estimate how long ago the organism the tissue came from died. The half-life of ^{14}C is about 5,730 years, so we can expect that for every 5,730 years that have passed since the organism died, the amount of ^{14}C in its remains has decreased by a factor of one-half.

Below are measurements of the total amount of carbon and the amount of ^{14}C in four samples. (The amounts of carbon are given in moles; one mole = 6.022×10^{23} atoms.) The last column in the table is the fraction of carbon in the sample that is ^{14}C. Note that the fraction of carbon in the atmosphere that is ^{14}C is about 1×10^{-12}.

Sample	Moles of carbon	Moles of ^{14}C	Moles ^{14}C/Moles carbon

1	10.2	5.55×10^{-13}	5.44×10^{-14}
2	55.8	1.40×10^{-11}	2.50×10^{-13}
3	0.9	3.66×10^{-13}	4.06×10^{-13}
4	22.1	2.58×10^{-12}	1.17×10^{-13}

23. Which of the samples is likely to be the oldest?

A. Sample 1
B. Sample 2
C. Sample 3
D. Sample 4

24. What is the best estimate for the age of Sample 2?

F. 2,900 years
G. 6,000 years
H. 11,000 years
J. 25,000 years

25. After 5,730 additional years have passed, about how much carbon-14 do you expect will be present in Sample 4?

A. 2.58×10^{-14} moles
B. 5.8×10^{-13} moles
C. 1.29×10^{-12} moles
D. 5.16×10^{-12} moles

26. The proportion of carbon-14 in the atmosphere has not been constant over the years. What effect does this have on carbon dating?

F. This would have no effect on the results of carbon dating because we are measuring the amount of carbon in organic objects, not in the atmosphere.
G. This would have no effect on the results of carbon dating because the amount of carbon-14 in the samples would always match the amount in the *current* atmosphere.
H. This could affect the results of carbon dating but could be accounted for if we learned how the amount of carbon-14 in the atmosphere had changed over time and used it to calibrate our results.
J. This causes an unavoidable error in carbon dating that there is no way to account for, and it means carbon dating is inherently unreliable.

27. In practice, carbon dating is useful only for objects up to 50,000 or 60,000 years old. For older objects, other methods of radiometric dating can be used, involving different isotopes. Why would carbon dating NOT be useful for an object 1 million years old?

A. ^{14}C did not exist 1 million years ago.
B. Too little ^{14}C would remain to be easily measurable.
C. There are no remaining objects that old that contain carbon.
D. By that time all of the ^{14}N in the objects will have decayed as well.

28. There are four main types of radioactive decay:

- *Alpha decay,* in which an atom emits two protons and two neutrons
- *Beta-minus decay,* in which an atom emits an electron and a neutrino and one of its neutrons turns into a proton
- *Beta-plus decay,* in which an atom emits a positron and a neutrino and one of its protons turns into a neutron
- *Gamma decay,* in which an excited atom emits a gamma ray but its nuclear composition doesn't change

Keeping in mind that carbon has an atomic number of 6 and nitrogen has an atomic number of 7, which of these four types of decay does ^{14}C undergo?

F. Alpha decay
G. Beta-minus decay
H. Beta-plus decay
J. Gamma decay

Refer to the following for questions 29 - 35:

A *phase diagram* is a chart that shows what physical state a substance is in—solid, liquid, or gas—at different temperatures and pressures. Typically, the axes of a phase diagram are labeled with temperature on the *x*-axis and pressure on the *y*-axis.

Below is shown the phase diagram for molecular nitrogen:

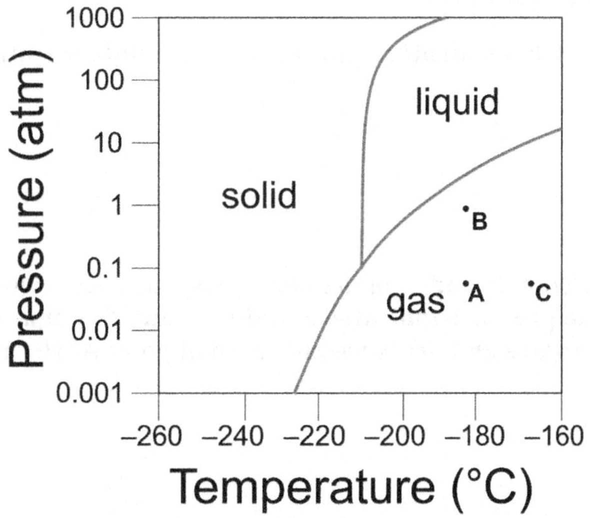

29. According to this diagram, which value is closest to the boiling point of nitrogen at atmospheric pressure?

A. -230 °C
B. -210 °C
C. -200 °C
D. -170 °C

30. What phase would the nitrogen be in at a temperature of -240°C and a pressure of 0.1 atmospheres?

F. Solid
G. Liquid
H. Gas
J. In equilibrium between two phases

31. The *triple point* of a substance is the temperature and pressure at which all three phases of the substance—solid, liquid, and gas—exist in equilibrium. According to the phase diagram, which of the following MOST accurately estimates the triple point of nitrogen?

A. –230 °C, 0.001 atmospheres
B. –190 °C, 10 atmospheres
C. –200 °C, 1 atmosphere
D. –210 °C, 0.1 atmospheres

32. At certain pressures, substances may undergo sublimation, transitioning directly between the solid and gas phases without passing through a liquid phase. In what range of pressures does nitrogen undergo sublimation, according to this diagram?

F. Below about 0.1 atmospheres
G. Only at a specific pressure of about 0.1 atmospheres
H. Above about 0.1 atmospheres
J. Nitrogen never undergoes sublimation

33. The *y* axis of this graph is labeled in atmospheres. What is another suitable unit this axis could have been labeled in?

A. mm^{-1}
B. J
C. N
D. atm

34. Consider the points labeled *A*, *B*, and *C* on the phase diagrams. How would the volume of a quantity of gas at the temperature and pressure indicated at points *B* and *C* compare to the volume of the same quantity of gas at the temperature and pressure indicated at point *A*? (It may help to recall the ideal gas law, $PV = nRT$.)

F. $V_B > V_A, V_C > V_A$
G. $V_B < V_A, V_C < V_A$
H. $V_B > V_A, V_C < V_A$
J. $V_B < V_A, V_C > V_A$

35. Water is an unusual substance in that it is denser in the liquid phase than the solid. Although most substances in their liquid state become solid if sufficient pressure is applied, for water the opposite is true—when pressure is applied to its solid state (at pressures above its triple point), it becomes liquid. In light of this information, which diagram could be a phase diagram for water?

A.

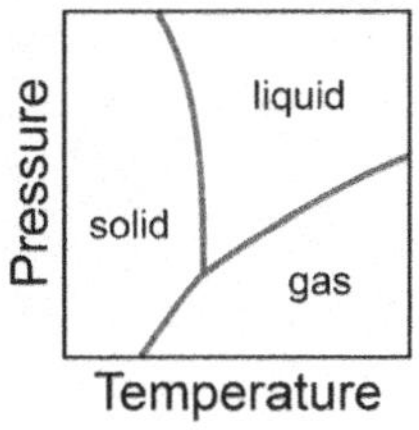

B.

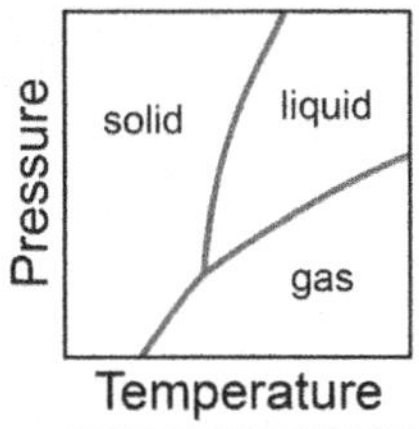

C.

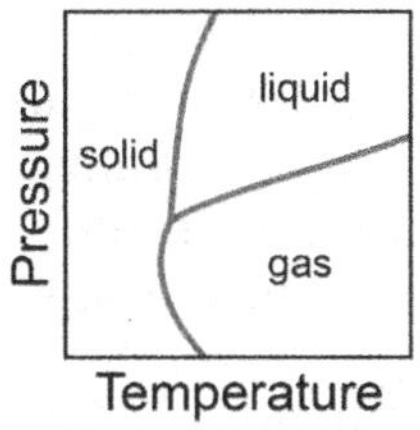

D.

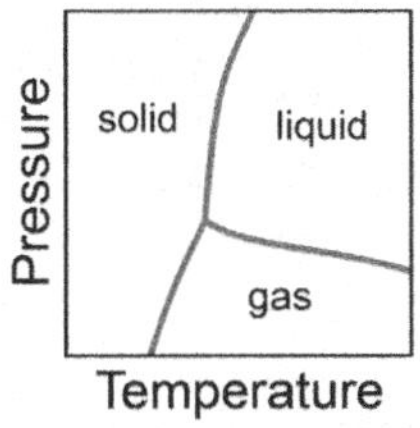

Refer to the following for questions 36 - 40:

Plants produce energy from sunlight by the process of photosynthesis carried out in organelles called chloroplasts within the plant's cells. During photosynthesis, the plant takes in carbon dioxide and water and uses them to synthesize carbohydrates that store energy for later use. The plants release oxygen as a waste product. The amount of oxygen produced by a plant can be used as a measurement of the rate of photosynthesis.

A student wants to study the rate of photosynthesis in a plant under varying conditions. To do that, the student acquires a sample of an aquatic plant, *Egeria densa*, and places it underneath an inverted funnel, submerged in water. The student then takes a test tube and inverts it, filled with water, over the spout of the funnel. As the plant releases oxygen, the oxygen is directed by the funnel into the test tube, displacing some of the water. After the setup is left undisturbed for 24 hours, the amount of oxygen in the test tube can be measured. A diagram of the experimental apparatus appears below.

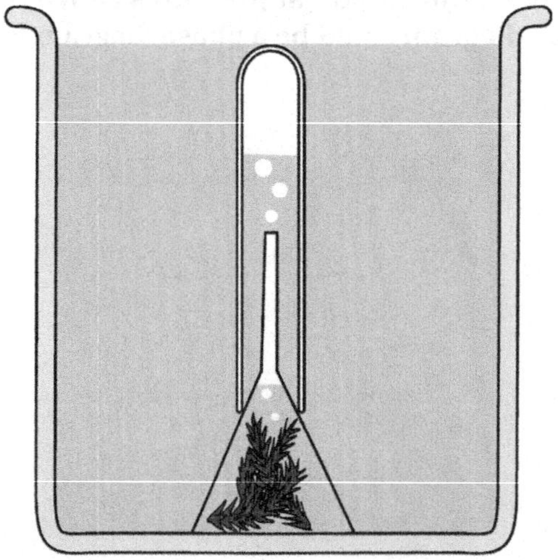

A student performs trials with eight different experimental setups. All of the setups are on the same table, but four of the setups are in bright light, and four are shaded by an awning and so in dim light. In four of the setups, the student stirs 1 gram of sodium bicarbonate into the water to add some additional carbon dioxide. The table below shows the student's results.

Trial	Light	CO_2 added?	Amount of oxygen produced
1	Bright	No	0.50 mL
2	Bright	No	0.60 mL
3	Bright	Yes	1.10 mL
4	Bright	Yes	1.05 mL
5	Dim	Yes	0.40 mL
6	Dim	Yes	0.35 mL
7	Dim	No	0.20 mL
8	Dim	No	0.20 mL

36. According to the student's data, under which set of conditions did the plants produce the most oxygen?

F. Bright light; CO_2 added
G. Dim light; CO_2 added
H. Bright light; no CO_2 added
J. Dim light; no CO_2 added

37. Which pair of trials involved the same conditions?

A. 4 and 5
B. 5 and 6
C. 6 and 7
D. 4 and 7

38. What is MOST likely to be a significant source of error in the student's experiment?

F. Variation in temperature
G. Variation in the amount of CO_2 added
H. Variation in the amount of oxygen collected
J. Variation in the size of the plants

39. The passage says that during the process of photosynthesis, the plant takes in carbon dioxide and water and synthesizes carbohydrates. As the name implies, carbohydrates contain carbon and hydrogen (as well as oxygen). From where does the plant most likely obtain this carbon and hydrogen?

A. From the water
B. From the carbon dioxide
C. Carbon from the water and hydrogen from the carbon dioxide
D. Hydrogen from the water and carbon from the carbon dioxide

40. Suppose the student wants to do further experiments to study the effects of some of the variables. Which variation on the experiment is MOST likely to yield fruitful results?

F. Varying the size of the test tube
G. Varying the amount of CO_2 added
H. Varying the amount of water in the beaker
J. Varying the amount of oxygen produced

Answer Key and Explanations

English

1. A: The answer choice "was founded in 1790," is not correct because a comma is not necessary in this sentence. "Were founded in 1790" is incorrect because the singular subject of *United States Coast Guard* needs the singular verb *was*. "Will have been founded in" is incorrect because it uses the future perfect verb tense but the event was completed in the past.

2. J: This sentence adds no information to the passage that is not already in the surrounding sentences, and it is unnecessary as a transition.

3. C: This is the best answer choice because the vague pronoun *It* has been replaced with a specific noun.

4. J: This is the best answer choice as it removes the unnecessary comma. The answer choice "from smugglers, and enforce" incorrectly removes the infinitive signifier *to* from the sentence. Changing the word *enforce* to *promote* alters the author's meaning from the laws being upheld to the laws being advertised.

5. D: A comma does not need to be added in joint with a conjunction. The word *combat* should be kept singular; making it plural is unnecessary.

6. G: The word *actually* is an unnecessary filler and should not be added. The answer choice "As part of the Department of Homeland Security, we know the United States Coast Guard to be a federal law enforcement agency" is incorrect because of the dangling modifier. Finally, it is not only the Department of Homeland Security that considers the Coast Guard to be a federal law enforcement agency, so the answer choice "The Department of Homeland Security considers the United States Coast Guard to be actually a part of a federal law enforcement agency" is incorrect.

7. D: The answer choices including the word *we* include a dangling modifier because *we* are not the ones enforcing maritime law. The sentence also requires a subject, so "law, also serving the United States Coast Guard" is incorrect.

8. J: An adverb (really) is needed in the sentence instead of an adjective (real). "Truly, this is not an important" is incorrect because it negates the statement. Finally, a comma is not needed between the adverb and its object.

9. B: *Explore* and *investigate* are synonyms, so it is redundant to use both terms. Thus, the other answer choices are incorrect.

10. G: The purpose of this passage is to provide a brief history of the Coast Guard and a brief overview of their duties. The author should use this sentence in a persuasive passage instead of an informative one in order to maintain the focus and the purpose of the passage. Additionally, the use of first person breaks from the more formal tone of the passage.

11. D: The question asks for "the requirements for becoming a member of the United States Coast Guard." The passage merely lists responsibilities of Coast Guard personnel and notes a key difference between this branch and the Navy. There is no information on how one can become a member of the Coast Guard.

12. H: This answer choice best sums up the information in this essay and rounds out the writer's discussion about the organization as a whole. Discussing careers with the Coast Guard isn't a theme in this essay. Opinion statements do not match the factual delivery of the passage, so they should not be used. Stating that the duties the Coast Guard carries out are unimportant contradicts the information and ideas presented in the essay, so this choice is incorrect.

13. C: As written, the sentence inappropriately uses a comma and has created a sentence fragment. The second choice is incorrect because it also creates a sentence fragment in addition to using the contraction of *it is* where a possessive pronoun should be used. The final choice is incorrect because it uses the preposition *with* where it should use a coordinating conjunction to show relationship.

14. H: The current verb tense is incorrect; it implies that this mission is no longer active and that the Coast Guard used to cover these responsibilities. "Responsibilities of this mission will include stopping" implies that the mission is not yet active. The word *might* indicates possible responsibility for the objectives of the mission.

15. A: The sentence is correct as is. Two of the other options create sentence fragments. "The mission of the department is to protect the coastlines, and American waters, through enforcing US and international laws" creates a non-defining clause where the information should be included in the main clause.

16. F: *Island* should be kept plural, as the following sentence states that New Zealand has "two large islands and a number of smaller ones." The preposition *between* is for comparing two things, but "all the Pacific islands" is an unknown number, likely more than two. The adjective *more* is comparative, which is used for two items, while the author is comparing New Zealand to "all the Pacific islands."

17. D: New Zealand's popularity as a tourist destination is not related to anything else the author discusses in this passage. The focus of the passage is on the history, geography, and culture of the islands.

18. H: The error in this sentence is the unnecessary comma after *islands*. Replacing *number* with *amount* is incorrect. Since the number of islands can be counted, the word *number* is the accurate choice for this sentence.

19. B: This choice is correct, as it includes all necessary information while remaining concise. Using verbiage such as *nevertheless* and *southward* is unnecessary. The information about migration occurring in the 15th century should not be deleted, and a comma should not be added after *legends*. Finally, merely rearranging material is unnecessary.

20. J: The main problem in the incorrect answer choices is the verb tense. The phrase *has been known already* signifies use of the present perfect tense, *will have been known already* uses the future perfect tense, and *who had probably* uses the past perfect tense. Only the correct choice uses past tense to match the rest of the passage, as well as using correct punctuation.

21. A: The word *southward* should remain uncapitalized. Also, each of the incorrect choices uses an incorrect verb tense that does not match the rest of the passage: present (*is limited*), past perfect (*had been limited*), and present perfect (*has been limited*).

22. G: Although this statement is placed in the correct paragraph, it is not useful to list foods that cannot be grown on either island, since this is not a factor in the Polynesian migration.

23. D: This statement is the best choice as the revision transitions from the previous sentence on the difficult climate and utilizes active voice, while maintaining the author's original meaning. Not changing the sentence preserves the meaning but uses passive voice. Stating that the settlers forced themselves to hunt, gather, and fish rather than stating the settlers were forced by the climate changes the meaning of the sentence. The phrase *will have been forced* uses both passive voice and the future perfect tense.

24. J: The two sentences are cause and effect. The first sentence gives the cause (that the settlers depended on hunting, gathering, and fishing), and the second sentence gives the effect (that the settlers stayed close to the sea where fish were abundant). *Therefore* is a good transition between cause and effect, so this choice is correct.

25. B: Including a comma after *fern* is unnecessary, and so is capitalizing the word *shellfish*.

26. J: This answer choice correctly uses a colon to introduce a list, creating a complete statement before placing the colon. The other choices all have sentence fragments before the colon.

27. B: The adverb *markedly* is meant to modify the verb *increased*, signifying that warfare grew significantly more prevalent after the easy food source was gone. The unchanged sentence incorrectly attempts to modify the noun *disappearance*. The remaining answer choices use a vague pronoun, which does not clearly indicate the moa.

28. F: This sentence functions best in its current location. The first sentence of the paragraph functions as a topic sentence on the sweet potato. The middle sentence explains how the sweet potato could grow in many areas and survive the winter months as well. This sentence adds the significance of the information: that this food allowed the human population to increase after the food shortage mentioned in the previous paragraph.

29. C: This choice is correct because it gives the most precise information, specifying the Maori population rather than general humanity.

30. F: The author has stated that "the most important farmed crop in prehistoric New Zealand was the sweet potato." In the final paragraph, the author has shared how the sweet potato was relied upon for food throughout the year and was responsible for population growth on the islands. So, the addition of how the Maori people lived alongside their sweet potato farmlands is more evidence to support the topic sentence of this paragraph.

31. C: This choice is the only one that uses past tense. The phrase *will have* is incorrect because it signifies use of the future perfect tense, while the remainder of the passage is in past tense. Additionally, using the word *flew* instead of *flown* with the future perfect *will have* is incorrect. The phrase *have flown* is present perfect tense and is therefore incorrect.

32. J: Using *that* creates a restrictive clause, so the comma after the word is not necessary. Using *which* creates a nonrestrictive clause, so a comma is necessary.

33. B: The other answer choices show a relationship between American pilots not having work because they gave up flying airplanes. The original sentences communicate the opposite: some American pilots returned from World War I and no longer had work as pilots. So, they had to give up flying altogether and find other jobs.

34. F: Removing the word *new* is incorrect because *new* and *creative* are not exact synonyms. Therefore, it is not redundant to say something is new and creative. Adding the word *attempted* is incorrect because using *attempted* and the words *to do* in the same sentence would be redundant. Exchanging the word *things* for *tricks* is incorrect. The following sentence highlights a pilot who transported news stories, which is a service, not a stunt.

35. C: Including the term *news* is redundant because it was introduced in the previous sentence. *Big news story* can be stated more concisely as *important story*. *Big* and *news* are also not coordinate adjectives in this context, so a comma between them would be incorrect. Finally, *broke* is more precise for the news industry than *arrived*.

36. F: A colon cannot be used to separate two independent clauses unless what comes after the colon is an explanation of the preceding statement or a lengthy and formal quote. Changing from an active voice to a passive voice is not the best choice, so that is incorrect. Finally, a semicolon should not be used with a conjunction, so that answer choice is incorrect.

37. B: This answer choice is the best selection as it provides context to the cost of an airplane ride without setting up a contrast. Using a parenthetical phrase is less smooth than including the information directly in the sentence. Setting up an "either-or" and a contrast is not the original intent of the sentence, so those choices are incorrect.

38. F: Exchanging the colon for a comma would create a comma splice, so that choice is incorrect. *Were once standing* is the past continuous tense, not regular past tense to match the surrounding sentences, so that choice is incorrect. The author intends to convey an example that these barnstormers attempted the feat at one point, not regularly, so removing the word *once* would be incorrect.

39. C: Point A is not the best choice because a context has not yet been established. Point B is not the best choice because the previous sentence introduces the idea that pilots had to resign from their flight careers. Point D is not the best choice because it interrupts a thought about the US Postal Service using aircraft to transport mail. Point C is the best selection as it is in the middle of a list of examples of activities that pilots undertook in this era.

40. J: If the author wanted the purpose of the passage to focus on the American public's opinion on what the pilots should pursue after returning from WWI, then readers would need to be provided with reasons for their concerns about men and women pursuing careers in flight.

41. A: This is a plural noun. *Barnstormer's* is a possessive noun. *Barnstormers'* is a plural possessive noun. *Barnstormer* is a singular noun.

42. G. In this context, *bail* means to jump from an airplane. *Bale* in the original sentence means to tightly bundle. *Baile* refers to a form of dance. *Bell* is a noun and does not fit the context, as a verb should be used.

43. D: The original sentence is written in future tense. This event happened in the past and requires a past tense verb. "Flight will take place on" is also future tense, and "flight was to take place on" implies that the flight did not occur.

44. F. This sentence requires a singular linking verb, which is present in the original sentence. "Will pass" is in future tense. "Can pass to make" uses a modal verb. "Were passed to make" uses a plural past tense verb.

45. C: This sentence requires a comma to separate the dependent clause from the following independent clause. "Before airmail; the post" uses a semicolon, but the statements being separated are not both independent clauses. "Before airmail: the post" incorrectly uses a colon as there is no dialogue or list following it or independent clause before it.

46. J: The need for revision with this sentence comes with the unnecessary adjective *American*. The passage implies that the American is already included since the sentence begins with "In Western society." The *individual self* should not be reduced to *self* as it is a term used in psychology fields and parallels with *collective self* later in the sentence. In addition, *Western* should be capitalized.

47. B: This is the best choice as there are multiple "Western societies." *Beside* is a term for physical/geographical proximity, which does not apply to societies. The preposition *among* compares multiple options whereas the preposition *between* compares only two options. *Underneath* again refers to location rather than culture. This choice also leaves *western* lowercase.

48. H: This is a good answer because it stresses that the purpose of the first paragraph is to introduce a tension and not to make judgments one way or another. In general, the first paragraph in an essay (of any length) introduces the discussion at hand or frames a particular debate. Most introductory paragraphs do not introduce extensive content. In this paragraph, there is no clear stance taken on either Buddhist or Western notions of the self. The term *egolessness* is not discussed until the second paragraph, so that answer choice is incorrect.

49. B: The clause after the semicolon reflects a contrast to the first clause (as *While* implies a contrast). Only the correct answer choice uses the transition *rather*, which also reflects contrast.

50. H: When using possessives for compounds, you need to be sure that the apostrophe works with the meaning of the sentence. The concerns of a person may be different from the concerns of a group, making the answer choice "places his or her concerns before any other person's or group's concerns" correct. Opting not to change the sentence is incorrect because *person* should be *person's*. The word *group's* should not be deleted, so that answer choice is incorrect.

51. A: This question is easy to overthink. In the second paragraph, "egolessness" and "ego-toxicity" are defined and contrasted. The purpose of this paragraph, then, should mention this in some form. This answer choice is correct because it captures the fact that these terms are distinguished in the paragraph. The paragraph only mentions the conflict that Buddhists feel—there is no judgment made on the conflict, so the answer choice "It makes light of the conflicts that Buddhists in Western societies experience" is incorrect. The paragraph also does not praise one perspective over another.

52. G: This is the only revision of the phrase that uses proper grammar and punctuation.

53. B: This is the best choice as the pronouns agree with the introductory clause and the future tense follows up on the hypothetical statement earlier in the sentence.

54. G: The original underlined portion has awkward phrasing that can be revised for clarity. Only "beings, and to do good is good for all beings, including" revises this phrasing to be clearer and more concise, while retaining the intended meaning—doing good to others is also good for you.

55. D: This statement is an explanation of the previous sentence, which states that a person can do good both to the world and him or herself. Opting not to change the sentence is incorrect because the word *in* does not make sense in this context. Removing the phrase *care for one's-self* incorrectly implies that a person can care only for the world, rather than caring for both self and the world. Stating that it *could be possible* to accomplish this is incorrect because the previous sentence states that it *is possible*.

56. H: In the first paragraph, the third sentence identifies increased tension in recent decades between individualism and collectivism in the West. This is developed in subsequent paragraphs by the discussion of ego-toxicity vs. egolessness that reflects individualism vs. collectivism. The second sentence provides evidence supporting the first sentence, not a main idea. The fourth sentence provides evidence supporting the third sentence. The first sentence focuses only on Western emphasis of individualism over collectivism, not on the tension between the two that is a main idea on which the following paragraphs elaborate.

57. D: The last sentence in each paragraph of this passage identifies "struggles," "caught between," and "The struggle...continues"—all referring to a main conflict between individualism and collectivism. The final sentence resolves these struggles by stating that abandoning ego-toxicity enables compassionate caring for self and others. Hence none of these sentences identifies only half of this conflict, and the final sentence does not complete these conflicts. The first sentence of each paragraph does not identify this main conflict; only the first sentence of the third paragraph does this. In the first paragraph, the first sentence identifies the Western emphasis of one over the other, not the conflict between them. In the second paragraph, the first sentence identifies the idea of "egolessness" central to Buddhist belief, not its conflict with ego-toxicity identified later in the paragraph. The final sentence does not simply reiterate the conflict but resolves it.

58. G. Ending a sentence with a conjunctive adverb requires a comma to precede it. As written, this sentence is incorrectly using a semicolon. The other choices either lack or misuse punctuation.

59. B. As written, this sentence uses the conjunction for *they are* where it should use the possessive *their*. "Show thru their actions that" uses an informal, idiomatic form of *through*. "Show threw they're actions that" uses the homophone *threw* (which is the past tense of *throw*) as well as the contraction for *they are*.

60. J. The paragraph before this sentence is written in present tense and the statement is referencing a group of people, making *face* the appropriate choice. As written, the sentence is past tense. *Faces* is a singular verb, which should only be used with a singular noun to have correct subject-verb agreement. "Did face" uses past perfect tense, which does not match the present tense of the rest of the passage.

61. B: The issue with this sentence is a comma that separates the subject from the verb. The other answer choices are incorrect because they do not remove the unnecessary comma. Additionally, changing the preposition within the sentence is not necessary, and neither is changing *time* to *day and age*.

62. J: The incorrect choices all remove an essential element of the sentence. It is also incorrect to set up a contrast that did not exist in the original passage. The correct answer choice does not remove a key part of the sentence or change the intent of the original. It merely revises the two original sentences by combining them.

63. A: The word *worldwide* is one word and does not need to be hyphenated. Additionally, changing the verb to past tense does not match the rest of the paragraph. Finally, adding the phrase *due to* changes the meaning of the statement from how basketball grew to why it grew.

64. F: The capitalization and punctuation in the sentence is correct as written.

65. C: The capitalization in this sentence is correct as written, but the comma is needed after the name of the state.

66. J: The verb needs to agree with the subject in number. The verb in this sentence comes before the subject since the subject is *two teams*. Adding a semicolon after *two-teams* is not correct because what follows the semicolon is not an independent clause. Adding a comma after *two-teams* is not correct because the comma and conjunction need an independent clause to separate the sentence.

67. A: The simple past tense is needed for this sentence, not the past perfect tense. A comma is also needed after *basketball*.

68. H: This sentence refers to the "smaller National Basketball League." This needs to be located after the sentence about the BAA's formation for comparison.

69. B: The error with this sentence is the failure to add a comma after the year. The incorrect answer choices do not include a comma after the year. The acronym *Basketball Association of America* should also be capitalized.

70. G: The correction to this sentence can be a revision of redundancy since basketball is already understood to be a sport. So, this is the best answer choice because it removes the unnecessary verbiage, "the sport of."

71. D: The error in the sentence is with the contraction *it's*. The author should replace it with the possessive pronoun *its*.

72. F: There is no error with describing the kind of fun that is characteristic of the sport. Also, a comma is needed in this situation, not a colon. Finally, the verb tense is correct in the original sentence, as the event started in the past and continues into the present.

73. B: Point B is the best choice because this sentence effectively introduces the paragraph that discusses the origins of the game. Point A is not the best option because the introduction is highlighting broad topics that will be discussed in the body paragraphs. Point C is not the best option because the focus of this paragraph is on the spread of the game after its invention and the development of organized basketball. Point D is not the best option because new information should not be introduced in the conclusion.

74. H: This writing is best characterized as an exposition or explanation of how basketball began.

75. D: This is the best choice because the question asks about the influence of the YMCA on multiple sports, and this passage only addresses basketball and its invention at the YMCA.

Mathematics

1. C: The cost of the ticket is constant and represents the value of the y-intercept (b) of the linear equation. The cost per ride is variable and represents the slope (m) of the linear equation. Substitute these values into slope-intercept form of a linear equation, $y = mx + b$. Therefore, the equation that can be used to find the total amount Elijah spent is $y = 3.50x + 30$, where x represents the number of rides Elijah rode and y represents the total amount Elijah spent.

2. H: To evaluate $g(2)$, substitute 2 for every occurrence of x in the equation $g(x) = 3x + x + 5$. Then simplify the result using order of operations.

$$g(2) = 3(2) + (2) + 5$$
$$g(2) = 6 + 2 + 5$$
$$g(2) = 13$$

3. D: The equation may be solved for x by first subtracting b from both sides of the equation. Doing so gives $ax = c - b$. Dividing both sides of the equation by a gives $x = \frac{c-b}{a}$. Therefore, the value of x is $\frac{c-b}{a}$.

4. J: When a number is raised to a power, you multiply the number by itself by the number of times of the power. For example, $2^3 = 2 \times 2 \times 2 = 8$. A number raised to the power of 0 is always equal to 1. So, 6^0 is the smallest number shown. Similarly, for the other numbers:

$$9 = 9;\ 10^1 = 10;\ 4^2 = 4 \times 4 = 16$$

Since $1 < 8 < 9 < 10 < 16$, we can write the order as $6^0, 2^3, 9, 10^1, 4^2$.

5. B: Use the table of values to first write equations for $f(x)$ and $g(x)$: $f(x) = 2x^3$ and $g(x) = 3x - 5$. Then, use those equations to find $f(g(3))$.

$$g(3) = 3(3) - 5 = 9 - 5 = 4$$
$$f(4) = 2(4)^3 = 2(64) = 128$$

So, $f\big(g(3)\big) = f(4) = 128$.

6. K: The area of the square is $A = s^2 = (30 \text{ cm})^2 = 900 \text{ cm}^2$. The area of the circle is $A = \pi r^2 = (3.14)(15 \text{ cm})^2 \approx 707 \text{ cm}^2$. The area of the shaded region is equal to the difference between the area of the square and the area of the circle, or $900 \text{ cm}^2 - 707 \text{ cm}^2$, which equals 193 cm^2.

7. C: The expression $(x - 3)^2$ can be rewritten as $(x - 3)(x - 3)$. Use the FOIL method to multiply the first terms, outer terms, inner terms, and last terms. Then, add these four terms together to get $x^2 - 3x - 3x + 9$. Combining like terms gives $x^2 - 6x + 9$.

8. J: To solve, first figure out how much money Tim has earned just for child care, then determine the bonus amount, and then add in the bonus amount:

$$childcare = 4 \text{ hours} \times \frac{\$5.00}{\text{hour}} = \$20.00$$

$$bonus = \$20.00 \times 0.20 = \$4.00$$

$$total = \$20.00 + \$4.00 = \$24.00$$

9. C: The y-intercept of the inequality is 20. The slope can be determined by calculating the ratio of the change in y-values per change in corresponding x-values. Choose any two points to calculate the slope. For example, the points (0,20) and (25,5) can be used.

$$m = \frac{y_2 - y_1}{x_2 - x_1} = \frac{5 - 20}{25 - 0} = \frac{-15}{25} = -\frac{3}{5}$$

Therefore, the slope is −0.6. Write the inequality in slope-intercept form. Use the less than or equal to sign (≤) because the line is solid and the graph is shaded below the line.

$$y \leq -\frac{3}{5}x + 20$$

10. H: When subtracting A from B, the difference matrix can be written as $\begin{bmatrix} 1-1 & -3-(-3) \\ -4-(-4) & 2-(-2) \end{bmatrix}$, which reduces to $\begin{bmatrix} 0 & 0 \\ 0 & 4 \end{bmatrix}$.

11. A: The picture is scaled so that each inch on the drawing represents two feet in real life. We can multiply 4 inches by 2 to find the actual height of the wall. Because $4 \times 2 = 8$, we know the real wall must measure 8 feet.

12. F: Matrices can be added or subtracted only if they have the same dimensions. Since both are 2×2 matrices, each position of the resulting matrix is the sum of the values of each matrix at the corresponding positions:

$$\begin{bmatrix} 4 & 2 \\ 7 & 12 \end{bmatrix} + \begin{bmatrix} -1 & 15 \\ 3 & -5 \end{bmatrix} = \begin{bmatrix} 4+(-1) & 2+15 \\ 7+3 & 12+(-5) \end{bmatrix} = \begin{bmatrix} 3 & 17 \\ 10 & 7 \end{bmatrix}$$

13. B: An arc is a piece of a circle. In the figure, $\widehat{AB}$ is the piece of the circle that starts at point A and ends at point B. In general, an arc length s is given by $s = \theta r$, where r is the radius of the circle containing the arc and θ is the angle created by radii drawn to the endpoints of the arc. In a unit circle, the length of an arc is simply the measure of the angle (in radians). Therefore, the arc length of $\widehat{AB}$ is equal to the measure of $\angle AOB$, so its length is $\frac{\pi}{3}$.

Alternatively, we can solve using the angle and circumference. We know that the arc length is the fraction of the circle corresponding with the angle. For instance, if an angle was $\frac{\pi}{2}$, we divide this by the measure of the full circle (2π radians) to find that the arc length is $\frac{\pi}{2} \div 2\pi = \frac{\pi}{2} \times \frac{1}{2\pi} = \frac{1}{4}$ of the circumference of the circle. So, in this case, we find that the fraction of the circle is $\frac{\pi}{3} \div 2\pi = \frac{\pi}{3} \times \frac{1}{2\pi} = \frac{1}{6}$. The circumference of the circle is $C = 2\pi r$, and since the radius is 1, the circumference is simply 2π. Multiplying this by the fraction yields $\frac{2\pi}{1} \times \frac{1}{6} = \frac{\pi}{3}$. Therefore, solving using the angle and circumference also results in an arc length of $\frac{\pi}{3}$.

14. G: The first function $L(g)$ gives the water level after g gallons are pumped into the tank. The second function $w(t)$ gives the number of gallons pumped into the tank after t minutes, which the first function calls g. Consequently, we can have L act on w: the composition of the functions $L(w(t))$ is the water level of the tank after t minutes. Calculate $L(w(t))$.

$$L(w(t)) = 0.3 \times w(t)$$
$$L(t) = 0.3 \times 1.2t$$
$$L(t) = 0.36t$$

Thus, the function $L(t) = 0.36t$ represents the water level of the tank after t minutes.

15. D: Standard form for complex numbers requires the denominator be completely real, meaning it has no imaginary part. When dividing complex numbers, $\frac{a+bi}{c+di}$, first multiply by a fraction equal to 1, written to make the product of the denominators completely real. This is accomplished by using the conjugate of the denominator over itself: $\frac{c-di}{c-di}$.

$$\frac{15-5i}{4-2i} \times \frac{4+2i}{4+2i}$$

Then, FOIL both the numerator and the denominator.

$$\frac{60+30i-20i-10i^2}{16+8i-8i-4i^2}$$

Finally, combine like terms and simplify. Remember that $i^2 = -1$.

$$\frac{60+10i+10}{16+4} = \frac{70+10i}{20} = \frac{10(7+i)}{10(2)} = \frac{7+i}{2}$$

16. F: The number of bacteria forms a geometric sequence: 100, 200, 400, 800, 1,600, etc. Notice that, if you ignore the two zeroes, these numbers are all powers of 2 (i.e. 2^0, 2^1, 2^2, 2^3, 2^4, etc.). In other words, they are all 100 multiplied by a power of 2, so the sequence can be written as an exponential function of the form $y = 100 \times 2^n$. However, since this sequence begins with an exponent of 0 on the first day, rather than 1, and an exponent of 1 on the second day rather than 2, you need to subtract 1 from n to get the correct power. Thus, the function $b(n) = 100 \times 2^{n-1}$ represents the number of bacteria on the nth day.

17. A: Multiply 60 mph by 15 hours to find out how far he drove on Day 1:

$$60 \text{ mph} \times 15 \text{ hr} = 900 \text{ mi}$$

If he does the same on Day 2, he will have driven a total of 1,800 miles. He will have 200 miles left to go on a 2,000-mile trip.

18. H: To determine the scale factor of the dilation, compare the coordinates of $\Delta J'K'L'$ to the coordinates of ΔJKL. J is at $(-2,-3)$ and J' is at $(-4,-6)$, which means that the coordinates of J were multiplied by a scale factor of 2 to get the coordinates of J'. K is at $(1,3)$ and K' is at $(2,6)$. L is at $(4,-1)$ and L' is at $(8,-2)$. The coordinates of K and L were also multiplied by a scale factor of 2 to get to the coordinates of K' and L'. Therefore, the scale factor of the dilation is 2.

19. D: To solve, convert the pounds to ounces (one pound is 16 oz): a quarter-pound of blueberries equals 4 oz; a half-pound of strawberries equals 8 oz; a half-pound of yogurt equals 8 oz, a quarter-pound of walnuts equals 4 oz.

$$4 \text{ oz} + 8 \text{ oz} + 8 \text{ oz} + 4 \text{ oz} = 24 \text{ oz}$$

$$24 \text{ oz} \times \frac{\$0.15}{\text{oz}} = \$3.60$$

20. H: To solve, first figure out how much she owes over the $3.00 base fee. For each five minutes, she pays an extra 15 cents. For each hour after the first one, she will pay:

$$12 \times 0.15 = \$1.80$$

She has used the service for an extra 2 hours and 10 minutes. Two hours of additional time is:

$$\$1.80 \times 2 = \$3.60$$

Ten minutes of additional time is:

$$\$0.15 \times 2 = \$0.30$$

Adding these two values gives an additional cost of \$3.90. Add this to the base fee of \$3 for the first hour to get a total bill of \$6.90.

21. C: If Abe goes 3 miles in one hour, he goes half of that or $1\frac{1}{2}$ miles in half an hour. Similarly, Beatriz can go half of 4, or 2 miles, in half an hour. Subtract to find how much more Beatriz can run than Abe in half an hour. $2 - 1\frac{1}{2} = \frac{1}{2}$, so Beatriz can run $\frac{1}{2}$ mile more than Abe in half an hour.

22. F: To solve, first figure out how much room is left when her car and the garage are taken into account: 19 feet − 15 feet = 4 feet. To center the car, it would have to be parked 2 feet from the front of the garage.

23. B: To solve for the percentage, set up a ratio: $\frac{36}{81} = \frac{x}{100}$. Cross-multiply: $81x = 3{,}600$. Solve by dividing both sides by 81: $x \approx 44$. Therefore, 36 is approximately 44% of 81.

24. H: Since $\overline{AB}$ is tangent to circle O, then $\overline{AB}$ forms a right angle with radius $\overline{AO}$. ΔAOB is then a right triangle, so the Pythagorean theorem can be used to find the measure of $\overline{OB}$.

$$\begin{aligned} c^2 &= a^2 + b^2 \\ (\overline{OB})^2 &= 8^2 + 15^2 \\ (\overline{OB})^2 &= 64 + 225 \\ (\overline{OB})^2 &= 289 \end{aligned}$$

Take the square root of both sides, to find that $\overline{OB} = 17$.

25. B: The volume of a square pyramid can be calculated using the formula $V = \frac{Bh}{3}$, where B is the area of the base and h is the height of the pyramid. Therefore, the volume of Natasha's tent is $\frac{x^2h}{3}$. If she were to increase by 1 ft the length of each side of the square base, the tent's volume can be calculated by substituting $x + 1$ for x in the original tent volume formula.

$$\frac{(x+1)^2h}{3} = \frac{(x^2+2x+1)(h)}{3} = \frac{x^2h + 2xh + h}{3} = \frac{x^2h}{3} + \frac{2xh + h}{3}$$

Notice this is the volume of Natasha's tent, $\frac{x^2h}{3}$, increased by $\frac{2xh+h}{3}$, or $\frac{h(2x+1)}{3}$. This is how much more interior space the tent would have.

26. J: Linear functions can be written in the form $g(x) = mx + b$. To determine the value of the slope, m, notice that $g(x)$ decreases by 3 every time x increases by 1: when x goes from 0 to 1, the value of the function goes from 4 to 1; and when x goes from 1 to 2, the function goes from 1 to –2. Since $g(x)$ decreases by 3, the slope is –3, so the function is $g(x) = -3x + b$.

Next, calculate the value of the y-intercept, b. The y-intercept is the value of y, or in this case $g(x)$, when $x = 0$. From the table, you can tell that $g(0) = 4$. Thus, the function is $g(x) = -3x + 4$.

27. B: We can express Andre's speed as the rate 65 miles to 1 hour, or $\frac{65}{1}$. Next, we can set up a proportion to determine how long it will take Andre to travel 195 miles. Since we are comparing miles to hours, our proportion should be $\frac{65}{1} = \frac{195}{x}$. To solve for x, we must determine how much greater 195 is than 65. We can do this using division. $195 \div 65 = 3$, which tells us that 195 is 3 times greater than 65. Now, we must multiply our denominator, 1, by 3 as well to keep our proportion balanced. The product of 1 and 3 is 3, making $x = 3$. It will take Andre 3 hours to travel 195 miles.

28. G: Data is said to be positively skewed when there are a higher number of lower values, indicating data that is skewed right. Data is said to be negatively skewed when there are a higher number of higher values, indicating that the data is skewed left. An approximately normal distribution shows an increase in frequency, followed by a decrease in frequency, of approximately the same rate, following a general bell curve. Therefore, Group A is positively skewed, and Group B is approximately normal.

29. C: Multiply $1,000 by 35% to get the amount deducted: $\$1,000 \times 35\% = \$350.00$. Subtract this value from the original amount: $\$1000 - \$350 = \$650$.

30. J: Since he does not replace the first card, the events are dependent. The sample space will decrease by 1 for the second draw because there will be one fewer card to choose from. Thus, the probability may be written as $P(A \text{ and } B) = \frac{13}{52} \times \frac{13}{51}$, or $P(A \text{ and } B) = \frac{169}{2{,}652} = \frac{13}{204}$.

31. E: The ratio indicates the number of people who chose veggie (60) to the number of people who chose turkey (45). Write the ratio 60 : 45 and then reduce it by dividing both parts by 15 so that it becomes 4 : 3.

32. H: The number of students who chose either turkey or egg salad is $45 + 15 = 60$. Adding the number of campers yields a total of 180, so we can write the fraction $\frac{60}{180} = \frac{1}{3}$, or approximately 33%.

33. B: Based on the location of the 34°, the 14 ft section is the adjacent leg and the ramp length is the hypotenuse of the right triangle. Therefore, in order to solve for x, it needs to be set up as $\cos 34° = \frac{\text{adjacent}}{\text{hypotenuse}}$ or $\cos 34° = \frac{14}{x}$. The value of x is found by rearranging the equation to be $x = \frac{14}{\cos 34°}$.

34. H: The relationship between Kate and her shadow is the same as the relationship between Sara and her shadow; that is, $\frac{Kate}{Kate's\ shadow} = \frac{Sara}{Sara's\ shadow}$. If Sara's shadow is 16 inches longer than Kate's, it is 48 inches long.

$$\frac{x}{48} = \frac{40}{32}$$
$$32x = 48(40)$$
$$x = \frac{1920}{32}$$
$$x = 60$$

35. C: Start by determining the area Sophie needs to paint. The area of a rectangle can be calculated by multiplying the length by the width.

$$A = l \times w = 15 \times 8 = 120$$

Therefore, she needs to cover 120 square feet of wall with paint. Since one gallon of paint can cover 36 square feet, divide 120 by 36 to determine how many gallons of paint she needs.

$$120 \div 36 = 3\frac{1}{3}$$

Sophie needs $3\frac{1}{3}$ gallons of paint to cover the room, but she needs to purchase 4 gallons since she can only purchase whole gallons of paint. 3 gallons would not be enough to cover the whole wall.

36. H: To find the temperature in degrees Fahrenheit, plug 20 into the formula for degrees Celsius and solve.

$$°\text{F} = \left(\frac{9}{5}\right)(20) + 32 = 36 + 32 = 68$$

Therefore, the temperature in degrees Fahrenheit is 68°.

37. A: To find Hector's price per gallon we must divide the total amount of money Hector paid, \$22.44, by the number of gallons he received, 12. $\$22.44 \div 12 = \$1.87$, so Hector paid \$1.87 per gallon of gasoline.

38. H: When the dress is marked down by 20%, the cost of the dress is 80% of its original price. Since a percentage can be written as a fraction by placing the percentage over 100, the reduced price of the dress can be written as $\frac{80}{100}x$, or $\frac{4}{5}x$, where x is the original price. When discounted an extra 25%, the dress costs 75% of the reduced price. This results in the expression $\frac{75}{100}\left(\frac{4}{5}x\right)$, which can be simplified to $\frac{3}{4}\left(\frac{4}{5}x\right)$, or $\frac{3}{5}x$. So the final price of the dress is three-fifths of the original price.

39. B: The sign of the constant inside the squared term is positive for a shift to the left and negative for a shift to the right. Thus, a movement of 5 units left is indicated by the expression $y = (x + 5)^2$. A shift of 4 units down is indicated by subtraction of 4 units from the squared term.

40. K: Out of the twenty students in the classroom, half are girls. That means there is a 1 in 2, or 50%, chance that the homework handed in will belong to a girl.

41. A: For any point outside a circle, there are exactly two lines tangent to the circle passing through that point. Further, the lengths of these line segments from the point to the circle are equal. In this problem, the two segments extending from Q both have a length of 7. The two segments extending from R have a length of 4. The two segments extending from S have a length of 2. The two segments extending from P have a length of 5. Therefore, the perimeter of quadrilateral $PQRS$ can be calculated as $7 + 7 + 4 + 4 + 2 + 2 + 5 + 5 = 36$. The perimeter of the quadrilateral is 36.

42. H: The linear function $s(h) = 27h + 720$ starts at 720 when $h = 0$ and increases by 27 every time h increases by 1. Therefore, for every hour after 40, the librarian earns \$27, so his salary is \$27 per hour.

43. C: To solve, find the perimeter (the distance around the outside) of each by adding the length of each side of the rectangles:

Garden A: 4 ft by 9 ft rectangle, 4 ft + 9 ft + 4 ft + 9 ft = 26 ft

Garden B: 12 ft by 3 ft rectangle, 12 ft + 3 ft + 12 ft + 3 ft = 30 ft

Garden C: 18 ft by 2 ft rectangle, 18 ft + 2 ft + 18 ft + 2 ft = 40 ft

The largest perimeter, Garden C, will require the most fencing.

44. J: The general form of the interest exponential is $A(t) = P(1 + r)^t$, where P is the initial principal, r the interest rate (as a decimal), and t the number of interest yield periods after the initial investment. P is \$315 in this case, which means that is the initial amount put into the account. Furthermore, the exponential function $b(t) = 315(1.05)^t$ equals 315 when $t = 0$. Therefore, John initially put \$315 into the bank account.

45. B: Since we are given a conversion factor, begin by setting up conversion fractions. We know that $\frac{1}{2}$ inch = 12 miles, and we are looking for how many inches would represent 84 miles. Set up the following conversion fraction.

$$\frac{\frac{1}{2}\text{ inch}}{12\text{ miles}} = \frac{x\text{ inches}}{84\text{ miles}}$$

Since the units are lined up properly, we can ignore them for the moment, cross multiply the values, and solve for x.

$$\frac{1}{2} \times 84 = 12x$$
$$42 = 12x$$
$$3.5 = x$$

Since $x = 3.5$, a distance of 84 miles would be represented by 3.5 inches on the map.

46. J: The theoretical probability of getting tails is $\frac{1}{2}$. Thus, she can expect to get a total of $\frac{1}{2} \times 1{,}000$ tails, or 500 tails.

47. D: To solve this problem, first figure our Dale's new rate by multiplying 45 by 0.07 (7% as a decimal) and adding this to his original rate ($45).

$$\$45 \times 0.07 + \$45 = \$3.15 + \$45 = \$48.15$$

Then, determine how many hours he would have worked last year to earn $135. Do this by dividing $135 by his hourly wage ($45).

$$\$135 \div \$45/\text{hr} = 3\text{ hrs}$$

Finally, multiply his new hourly wage ($48.15) by 3 to figure out how much he would have earned for the same project this year.

$$\$48.15 \times 3 = \$144.45$$

48. K: If $\frac{1}{4}$ inch represents 8 miles, then 1 inch represents $4 \times 8 = 32$ miles. Two inches represents $2 \times 32 = 64$ inches. Since $\frac{1}{8}$ is half of $\frac{1}{4}$, we can take half of 8 to find that $\frac{1}{8}$ inch represents 4 miles. Then $2\frac{1}{8}$ inches represents $64 + 4 = 68$ miles.

49. B: To determine how much Brenda would have saved, first find out the sale price of the shoes and then subtract this price from the amount Brenda paid. The sale price of the shoes is:

$$\$62 \times 0.75 = \$46.50$$

Then, subtract this amount from the amount Brenda paid:

$$\$62 - \$46.50 = \$15.50$$

Brenda would have saved $15.50 if she had waited a day.

50. J: We know the ratio of boys to girls is 3 to 4, which means there are 3 boys for every 7 students (because $3 + 4 = 7$). We can write the ratio of boys to total students as $\frac{3}{7}$. We also know that there are 12 boys in the class, so we can create the following proportion.

$$\frac{3}{7} = \frac{12}{x}$$

To solve for x, use cross multiplication, and then solve as a regular equation.

$$3x = 12 \times 7$$
$$3x = 84$$
$$x = 28$$

Since $x = 28$, this means there is a total of 28 students in the class.

51. D: Begin by calculating the total rainfall in the summer and autumn months by adding all the values together. The total rainfall is 25.38 inches. Then, create a ratio comparing the rainfall in October to the total rainfall. The ratio $\frac{4.5}{25.38}$ represents the fraction of rainfall received during October. Convert the ratio to a percentage by dividing the numerator by the denominator and then multiplying by 100: $\frac{4.5}{25.38} \approx 0.177 = 17.7\%$. Therefore, about 17.7% of the rain fell during October.

52. K: Recall that, for a rectangle, area (A) is length (l) times width (w).

$$A = l \times w = 10 \text{ ft} \times 15 \text{ ft} = 150 \text{ ft}^2$$

Therefore, the area of the rectangle is 150 ft^2.

53. D: If James paid 30% of the prize in taxes, this means he has 70% left. If 70% of the original prize is \$14,000, we can set up the equation: $0.7x = 14{,}000$. We divide both sides by 0.7 to find that $x = 20{,}000$, so James originally won \$20,000.

54. K: The degree of $f(x)$ is 1, the degree of $g(x)$ is 2, and the degree of $h(x)$ is 3. The leading coefficient for each function is 2. Functions $f(x)$ and $h(x)$ have exactly one real zero ($x = 1$), while $g(x)$ has two real zeros ($x = \pm 1$):

$f(x) = 0$	$g(x) = 0$	$h(x) = 0$
$2x - 2 = 0$	$2x^2 - 2 = 0$	$2x^3 - 2 = 0$
$2x = 2$	$2x^2 = 2$	$2x^3 = 2$
$x = 1$	$x^2 = 1$	$x^3 = 1$
	$x = 1; x = -1$	$x = 1$

All of the functions have two terms, which makes them binomials instead of trinomials.

55. B: Start by multiplying the coefficients and then multiply the i-terms. $-2 \times 7 = -14$ and $i \times i = i^2$. The expression simplifies to $-14i^2$. Remember, $i^2 = \sqrt{-1} \times \sqrt{-1} = -1$, so the expression becomes $-14 \times (-1) = 14$. Therefore, the expression is equal to 14.

56. H: To find the probability that a student is enrolled at TAMU or that a student prefers lattes, the addition rule needs to be used. The addition rule adds the probabilities of two independent events and subtracts the probability that both events are true to avoid double counting. The probability may be written as $P(A \text{ or } B) = \frac{750}{1{,}650} + \frac{675}{1{,}650} - \frac{350}{1{,}650}$, which simplifies to $P(A \text{ or } B) = \frac{1{,}075}{1{,}650} \approx 65\%$. Therefore, the probability is approximately 65%.

57. B: Multiply $12,000 by 10% to get $1,200. Add these figures together to find out the total amount. Molly will repay $13,200. Divide this by 24 months to find out the monthly payments:

$$\frac{\$13{,}200}{24} = \$550$$

58. J: The volume of the box is the product of $\sqrt{3}$, $2\sqrt{5}$, and 4. To multiply two or more square root radicals, multiply the coefficients and then multiply the radicands.

$$\sqrt{3} \times 2\sqrt{5} \times 4 = 8\sqrt{3}\sqrt{5} = 8\sqrt{15}$$

Then, simplify the radicand if possible by factoring out any squares. Since 15 cannot be factored into any square factors, it cannot be simplified further.

59. C: To solve the equation, cross-multiply

$$\frac{2}{x-8} = \frac{3}{x}$$

$$2(x) = 3(x-8)$$

Distribute into the sets of parentheses.

$$2x = 3x - 24$$

Combine like terms by subtracting $3x$ from each side.

$$-x = -24$$

Finally, divide both sides by −1.

$$x = 24$$

60. K: Since the two triangles have all three corresponding pairs of sides and corresponding pairs of angles marked congruent, then the two triangles are congruent. Similar triangles are the same shape but not necessarily the same size; they have congruent angles. All congruent triangles are similar triangles, so the correct choice is that the triangles are both similar and congruent. An equilateral triangle has three congruent sides and angles measuring 60° each, so these triangles are not equilateral.

Reading

1. A: Lines 57–65 most clearly state this idea that America is evolving toward a better situation. FDR states that throughout US history "we have been engaged in change ... a revolution which goes on steadily ..." None of the other statements directly reflect this idea.

2. G: The argument that needs to be evaluated is that people will be happy to give more money in taxes to the government. It would be safe to raise the counterargument that the general population may already believe they are paying enough in taxes and don't think the government is spending that money wisely. Not everyone will be happy to give more to the government to spend. The incorrect answer choices either do not address the question or agree with FDR's argument.

3. D: This speech is typically referred to as the "Four Freedoms" speech. In it, FDR articulates the basic freedoms he believes in. These freedoms are the central focus of the speech, since it supports the other ideas that he is focusing on (i.e., social issues). The importance placed on ensuring all people have access to the benefits of an old age system is a simple detail within the speech, not the main idea. The remaining answer choices are not points expressed within the speech.

4. H: FDR spoke of freedom, defining it earlier in the paragraph as "the supremacy of human rights everywhere." This is the "high concept" he refers to in the following paragraph/sentence. In this context, the "end" of victory does not mean death. It does not precisely mean purpose, as in the common phrase "a means to an end" (a way of achieving a purpose): he was not saying victory was the only purpose of the concept, but rather that this concept could have no other outcome or result than victory. "End" can also mean conclusion, i.e., the termination or finishing of something, which does not fit the meaning in this context quite as precisely as because it does not imply cause and effect as "outcome" does.

5. D: After describing the four freedoms he identified, FDR said the vision of a world founded on those freedoms was "no vision of a distant millennium" but "a definite basis for a kind of world attainable in our own time and generation. That kind of world is the very antithesis of the so-called new order of tyranny..." referring to the "order" that dictators wanted to impose, to which "we oppose the greater conception—the moral order." He further described the "cooperation of free countries, working together in a friendly, civilized society" as the "world order which we seek". This context establishes that "order" most nearly means a system of societal and world politics rather than a military leader's command; an authoritative decision or direction, e.g., a court order or a doctor's order; or an arrangement in sequence, e.g., alphabetical, numerical, or chronological order.

6. F: In lines 13–15 FDR said, "A part of the sacrifice means the payment of more money in taxes" for "a greater portion of this great defense program."

While he called for taxpayers to support the military, in this passage he did not equate personal sacrifice with serving in the military. Although he described worldwide arms reduction, he did not equate this with personal sacrifice, but with the fourth freedom: freedom from fear. The four freedoms he identified were "essential human freedoms," i.e., things all human beings had rights to, not examples of personal sacrifice.

7. D: In lines 59–61 Roosevelt describes his view of change as "a revolution which goes on steadily, quietly adjusting itself to changing conditions." He lays out specific goals earlier in his speech and hopes that they are attainable in "our own time and generation" (line 48). But in this paragraph, he says that change, as seen throughout American history, is gradual and prone to adjustments as circumstances require. Although FDR refers to wars and their atrocities, he is merely making the point that America changes peacefully rather than through war. FDR's plans for social and financial reform are not referenced in this paragraph. Although this paragraph refers to "the cooperation of free countries" (lines 63–64), this is not the main idea of American change that FDR is explaining.

8. H: In this passage there is no mention of expanding the draft of citizens into military service. As examples of aspects of the social economy needing "immediate improvement," FDR cited, "We should bring more citizens under the coverage of old-age pensions"; "We should widen the opportunities for adequate medical care"; and "We should plan a better system by which persons deserving or needing gainful employment may obtain it".

9. D: In this passage, FDR did include some simple sentences, but they are typically not short. The shortest sentences in the passage have six and seven words respectively and are the only ones that short. The structure used most frequently is the complex sentence; these are typically long. He also included some long compound sentences; and some long complex-compound sentences.

10. J: While the President does name some of the rights that come under the First Amendment, he is not merely reciting or trying to paraphrase the First Amendment. Although President Roosevelt uses the phrase "everywhere in the world" several times, readers should also acknowledge that "everywhere in the world" includes the United States of America and neither the world nor America is emphasized as being more important than the other. In addition, the President says that the Americans are seeking to make the world more secure, and he asserts that this can be achieved when all people around the world enjoy the same freedoms as Americans. Additionally, while the task is challenging and immense, the President does not seem to be wavering or doubtful on his hope for that dream.

11. A: Only this choice provides support for the idea of special relativity. The answer choice "Galilean co-ordinate systems and their application in classical mechanics" is used in the explanation but does not provide support on its own. The answer choice "the idea of chance in quantum mechanics" is actually part of a counterargument to relativity. The answer choice "The two different parts of relativity" only indicates that there are two sections and does not provide any support.

12. G: Only this choice deals closely with an argument against relativity. The incorrect answer choices either agree with Einstein's theory of relativity and are therefore not arguments, do not pose an argument against relativity, or focus on a detailed question rather than the entire theory.

13. C: The word "truth" was quoted because Einstein was referring to the understanding of the laws of motion we had before relativity, which did indeed seem to provide the correct answers for a great deal of physics questions. However, according to the other sentences around this word, we can conclude that it does not refer to an absolute truth because relativity turns classical ideas on their heads.

14. G: Corresponding to the noun "delicacy," one meaning of the adjective "delicate" is fragile or easily damaged. This meaning is not supported by the context. As it modifies "detail," delicacy here refers to how sensitively and specifically classical mechanics describes the movements of stars, planets, etc. Another meaning of a delicacy is an expensive and/or rare delight, especially regarding food; e.g., caviar is considered a delicacy. This meaning makes no sense in this context. Delicacy can also refer to soft texture, e.g., the delicacy of a lace fabric. This meaning does not relate to the subject matter.

15. D: *A priori* is Latin, meaning literally "from the one before." In the context of Einstein's discussion, he means that because the principle of relativity can be generalized so broadly across domains, its applying so precisely in one domain predicts it would apply with comparable accuracy in another domain; and therefore, that its being valid for one domain but not another is not very likely. It is *a priori* not very likely when considering this application of a general principle to a specific domain, and this unlikeliness is logically true/valid independent of observation or experience.

16. F: The quoted phrase is most likely an example of understatement. To emphasize through reversal how exquisite he found the detail provided by classical mechanics, Einstein downplayed it by describing it as less than wonderful, but only a little less. He further qualified this by not writing "*nothing* short of wonderful," but "*little* short of wonderful," making it comparative rather than absolute. An example of overstatement or hyperbole in this case would be something like "the most wonderful ever seen," "too wonderful to be believed," etc. Amplification is repeating a word/phrase but with added details or expanded description for emphasis; e.g., "...it supplies us with the actual motions of the heavenly bodies with a delicacy of detail—a delicacy of detail so fine that it can only be perceived as wonderful." Metabasis is a transitional summary that recapitulates what was said previously and predicts what will be said next, to clarify and organize discourse.

17. C: As Einstein indicated in the sentence following this one, "This statement is called the principle of relativity (in the restricted sense)." The statements in the incorrect choices are all conclusions predicated upon the condition that this principle was NOT true. The choice including lines 69–73 begins with "If the principle of relativity (in the restricted sense) does not hold," continuing with the "then" clause quoted. The choice including lines 74–80 continues, saying, "In this case we should be constrained to believe that..." finishing with the clause quoted. The choice containing lines 106–112 is prefaced by, "If the principle of relativity were not valid" and continues with the clause quoted.

18. H: The word "truth" was quoted because Einstein was referring to the understanding of the laws of motion we had before relativity, which did indeed seem to provide the correct answers for a great deal of physics questions. However, according to the other sentences around this word, we can conclude that it does not refer to an absolute truth because relativity turns classical ideas on their heads.

19. C: Of the first five paragraphs, the first four are completely positive in Einstein's assertions and explanations of his claims; the fifth is also mainly positive, with only a hint of counterclaim in its last sentence refuted to emphasize the claim's validity ("But that [this] principle...should hold...in one domain...and yet...be invalid for another, is a priori not very probable."). The last two paragraphs present counterclaims, introduced by "If the principle of relativity does not hold..." and similar clauses, followed by "then..." conclusions illustrating the logically necessary yet improbable results of such counterclaims.

20. H: Einstein's identification of "two general facts" introduces two arguments wherein he explains reasoning to support the principle of relativity. Lines 121–123 is the last sentence in the excerpted passage, summarizing rather than introducing his preceding evidence. Lines 66–67 introduce the second of his two "arguments" or "general facts" rather than introducing both of them. Lines 1–3 is the first sentence in the excerpted passage, but it is obvious from the clause "let us return to our example" that he is revisiting an example he introduced in a previous part of his paper not included in this excerpt; hence he is not introducing new evidence there, but rather reusing previously introduced evidence to make additional points.

21. B: The entire passage makes the argument that Black History Month should be abolished, offering various reasons why this is the best course of action.

22. J: The context of the sentence suggests that post-racial refers to an approach in which race is not a useful or positive organizing principle.

23. D: The author of Passage A never suggests that people do not learn about African American history during Black History Month.

24. G: Passage B states that W.E.B. DuBois was born in 1868; his birth was therefore the first of the identified events.

25. C: The author points out in paragraph 3 of Passage B that the debate about how to meet the need to teach children about African American history can remind parents that this need is not yet fully met.

26. F: In paragraph 4, the author of Passage B states that the material available is rich and varied.

27. C: The author of Passage B points out that just because there is a month focused on African American history, this doesn't mean that African American history must be ignored for the rest of the year.

28. J: This choice is the best option because both authors agree that revisions to curriculum in the education system are necessary to improve the understanding of black history. The answer choice "voted for Barack Obama to become president" is not the best option because, while the authors seem to be supportive of him, there is not enough information in the passages to draw that conclusion. Additionally, the author of Passage A merely quotes an article, and the author of Passage B makes no mention of the media. The statement that the authors "think that February is not the best time for Black History Month" suggests that the authors would be supportive of Black History Month if it were moved to another month. However, the author of Passage A wants to remove the recognition of Black History Month, not merely change the dates.

29. D: Clearly both authors think it is important for students to learn about the achievements and experience of African Americans; their debate is whether observing Black History Month is the best way to achieve this goal.

30. J: The last paragraph of Passage B states that Abraham Lincoln and Frederick Douglass were essential civil rights activists.

31. D: The incorrect choices all have similar meanings and match the text's description of Lubitsch's film style as elegant or sophisticated.

32. H: This phrase is used in the last sentence to describe the Lubitsch style.

33. B: Lubitsch's focus on seemingly irrelevant details as symbols is described in the text as his signature style (Lines 21–23).

34. H: Lubitsch was invited in 1923 by Albert Zukor (Lines 18–19).

35. D: Made in 1912, the film could not have been a talkie, as it was not until 1923 that Lubitsch went to Hollywood to use sound technology. And the text tells us nothing of the film's content or personnel.

36. F: Monescu and Lily were both thieves who posed as members of high society. Mariette was a real heiress, and Lubitsch, of course, was a director, not a character in the film.

37. C: This, indeed, is the underlying theme of the entire movie, as shown by the characters of Monescu and Lily, who appear to be elegant but are, in fact, thieves.

38. G: Lily has no wealth of her own, but Monescu finally chooses her over Mariette and her fortune (Lines 71–75).

39. B: Lily passes herself off as a countess and Monescu poses as a baron (Lines 66–68).

40. G: Lines 82–83 tells us that he made films in English, German, and French, suggesting that part of his film career was spent in France.

Science

1. A: Scientist 1 argues that due to the limitations on the range of the strong nuclear force, elements cannot exist with an atomic number greater than about 173. Scientist 2 explicitly says in the last sentence that the periodic table can probably be extended indefinitely. Although Scientist 2 does mention "islands of stability," they do not form a major part of Scientist 2's argument, nor do they contradict Scientist 1's claims; Scientist 1 says only that the number of elements yet to be discovered is limited, not that undiscovered elements cannot be stable.

2. G: Both scientists agree that there are more elements remaining to be discovered, although they disagree as to *how many* such elements there are—Scientist 1 thinks they will stop around element 173, whereas Scientist 2 thinks the elements could go on indefinitely. Scientist 2's mention of "islands of stability" contradicts the thought that the higher an atomic number, the less stable the element, and neither scientist expresses any opinion on the procedure for naming elements or on which elements might exist in nature. (The passage does state that only 94 elements exist in nature *on Earth*, but this doesn't preclude heavier elements existing, e.g., inside ultra-dense neutron stars.)

3. A: Scientist 1 argues that no element with an atomic number greater than about 173 could exist. The discovery of an element of atomic number 200 would be a clear contradiction of this and would support Scientist 2's argument that the periodic table continues indefinitely (although it would not prove Scientist 2 correct—e.g., it could still be that the periodic table stops at element 220). The discovery of elements with atomic numbers between 150 and 160 would not damage Scientist 1's argument because those are still less than 173. The stability or instability of element 126 has little to do with either scientist's argument—Scientist 2 does mention the possibility of an "island of stability" there, but it is not important to the overall argument and has no bearing on Scientist 1's argument at all.

4. G: Both scientists make reference to discovering new elements and accept that elements that do not occur in nature can be created in the lab. (Indeed, considering the number of elements that *have* been created in the lab, it would be odd for any chemist *not* to accept this.) Neither scientist says anything about safety precautions, nor does either rule out the possibility of detecting elements with atomic numbers above 126—indeed, Scientist 2 even mentions a possible "island of stability" around atomic number 164. Although Scientist 1 might accept the idea that the arrangement of the particles in an atom changes in predictable ways as the atomic number increases, Scientist 2 certainly wouldn't, as Scientist 2 explicitly mentions that we "know too little about the arrangement of heavy atoms to confidently name a limit to their size."

5. C: Although Scientist 1 refers to both the strong nuclear force and electromagnetism, Scientist 1 states that the former holds nuclei together. It is the fact that protons repel each other through electromagnetism that, according to Scientist 1, would place a limit on the size of an atomic nucleus. Scientist 1 makes no mention of either the weak nuclear force or gravity—although as an attractive force, gravity, if anything, would also help hold the nucleus together. (In fact, however, gravity is far too weak a force to have any significant effect at all on the nuclear scale.)

6. H: Scientist 2 speaks of possible "islands of stability" centered on elements 126 and 164. If these islands of stability exist there, then elements 126 and 164 themselves would be relatively stable in comparison to the elements around and between them—and element 145 in particular, lying halfway between these "islands of stability," would *not* be expected to be as stable. As for element 8, the discussion of "islands of stability" refers to relative stability among the heavy elements that don't exist in nature and have yet to be created in the lab. Element 8 is not such an element—with that low atomic number, it's a light element that exists in nature and is certainly stable. (As a matter of fact, element 8 is oxygen, which is not only abundant in the Earth's atmosphere, lithosphere, and oceans but is by mass the most abundant element in your body!)

7. D: For the bands to match between the two profiles, a band in Profile 2 must appear in the same position as the band in Profile 1. Only Band D has a match in Profile 2:

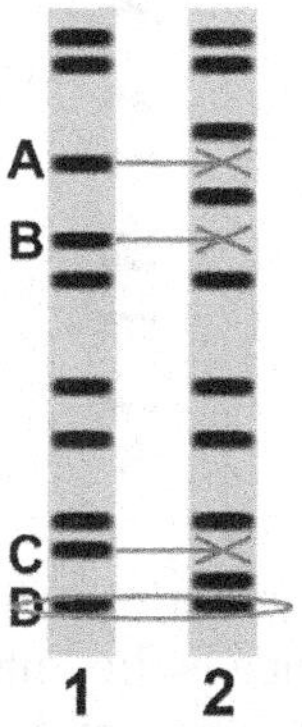

8. H: Seven bands match between Profiles 1 and 2:

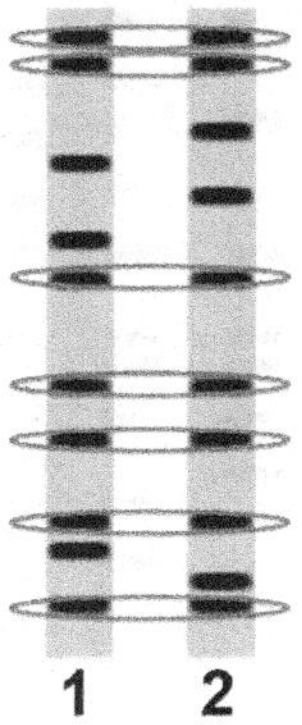

This is slightly more than would be expected by chance; on average, we would expect half the bands to match between a parent and child—so because there are 10 bands, we would expect five matches on average. However, this is only an average, and a slight deviation isn't that surprising; seven matches instead of five is not especially improbable.

9. D: According to the passage, any bands in the child that are *not* present in one parent must be present in the other. This means that any band in Profile 1 and not in Profile 2 must be in the profile of the father. These are the bands we should expect to find:

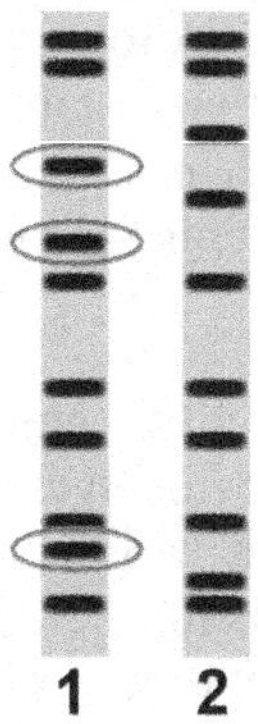

The only profile to have all of these bands is Profile 6:

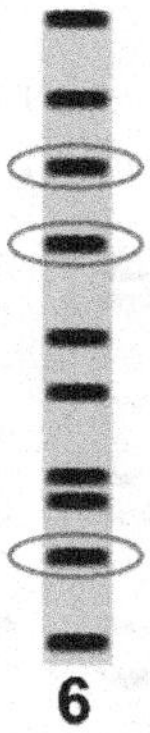

10. G: As stated in the passage, each mark in the genetic profile of a child should also appear in one (or both) of the parents. The profile in the second profile choice is the only one for which this is true. All the other choices have some marks that do not appear in either Profiles 3 or 4.

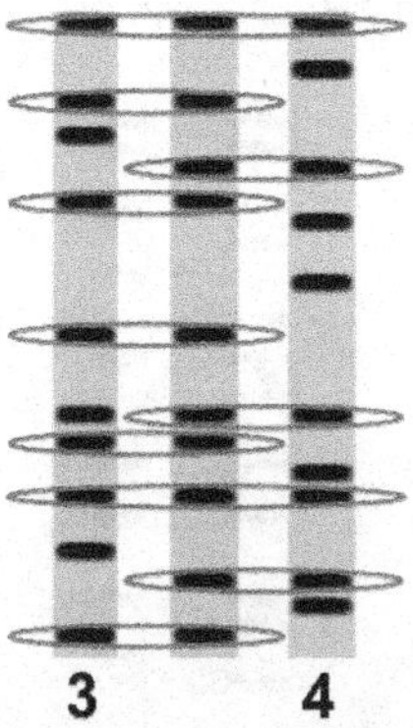

11. B: The passage explicitly says that the number of markers shared by siblings is unpredictable. Therefore, there's no firm reason to conclude that Profiles 5 and 6 could not belong to siblings. However, they do not share more than half of their markers. They do share some markers, but only four of the 10 markers are shared, which is less than half.

12. H: The number of loops is recorded in the third column in the student's data tables. Trial 5 used 250 loops, which is more than the number used in any other trial.

13. B: Table 1 shows that the magnetic field strength increases with the number of coils, which is what should be expected from the passage—except for Trial 4, which has a larger number of coils but a smaller magnetic field strength than Trials 2 or 3. If Trial 4 is removed, then the pattern of increasing field strength with increasing number of coils is consistent. Therefore, Trial 4 is the outlier and is the most likely trial to be a mistake.

14. F: Aside from the single outlier in Trial 4, in Table 1 the rows with the higher numbers of loops also have higher magnetic field strength. This shows that increasing the number of loops increases the strength of the magnetic field. Likewise, Table 2 shows that increasing the diameter of the core increases the magnetic field strength.

15. D: One way to eliminate the effect of the Earth's magnetic field is to measure it and account for it, which is best done by measuring the field strength without the electromagnet there and then subtracting it from the value read when the electromagnet is present. For the best results, the electromagnet should be aligned parallel to the Earth's magnetic field so that the magnitudes of the fields simply add together.

None of the other choices describes a good way of accounting for the Earth's magnetic field. Performing the experiment in a closed room will not help; the Earth's magnetic field is still present indoors, as evidenced by the fact that compasses work indoors. (There is a type of enclosure called a Faraday cage specifically designed to eliminate magnetic fields, but it's more involved than a closed room—and in any case it only stops *changing* magnetic fields, not static (or slowly changing) magnetic fields like the Earth's.) Aligning the electromagnet perpendicular to the Earth's magnetic field would not eliminate the effect of the latter; it only means that the magnetic field of the electromagnet and the Earth would add like perpendicular components of a vector:

$$B_{total} = \sqrt{\left(B_{magnet}\right)^2 + \left(B_{earth}\right)^2}$$

Finally, the speed at which the experiment is performed has no bearing on the effect of the Earth's magnetic field; the Earth's magnetic field is (for practical purposes) constant and does not take time to affect the results.

16. F: If the student's hypothesis is correct, we would expect that when the current is held constant, the magnetic field strength is proportional to the number of coils. That is indeed what we see in the data in this table. When the number of coils is doubled from 50 to 100, the magnetic field strength is doubled from 1.16 T to 2.32 T; when the number of coils is tripled from 50 to 150, the magnetic field strength is tripled from 1.16 T to 3.48 T, and so on. Because we do see the result we would expect to see if the student's hypothesis were correct, these data support the student's hypothesis.

17. C: If wires of the same length are used for each trial, this would effectively eliminate the discrepancy due to the different resistance of wires of different lengths. None of the other choices is a viable option. There is no reason why a prime number of coils would be preferable, and using wires of different metals adds an additional confounding factor. Adding a wire directly connecting the ends of the electromagnet would certainly be counterproductive because such a short circuit would prevent the electromagnet from working at all—all the current would flow through the short circuit and none through the electromagnet.

18. J: The purpose of a scientific control is to make sure that any observed effect is solely due to the variable under investigation. In this case, the variable being investigated is the concentration of the antibiotic; we want to make sure that adding a drop of liquid doesn't produce a similar effect—or at least to see what effect it does produce so that it can be taken into account in the analysis. Because we want to investigate the effect of the antibiotic, using different concentrations of the antibiotic would not be a suitable control—nor would using a different antibiotic because our experimental solutions do not contain this other antibiotic. We want something as close as possible to the solution we are investigating but without the presence of the antibiotic, so the best choice is to use pure water.

19. B: For the switch in labels not to affect the scientist's results, they must have been on dishes that had the same concentration of the antibiotic. Petri dishes 4 and 6 were both treated with the antibiotic solution at a concentration of one part per thousand; switching the labels on these two dishes would not have affected the scientist's results. All of the other choices describe pairs of dishes in which one was treated with the antibiotic and the other was treated with the control solution. Switching the labels on any of these pairs of Petri dishes would certainly have affected the results.

20. H: All the Petri dishes treated with the antibiotic show a clear circle free of bacterial growth. It is clear that the antibiotic impedes bacterial growth at both tested concentrations. However, there is no obvious significant difference between the dishes treated with the antibiotic solution at a concentration of one part per thousand and those treated with a solution at a concentration of two parts per thousand. This means that the effect does *not* necessarily scale with increasing concentration.

21. B: Dish 8 is one of those treated with the control liquid. Because the control liquid should have no effect on bacterial growth, there is no reason why the Petri dish should develop a clear circle in the middle. Furthermore, there is no reason to expect the sizes of the bacterial colonies to decrease. If anything, we would expect the bacterial colonies to grow further.

22. J: If there are no bacteria present at the higher temperature, it could be that the antibiotic was more effective and killed them all, but given the lack of a control, it could also be that the bacteria could not grow at that higher temperature in the first place. If the bacteria did grow at that higher temperature, then if the antibiotic were *less* effective, we would expect the Petri dishes to contain *more* bacteria, not for the bacteria to be absent. If the bacteria could not grow in agar, then there would have been no bacteria in the first scientist's experiment either.

23. A: The older the sample is, the more of its ^{14}C will have undergone radioactive decay. The oldest sample is therefore the one with the smallest proportion of ^{14}C left, which is sample 1. Note that sample 3 has the least ^{14}C left in absolute terms, but it had a smaller amount of carbon to start with; the *fraction* of ^{14}C to carbon is smaller for sample 1, which is what matters.

24. H: The fraction of carbon-14 in Sample 2 is 2.5×10^{-13}. The fraction of carbon-12 in the atmosphere is given in the passage as about 1×10^{-12}. The amount of carbon-12 in Sample 2 has therefore decreased by a factor of $2.5 \times 10^{-13} \div 1 \times 10^{-12} = 0.25$, or $\frac{1}{4}$. This means two half-lives must have passed: after one half-life, half the carbon-14 is left, and after two half-lives, the amount is halved again. So, the age of Sample 2 must be about twice the half-life of carbon-14, 2×5730 years $\approx 11{,}000$ years.

25. C: The half-life of carbon-14 is equal to 5,730 years, so after an additional 5,730 years the amount of carbon-14 in Sample 4 should be half what it is now. Half of 2.58×10^{-12} moles is 1.29×10^{-12} moles.

26. H: If the amount of carbon-14 in the atmosphere changes over time, then this certainly would affect the results of carbon dating because it requires the assumption that the fraction of carbon-14 in an organism when it dies is the same as the fraction in the atmosphere at that time. However, it can be accounted for if we can learn how the amount of carbon-14 in the atmosphere has changed over time. In fact, this *is* a known issue with carbon dating, but scientists have measured the change in the amount of carbon-14 in the atmosphere over time from tree rings, cave formations, and other sources and use that to calibrate the carbon dating process.

27. B: One million years would be well over 100 times the half-life of ^{14}C. After 100 half-lives, the amount of ^{14}C remaining would be $\left(\frac{1}{2}\right)^{100}$ the original amount, which is an extremely small number—about 10^{-30}. Given that the fraction of carbon that is ^{14}C to begin with is already small, about 10^{-12}, taking $\left(\frac{1}{2}\right)^{100}$ of that would result in such a small proportion remaining as to be completely negligible and impractical or impossible to measure—indeed, unless the sample is quite large, it's possible that there will be no atoms of ^{14}C left undecayed by then.

None of the other choices is a reasonable answer. Certainly, ^{14}C existed a million years ago—if it's being produced today by cosmic rays interacting with atmospheric gases, there's no reason it wouldn't have been produced the same back then; the atmosphere and cosmic radiation haven't changed that much in the past million years. There *are* objects containing carbon that are more than a million years old: coal, for instance. Finally, the passage says that ^{14}N is stable, and therefore wouldn't undergo radioactive decay, but even if that wasn't the case, nothing in the passage indicates that we would need to know the amount of ^{14}N in the sample to use radioactive dating.

28. G: To answer this question, note the effect that each type of decay would have on the isotope's atomic number. Recall that the atomic number is equal to the number of protons in the element. If two protons are ejected in alpha decay, then the isotope's atomic number must decrease by 2. If in beta-minus decay a neutron is changed into a proton, then the isotope's atomic number must increase by 1. Conversely, if in beta-plus decay a proton is changed into a neutron, then the isotope's atomic number must decrease by 1. Finally, the question says that gamma decay does not change the isotope's nuclear composition, so its atomic number is unchanged.

According to the passage, the decay of ^{14}C involves the change of an atom of ^{14}C into ^{14}N. This means that the isotope's atomic number changes from 6 to 7—that is, it increases by 1. The only type of radioactive decay that increases the isotope's atomic number by 1 is beta-minus decay.

29. C: The boiling point is the temperature at which the nitrogen transitions from liquid to solid. It is therefore represented on the phase diagram by a point on the line between the liquid and solid phases. If we trace across horizontally from 1 atmosphere on the *y* axis until we hit this line, we see that it corresponds to a position on the *x* axis of about –200 °C. (Specifically, the boiling point of liquid nitrogen at atmospheric pressure is –195.7 °C, although we can't get that level of specificity from the graph.)

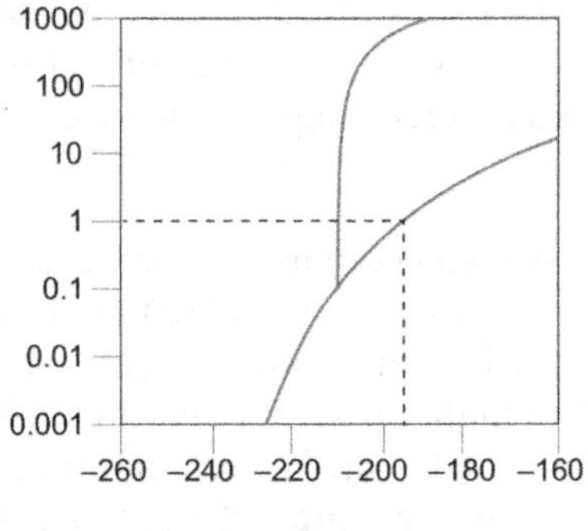

30. F: This point on the graph lies within the region labeled as solid:

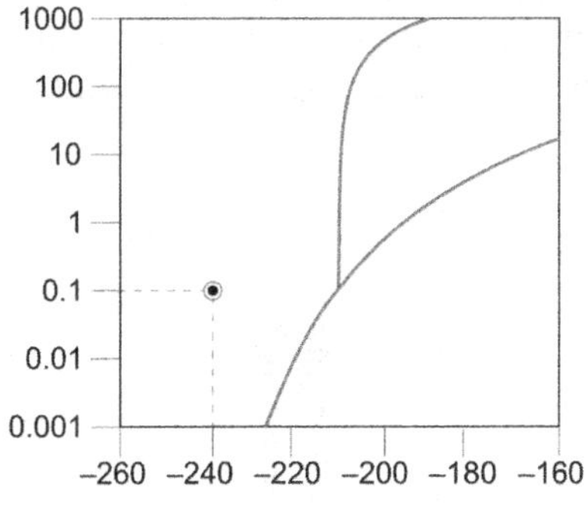

The nitrogen would be in equilibrium between two phases only if this point lay on one of the lines dividing the regions. This is not the case; the point is well within the solid region.

31. D: The triple point is represented on the graph by the point at which the three regions of the graph all touch—which is to say, the point where the lines separating the regions intersect, circled in the diagram below.

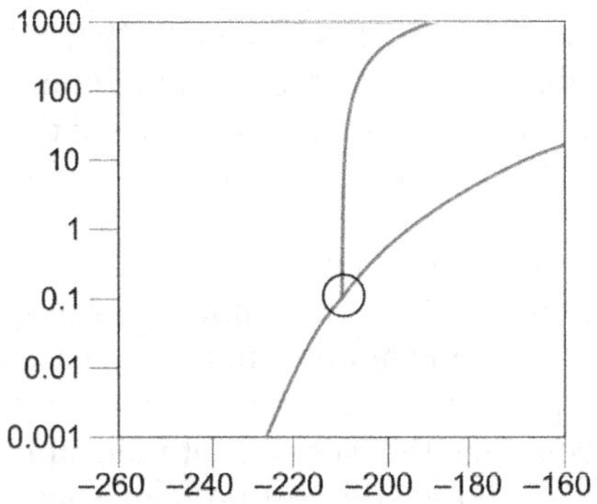

This point is at a temperature of about −210 °C and a pressure of about 0.1 atmospheres. (More specifically, it's at a temperature of −210 °C and a pressure of 0.1236 atmospheres, but again it's not possible to get that much accuracy from the graph alone.)

32. F: For nitrogen to undergo sublimation, it must be possible for it to pass directly from the solid state to the gas state without passing through the liquid state in between. This means it can only happen in a region on the phase diagram where the regions corresponding to solid and gas directly border each other. This is the case for pressures lower than about 0.1 atmospheres. (More specifically, it's for pressures lower than the pressure of the triple point, which as mentioned in the solution to the previous question is about 0.1236 atmospheres.)

33. D: Atmospheres are a unit of pressure, which matches what is stated in the passage about the y axis of a phase diagram usually representing pressure. It could also have been labeled with a different unit of pressure but not with a unit measuring an unrelated quantity. Of the given options, atmospheres is the only one that is a unit of pressure. The unit mm^{-1} measures inverse length, joules are a unit of energy, and newtons are a unit of force.

34. J: From the ideal gas law, $PV = nRT$, we expect that for a particular quantity of gas, the volume is directly proportional to the temperature and inversely proportional to the pressure. (In practice, of course, the ideal gas law does not hold exactly for real gases, but under most circumstances it still holds to a good approximation.) The pressure at point B is higher than at point A which, because volume is inversely proportional to pressure, means the volume is lower. The temperature at point C is higher than at point A which, because volume is directly proportional to temperature, means the volume is higher.

35. A: If solid water (i.e., ice) becomes liquid when sufficient pressure is applied, that means that the line separating the solid and liquid phases must be directed upward and to the left—that way, when pressure is increased, corresponding to moving upward in the diagram, the system will cross the line and transition from the solid phase into the liquid phase.

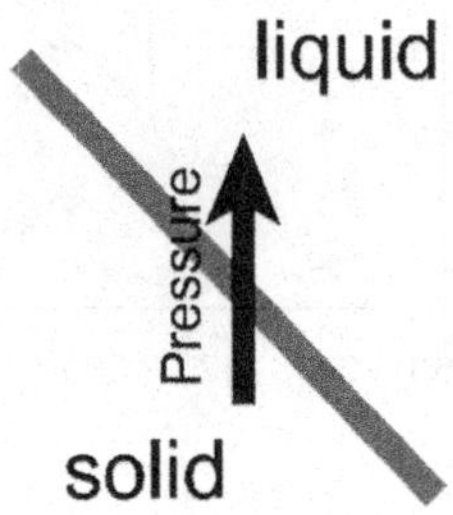

The correct choice is the only option that shows the line between the solid and liquid phases oriented in this direction.

36. F: According to the data table, the two trials in which the most oxygen was produced were trials 3 and 4. Both of these trials involved bright light and added CO_2.

37. B: According to the data table, Trials 5 and 6 both involved dim light and added CO_2. Each of the other pairs of trials named in the choices differ either in the amount of light or in whether or not CO_2 was added.

38. J: Nothing in the passage indicates that the student made any attempts to control for the sizes of the plants; all else being equal, it seems likely that larger plants would produce more oxygen. Because all the plants were on the same table, it is unlikely that there was significant variation in temperature. The passage specifies that the student put 1 gram of sodium bicarbonate in each setup that had added CO_2, so it seems there was no significant variation there. Finally, the amount of oxygen produced was what the student was measuring; any variation in this amount would have been a *result* of error, not a cause of it.

39. D: The chemical formula of water is H_2O—each molecule of water contains two atoms of hydrogen and one atom of oxygen. Water does not contain carbon, so although the plant could acquire hydrogen from water, the carbon must have come from somewhere else. Conversely, the chemical formula for carbon dioxide is CO_2—each molecule of carbon dioxide contains one atom of carbon and two atoms of oxygen. So, carbon dioxide contains carbon and oxygen (as you might guess from the name, even if you didn't know the chemical formula) but no hydrogen. So, the hydrogen must have come from the water, and the carbon from the carbon dioxide.

40. G: Although the student did test whether adding CO_2 to the water (by stirring in sodium bicarbonate) affected the results, the test was purely binary—either the setups had added CO_2 or they didn't, and the student added the same amount of sodium bicarbonate (1 gram) to all the setups that did. It might be interesting to vary the amount of CO_2 added to see if the amount of oxygen produced keeps increasing as more CO_2 is added or whether a point of diminishing returns is reached. There is no reason to expect that varying the size of the test tube should affect the results nor the amount of water in the beaker—the experiment will work only if the funnel is fully submerged, but beyond that any added water is unlikely to have an additional effect. Finally, the amount of oxygen produced is the dependent variable being measured; the student cannot vary it directly.

Another potentially interesting extension of the experiment could be to vary the amount of light the setup is exposed to (and to find a way to quantify the lighting beyond simply "bright" or "dim"), but this was not one of the choices.

ACT Practice Tests #2 and #3

To take these additional ACT practice tests, visit our bonus page:
mometrix.com/bonus948/act

SCAN HERE

Appendix A: Time Statistics for the ACT

ACT Time Constraints				
	English	Math	Reading	Science
Passages	5	N/A	4	6
Questions	75	60	40	40
Time (in minutes)	45	60	35	35
Questions/Passage	15	N/A	10	6.67
seconds/question	36	60	52.5	52.5
min/passage	9	N/A	8.75	5.83
words/passage	260	N/A	780	350
words/question	43	N/A	43	52
Reading rate (WPM)	200	200	200	200
Time used for passages (min)	7.5	N/A	12	10.5
Time left for questions	30	N/A	34.5	24.5

Appendix B: Area, Volume, and Surface Area Formulas

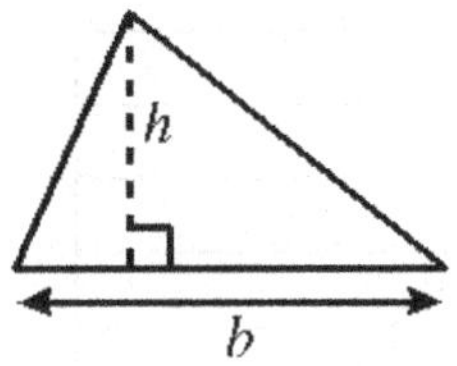

$A = \frac{1}{2}bh$

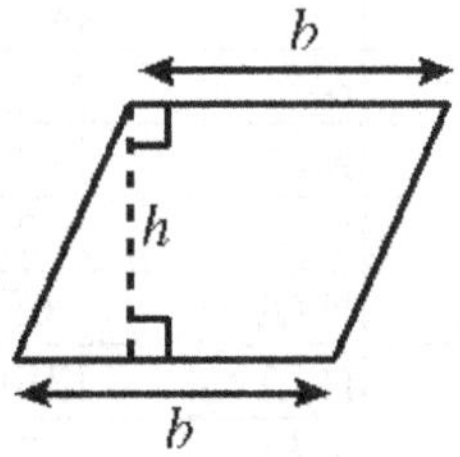

$A = bh$

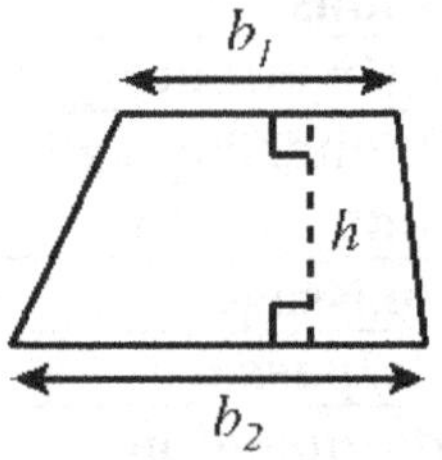

$A = \frac{1}{2}h(b_1 + b_2)$

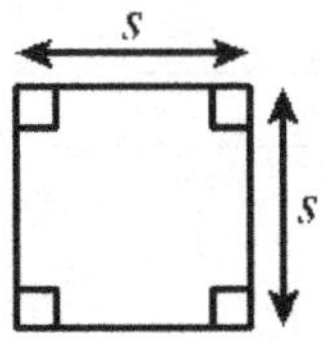

$p = 4s$

$A = s^2$

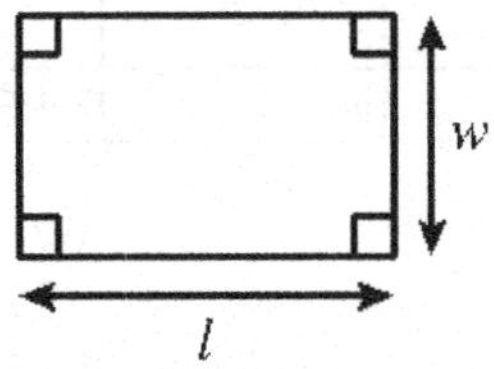

$p = 2l + 2w$

$A = lw$

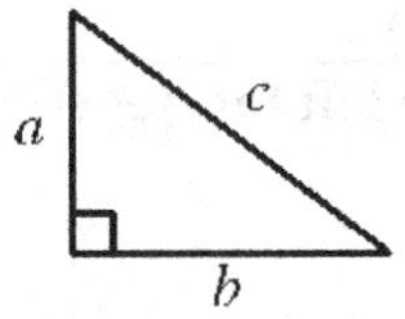

$c^2 = a^2 + b^2$

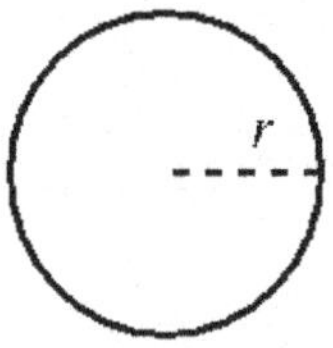

$C = 2\pi r$

$A = \pi r^2$

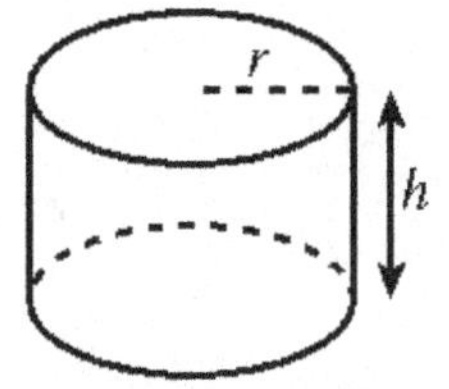

$V = \pi r^2 h$

$S.A. = 2\pi rh + 2\pi r^2$

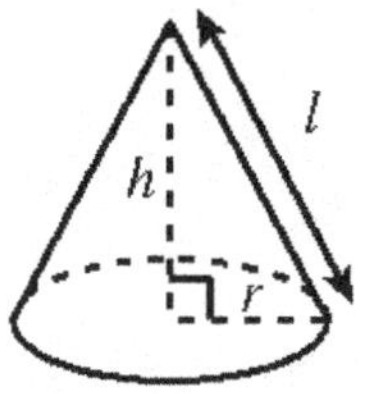

$V = \frac{1}{3}\pi r^2 h$

$S.A. = \pi rl + \pi r^2$

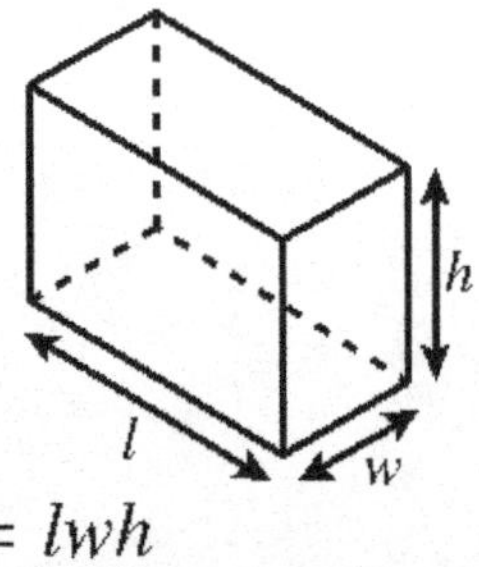

$V = lwh$

$S.A. = 2lw + 2lh + 2wh$

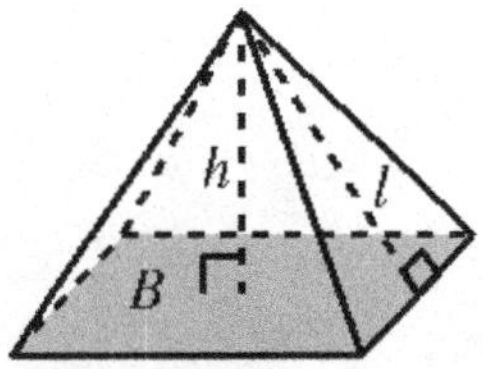

$V = \frac{1}{3}Bh$

$S.A. = \frac{1}{2}lp + B$

Pi

$\pi \approx 3.14$

How to Overcome Test Anxiety

Just the thought of taking a test is enough to make most people a little nervous. A test is an important event that can have a long-term impact on your future, so it's important to take it seriously and it's natural to feel anxious about performing well. But just because anxiety is normal, that doesn't mean that it's helpful in test taking, or that you should simply accept it as part of your life. Anxiety can have a variety of effects. These effects can be mild, like making you feel slightly nervous, or severe, like blocking your ability to focus or remember even a simple detail.

If you experience test anxiety—whether severe or mild—it's important to know how to beat it. To discover this, first you need to understand what causes test anxiety.

Causes of Test Anxiety

While we often think of anxiety as an uncontrollable emotional state, it can actually be caused by simple, practical things. One of the most common causes of test anxiety is that a person does not feel adequately prepared for their test. This feeling can be the result of many different issues such as poor study habits or lack of organization, but the most common culprit is time management. Starting to study too late, failing to organize your study time to cover all of the material, or being distracted while you study will mean that you're not well prepared for the test. This may lead to cramming the night before, which will cause you to be physically and mentally exhausted for the test. Poor time management also contributes to feelings of stress, fear, and hopelessness as you realize you are not well prepared but don't know what to do about it.

Other times, test anxiety is not related to your preparation for the test but comes from unresolved fear. This may be a past failure on a test, or poor performance on tests in general. It may come from comparing yourself to others who seem to be performing better or from the stress of living up to expectations. Anxiety may be driven by fears of the future—how failure on this test would affect your educational and career goals. These fears are often completely irrational, but they can still negatively impact your test performance.

Elements of Test Anxiety

As mentioned earlier, test anxiety is considered to be an emotional state, but it has physical and mental components as well. Sometimes you may not even realize that you are suffering from test anxiety until you notice the physical symptoms. These can include trembling hands, rapid heartbeat, sweating, nausea, and tense muscles. Extreme anxiety may lead to fainting or vomiting. Obviously, any of these symptoms can have a negative impact on testing. It is important to recognize them as soon as they begin to occur so that you can address the problem before it damages your performance.

The mental components of test anxiety include trouble focusing and inability to remember learned information. During a test, your mind is on high alert, which can help you recall information and stay focused for an extended period of time. However, anxiety interferes with your mind's natural processes, causing you to blank out, even on the questions you know well. The strain of testing during anxiety makes it difficult to stay focused, especially on a test that may take several hours. Extreme anxiety can take a huge mental toll, making it difficult not only to recall test information but even to understand the test questions or pull your thoughts together.

Effects of Test Anxiety

Test anxiety is like a disease—if left untreated, it will get progressively worse. Anxiety leads to poor performance, and this reinforces the feelings of fear and failure, which in turn lead to poor performances on subsequent tests. It can grow from a mild nervousness to a crippling condition. If allowed to progress, test anxiety can have a big impact on your schooling, and consequently on your future.

Test anxiety can spread to other parts of your life. Anxiety on tests can become anxiety in any stressful situation, and blanking on a test can turn into panicking in a job situation. But fortunately, you don't have to let anxiety rule your testing and determine your grades. There are a number of relatively simple steps you can take to move past anxiety and function normally on a test and in the rest of life.

Physical Steps for Beating Test Anxiety

While test anxiety is a serious problem, the good news is that it can be overcome. It doesn't have to control your ability to think and remember information. While it may take time, you can begin taking steps today to beat anxiety.

Just as your first hint that you may be struggling with anxiety comes from the physical symptoms, the first step to treating it is also physical. Rest is crucial for having a clear, strong mind. If you are tired, it is much easier to give in to anxiety. But if you establish good sleep habits, your body and mind will be ready to perform optimally, without the strain of exhaustion. Additionally, sleeping well helps you to retain information better, so you're more likely to recall the answers when you see the test questions.

Getting good sleep means more than going to bed on time. It's important to allow your brain time to relax. Take study breaks from time to time so it doesn't get overworked, and don't study right before bed. Take time to rest your mind before trying to rest your body, or you may find it difficult to fall asleep.

Along with sleep, other aspects of physical health are important in preparing for a test. Good nutrition is vital for good brain function. Sugary foods and drinks may give a burst of energy but this burst is followed by a crash, both physically and emotionally. Instead, fuel your body with protein and vitamin-rich foods.

Also, drink plenty of water. Dehydration can lead to headaches and exhaustion, especially if your brain is already under stress from the rigors of the test. Particularly if your test is a long one, drink water during the breaks. And if possible, take an energy-boosting snack to eat between sections.

Along with sleep and diet, a third important part of physical health is exercise. Maintaining a steady workout schedule is helpful, but even taking 5-minute study breaks to walk can help get your blood pumping faster and clear your head. Exercise also releases endorphins, which contribute to a positive feeling and can help combat test anxiety.

When you nurture your physical health, you are also contributing to your mental health. If your body is healthy, your mind is much more likely to be healthy as well. So take time to rest, nourish your body with healthy food and water, and get moving as much as possible. Taking these physical steps will make you stronger and more able to take the mental steps necessary to overcome test anxiety.

Mental Steps for Beating Test Anxiety

Working on the mental side of test anxiety can be more challenging, but as with the physical side, there are clear steps you can take to overcome it. As mentioned earlier, test anxiety often stems from lack of preparation, so the obvious solution is to prepare for the test. Effective studying may be the most important weapon you have for beating test anxiety, but you can and should employ several other mental tools to combat fear.

First, boost your confidence by reminding yourself of past success—tests or projects that you aced. If you're putting as much effort into preparing for this test as you did for those, there's no reason you should expect to fail here. Work hard to prepare; then trust your preparation.

Second, surround yourself with encouraging people. It can be helpful to find a study group, but be sure that the people you're around will encourage a positive attitude. If you spend time with others who are anxious or cynical, this will only contribute to your own anxiety. Look for others who are motivated to study hard from a desire to succeed, not from a fear of failure.

Third, reward yourself. A test is physically and mentally tiring, even without anxiety, and it can be helpful to have something to look forward to. Plan an activity following the test, regardless of the outcome, such as going to a movie or getting ice cream.

When you are taking the test, if you find yourself beginning to feel anxious, remind yourself that you know the material. Visualize successfully completing the test. Then take a few deep, relaxing breaths and return to it. Work through the questions carefully but with confidence, knowing that you are capable of succeeding.

Developing a healthy mental approach to test taking will also aid in other areas of life. Test anxiety affects more than just the actual test—it can be damaging to your mental health and even contribute to depression. It's important to beat test anxiety before it becomes a problem for more than testing.

Study Strategy

Being prepared for the test is necessary to combat anxiety, but what does being prepared look like? You may study for hours on end and still not feel prepared. What you need is a strategy for test prep. The next few pages outline our recommended steps to help you plan out and conquer the challenge of preparation.

Step 1: Scope Out the Test

Learn everything you can about the format (multiple choice, essay, etc.) and what will be on the test. Gather any study materials, course outlines, or sample exams that may be available. Not only will this help you to prepare, but knowing what to expect can help to alleviate test anxiety.

Step 2: Map Out the Material

Look through the textbook or study guide and make note of how many chapters or sections it has. Then divide these over the time you have. For example, if a book has 15 chapters and you have five days to study, you need to cover three chapters each day. Even better, if you have the time, leave an extra day at the end for overall review after you have gone through the material in depth.

If time is limited, you may need to prioritize the material. Look through it and make note of which sections you think you already have a good grasp on, and which need review. While you are studying, skim quickly through the familiar sections and take more time on the challenging parts. Write out your plan so you don't get lost as you go. Having a written plan also helps you feel more in control of the study, so anxiety is less likely to arise from feeling overwhelmed at the amount to cover.

Step 3: Gather Your Tools

Decide what study method works best for you. Do you prefer to highlight in the book as you study and then go back over the highlighted portions? Or do you type out notes of the important information? Or is it helpful to make flashcards that you can carry with you? Assemble the pens, index cards, highlighters, post-it notes, and any other materials you may need so you won't be distracted by getting up to find things while you study.

If you're having a hard time retaining the information or organizing your notes, experiment with different methods. For example, try color-coding by subject with colored pens, highlighters, or post-it notes. If you learn better by hearing, try recording yourself reading your notes so you can listen while in the car, working out, or simply sitting at your desk. Ask a friend to quiz you from your flashcards, or try teaching someone the material to solidify it in your mind.

Step 4: Create Your Environment

It's important to avoid distractions while you study. This includes both the obvious distractions like visitors and the subtle distractions like an uncomfortable chair (or a too-comfortable couch that makes you want to fall asleep). Set up the best study environment possible: good lighting and a comfortable work area. If background music helps you focus, you may want to turn it on, but otherwise keep the room quiet. If you are using a computer to take notes, be sure you don't have any other windows open, especially applications like social media, games, or anything else that could distract you. Silence your phone and turn off notifications. Be sure to keep water close by so you stay hydrated while you study (but avoid unhealthy drinks and snacks).

Also, take into account the best time of day to study. Are you freshest first thing in the morning? Try to set aside some time then to work through the material. Is your mind clearer in the afternoon or evening? Schedule your study session then. Another method is to study at the same time of day that you will take the test, so that your brain gets used to working on the material at that time and will be ready to focus at test time.

Step 5: Study!

Once you have done all the study preparation, it's time to settle into the actual studying. Sit down, take a few moments to settle your mind so you can focus, and begin to follow your study plan. Don't give in to distractions or let yourself procrastinate. This is your time to prepare so you'll be ready to fearlessly approach the test. Make the most of the time and stay focused.

Of course, you don't want to burn out. If you study too long you may find that you're not retaining the information very well. Take regular study breaks. For example, taking five minutes out of every hour to walk briskly, breathing deeply and swinging your arms, can help your mind stay fresh.

As you get to the end of each chapter or section, it's a good idea to do a quick review. Remind yourself of what you learned and work on any difficult parts. When you feel that you've mastered the material, move on to the next part. At the end of your study session, briefly skim through your notes again.

But while review is helpful, cramming last minute is NOT. If at all possible, work ahead so that you won't need to fit all your study into the last day. Cramming overloads your brain with more information than it can process and retain, and your tired mind may struggle to recall even previously learned information when it is overwhelmed with last-minute study. Also, the urgent nature of cramming and the stress placed on your brain contribute to anxiety. You'll be more likely to go to the test feeling unprepared and having trouble thinking clearly.

So don't cram, and don't stay up late before the test, even just to review your notes at a leisurely pace. Your brain needs rest more than it needs to go over the information again. In fact, plan to finish your studies by noon or early afternoon the day before the test. Give your brain the rest of the day to relax or focus on other things, and get a good night's sleep. Then you will be fresh for the test and better able to recall what you've studied.

STEP 6: TAKE A PRACTICE TEST

Many courses offer sample tests, either online or in the study materials. This is an excellent resource to check whether you have mastered the material, as well as to prepare for the test format and environment.

Check the test format ahead of time: the number of questions, the type (multiple choice, free response, etc.), and the time limit. Then create a plan for working through them. For example, if you have 30 minutes to take a 60-question test, your limit is 30 seconds per question. Spend less time on the questions you know well so that you can take more time on the difficult ones.

If you have time to take several practice tests, take the first one open book, with no time limit. Work through the questions at your own pace and make sure you fully understand them. Gradually work up to taking a test under test conditions: sit at a desk with all study materials put away and set a timer. Pace yourself to make sure you finish the test with time to spare and go back to check your answers if you have time.

After each test, check your answers. On the questions you missed, be sure you understand why you missed them. Did you misread the question (tests can use tricky wording)? Did you forget the information? Or was it something you hadn't learned? Go back and study any shaky areas that the practice tests reveal.

Taking these tests not only helps with your grade, but also aids in combating test anxiety. If you're already used to the test conditions, you're less likely to worry about it, and working through tests until you're scoring well gives you a confidence boost. Go through the practice tests until you feel comfortable, and then you can go into the test knowing that you're ready for it.

Test Tips

On test day, you should be confident, knowing that you've prepared well and are ready to answer the questions. But aside from preparation, there are several test day strategies you can employ to maximize your performance.

First, as stated before, get a good night's sleep the night before the test (and for several nights before that, if possible). Go into the test with a fresh, alert mind rather than staying up late to study.

Try not to change too much about your normal routine on the day of the test. It's important to eat a nutritious breakfast, but if you normally don't eat breakfast at all, consider eating just a protein bar. If you're a coffee drinker, go ahead and have your normal coffee. Just make sure you time it so that the caffeine doesn't wear off right in the middle of your test. Avoid sugary beverages, and drink enough water to stay hydrated but not so much that you need a restroom break 10 minutes into the test. If your test isn't first thing in the morning, consider going for a walk or doing a light workout before the test to get your blood flowing.

Allow yourself enough time to get ready, and leave for the test with plenty of time to spare so you won't have the anxiety of scrambling to arrive in time. Another reason to be early is to select a good seat. It's helpful to sit away from doors and windows, which can be distracting. Find a good seat, get out your supplies, and settle your mind before the test begins.

When the test begins, start by going over the instructions carefully, even if you already know what to expect. Make sure you avoid any careless mistakes by following the directions.

Then begin working through the questions, pacing yourself as you've practiced. If you're not sure on an answer, don't spend too much time on it, and don't let it shake your confidence. Either skip it and come back later, or eliminate as many wrong answers as possible and guess among the remaining ones. Don't dwell on these questions as you continue—put them out of your mind and focus on what lies ahead.

Be sure to read all of the answer choices, even if you're sure the first one is the right answer. Sometimes you'll find a better one if you keep reading. But don't second-guess yourself if you do immediately know the answer. Your gut instinct is usually right. Don't let test anxiety rob you of the information you know.

If you have time at the end of the test (and if the test format allows), go back and review your answers. Be cautious about changing any, since your first instinct tends to be correct, but make sure you didn't misread any of the questions or accidentally mark the wrong answer choice. Look over any you skipped and make an educated guess.

At the end, leave the test feeling confident. You've done your best, so don't waste time worrying about your performance or wishing you could change anything. Instead, celebrate the successful completion of this test. And finally, use this test to learn how to deal with anxiety even better next time.

Review Video: Test Anxiety
Visit mometrix.com/academy and enter code: 100340

Important Qualification

Not all anxiety is created equal. If your test anxiety is causing major issues in your life beyond the classroom or testing center, or if you are experiencing troubling physical symptoms related to your anxiety, it may be a sign of a serious physiological or psychological condition. If this sounds like your situation, we strongly encourage you to seek professional help.

Additional Bonus Material

Due to our efforts to try to keep this book to a manageable length, we've created a link that will give you access to all of your additional bonus material:

mometrix.com/bonus948/act

Made in the USA
Monee, IL
14 July 2024

61800013R00181